EUROPE, OR THE INFINITE TASK

MERIDIAN

Crossing Aesthetics

Werner Hamacher

Editor

*Stanford
University
Press*

*Stanford
California
2009*

EUROPE, OR THE INFINITE TASK

A Study of a Philosophical Concept

Rodolphe Gasché

Stanford University Press
Stanford, California

© 2009 by the Board of Trustees of the
Leland Stanford Junior University. All rights reserved.

No part of this book may be reproduced or transmitted in any form or by any means, electronic or mechanical, including photocopying and recording, or in any information storage or retrieval system without the prior written permission of Stanford University Press.

Printed in the United States of America
on acid-free, archival-quality paper

Library of Congress Cataloging-in-Publication Data

Gasché, Rodolphe.
Europe, or the infinite task : a study of a philosophical concept / Rodolphe Gasché.
  p. cm.—(Meridian, crossing aesthetics)
Includes bibliographical references and index.
ISBN 978-0-8047-6060-7 (cloth : alk. paper)
ISBN 978-0-8047-6061-4 (pbk. : alk. paper)
1. Europe—Philosophy—History. 2. Phenomenology.
3. Philosophy, European—20th century. I. Title.
II. Series: Meridian (Stanford, Calif.)
B105.E68G38 2009
190—dc22
                                          2008022531

Contents

Acknowledgments ix

Abbreviations xi

Introduction 1

PART I. EDMUND HUSSERL

1 Infinite Tasks 21
2 Universality and Spatial Form 44
3 Universality in the Making 64

PART II. MARTIN HEIDEGGER

4 Singular Essence 95
5 The Strangeness of Beginnings 124
6 The Originary World of Tragedy 144

PART III. JAN PATOČKA

7 Care of the Soul 211
8 The Genealogy of "Europe-Responsibility" 237

PART IV. JACQUES DERRIDA

9 European Memories — 265
10 "This Little Thing That Is Europe" — 287
11 De-closing the Horizon — 303

   Epilogue — 339

   Notes — *349*
   Bibliography — *397*
   Index — *409*

Acknowledgments

This book began as a lecture that I delivered in 1995 on the occasion of a symposium titled "Ethics and Politics in Contemporary European Thought" at Thammasat University in Bangkok. I cannot be grateful enough to Utong Kovindha and Charles Freeland, not only for having organized that event but also for their unwavering friendship. Several extended visits as a guest scholar at the Max Planck Institute for the History of the Sciences, in Berlin, provided ideal conditions for doing the necessary research involved in the project, particularly, for the parts devoted here to Husserl and Patočka. My deepest thanks go therefore to my friend Hans-Jörg Rheinberger, the director of Section III at the institute, who provided generous support for this project. Among the many other important moments for tryouts of chapters and sections of this book, let me mention only the following: In 2003 an invitation to conduct a cycle of three seminars at Northwestern University, collectively titled "The Crisis of the European Sciences and Transcendental Phenomenology," allowed me to put the final touches to the section of the book that deals with Husserl's elaborations on Europe. In 2004 another three seminars at Villanova University on Husserl's and Heidegger's conception of Europe gave me an opportunity to test the corresponding parts of the book. The three seminars in the summer of 2005 devoted to Patočka at the Collegium Phenomenologicum at Citta di Castello, Italy, as well as another set of three seminars that year on Patočka and Derrida at Johns Hopkins University, helped me to finalize the book chapters in question. I greatly benefitted from the searching discussions by the participants in these seminars, as well as from the advice that has come to me by so many who attended these events. Especially important, however, were the thoughtful suggestions by my close friends and colleagues Juan Manuel Garrido, David Johnson, and Kalliopi Nikolopoulou.

Some of the chapters, or earlier versions of them, have already appeared in print and are reprinted here with the permission of the publishers. A first version of Chapter 1 was published under the title "Self-Responsibility, Apodicticity, Universality," in a Japanese translation, in *Menschenontologie* 10 (2004): 17–37. Chapter 3 appeared under the title "Universality in the Making—On Edmund Husserl's Conception of the One World," in *Interdisziplinäre Phänomenologie* 1 (2004): 91–115. An earlier version of Chapter 4, entitled "Mal assuré: Du destin de l'Europe," is featured in *Heidegger, Le danger et la promesse*, ed. G. Bensussan and J. Cohen (Paris: Kimé, 2006), 195–210. Portions of Chapter 5 were first published under the title "Ausserordentlich befremdlich: Europa als Anfang" in *Nachleben der Religionen: Kulturwissenschaftliche Untersuchungen zur Dialektik der Säkularisierung*, ed. Martin Terml and Daniel Weidner (Paderborn: Wilhelm Fink Verlag, 2007), 75–87. Chapter 9 was first published under the title "European Memories: Jan Patočka and Jacques Derrida on Responsibility" in *Critical Inquiry* 33, no. 2 (winter 2007): 291–311, and has been reprinted in *The Late Derrida*, ed. W. J. T. Mitchell and A. I. Davidson (Chicago: University of Chicago Press, 2007), 73–93. Finally, Chapter 10, "'This Little Thing That Is Europe,'" originally appeared in the *CR: New Centennial Review* 7, no. 2 (fall 2007): 1–19.

Abbreviations

BW	Martin Heidegger, *Basic Writings*
C	Edmund Husserl, *The Crisis of European Sciences and Transcendental Phenomenology*
DP	Plato, *The Dialogues of Plato*
EGT	Martin Heidegger, *Early Greek Thinking*
EHP	Martin Heidegger, *Elucidations of Hölderlin's Poetry*
GD	Jacques Derrida, *The Gift of Death*
HE	Jan Patočka, *Heretical Essays in the Philosophy of History*
HHA	Martin Heidegger, *Hölderlins Hymne "Andenken"*
HHGR	Martin Heidegger, *Hölderlins Hymnen "Germanien" und "Der Rhein"*
HHI	Martin Heidegger, *Hölderlin's Hymn "The Ister"*
IM	Martin Heidegger, *Introduction to Metaphysics*
LS	Jan Patočka, *Liberté et sacrifice: Ecrits politiques*
MNM	Jan Patočka, *Le monde naturel et le mouvement de l'existence humaine*
MNPH	Jan Patočka, *Le monde naturel comme problème philosophique*
OH	Jacques Derrida, *The Other Heading: Reflections on Today's Europe*

P	Martin Heidegger, *Parmenides*
PE	Jan Patočka, *Plato and Europe*
PEF	*Penser l'Europe à ses frontières*
PGHP	Jacques Derrida, *The Problem of Genesis in Husserl's Philosophy*

EUROPE, OR THE INFINITE TASK

Introduction

The unmistakable sense of urgency that characterizes Edmund Husserl's explicit thematization of, and central focus on, Europe and the West in his reflections in the late 1930s must certainly be understood as a response to a precise historical and political reality—namely, the rise of fascism. And, where intellectual life is at stake, it must be seen as a response to German Nazism's hostility toward spirit (*Geist*). If, however, these late works are viewed exclusively from such an angle, then Husserl's recourse to Europe's cultural history and its origins in Greek philosophy as a means to counter the barbarism of the time may appear hopelessly naive—the response of a philosopher living in the thin air of his high-flown abstractions—particularly if one thinks of the atrocities that were still in the offing.[1] Nonetheless, the political realities of the day do not entirely explain the central importance granted to Europe in these writings. Indeed, in the so-called Vienna lecture, titled "Philosophy and the Crisis of European Humanity," and subsequently in his unfinished work, *The Crisis of European Sciences and Transcendental Phenomenology*, though Husserl clearly has fascism's grip on Europe in view, he in fact diagnoses a disease and a crisis in which Nazism is simply the most blatant symptom. It is a crisis of such drastic proportions that only a complete shake-up of Europe's traditions—its entire intellectual and cultural history—could offer hope of bringing about a reversal of Europe's otherwise inexorable decline and end. If Europe becomes so prominent in Husserl's late thought, and if he conjures its Greek heritage in the idea of a universal rational science, then it is because for him Europe is intimately tied to the very idea and promise of reason and rationality. What is called

"Europe" in Husserl's thinking is certainly not limited to a geographical entity. Nor is it to be equated simply with a historical, cultural, political, or economic reality. Europe, insofar as it can be traced back to its origins in the Greek idea of a universal rational science—philosophy—is inseparable from the project of a life predicated on reason. From this perspective, Husserl's later works only make explicit something that was a fundamental presupposition since the beginning of phenomenological thought: that philosophy, and phenomenological philosophy in particular, is not merely a finite European phenomenon but a life project that, although it goes by the name of *Europe*, nevertheless concerns humanity as a whole. Consequently, what happens to Europe necessarily affects all of humankind. Given this crucial importance of the question of Europe, it comes as no wonder that about the same time that Husserl conceived of the Vienna lecture and began writing *The Crisis of the European Sciences*, other thinkers within the same tradition of philosophical thought—Martin Heidegger, as well as Jan Patočka—offered their own accounts of Europe. Furthermore, phenomenological thought's emphasis on the intricate relation between philosophy and Europe has been the reason why, in the aftermath of Husserl, Heidegger, and Patočka, many thinkers' reflections on Europe (whether they are neo- or postphenomenologists) are not just occasional or haphazard events. If these thinkers—with Jacques Derrida being first and foremost among them—have broached, critically or not, the issue of Europe, it is precisely owing to what became explicit with Husserl, namely, that philosophy and Europe are linked in more ways than one.

In this book—which, at first glance, may resemble a history of ideas, or a conceptual history—I intend to discuss the different conceptions of Europe in the works of Husserl, Heidegger, Patočka, and Derrida. In short, this is a philosophical inquiry into "Europe," one that is exclusively restricted to elaborations of Europe within the phenomenological tradition. In spite of the prominence that the term *Europe* (as well as the term *Occident*, which more often than not is closely aligned with it) enjoys in philosophical thought from the eighteenth century on—one thinks of Novalis, Friedrich Schlegel, and especially Nietzsche—this philosophical prehistory of the phenomenological reflections on Europe will not be enlarged on here. Nor will there be any discussion of the huge literature on the subject that emerged in the wake of each of the Great Wars. Since the thrust of this work is exclusively philosophical, it may also be appropriate, in the beginning, to say what this work does *not* pretend to be about. Though it is indeed a book on Europe, it does not deal with "Europe" simply as some past or present entity or as some geopolitical, legal, and cultural entity that is yet to be created. In spite of the fact that, at this precise historical juncture, Europe is seeking to become integrated—something that, notwithstanding the inevitable temporary setbacks, has not only yielded already, historically speaking, monumental results—the adoption of the euro, for instance—but has also created in response to the anxieties that it produces (in the United States for instance) the phenomenon called "Europhobia"—I do not intend to broach the intricate problems that this unification, and the establishment of a transnational European identity, pose in practice. There will be no discussion of the long and difficult history of Europe's inner and outer borders nor of all the trouble this history continues to represent today in a united Europe. I will not address the issue of what sort of legal and political unity a united Europe should have, that is, whether it can be modeled after a federal conception of the state, as is the case in the United States, or whether Europe's manifold cultures, languages, and histories (if not even contradictions) call for a different model of integration, one that would possibly be distinct from that of a state to begin with.[2] This book will also not be concerned with the Europe promoted by the current economical and financial Caesarian powers of the continent, in short, with the undoubtedly crucial question of whether the attempts to turn Europe into a primarily economic zone, or to shape it into a political construction on the basis of a still to be adopted (provisional or definite) European constitution, are sufficient to construct a Europe that would meet the various expectations at the heart of the project of a United Europe. Undoubtedly, the question of whether or not a Europe (understood as an economic power that is competitive among the world markets and that is politically united by a constitution whose prime goal is merely to further cement its economic clout) does justice to the expectations and dreams for Europe that are fostered by its cultural, political, and legal traditions is a highly significant one. But this issue will have to remain in the background here. Finally, this book will not inquire into the resistance that the unification of Europe actually encounters on a daily basis, at every step, in its inner or outer conflicts—whether merely ideological or violent and bloody—conflicts that have repeatedly bedeviled the establishment of a United Europe.

What, then, will this book on Europe be about, if it does not even bother to address the topical issues that are confronted on a daily basis? Is it merely an exercise in futile and abstract reflection about some high-flown conception of what "Europe" might mean? At a moment in history when truly pressing issues besiege the formation of a new Europe, why devote an entire book to philosophical speculations about a "Europe" that are perhaps only a pipedream, or even a hallucination? Is this not simply a waste of time? And furthermore, does it not, in taking the theme of Europe seriously, reek of Eurocentrism?

The philosophically, and especially the phenomenologically, schooled reader, even though he or she may not have paid special attention to the recurrent theme of Europe in phenomenological thought, will, I dare hope, recognize the rationale for devoting a whole study to the philosophical status of Europe in the tradition of thought inaugurated by Husserl. Such a reader will at least be sympathetic to an effort that takes the theme of "Europe" as seriously as any of the other terms of phenomenological thought, as well as the attempt at establishing, in as precise a manner as possible, what the different thinkers of Europe understood by this term; how each conception arose from a critique, displacement, and, in certain cases, a radicalization of Europe—a radicalization by means of the extrapolation of implications of a predecessor's conception of Europe that had yet to be thematized. However, this has not been my sole reason for writing this book. More is at stake in this study of Europe as a philosophical topos than just a methodologically sound, scholarly investigation. Considering the intricate relation that phenomenological thought has established between Europe and philosophical thought, it will not escape the astute reader's attention that what is at stake in such an investigation is philosophy itself, as well as some of its most central issues: universality, rationality, apodicticity, responsibility, and world. At stake, therefore, is something that also transcends Europe and Europeans, something that, in principle, also concerns non-Europeans. For the time being, however, to respond to the critical reservations one might have about the idea of devoting a whole book to Europe as a philosophical question, one could pose a simple question. Given that it is an admittedly urgent task to come up with ways to address the problems that arise with the efforts to bring about a unified Europe, what conception of Europe should one put forth in seeking solutions to these concrete difficulties? Furthermore, what are the categorial resources one should draw on to address the social, cultural, and political problems that such a unification ought to consider? Likewise, how do such categorial resources relate to these very realities? In fine, the question is directed at the kind of Europe that one should try to realize in addressing current pragmatic problems. In short, it is directed at the very concept or idea of Europe—supposing there is such a thing—that should serve as the norm, or horizon, for tackling these pressing concrete issues. Should the standard be a Europe understood as an economic world power capable of successfully competing in the globalized world, one that is based on a constitution that merely enshrines the legal and political requirements to achieve this goal? Or might not "Europe" be the thought of a different conception of the world than the one that is based solely on the economic and political exigencies of a globalized environment? Is it not the case that "Europe" is precisely what is about to disappear in what is currently being created, as an economic and political bloc, in the name of Europe?

As I have already intimated, this study of Husserl's, Heidegger's, Patočka's, and Derrida's conceptions of Europe may resemble either a history of ideas or a history of concepts. In fact, it will resemble more a history of concepts to the extent that such a project examines the historical transformation of the meaning of relatively stable terms or notions, whereas a history of ideas traces the changing terminological formations of supposedly fixed complexes of meaning. Indeed, although "Europe" has been characterized indiscriminately as an idea or a concept (and, as we will see, it has been named many other "things" as well, including the characterization of its being "a little thing"), the history that this book follows is the history of the successive critical transformations and expansions of the cluster of the implications that are associated with the term. And, the fact that "Europe" is sometimes simultaneously called an idea and/or a concept (and a host of other things) may also imply that this "thing" is perhaps neither one nor the other. Consequently, the study of the evolution of the notion of "Europe" in phenomenological thought may not even be a history of a concept or of an idea in any rigorous sense. As will hopefully become clear in what follows, there is something about "Europe" that paradoxically forbids enclosing its meaning, reach, and sweep within notions that are intrinsically European themselves, including the very notions of "concept" and "idea." Indeed, rather than something one confidently knows—and a concept implies knowledge—"Europe" may be something exceedingly strange to the extent that one does not know what precisely its name is assigned to or what the full range of its determinations are. And yet the notion of "Europe" plays a definitively crucial role within phenomenological thought. Rather than a history of a concept or idea, the proposed history—if it can still be called one—would thus be the history of the successive attempts to invent a concept or an idea of Europe and, since it is not in advance clear what exactly this concept or idea means, to fill this blank or empty signifier. But, one may object, is there anything more futile than such an exercise? And what if the specificity of "Europe," rather than providing a fixed and stable identity, were instead a form of identity intrinsically tied to the relentless demand of having to be critically rethought, reinvented, and recast, time and again, at any given turn in history, in short, at every moment, every day? What if this were the force and the significance of this thing called "Europe"?

A book on Europe, and one moreover that affirms the idea or concept of such a thing, along with all of its constitutive exigencies (such as universality, rationality, apodicticity, responsibility, and so forth), will inevitably face the accusation of anachronism. Not only has Europe lost its economic and political clout as the sole major player in the world, but the history of its relations to the non-European world, as well as its relation to the others within its own borders, has cast a seemingly final verdict on the superiority and integrity of European "values." Even though I do not intend to expand in any detail on the ideological function that concepts such as universality, occidental rationalism, and the concept of Europe itself, have systematically played—nor how the alleged merits of these concepts, and the imaginary humanity that they imply, have repeatedly served the hegemonic and imperialist interests of the continent—this does not mean that I intend to put such judgments to rest. To this historically well-founded judgment on the past arrogance and violence of a power-hungry European civilization, another, equally historical, aspect of European culture needs to be counterposed, one whose span, even though it may not to be equal in size to this first prong of European culture, nonetheless remains a quite unique feature of it. Indeed, at the same time that European values have served to justify and occlude the exploitation and humiliation of much of the rest of the world, these very concepts and ideas have also made it possible for Europe to question its own traditions and the crimes that have been committed in their name. Undoubtedly, this unique feature of critical self-evaluation is repeatedly celebrated by all the grand discourses on Europe; thus, it should also be subject to some suspicion. One may also ask how pervasive this tradition has been in Europe and to what extent it has effectively shaped European history. Yet the fact remains that there is such a tradition and such a culture in Europe. Whether or not one holds that this undeniable phenomenon of self-criticism, with the Enlightenment as one of its most prominent historical expressions, has gone far enough, or too far (for indeed, Europe's practice of critically putting itself into question is also a regular subject of lament), such self-criticism is something quite unique that sets Europe apart. Indeed, this culture of reflection and critical self-referentiality allows European discourses to bring violations of Europe's own proclaimed standards to light, just as it allows, in principle, all other voices and opinions to be heard. Rooted in the undoubtedly Western concern with universality, rationality, evidence, and so forth, this self-critical discourse and practice is a definite feature that has profoundly shaped European history and culture. And, though this feature is not ubiquitously manifest in Europe—indeed many occasions could be cited as evidence of violence against it—it is this very *demand*, to put it differently, of relating in a negative fashion to oneself and the ensuing openness to all others that is constitutive of a European "identity." Whatever the factual limits of this culture of critical reflection in Europe's long history are—which on the basis of its empirical credentials alone cannot therefore be declared the best possible culture, nor can it be categorically distinguished as superior to all other cultures—such a culture, even empirically speaking, is not a matter of course.[3] It is not simply ironic that all critique of Europe must ultimately seek its resources in the theory and practice of self-questioning that is itself characteristic of European "identity."

Nonetheless, this study will not be concerned with Europe as an empirical entity with its factual tradition of self-questioning as an overture to the non-European. Rather, it will be an attempt to analyze the concept or idea of Europe—an attempt at a "Euroanalysis," to borrow a concept—as one finds it in phenomenological approaches from Husserl to Derrida.[4] My aim is to extrapolate the main issues that are intertwined with the philosophical concept or idea of Europe, to analyze the transformations they undergo at the hands of the various thinkers, and to probe the possibility of a yet untapped critical potential in this notion. As I have pointed out, there are a number of interrelated issues involved in the notion of

Europe: universality, apodicticity, responsibility, and world. Yet, one will argue, these are "values," or more precisely, exigencies, injunctions, or demands and, as such, are not specific to Europe alone but to the West as a whole—that is, to America (and the Americas) as well.[5] And, while this is undoubtedly true, it is Europe that is linked by name to these "values" to the extent that they have been central to European philosophy, being the subject of continuous reflection and elaboration throughout its history. Since these "values" originate in Europe, they reflect a specifically European history and development, one may further argue. But since these ideas (such as universality, apodicticity, self-responsibility, and so forth) first emerged in Europe, and have remained intrinsically tied up with its history, are they therefore less universal, less demanding? Or, is not the putting into question of these ideas, on the basis that they have originated in one part of the world, not already indicative of how inescapable these demands are? By simply arguing against these "values" on the basis that they are Eurocentric, for instance, one presupposes and participates in what one has denounced as the hubris of the logos, namely, in the very demand for universality. Furthermore, by holding that European rationalism is situated, and hence relative, one either assumes an absolute position from which the relative value of all discourses can be established, or one deprives oneself of the possibility of even arguing for the validity of one's own position, unless one does so by reifying a selective worldpicture. But such opposition to the concept or idea of Europe in phenomenological thought is further defeated by the fact that, as we will see, this concept or idea is shaped not only by the fundamental demand to transcend whatever is particular but also that which still tinges this idea itself with particularity. As a result, the idea of Europe—the knot that binds together the different exigencies that make it up—is as exacting a demand on the Europeans as it is on anyone else. As a result, one of the questions that we will have to take up, especially at the end of this study, is why one should still refer to all these exigencies that form the cluster of what "Europe" refers to, by the name of *Europe*.

For now, however, let me return to the suggestion that the following inquiry into the phenomenologists' understanding of "Europe" resembles a history of concepts or ideas. If, rather than providing a systematic exposition of the idea or concept of Europe, I have chosen to present a kind of narrative of the different positions of four major phenomenologists on this topic—something that further entails embedding their treatment of it within outlines of the major tenets of their work, and hence this book can also be seen as a configuration of four monographs—it is also in order to preclude the suggestion that "Europe" is a fixed meaning, identity, or essence. As we will see, "Europe" is not only a set of interrelated demands, which entails a disappropriation and decentering of substance or essence. It is also a conception that is always only in the making, never closed off, and structurally open to future transformation and change. Thus the question arises of what precisely it is that one calls by the name of *Europe*. And this does not simply ask what the name *Europe* refers to, but, in addition, it asks about the kind of term *Europe* is. To begin with, is this term a name? And, is it first of all a proper name? Until now I have spoken indiscriminately of the concept or the idea of Europe. Indeed, these are the principal terms in which "Europe" is cast by the thought of the philosophers we will discuss. But does not the fact that the terms *idea* and *concept* serve to designate "Europe" without discrimination between them, suggest that "Europe" is, perhaps, neither an idea nor a concept? In this case the history sketched out in this book would be neither a history of the idea nor of the concept of Europe. Could it be that there is something about the thought of Europe that inhibits its becoming an idea or a concept such that one could then write its history?

The philosophical treatment of Europe that I will propose here, suggests, of course, that we will be dealing with a concept or an idea, all the more so since the *Historisches Wörterbuch der Philosophie*, a standard work whose approach is that of a history of concepts, and which features an entry on Europe (the first, to my knowledge, by a philosophical dictionary), would seem to provide indisputable authority to such an approach.[6] In addition, in both the Vienna lecture and *The Crisis of the European Sciences*, Husserl explicitly calls Europe a concept and/or an idea. Even though one may miss a similar univocal subsumption of the theme of Europe under these designations in Heidegger, Patočka, and Derrida, their treatment of the theme in question is not conceivable without the conceptual or ideational status that Husserl gave to it. At this point, however, it must be noted that in the relevant philosophical literature on Europe, "Europe" is not only referred to as a concept or an idea. A frequent appellation is also that of a "figure." And there is a long list of other names as well: an image (Paul Valéry),[7] a category (Alain Badiou),[8] a schema (Denis Guénoun),[9] and even, reflecting the ambiguities and limitations of all these terms, "a little thing" (Jacques Derrida).[10] For our purpose it should suffice to comment briefly on the name of *Europe*—*Europe* as a name for Europe—before proceeding to an elucidation of "Europe" as a philosophical concept or idea (both of which point to all the philosophy—if not to philosophy itself—that is wedded to this term). As a toponym, the name *Europe* already reveals some interesting features that are not extrinsic to "Europe's" philosophical implications. Even though the name of *Europe* stands since the seventh century BC for central Greece, and was subsequently extended to Thrace and Macedonia, it is also the case that, according to Aristotle, the Greeks did not consider themselves Europeans. On the contrary, as Aristotle remarks, the Greeks understood themselves as the people of the middle, situated between Asia and Europe.[11] In this context of the Greeks' own self-understanding, the term *Europe* does not signify a specific region, country, or site but only a direction toward an obscure western land mass. It is a word of presumably Semitic origin—whose root, *ereb* (*erebos*, in Greek), means darkness or evening—that was handed down to the Greeks by the Phoenicians living on the coast of Asia Minor and that gestures toward the western land where the sun sets. "Europe" then, in this originary sense, names the onset of darkness after the sun has gone down on the western shore of the Aegean Sea, designating a still shapeless land over there—that is, the land of the evening (*Abendland*), or Occident. Not only is it the case that "Europe" does not come to designate a precise geographical entity until very late—in the ninth century AD, first in relation to the Western Empire newly founded in the wake of the dissolution of the western part of the Roman Empire, and subsequently, as a name for the whole Latin Occident (in short, the Latin half of Christianity, that is, before the Reformation and the subsequent schisms)—but, it is also the case that Europe did not invent this name for itself. It not only borrowed it from the Greeks, who are generally taken to have been the cradle of European culture, although paradoxically they did not consider themselves part of it, but ultimately from the inhabitants of Asia Minor.[12] By referring to itself as "Europe," Europe, therefore, avails itself of "the first glance upon Europe that occurred from outside it—from Asia."[13] In other words, by calling itself by "the name of an other," Europe looks at itself, and grasps itself reflectively only through the opaqueness of a name that comes to it from the other.[14]

The familiar myth of Europa, the daughter of the Phoenician king Agenor and his wife, Telephassa, born in the port of Tyre on the oriental coast of the Mediterranean, and abducted to Crete by Zeus disguised as a bull of dazzling whiteness, from whom a nameless Europe may also have received its name, further highlights the non-European origin of Europe's name. As Herodotus points out, this Europa—the most celebrated figure of this name—was "an Asiatic [who] never visited the country which we now call Europe" and who "sailed from Phoenicia to Crete and from Crete to Lycia" (that is, back to Asia).[15] If Europe should indeed owe its name to Europa, then rather than being a name that it gave to itself, identifying itself as such, it is one that comes to it from outside of itself, a name that, furthermore, signifies the abduction from the native land (Asia) toward a still anonymous land. As Denis Guénoun remarks in a fine analysis of the legend in question, this name refers above all "to the movement of tearing away, and carrying off from the paternal lands, from Asia as land . . . toward the strange site without a name. Europe, this is: the tearing away from Asia . . . toward the West, necessarily, because this movement is also the one that carries, and carries the sun with itself, which rises, and then sets as well."[16] Undoubtedly, what this myth suggests is that Europe constitutes itself by separating itself from and pitting itself against Asia, encapsulating itself in the same movement within itself by setting itself apart from its main other. This is a recurrent topos that has remained tied to Europe's self-understanding until recently and that resonates even in its geographical definition by many geographers, but most prominently by the poet Paul Valéry, as a little promontory or cape of the Asian continent. But in addition to naming this passage from Asia to itself, "Europe" also names the tearing away from a fatherland and the transport and exposition to what is other, strange, and not of oneself. What the name *Europe* refers to is thus not primarily the proper name of a land but a name for a movement of separation and tearing (oneself) away in which everything proper has always already been left behind. It is thus an extension prior to all confinement within oneself, thus constituting an exposure to the foreign, the strange, the indeterminate.[17]

Approaching the question of Europe from the glance, or sight that would be specific to it, Jean-Luc Nancy has resorted to an (admittedly questionable) etymology of Europe to further support his argument that Europe is an idea of vision. Rather than resorting to the Greek term for Europe, a term that itself originated in Asia Minor—that is, from "Europe" as the land of the setting sun opposite to Asia, or from Europa, the Asian woman abducted to Crete by Zeus—Nancy wonders whether its etymological origin should not be retraced to the Greek word *Euruopa*. The term *Euruopa*, which in Homer always appears as a companion adjective to Zeus—*Zeus euruopè*—means wide-looking, wide-eyed, far-seeing, looking far into the distance, or wide-sounding as in the far-thundering Zeus. It would thus appear questionable to link this masculine form of Zeus's epithet to the name of *Europe*. However, this epithet also has a feminine correspondent: *eurôpé*, as Gonzague de Reynold has argued. As Europa's name indicates, the eyes of the daughter of King Agenor were so beautiful that Zeus fell in love with her. De Reynold concludes: "*Eurôpé* is . . . a woman with large eyes, a lovely way of looking, a beautiful face. The kinship between Europe and the Homeric epithet is thus obvious."[18] Understanding the name of Europe by relying on the resources of this word *Euruopa*, signifying a look far into the distance, "Europe" becomes for Nancy the idea of a vision that is essentially a look into the distance, always ahead of itself, at what is other than itself, namely, first the world, the horizon, and the universal, though it ultimately aims beyond all these. In any case, understood from Zeus's glance into the distance, the name *Europe* thus reveals itself once again as a name that articulates a movement—this time on the level of vision—that from the beginning is already ahead of itself, a look that has never first been a look at itself from which one then departs.[19]

Undoubtedly, by naming "Europe"—and especially by writing a whole book on it—one assumes that this name refers to an identifiable bearer or referent, precisely, one that exists independently of this name and to which this name refers. As a proper name, "Europe" should refer to a singular and identifiable referent, as is the case with the names of Canada, Germany, France, or Luxembourg. This would also suggest that one knows what is called "Europe," in the same way as one knows what Canada, Germany, France, or Luxembourg are when one speaks of them. Nonetheless, it is nearly impossible to find any consensus about what the proper name *Europe* refers to. That which carries this name is a rather checkered thing—from the indeterminate region in the West, where the sun sets, to the historical narratives that, at each particular moment of European history, have determined what was understood as Europe, to the contemporary uncertainty displayed by the discussions of what belongs geographically and culturally to Europe. Geographically, European space is difficult to delimit since no natural boundaries exist on its eastern flank. Because of this difficulty, cultural definitions have been proposed. To quote Karl Jaspers:

> If we want to call it by the name Europe, then Europe is the Bible and antiquity. Europe is Homer, Aeschylus, Sophocles, Euripides; it is Phidias, Plato and Aristotle and Plotinus; it is Virgil and Horace, Dante, Shakespeare, Goethe; it is Cervantes and Racine and Moliere; it is Leonardo, Raphael, Michelangelo, Rembrandt, Velasquez; it is Bach, Mozart, Beethoven; it is Saint Augustine, Anselm, Thomas, Nicolas Cusanus, Spinoza, Pascal, Kant, Hegel; it is Cicero, Erasmus, Voltaire. Europe is in domes and palaces and ruins; it is Jerusalem, Athens, Rome, Paris, Oxford, Geneva, Weimar. Europe is the democracy of Athens, of republican Rome, of the Swiss, the Dutch, and the Anglosaxons. We would come to no end if we counted everything that is dear to our heart, an immeasurable richness of spirit, morality, and faith.[20]

Precisely. And furthermore, if one were able to close this list, what in the end would positively unify these multiple heritages? As a consequence it has been proposed that one define Europe's cultural unity negatively, that is, by inserting it into a series of oppositions. This has been Rémi Brague's approach in *Europe, la voie romaine*. However, rather than establishing a firm identity of Europe, Brague, by emphasizing Romanity and Latinity as what is proper to Europe, is led to define the cultural identity of Europe as "an excentric identity" where that which is proper to it is not its own. Considering the indeterminateness of what is Europe—both geographically and culturally—must one not assume that, from the beginning, the name *Europe* seeks to impose some intelligible and normative contours onto Europe itself? If this name is the proper name for Europe, is it not primarily to the extent that it seeks to project on Europe a unity as a desideratum? But can it still be a proper name then? As we have seen, this name is itself a highly strange one. In principle, a proper name should be a meaningless word for a singular thing. But, as our discussion of the semantics of the name has shown—which, needless to say, is interested neither in embedding this name within some unshakable etymon nor in the veracity of the different etymological tracings, but only in how its different meanings may have been at work in the grand discourses about Europe—*Europe* is not a proper name in a strict sense. To recap, the singular and seemingly proper name of *Europe* is a name that comes to Europe from somewhere other than itself; as such it designates a still indeterminate and obscure part of the world where the sun sets. It is the name for a region or thing that still remains, and will perhaps forever remain, indeterminate. The name itself names Europe's origin in a movement of departure from everything native. It also establishes what the "essence" of Europe is: a relentless uprootedness that is always glancing far into the distance, being always already ahead of itself with the other. It is never a static and determined identity first, one that would subsequently open itself to the other—one whose remainders would prevent its full exposure.[21] As a name, *Europe* then designates "nothing" but an originary separation from the native, a fundamental openness to the world, and an originary transcendence toward what it is not. Although a proper name for a singular existence—one particular continent—the name *Europe*, then, also suggests that some very determinate meaning inheres in the space between this name and what it refers to. Consequently, it is much more than just a proper name for an individual referent. However brief our discussion of the name *Europe* has been, it should be clear that this name is not simply a meaningless marker, the way a proper name for an individual existence should properly be. Instead it is eminently intelligible.[22] As Gottfried Wilhelm Leibniz holds, *"proper names have been ordinarily appellatives, that is to say, general in their origin."*[23] Of the many examples that Leibniz provides to support his point, suffice it to mention that "Caesar was the name of a child drawn by incision from the womb of his mother."[24] For example, although the names of countries, towns, and mountains are names for particular things, as Leibniz argues, they are also formed on similitude with more general terms, which themselves signify general ideas. Let me point out that this generality is primarily one of species and genera. Now, even though Leibniz does not mention Europe, what he has established about proper names would apply to it as well. Although designating an individual thing, the name of Europe carries a meaning that projects well beyond the finite, singular, situatable, and irreplaceable bearer of this name. But is this intelligible charge of the name *Europe* of the order of a generality understood in terms of species and genera? Is it generic in any sense? And, above all, is it something general to begin with? Finally, is the intelligibility carried by this proper name of the order of a concept or an idea such that it turn the proper name of *Europe* itself into a concept or idea of Europe?

Before setting out to answer this question, I wish to linger first on the frequent, and equally important conception of Europe as a figure, even though this conception will not be further examined in this book.²⁵ When it is applied to Europe, the notion of figure suggests that it is the distinct exterior form that its subject—Europe—takes. As such, it traces Europe's shape as something that is most properly its own. And within its limits Europe can properly unfold all the attributes of its presupposed interiority or essence. As opposed to speaking of the figures of Europe in the plural, which ordinarily refer to the historical manifold of specific *topoi* that have been affiliated with the cultural history of Europe, speaking of the figure of Europe in the singular links the notion of the figure directly to the question of Europe's identity. As a figure, Europe is predicated on a distinct essence that identifies it without a doubt. In this respect the figure of Europe also becomes inseparable from the problematic of the borders of Europe—not only in the geographical sense but in all the possible senses of the outlines in which cultural, economic, and political configurations can be drawn and thus set apart from other such configurations. It is within these borders that a pre-assumed identity of Europe can manifest itself in all its different shapes. Furthermore, if figure is conceived as *Gestalt*, henceforth as the product of a *Gestaltung*—a figuration, or formation, by way of a form that is imposed on some matter—then the figure of Europe shows itself to be the making, or work, of Europe itself as subject of this identity, if not by a subject that claims to represent Europe, to stand for it, and to be in charge of it. It is furthermore in this figure that this subject seeks to recognize itself and to accomplish the closure of its subjectivity. As a figure, Europe is understood as an entity that clearly stands out within its borders and that, as the actualization of a self-identical subject, sets itself apart from everything else. Undoubtedly, of the many figures of the figure of Europe, not only are there several that, rather than being static entities, have fluid boundaries that do not inhibit their transgression. Some are so fluid as to undo the very metaphysical logic of the figure—such as that of the archipelagos as a specifically European figure.²⁶ But as regards the conception of Europe as a figure (in the singular), the question arises of whether the intelligible content of the name of Europe can at all be constituted within such a thing as a figure or by way of a manifold of figures. In naming the passage away from everything native toward indeterminate otherness—as well as in allowing for the essential ability for transformation in response to what is other—does not what the name *Europe* evokes undermine all actualization of an identity within the sharp borders of a figure? But does identity always have to be figural in the first place? Does it always have to be thought in accordance with the metaphysical logic of the figure? Let me first remark that what the name *Europe* suggests is not a dismissal of identity or identification as such but only of a supposedly natural identity; identity or identification is not to be done away with as such. Identity and identification remain as a task, all the more so as the starting point of the identificatory process can only be the disappropriating exposure to otherness. But even such a process of identification cannot do without figuration, that is, without continuing to draw on the resources of form and figure. Understood in the sense of fashioning, molding, or modeling, figuration—from *fingere*, even in the sense of inventing, feigning, fictionalizing, rather than from its product—remains essential to shaping the response to otherness. Rather than leading to an identity aimed at buttressing itself against all intrusion, the figuration of identity in which construction does not become occluded remains indebted to the other and hence also open to change. Taking seriously what is suggested by the name of *Europe*, a figure of Europe based on such premises, would therefore have to be the "figure of a non-figure."[27] Understood in this way, the borders of Europe, rather than being confines within which a pre-assumed essence can unfold, must be rethought as limits that are always already crossed or as a horizon that is always already perforated.[28]

To elicit the name *Europe* is not only to evoke the continent and its history—Europe as a geographical and political entity, as well as the history of its many accomplishments and its many failures—but something else as well (even though one does not know exactly what this is). Undoubtedly, there are many who confidently pretend to know what exactly Europe has stood for, and continues to stand for—namely, a hegemonic phantasm and moribund worldview. By depicting Europe and the West as a homogeneous power of domination over the rest of the world, postcolonial criticism of European imperialism, and its construction of non-European cultures, knows perfectly what Europe is. Indeed, it knows it so well that it itself indulges in the same lack of differentiation of which it accuses the West in its relation to its others. It thus turns "Europe" into the blind spot of its own discourse.[29] As indicated, to invoke the name *Europe*, apart from referring to its location, culture, and history, is also to intimate something else: it is to suggest a concept or idea—a concept or an idea called "Europe"—even though it may not be immediately clear to what content such a concept or idea is assigned. I have pointed out before that, although "Europe" has been something like a philosopheme since at least the eighteenth century, it is in phenomenological thought in particular that Europe is explicitly discussed as either a concept or an idea—in other words, as something that is clearly of the order of the philosophical. For Husserl, to say that Europe is a concept or an idea is to say in the same breath that Europe is philosophy: the idea of Europe is the idea *of* philosophy—an idea of a universal rational science congruent with philosophy. Born in Europe, it elevates "Europe" to the status of an idea as well—a pure signified, or, as it were, an a priori signification independent from Europe in all its facticity. In short, as a concept or idea Europe is a project, the task of thinking and accomplishing universality. And, as we will see, to the extent that this task is infinite, it is itself a universal idea. Now, let us also point out that by thus figuring or representing itself—as it has indeed done throughout its history—Europe must make use of the very notions of concept and idea, which themselves are distinct philosophical means for gathering and unifying manifolds. (Since Husserl, like his followers, speaks of Europe without clearly distinguishing between concept and idea—the first implying, from a Kantian perspective, the grasping of cognition, the second, thought itself—I will leave this question unresolved.) But Josef Simon has also drawn our attention to the obvious, namely that "the concept 'idea' is itself already something European, and this is also the case with the concept of 'concept.'"[30] Europe's attempt at self-understanding and self-representation is therefore, at first sight, European through and through. However, as our discussion of the name *Europe* has shown, and as will hopefully become progressively clear throughout this examination of the concept or idea of Europe in phenomenological thought, the idea or concept of universality that is linked up with Europe cannot ultimately be brought within the compass of the concept or the idea. Unquestionably, what Europe is, or what it promises to be, needs to be identified, figured out, and imagined. It needs figuration. But above all, it requires incessant thinking and projection ahead as a project and a goal. The concept and the idea are unquestionably the prime discursive means to accomplish this task. But, at the same time, no concept or idea—that is, nothing of the order of the *genos* or the general—is in the end capable of integrating the infinite task named "Europe." That is, Europe as a merely discursive figure is not adequate to the kind of universality that is characteristic of the name of *Europe*.

If "Europe" is, then, ungraspable in the sense that the infinite task that it names cannot be confined and mastered by a concept or an idea, it is also because, as the grand discourses on Europe under consideration here will show, "Europe" is a discourse—the ceaseless attempt at discursively rethinking and refining the infinite, hence, universal task of a world, that by being a world hospitable without reservation or reserve to the other would alone be a world. Put differently, if this infinite task named "Europe" does not let itself be enclosed in figures (discursive or otherwise), concepts, or ideas, but instead requires a constant exposure to thought, then "Europe," rather than lending itself once and for all to an arrest in an identifiable conception and project to which it could be confined, projects beyond these boundaries. As Jean-Luc Nancy has suggested:

> There is something about "Europe" which we don't decide, something which, by the way, no one has decided, something that, by contrast, one needs to be capable of welcoming. Perhaps Europe, or the "essence" of Europe if one can still speak in this way, is first and foremost more of the order of a *birth* than a project. Undoubtedly, the projects of Europe that have been in the works for more than forty years have played their determinate role, and they will continue to do so. But Europe is *born* as well—or to put it differently, it *arrives* with everything unpredicted, unpredictable, if not improvident, incomplete, inchoate, and unfinishable. One ought not to ask (*vouloir autour*) too much of a new born.[31]

This newborn, as should already be evident, is philosophy itself. And it is a most demanding newborn furthermore.

PART I

Edmund Husserl

§ 1 Infinite Tasks

In his unfinished work *The Crisis of European Sciences and Transcendental Phenomenology*, Husserl construes the sciences as the defining essence of Europe. They are intrinsically linked to what in the Vienna lecture is called "the phenomenon 'Europe,'" "the concept of Europe," and, in *The Crisis*, the "absolute idea" of Europe (*C*, 299, 16). Doubtless, the unquestionable success of the exact, or natural sciences, as well as that of the formal discipline of mathematics, since the Renaissance, has been the reason for Europe's scientific and technological superiority; it is one of the major reasons for the subsequent phenomenon of the Europeanization of almost all of the rest of the world. But the sciences, as Husserl understands them, are also tied to an all-inclusive sense of what is. Thus, the idea of Europe, to the extent that it is wed to that of the sciences, coincides with the very idea of universality itself. For Husserl, however, universality is not predicated on a factual domination of the world by Europe nor upon the factual status of the sciences from the Renaissance to the present. Despite the intricate concatenation of the sciences, universality, and "Europe," found in *The Crisis*, European scientific and technological success is, for Husserl, in no way an index of the sciences' nor of Europe's universality implicated by extension. One could go as far as to say that, according to Husserl, the undeniable superiority of the idea and praxis of scientific cognition of the world is the clear indication of instrumental reason's interestedness, of its remaining tied up with one particular historical, cultural, national, and so on, mind-set, and thus with one anthropological type and its particular tradition. In fact, one could argue that Husserl's point in *The Crisis* is that the European success is the effect of precisely not meeting the challenge that science, as a universal and rational undertaking, presents. Predicated on universalist pretensions that are at the service of determinate interests, the sciences forfeit the very universality that they promise. The spiraling technism of the method of inquiry, its complete formalization in modern times, is for Husserl an unmistakable sign that the sciences are not seeking to achieve knowledge of the *one* world—the total horizon of the world—which all humans as humans share and that is presupposed by the very notion of universality. In fact, the crisis of the sciences, diagnosed by Husserl, is due precisely to the mathematization and formalization of the sciences: those qualities that have made them so successful. Indeed, according to Husserl, the positivist sciences have lost all relationship to the whole—the life-world—within which they would be meaningful. The crisis in question is the result of the scientific surreptitious substitution of the mathematized objective world of nature for the *one* world, the true world. Stated differently, the crisis on which Husserl elaborates is one that results from the abandonment by the successful sciences, and the concomitant technologization of knowledge, of an all-embracing science, or philosophy, one that would be not only all-encompassing, and universal, but whose methodology would rest on universal principles. In short, the crisis of the European sciences is rooted in the abandonment of the idea of science itself. The ensuing result of this abandonment is what Husserl terms "an existential catastrophe of the European human being," for indeed, "once science does no longer fulfill its ultimate meaning as science, the European human being does no longer fulfill his ultimate meaning, that is to say, as European human being."[1]

In what sense, then, can the sciences still be said to represent the foundation of "Europe"? To answer this question, we must first clarify what the title "Europe" refers to. In the lecture from 1935 entitled "Philosophy and the Crisis of European Humanity"—the Vienna lecture—Husserl emphasizes that the designation "Europe" is not to be "understood geographically, as on a map, as if thereby the group of people who live together in this territory would define European humanity" (*C*, 273). "Europe" is not to be defined in natural, nor even conventional, terms whatever their kind or shade. Instead, "Europe" is said to be of the order of a "supranationality of a completely new sort" (*C*, 289), that is, of the order of a "spiritual shape [*geistige Gestalt*]." As a spiritual shape, Husserl holds, "Europe" is the name for "the unity of a spiritual life, activity, creation, with all its ends, interests, cares, and endeavors, with its products of purposeful activity, institutions, organizations" (*C*, 273). Rather than a geographical entity, or an entity identified in terms of race, Europe is a practical objective—a life project—an immanently practical project, one that embraces all aspects of life.[2] What structures this project animated by "a spirit of free critique and norm-giving aimed at infinite tasks" (*C*, 289), is the spiritual end by which life is to be shaped here. If the sciences are instrumental to the spiritual life project called "Europe," it is only to the extent that they define the idea that animates this life project. As Husserl suggests at the beginning of *The Crisis*, what "Europe" stands for is the project of reshaping humankind in light of "the questions which are decisive for a genuine humanity" (*C*, 6), in other words, questions that concern humanity's, and not geographical Europe's, self-understanding. "Europe," then, is the project of a reshaping of the relations among individuals, groups, and nations, in light of what it means to be human rather than in terms of membership in an ethnia, with its particular customs and traditions. Now, if the sciences are constitutive of "Europe" as a spiritual shape, it is because they are not simply contemplative and disinterested enterprises. *Episteme*, as a posture or state of mind (that is, as a form of *hexis*) regarding the things it relates to, is practical not only because it is in possession of concrete knowledge about these things that can be taught and learned, thus requiring experience and time, but also because such knowledge comes with certain requirements, or ideal injunctions, whose realization, by contrast, demands to be enacted in full at every moment. The sciences, according to their idea, are linked from the outset—that is, from their emergence in Greece and their subsequent transformation in the Renaissance—to an eminently practical project of enabling humanity to understand and reshape itself, in other words, to constitute itself *as* humanity.[3] Even though factically the sciences emerge in Greece, they are immediately geared toward what is universal, and the concerns of humankind as a whole. Husserl submits that with the emergence of universal philosophy, Greek humanity became "the first breakthrough to what is essential to humanity as such, its *entelechy*" (*C*, 15). In spite of their origin in a specific region of the world, the sciences are not a contingent affair but, in Husserl's words, the expression of "humanity struggling to understand itself" (*C*, 14). Consequently, if the European sciences are suffering a crisis, it is precisely because they have cut themselves loose from this specific task that defines, both theoretically and practically, the sciences' initial meaning.[4] Let me point out, right away, that this reference to a task defining the sciences entails that what they are to achieve does not consist of placing an easily and comfortably available knowledge at one's disposal, one that would simply have to be applied. Now, only insofar as the sciences are involved in fostering the emergence of humanity itself—of humanity conscious of itself *as* humanity—can they be said to be the driving force of the idea of Europe—its origin and *telos*. This, however, means that the various sciences be not merely fact-minded but that they understand themselves as deriving their relational meaning, or truth, from their foundation in an all-embracing science, or philosophy, concerned with what is universal.

As the agents of universality, the sciences animate the spiritual shape of Europe. They constitute the *idea* of Europe, and endow Europe with a "remarkable [*merkwürdige*] teleology, inborn, as it were, only in our Europe" (*C*, 273). The idea of the universal, which guides Europe as a spiritual shape (as well as the equally spiritual history of that shape), is not merely remarkable because it would set Europe apart from other parts of the world.[5] This telos is remarkable primarily because it is, as the German *merkwürdig* suggests, a very peculiar, strange, or odd telos. Without a full grasp of what is profoundly odd about the very idea of universality, and hence about the title "Europe," it is impossible, I hold, to do justice to precisely how Husserl understands these terms, and what the presuppositions and implications are of speaking of Europe as an absolute idea. Without taking stock of the strangeness of this idea—one strange enough as to be even at odds with Europe as a geographical and ethnical entity—the very charge that universality is Eurocentric is, at best, a symptom, to use Husserlian language, of "lazy reason" (*C*, 16). In the following discussion of the idea of Europe, I will seek to highlight this strangeness.

Part 2 of *The Crisis of European Sciences* is mainly concerned with the resurgence of the idea and ideal of a universal science during the Renaissance and with the subsequent abandonment of that ideal (vital to humanity) by the objective sciences, which has caused the contemporary crisis. What the Renaissance rediscovers, and then loses again, is the Greek idea of a rational and universal science. That Greek idea, however, is not a conception that had always been familiar to the ancient Greeks. Rather, this idea is the unfamiliar itself. As Husserl observes in the Vienna lecture, this idea is "intimately involved with the outbreak or irruption [*Aufbruch und Einbruch*] of philosophy and its branches, the sciences, in the ancient Greek spirit" (*C*, 273) and inaugurates a breakthrough (*Durchbruch*) of a new human epoch. As the expressions, "outbreak," "irruption," and "breakthrough," suggest, this idea (violently) bursts into existence, as it were; it intrudes on and disturbs previous ways of thinking and acting. To use an expression coined by Eugen Fink to describe the structure of philosophical wonder, an "Entsetzung"—a shocking dis-placement, or uprooting from the human being's prepossession by the world, his or her familiarity with it and sense of security within it—accompanies the irruption of the idea in question.[6] Only something bewilderingly strange can produce such effects. Indeed, rather than providing security, "the great and genuine ethos which constitutes philosophy—great and genuine philosophy," that is, Greek philosophy, in particular, rather than providing "security," comes with the most unsettling exigencies.[7] Husserl characterizes not only "the originary demand given through the intention of philosophy, as containing in the evident conditions of possibility of philosophy's fulfillment, a categorical imperative," but he also describes the aspiration to a life according to higher values "as the search to reach out for something that in the end is contrary [*zuwider*] [to the ego], a way of life and aspiring that brings it into conflict with itself."[8] If ancient Greece enjoys a unique position with respect to the rest of the world, it is exclusively because of this irruption of philosophy as the alienating demand to live according to universal ideas and because Greece espoused this strange demand and shaped its institutions accordingly. Described as the idea of an all-encompassing science, the breakthrough of philosophy in ancient Greece might not strike us immediately as a particularly odd event. Since the claim to be all-encompassing is frequently viewed not only as illusory but also as arrogant, the emergence of this idea is rather felt to be that of a preposterous claim; consequently, what this idea demanded of Greece itself—the demand to rise above itself as a particular people—is obfuscated. In any case, before it can be shown that the idea that irrupts in ancient Greece is precisely the *idea* of an all-encompassing science, that is, of the universal task to theoretically and practically realize such a science, one must underscore a number of the features of this idea of a universal and rational science that not only reveal its strangeness but that also clarify how one is to understand the all-encompassing nature of the science in question.

Reflecting on the idea immanent to Europe (or, what is the same, the teleology that animates it), Husserl writes in the Vienna lecture that this idea "makes itself known [*die sich vom Gesichtspunkt der universalen Menschheit überhaupt kenntlich macht*], from the standpoint of universal mankind as such, as the breakthrough and the developmental beginning of a new human epoch—the epoch of mankind which now seeks to live, and only can live, in the free shaping of its existence, its historical life, through ideas of reason, through infinite tasks" (*C*, 274). The idea of philosophy that irrupts into the world of the ancient Greeks—who, it should be noted, not only were of heterogeneous origins but whose early philosophers were, moreover, foreigners, or exiles[9]—is the idea of a science that answers for itself before "universal mankind," in other words, no longer in terms particular to the cultural, traditionalist, and religious idioms of the various ethnicities that made up Greece. This idea of philosophy is not merely one of tasks (*Aufgaben*, literally, assignments) depending on a programmatic and normative knowledge that merely needs to be applied but of infinite tasks—a concept that Husserl probably borrowed from the neo-Kantian Hermann Cohen, who has systematically highlighted the importance of the concept of "task" in Kant—and concerns tasks that devolve from ideas that, because infinite, constitute universal tasks.[10] Even before we speak of the content of this new conception, it is important to realize that the very way the idea of philosophy comes into being runs against all established ethnic, cultural, and traditionalist views or norms. Indeed, Husserl's reference to the standpoint from which the idea of philosophy makes itself known implies that philosophy does not impose itself as just another self-evident, culturally specific product. Rather, from the outset it justifies itself in terms that call on everyone, regardless of customary ways of thinking. What makes this idea so odd is that it answers for itself and does so with a view toward principles and rules that can be followed and reconstructed by everyone on condition that particular modes of thinking are bracketed. The self-presentation from the standpoint of universal humankind shows this idea to be one of humankind itself. Indeed, the breakthrough that takes place in early Greece is the irruption into consciousness of the very concept of humanity itself as a concept transcending all particular humanities.[11] Whether or not the Greek notion of universality was still tinged by Greekness, a norm—and with it, a task—arose that constitutes a demand that remains, I contend, universally valid. Furthermore, by justifying itself in terms that appeal to everyone, rather than to the constituents of one's home world, the idea of philosophy is introduced as bearing from the outset on the human being's life. It is the request that everyone shape his or her life freely—free from all traditionalist conceptions—by not acting or advancing anything that cannot be accounted for in terms transparent to all. This is a very demanding demand, one that goes against the grain of all habitual ways of thinking, because in order to secure an opening to the other, and hence be answerable to the other, it requires not only thoroughly coherent but also "uniform" thinking and acting by yielding to universally recognizable principles. Indeed, this demand, which the Greeks called *logon didonai*, is the demand to be self-responsible and to assume this responsibility by accounting for one's claims and actions rather than having recourse to inveterate beliefs and ingrained habits of thinking. With this demand emerges the possibility of a new type of history, the history of a life shaped through ideas and reason, in short, a history of humankind itself. Now, since humankind can itself become a reality only when human beings shape their lives according to reason, that is, by becoming self-responsible, the emergence of philosophy and its demand is that of a task. Rather than furnishing the human beings with the sense of a common essence always already given in advance, the idea of philosophy coincides with the unsettling demand to ceaselessly account for oneself and to secure thus something that merits being called "universally human." Even though Husserl considers every human being to be an *animal rationale*, hence, capable of reason, this defining trait of what is human is not only primarily a teleological project, that is, something still to be accomplished, but it also consists in nothing but the critical ability to transcend given identities. Such transcending alone is what constitutes the human.[12] Considering what philosophy demands of the human being, the kind of life for which it holds out the prospect is a life of "infinite tasks." Rather than approximating a positive state, the suspension of the limitation caused by particularities is the goal of this infinite task. Indeed, the very act of suspending all traditionalisms is the way of reason, and it coincides with the accomplishment of the idea of humanity.[13] If this idea, then, is what constitutes, and immanently unifies, "Europe," it is an idea that breaks open Europe's self-immanence toward a transcendence, toward the other, and what is other than Europe. It is, therefore, no doubt, a quite unsettling idea, one that disturbs the very homeliness of any world, including the world of the Europeans.[14]

It also follows from this that it is the very strangeness, if not even foreignness, of this idea that determines its introduction into other home worlds. If this idea is to be taken on by other nations, or cultures, in short, if there is to be, what Husserl terms "a universal Europeanization," the idea in question must be for these nations and cultures a novel idea, one that originated elsewhere and is, necessarily, experienced as foreign. Without such foreignness, the idea of Europe, which as we have seen is foreign to Europe as well, would not, if introduced in another nation, become more than "a mere custom, one that is exclusively valid and binding for the members of a nation," and would not permit acting on other nations in a binding way, compelling them to enter into a rational relation of transnational or international togetherness. In a 1934 preliminary study to *The Crisis* entitled "Human Life in Historicity," Husserl suggests that only a principle that has been taken over, and that is a foreign acquisition, can possibly become binding for a nation that first lived with other nations in "an exterior togetherness, . . . in inner distance, reciprocal foreignness, lack of understanding, and the refusal of the foreign validities, surrounding worlds, cultural values, and so forth," if it is to give rise to "continuous communal life and a communal traditionality of univocity, to an agreement of continuously taking over validities, foundations of validity, and reciprocal criticism, correction, and unification, that have been acquired abroad [*in der Fremde erworbenen*]." The unity of nations Husserl refers to is one of "a supranation born from the sources of objective reason, just as the one that Europe has become, that is, one of an expanded Europe."[15]

Before further fleshing out the idea that irrupts in Greece, let me emphasize that it is not a merely theoretical idea. Although the "attitude of the *thaumazein*" (*C*, 284), which founds the theoretical attitude directed toward "the all-encompassing unity of all that is [*Alleinheit alles Seienden*]" (*C*, 276) and turns away from all practical interests, it is only insofar as these interests are connected to particular concerns within the concrete worlds of specific humanities. Since Husserl views these practical interests as deriving from a concern with human fate in worlds dominated by mythical, that is, also always particular, powers, praxis and practical knowledge are taken to be subservient to mythical world conceptions (*C*, 283–84). However, *theoria*'s gaze at the world itself, and its concern with a truth that is no longer "tradition-bound, everyday truth, but an identical truth which is valid for all who are no longer blinded by tradition, a truth-in-itself" (*C*, 286), is practical as well, but in an entirely different sense. *Theoria* becomes practical, first, in that it shapes the life of the thinker. Husserl writes in the Vienna lecture: "Part of the theoretical attitude of the philosopher . . . is his constant and prior resolve to dedicate his future life always, and in the sense of a universal life, to the task of *theoria*, to build theoretical knowledge upon theoretical knowledge *in infinitum*" (*C*, 286). The "new sort of humanity [that arises as a result of the theoretical attitude, and which] living in finitude, lives toward poles of infinity" (*C*, 277), produces a new form of community (*neuartige Vergemeinschaftung*), one based on "mutual help through mutual critique" (*C*, 286) and subsequent correction.[16] Indeed, it is as a critique of tradition-bound truths that theory becomes practical. Progressively this movement includes outsiders who either become philosophers themselves or learners, and since, "unlike all other cultural works, philosophy is not a movement of interest which is bound to the soil of the national tradition," it, finally, spreads to other nations (*C*, 286). As Husserl claims in the Vienna lecture, this movement does not end with the transnational unity of Europe. Its aim is an "ideally directed total society [*idealgerichtete Allsozietät*]" (*C*, 289). Even though Husserl readily admits that other cultures manifest "world-encompassing" interests, and, like Greek philosophy, have produced "universal knowledge of the world" (*C*, 280), this knowledge remains entangled in mythical-religious, that is, always, particular, forms that prevent them from gaining universal appeal (*C*, 283).[17] What distinguishes Greek philosophy from these "philosophies" is, according to Husserl, first of all, that *theoria* is "taken up into the will [by the whole Greek community] with the sense of an infinite and common [*allgemeinsamen*] task" (*C*, 280). Here the universal, construed as the odd demand to divest oneself of everything particular, and to live in view of the total horizon of the world, becomes a life-interest that transforms the whole local and particular culture so as to reform the community as a whole in view of the pursuit of universality as an infinite task.

What constitutes "Europe" and unifies the history of its spiritual shape is this idea, congruent with philosophy or universal science, of the task to think theoretically and act practically in view of what is universal. No superiority, let it be said, derives from the factual firstness of this idea in Europe. This task, generated by Europe, is not something that belongs to Europe as a private possession. To the extent that "Europe" is the idea of universal humanity, this task belongs to (and thus obligates) everyone;

it is a common task, whereby its original proprietor is instantly dispossessed. It is, therefore, not the *proprium* of Europe. Although anyone can lay claim to this task, and rename it accordingly, "Europe" remains the name for this task, and for the responsibility to and for this task, because, having emerged in Europe for the first time, it binds the Europeans, first and foremost.[18] But if the European *eidos* does not bestow any superiority on Europe, it is also because this idea is only that of a task, the odd task of overcoming all natural and traditionalist determinations and thus everything that characterizes Europe as a particular humanity. Before further probing its oddity, let me take a closer glance at this Husserlian notion of task. I take my first clue from Husserl's elaborations in *The Crisis* on the contemporary European thinkers' efforts to discern within the maze of all past and present philosophical projects in Europe, "the historical task which we can acknowledge as the only one which is personally our own" (*C*, 70). According to Husserl, the nature of this task can only be elucidated "through a critical understanding of the total unity of history—*our* history" (*C*, 71). In other words, the task that is specific to the European thinker, the one that is expressly his or hers personally, his or hers innermost own (*eine wahrhaft uns eigene Aufgabe* or *die eigenste Aufgabe*), can only come from within and with respect to the philosophical heritage that historically and spiritually has formed the philosopher. More precisely, the European philosopher must respond to the tradition bequeathed to him or her; it is for and to the task with which this tradition confronts the philosopher that he or she is responsible, and a responsible response to what the heritage demands of him or her defines his or her innermost task. To critically understand the heritage that has formed the European thinker, it is necessary to screen out all past and present *Weltanschauungen*, whether they are of European extraction or of foreign origin, and to seek out what, despite all its diversity and even contradiction, gives unity to European philosophical thought.

In the modern period, European philosophical history's unity and driving force is the task that, as we have already seen, emerges "through a primal establishment [in the Renaissance] which is at once a reestablishment and a modification of the Greek primal establishment. In the latter lies the *teleological beginning*, the true birth of the European spirit as such" (*C*, 71). In the final analysis, then, and insofar as they are the "functionaries of modern philosophical humanities" (*C*, 71), the innermost proper task of the contemporary European philosophers has to be understood from the teleological beginning of the European spirit as such in the Greek primal establishment.[19] For, indeed, the legacy, with respect to which the task of contemporary philosophy becomes intelligible, to and for which Europe is responsible, is no other than the Greek founding conception of philosophy as a universal task, a task that is not only one of individual and collective, but universal responsibility toward what is universal to humankind. Speaking in "Philosophy as Rigorous Science," of the research aspiration concerning a rigorous and scientific philosophy, Husserl submits that this aspiration, although fully conscious that it can "in no wise be the complete creation of the individual [philosopher], still devotes its fullest energies to promoting in cooperation with men of like mind, the break-through and gradual progress of a scientific philosophy."[20] Differently worded, the task of a rigorous philosophy is one that, to borrow a term that characterizes the early romantics' project of a progressive universal poetry, can only be achieved as a *symphilosophy*.[21] Its subject ultimately is not the individual philosopher but the community of philosophers and, ultimately, humanity itself. If the concept of a specifically European task is meaningful at all, it is only in this sense of being a task that is everybody's task, whether European or not, a universal task. This task, then, and it alone, is what Greece has bequeathed to the contemporary European thinker. To it alone, and for it alone, is he or she responsible. Paradoxically, without this task, which demands that one free oneself from what is particular about oneself, there is no specificity and no property or propriety of, or for, the European thinker. By reactivating that task, and taking it on, the philosopher severs himself from himself as a private individual, and becomes what Husserl calls somewhat awkwardly, "a functionary of mankind." He writes: "In *our* philosophizing we are *functionaries of mankind*. The quite personal responsibility for the true being as philosophers, our inner personal vocation, bears within itself at the same time the responsibility for the true being of mankind; the latter is, necessarily, being toward a *telos* and can only come to realization, *if at all*, through philosophy—through *us*, *if* we are philosophers in all seriousness" (*C*, 17).[22] The unfortunate expression *functionaries* has often been derided for its pompousness but also because of its bureaucratic ring, even though Husserl, when referring explicitly to civil servants, or government officials in general, uses as a rule the German term *Beamte*. Husserl understands the notion of functionary primarily from its Latin root, *fungi*, to busy oneself with, be engaged in, to perform, to execute, and so forth, from which also derives the German word *fungieren*, frequently used in his writings. For Husserl, philosophy is a profession, and as a professional one is a functionary in the sense that one has assumed a duty regarding the general expectations and constantly reiterated requirements of the community with respect to which this profession is exercised.[23] Since in the case of philosophy, this community is ultimately humankind at large, all Husserl wishes to say is that if, indeed, philosophy is about the universal, then to philosophize is to work toward, and to bear responsibility to, bringing the genuine being of humankind about. However stilted, the bureaucratic expression "functionaries of mankind" also suggests the essentially public nature of philosophy. The philosopher thus also differs from the sage, whether Greek or non-Greek, who as a personality teaches wisdom by directing himself to personality.[24] Not only is the philosopher when committed to universality a public figure and, hence, distinct from himself as a private, particular thinker, but he is also publicly accountable, answerable for the claims of universality he makes. Indeed, the idea of a universal philosophy is the idea of a responsible philosophy, that is, one that is responsible to humanity as such in that it seeks the full transparency of everything it asserts. Finally, since universal humanity comes to realization in the essentially public nature of answering for any claim one makes, the responsibility of the philosopher is, ultimately, a responsibility to and for responsibility itself.

Philosophy's true task, assigned to it at its advent in Greece, remains the idea of a universal science responsible to humanity as such. If this task is *assigned to* (*aufgegeben*) the philosopher, it is not least because the demand in question is not self-evident. It does not go without saying. Indeed, the notion of a task implies that what is to be accomplished has to be brought about against the resistance of that which exists. It requires a transgression of the given and is directed toward something beyond what is. Furthermore, if philosophy is a task, it is also because there are limits to accomplishing it. If the task could be met once and for all, it would not be a task. The notion of task may even inscribe within itself the need to confront the impossible and the impossibility of its ever being completed once and for all. To get a better understanding of the nature of this task assigned to the philosopher, some remarks about its teleological character are warranted.

In contrast to all determinations of European identity that rely on natural or conventional characteristics (all of which are accidental), the task of achieving true humanity alone can convey a distinct property and propriety to European humanities, precisely, by making these humanities differ from themselves, by uprooting them from their natural or cultural grounds. As Tadashi Ogawa has suggestively remarked, what Europe thus demands of itself is nothing less than the very de-Europeanization of European life and thought.[25] Since what constitutes the identity of Europe is a function of its own separation from itself, Europe's identity is not a given. With the birth of Greek philosophy, that is, with the idea of a "humanity which seeks to exist, and is only possible, through philosophical reason, moving endlessly from latent to manifest reason and forever seeking its own norms through this, its truth and genuine human nature," a task has been set for Europe—a *telos* with respect to which it is to define itself in order to be properly itself. "Inborn in European humanity," this telos of the realization of true humanity, is the end toward which it must stretch in order to be "Europe." In order to grasp the precise sense in which *telos* must be understood, it is perhaps appropriate to briefly evoke the two concepts of "end" known by the Greeks. Aristotle, for example, distinguishes between the good at which all things aim and the mark at which archers aim. According to Aristotle, in the "Nicomachean Ethics," to have the knowledge of what is good should have an influence on life in the same way that having a mark on which to fix his or her eyes helps the archer to hit the target. The distinction is one between *telos* and *skopos*.[26] Discussing this distinction with respect to Stoicism—both *telos* and *skopos* are concepts of "end" and, hence, of "task"—Jean-Luc Nancy notes that

> the *skopos* is the target one has in view and at which one aims. It is the goal presented and clearly offered to a sighting and aiming which this goal determines in turn. . . . By contrast, the *telos* is the accomplishment of an action or of a process, carrying it through to completion, to its end term. . . . The *end* that is the *telos* is not an end sighted and thus aimed at; it is an end insofar as it is the greatest possible development of something, beyond which there is nothing that this something could still become. This is why the *telos* is inseparable from existence. The *telos* is, as it were, entelechial rather than teleological. . . . [A *telos*, then,] is not made up of a model given in advance, an original that is to be joined again or taken back.[27]

It is, as Husserl has occasionally said, "only a 'formation of thinking' [*Denkgebilde*], and hence it cannot be intuitively experienced in concrete intercultural experiences of unanimity."²⁸ A *telos* is an end that is constituted in the process of aiming at it, and which only *will have been* the end in sight of which action has taken place, that is, in an anterior future. It follows from this that the telos inborn in Europe, and which is what, without being a *proprium*, defines Europe most properly, is not only of the order of something that must, at all times, be critically activated through Europe's separation from itself, but it also consists in nothing other than the performance of this separation itself. Greece, as we will see, is not a model simply to be imitated. The idea that first emerged in Greece in order to soon fall into oblivion can only be freely (that is, critically) reactivated, in other words, reconfigured. It is, after all, the idea of what Husserl calls "universal criticism" (*C*, 283).

Before I continue to explore the nature of the sciences that are said to represent the defining telos immanent to Europe, and to investigate further the intrinsic foreignness of all explicit universal thought to the particular home worlds in which human beings live, let me first address an easily foreseeable objection. Given that the current resistance to universality is predicated on the conception that the universal is an abstraction that suppresses particularity, and particularisms, its intrinsic strangeness could easily be construed as proof of its outright incommensurability to the defining home worlds of human beings. Undoubtedly, the planetary expansion of the technosciences has produced an alarming leveling of many ethnic and religious differences. If, however, the seemingly unstoppable expansion of the positivistic and technological sciences that originate in Europe and the West, not to speak of today's trend toward a commodified unitary culture, is certainly detrimental to particularities, this globalization is not, as we will see in the next chapter, to be mistaken for an index of universality. The European conception of the universal and the technological, economic, and cultural leveling and globalization of the world by the West may well be related in some manner, but the foreignness intrinsic to the universal is a foreignness of a different order from that of the technosciences that have gone global. Even though I have described the universal as radically contrary to the particular customs, traditions, and beliefs of the home worlds, the universal is not simply foreign to these worlds. Just as in Kant's ethics, where the individual must submit to a law that without exception is valid for all ethical subjects and, at the same time, affirm this intransigent law as its very own, so the universal that appears as alien to the subject as a particular human being must resonate with the subject in some essential manner. The main task of transcendental phenomenology is to explain how this is possible. Before I expand in greater detail on this issue, the following hints must suffice. As Husserl points out, the explicit task to bring about the true nature of human beings in the struggle with *doxa*, although this true nature is contrary to all inveterate prejudices, is a goal implicitly known by everyone in everyday life. It is prefigured by the concerns of daily life with truth. According to *The Crisis*, "this prefiguration is surpassed by philosophy" (*C*, 13). Philosophy, rather than a lofty construct, is, therefore, only the explicit thematization and unfolding of a difference—the difference between truth and opinion—that "every person" (in other words everyone, European or not) knows from everyday life, but which he or she ordinarily knows of in "merely isolated and relative fashion" (*C*, 13). Philosophy takes the ideal goal of true being to its full consequence. If, "in its first, original establishment, ancient philosophy, . . . conceives of and takes as its task the exalted idea of universal knowledge concerning the totality of what is" (*C*, 13), it is because, notwithstanding the subjectively relative ways in which the world is given to us in prescientific sense-experience, one is always somehow aware that there is the *one* world, the world shared by all particular humanities. Hence, rather than affecting the home worlds from the outside, the universal emerges within these worlds themselves and is intimately linked to specific concerns of these particular worlds. While a world experienced as one's home world implies a reference to other worlds, and hence to a total world, the vital concerns constitutive of the home worlds lead to the production of identically repeatable shapes that are instrumental in coming to grips with certain practical tasks but that, at the same time, prefigure the total horizon of the world. However, once this dimension of universality that is anchored in the particular life-worlds becomes conscious of itself (as has been the case in ancient Greece) and its more general implications are thematically thrown into relief, the universal acquires a practical meaning that is definitely at odds with the beliefs, customs, and habits of the home worlds in that it confronts these worlds with a praxis of a different order, one no longer limited to the interests of local humanities. The strangeness characteristic of universality is thus only relatively strange. Even though universality is not in absolute difference from the particular (and, as I would argue, manifests itself only as tinged by particularity), neither is it reducible to the particular. They remain in a relation of essential strangeness.

Let me enlarge on the task that comes into being with the breakthrough of the idea of a universal science in ancient Greece. The science in question, which is an all-encompassing science in a sense still to be elucidated, concerns itself with what is universal, that is, with the *one* world, or total horizon, that we, as human beings, share, regardless of all our differences. The science whose birth certificate is established in Greece is, therefore, as Husserl puts it in *The Crisis*, an expression of "humanity struggling to understand itself" (*C*, 14). The idea of a universal science that emerges in ancient Greece concerns humanity as such, not just Greek humanity. Philosophy as universal science fights for the true being of the human by conceiving of the human being in terms of the horizon that he or she shares with all others. This struggle of humanity to understand itself, which is fought in the name of ideas and reason, is a struggle precisely because it must be won against the interests that characterize regional humanities. Moreover, it is a struggle because that in the name of which this struggle takes place is not a given. Husserl writes: "This true being [of man] is not something he always already has, with the self-evidence of the 'I am,' but something he only has and can have in the form of the struggle to make himself true. True being is *everywhere* an ideal goal, a task of *episteme* or 'reason,' as opposed to being which through *doxa* is merely thought to be, unquestioned and 'obvious'" (*C*, 13). Even though the "capacity to secure rational meaning for his individual and common human existence" belongs to human beings, one's true being, that is, his or her being within the total horizon of the world, consists exclusively in the "struggle to make himself free." Yet this true being does not reside in some positive free state to be attained through the struggle, but merely in the state of the "struggle for his truth" itself (*C*, 13). Phrased differently, the life of reason that the sciences make possible is not a goal separate or beyond *doxa* but is realized only in the clinch with *doxa*. The human being's true nature concurs with the very task itself of struggling with *doxa* and is not the positive outcome of a clear-cut rupture with it.

From everything we have developed so far concerning philosophy's demand to suspend through critique the prejudices (opinions, beliefs, habits, etc.) associated with the particular home worlds, in order to bring the *one* world shared by all into relief, Husserl would seem to pursue the one of two seemingly disjunctive ways that Parmenides had recommended to the lover of truth. Distinct from the way of *doxa* and its ever-changing illusions, this way provides access to an everlasting world in itself. The use of the term *episteme* to designate the only knowledge commensurate with philosophy, and that he opposes to *doxa*, would only seem to further support the suspicion that Husserl confronts the life-forms of human beings with an eviscerated and abstract, universal, aloof from the life-world. Undoubtedly, everything philosophy has to keep in check to accomplish its task—that is, both natural and conventional determinations—is of the order of what traditionally has been called *doxa*. But the life-world in which the reference to the *one* world is anchored, that is, the domain of primitive evidences, which is the ground from which the first idealities emerge, and from which Husserl extrapolates not only the idea of a universal science, but with respect to which also all opinions, traditionalisms, customs, and so forth, are criticized, is also, according to Husserl, "nothing other than the world of *doxa* treated so scornfully by the tradition."[29] The importance that *doxa* thus acquires is owed to the fact that *doxa*, or the life-world, is that which all *episteme*, whether that of universal science or of the objective sciences, always already presupposes.[30] As Walter Biemel notes, *doxa* is "that which always already is pre-given and that means it is that which is presupposed, the original." In other words, *doxa*, as the life-world, has the "function of a ground" for the scientific ideal in general. Its fundamental role consists in being the original establishment on which all other establishments are built, in particular that of the objective sciences.[31] The idea of science, with its constitutive demarcation from *doxa*, arises thus from *doxa* itself. Phenomenology, seemingly separated by an abyss from *doxa* insofar as it is the universal science of the life-world, is tied into the life-world. As Karl Schumann remarks, phenomenology, as universal *episteme*, "presents itself as simultaneously a transgression and as the merely immanent highest form of the natural life of consciousness."[32] Indeed, the science interested in the life-world is, according to Husserl, "a peculiar science, to be sure, since it concerns the disparaged *doxa*, which now suddenly claims the dignity of a foundation for science, *episteme*" (*C*, 155–56). As we will see in Chapter 3, the goal of the analysis of the life-world is not only to lay bare the foundations of objective science but to reach back beyond the sedimentations of the life-world to a horizon of the world that can serve as the ground for an *episteme* that differs from objective, or logical, scientificity. It follows from this that rather than bringing to bear an abstract concept of universality on the life of human beings, the task of philosophy, as conceived by Husserl, seeks to induce a sense of universality from the subjectively relative world that is constantly obfuscated not only by the objective sciences but also by the beliefs and opinions that make up this same world. To Paul Ricoeur's question of how this new *episteme* "can also do justice to its most despised opposite, *doxa*," it is thus possible to answer by saying that its new scientificity arises by way of pitting *doxa* against *doxa*, that is, by wrenching itself from the life-world in a constant struggle with the sense-sedimentations that in this world cover it over.[33] A further consequence is that although universality requires transcendence of the particular, genuine universality does not, like the universality of globalization, destroy the particular.

Husserl offers several ways in which to think the relation between the universal and the particular. As we have seen, the universal does overcome *doxa* but ceaselessly struggles with it. Furthermore, as the elaborations on religion in the Vienna lecture suggest, the particular lets itself be transformed at the hands of the universal. Additional ways in which the universal and the particular relate are to be found in the many appendices to the main text of *The Crisis*.[34] Let me also say at this point that although philosophy comes into being in Greece as the project of a radical uprooting—one that Husserl also describes as "the cutting-off [*Entwerdens*] of finite mankind's development as it becomes mankind with infinite tasks" (*C*, 279)—the attempt to ground the universal in the life-world is also acknowledgment of the exacting demands of the life-project in question, which must allow for negotiation with the particularities of concrete life. Husserl writes: "The individual men who reorient themselves, as men within their universal life-community (their nation), continue to have their natural interests, each his individual interests; through no reorientation can they simply lose them; this would mean that each would cease to be what he has become from birth onward" (*C*, 281). Rooting the universal in the life-world is thus also an attempt to keep in check an immanent danger that lurks in the European idea of a completely uprooted human being (*aoikos*). This is the danger that an uprooted, nomadic existence—one that is "merely uprooted," and independent of all ethos—turns homogeneous, relinquishes its autonomy, and seeks the guidance of a leader.[35]

But let me return to Husserl's characterization of a life in accordance with reason. What he understands by reason is nothing but the capacity just described, to critically engage everything particular from the standpoint of universal humankind, and this in a process that can never claim to have reached its goal. The developed capacity of reason consists in nothing other than "to submit one's actual life and the results of once life to self-criticism, collective criticism [*Gemeinschaftskritik*], and to critically correct it."[36] Universal humanity is not the realization of a determined essence, model, or abstract substance, of the human being; it coincides with the unrelentingly performed task of critically engaging particularisms and transcending particularism in a self-responsible manner. It is in this sense that Husserl can even speak of reason as the profession of mankind.[37] Speaking of the "reorientation [*Umstellung*]" (*C*, 280) that necessarily accompanies the theoretical attitude in its differentiation from the natural and pretheoretical attitude (in that the theoretical attitude makes the universal horizon of the world thematic), Husserl defines the new sort of praxis that goes hand in hand with theory, in the Vienna lecture, as "that of the universal critique of all life and all-life-goals, all cultural products and systems that have already arisen out of the life of man; and thus it also becomes a critique of mankind itself and of the values which guide it explicitly or implicitly" (*C*, 283). By radically uprooting all forms of natural life in light of the total horizon of the world, and demanding that these forms be universally justified, the task of this universal critique is "to elevate mankind through universal scientific reason, according to norms of truth of all forms, to transform it from the bottom up into a new humanity made capable of an absolute self-responsibility [*Selbstverantwortung*] on the basis of absolute theoretical insights" (*C*, 283). Greece, and by extension "Europe," is thus synonymous with the idea of self-responsibility, that is, of a life of freedom—a freedom from the constraints of customs, beliefs, traditionalisms, and so forth—and a life in which one answers publicly for one's life, "from the standpoint of universal mankind as such." The demand to shape one's life according to principles of reason is not the demand to subject it to a determined essence of the human being, to some transcendental content as it were;[38] rather, it is the demand to exercise, without compromise and without rest, universal critique and, thereby, to take responsibility, "from the standpoint of universal mankind as such," for all one's claims and actions. It also follows from this that the exercise of universal critique alone is what raises an individual, group, or nation to universal humanity. It is with this infinite task, one that is adverse to all the values of the natural attitude—a task that in the perspective of the immediate and natural attitude is the most outlandish imposition—that the Greeks confronted themselves; it remains the task, according to Husserl, that Europe has to take upon itself.

This task of self-responsibility and universal answerability that emerges in ancient Greece, and that, given Europe's heritage, constitutes its teleology, is linked to the idea of a universal all-embracing science, to *theoria*, in short. As Husserl notes in *The Crisis*, the Greeks conceived of science not as a singular science but as "the one all-encompassing science, the science of the totality of what is" (*C*, 8). *Theoria*, as science in the singular, enters history in Greece "with its universal subject matter (*Thema*) of everything that is at all, a totality and an all-encompassing unity of what is" (*C*, 345). Without any restrictions whatsoever, science is directed toward all that can be experienced and thought. Science is not only therefore universal; its task is infinite, hence also, ultimately, without completion.[39] But since the theme of theory is also made up of "the most general and invariant characteristics of the world" (*C*, 345), theory for the Greeks contains within itself not all the concrete and singular things in the world but only all the sciences with their respective concrete and singular objects. Yet it is all-embracing, not in the sense that it would be the sum total of all individual sciences but in the sense that it reunites the knowledge that the particular sciences have of their specific objects. *Theoria* is the knowledge that interlinks all the particular knowledges; consequently, it is a knowledge that concerns the meaning of the regional sciences. Yet if "all-encompassing" also points to the "most general and invariant characteristics of the world," it furthermore suggests that *theoria*, or philosophy, is free from all traditionalisms and brings into view something that transcends all ethnic, customary, religious meanings, something that, consequently, is universal. If *theoria* is said to be the all-embracing science, it is because it concerns that which is part of the universe shared by humanity as a whole. According to this additional sense, then, *theoria* is all-embracing because it is about the *one* world shared by all.[40] "All-embracing" has still another meaning that must be mentioned here. As an all-embracing science, one that does not separate into "the juxtaposition of specializations of cultural formations," *theoria* is the science that is supposed to achieve "universal knowledge as universal reflection and a resulting self-understanding by which the hidden and undeveloped reason becomes reason, that is, reason that understands and regulates itself." In short, "all-embracing" means also that such a science accomplishes "the ultimate self-understanding of humanity."[41]

With the discovery that there is something that is identically the same in and for all humanities, hence ideal, there also arises for the first time the possibility (and necessity) of proving the truth (the *one* ideal world) that *theoria* asserts. Without the reference to a total horizon no truth claims are strictly possible. The breakthrough of an all-embracing science in Greece is coeval with the emergence of rationality and apodictic demonstration, even though, as Husserl admits, "the demand of apodicticity" emerges only explicitly with Descartes (*C*, 339). This notion of apodicticity that originates in formal logic, and designates, as Husserl remarks in *Ideas I*, "the consciousness of a necessity, or more specifically, a consciousness of a judgment, in which we become aware of a certain matter as the specification of an eidetic generality," must be distinguished from assertoric evidence that refers to the "*seeing of an individual*, for instance, the 'awareness' of a thing or of some individual state of things."[42] Apodictic is what is "absolutely" (*schlechthin unaufhebbar*),[43] and, indeed, commonly, "apodictic" is understood to denote the unconditionally necessary and immediately evident. But "the genuine and imperishable sense of apodicticity (apodicticity as a fundamental problem)" (*C*, 340), which Husserl has in mind in *The Crisis*, is not to be confused with "the usual sense taken from traditional mathematics" (*C*, 72). By linking the problem of apodicticity to the Cartesian demand of "the absolutely apodictic foundation of knowledge," apodicticity is raised to the status of the "originary condition [*Urbedingung*] of the possibility of a philosophy."[44] Only where philosophy, or science, achieves absolute apodicticity in this sense, in short where Descartes' demand is met to advance only such claims "for which one can stand in before oneself and all others," is there philosophy, or science, in a rigorous sense.[45] Only insofar as philosophy "makes the claim to justify, and not to advance any proposition, and any mediate or immediate discovery, as truth, without proving it in thoughtful self-responsibility," can philosophy claim the title of a rigorous science.[46] But if, as we have seen, by answering for all the claims that one makes one exercises self-responsibility, and understands oneself "*as being in being called to a life of apodicticity*" (*C*, 340), the problem of apodicticity amounts to that of "philosophical self-responsibility."[47] What Husserl calls "the fundamental demand of apodicticity" (*C*, 340) is thus finally a concern with "the ultimate responsibility of the autonomous human being for self-reflection."[48] As Paul Ricoeur has noted, in the context of *The Crisis*, apodicticity has been "enlivened by the new Idea of man" and the idea of the "total task" whose accomplishment is demanded by reason.[49]

I recall that *apodictic* derives from *apo*, "from," and *deiknynai*, "to show that which one must prove." The way the fundamental sense of apodicticity is to be conceived becomes manifest when Husserl speaks of the necessity to bring the task of philosophy to "consummate clarity and thus to an apodictic method which, in every step of achievement, is a constant avenue to new steps having the character of absolute success, i.e., the character of apodictic steps" (*C*, 72). The incontestable and absolute certitude of apodicticity thus rests on its clear demonstrability. The theoretical praxis that opens with the discovery of universals is coeval with the production of discursive forms that make it possible for all to see what is asserted, by answering in universal terms and according to universal norms for what is claimed. These discursive and rational forms are forms that are at odds with customary modes of argumentation. They are not time-proven modes of argumentation or persuasion but forms that present themselves, in other words, that account for themselves, and offer themselves to verification. Although Husserl does not explicitly say so, the critique of *doxa*, which extends to the latter's ways of shaping its discursive forms, clearly inscribes into the practice of argumentation the relation to all others, thus securing intersubjectivity. Uprooting traditional modes of argumentation, rational argumentation is universal in that by accounting for itself, that is, in being self-responsible, it presents itself, that is, addresses itself, and answers to others—all others. In any event, theoretical openness to the one world and universal answerability thus go hand in hand. For Husserl, as Klaus Held has noted, the inaugural event of science in ancient Greece, as precisely this unity of *theoria* and *logos*, is something entirely new in the history of humankind. Held writes:

> The openness for the one horizon of the world, which in all particular worlds appears only in limited and one-sided fashion, breaks with the self-evident and unquestioned attitude which up to then made up the life of men in all cultures, and which only now, that is in the light of the break with it, becomes known *as* an attitude. As the unity of *theoria* and *logos*, the doxa-critical openness to the world overcomes this now understood "natural attitude," and fosters on the basis of the Greeks a culture in Europe, which is

fundamentally different from everything that existed before because of this change of attitude.⁵⁰

The science that, according to Husserl, emerges in Greece, and that constitutes the idea of "Europe" and the teleology of its spiritual history, is a universal rational science. What *universal* means in this context should by now be clear: openness to the total horizon of the world, self-responsibility, and thus answerability to all others. Of course, the concept of universality presupposes that, indeed, there is *one* world, *one* horizon that encompasses all the particular worlds of humankind with their horizons. Or rather, it presupposes it, not as a world that is already constituted but as a telos infinitely to be striven for through universal critique.⁵¹ Yet, without this assumption, openness to the one world, and answerability to others as others, would be strictly impossible. As *The Crisis* also makes clear, the way in which the exact sciences have construed this one and same world as one that is limited to the objective world of shapes and shape-correlated plena, does not secure a universality that is truly apodictic. I leave the discussion of the analyses of the status of the one objective world of the exact sciences, and of the type of idealization that it implies, in abeyance—analyses that represent the background against which transcendental phenomenology will seek to recover a concept of universality from the life-world that meets the Greek challenge. In the meantime, let me emphasize one more time that openness to the one world, self-responsibility, apodicticity, and responsibility to others can only be achieved through the universal criticism of everything particular, that is, through a certain self-alienation, self-estrangement, self-othering. The constitutive foreignness of this intrusive task to oneself, as an individual, group, or nation with its particular customs, traditions, and beliefs, is obvious. It is all the more foreign to oneself as an individual, group, or nation in that its very strangeness is the strangeness of the other, the foreigner. But it is the condition sine qua non for acceding to the *one* world and encountering an other who is not reduced to *my other*, or who remains inaccessible because absolutely other. Without a definite adversity to all ingrained modes of thinking and acting, the universal would not be the universal. It would remain a mere particularity.

§ 2   Universality and Spatial Form

According to Husserl, "the *teleological beginning*, the true birth of the European spirit as such" (*C*, 71), lies in the Greek primal establishment of the idea of a universal science whose foundation in intersubjectively reconstructible truths makes it a science that in absolute self-responsibility accounts for all of its claims. Although the European spirit is born in Greece, it manifests itself properly only with another primal establishment, which occurs in the Renaissance, and "which is at once a reestablishment [*Nachstiftung*] and a modification of the Greek primal establishment" (*C*, 71). Indeed, the European spirit comes into existence in the shape of the modern sciences that owe their existence to a reactivation in the Renaissance of the Greek idea of an all-encompassing universal and rational science. But the reestablishment of this idea at the beginning of modernity is not a wholesale underwriting of the Greek heritage. It is a modification that transforms the idea in question. This reestablishment is responsible not only for the modern sciences' indisputable accomplishments but also for the current crisis of the sciences, that is, for what Husserl diagnoses as the sciences' inability to account for the meaning of their own activity and hence their loss of any relation to humanity's basic concerns. Perhaps more important, the success and simultaneous crisis of the European sciences is also an indication of the problematic nature (if not narrowness) of the concept of universality that informs the modern sciences. Indeed, as Husserl remarks, "a definite [*bestimmtes*] ideal of a universal philosophy and its method forms the beginning; this is, so to speak, the primal establishment of the philosophical modern age and all its lines of development" (*C*, 12). Hereafter, I will discuss in some detail the founding event of the modern sciences in the Renaissance, primarily to elicit what, precisely, this specific concept of universality amounts to and what its intrinsic limitations are compared to the Greek idea of universality. The aim of this elucidation is to show that, for Husserl, the concept of universality that dominates the modern sciences fails to make good on the promise of a universal horizon that emerged as a task with Greek philosophy. Furthermore, since Husserl links the European spirit to this promise, one must conclude that, essentially, the modern sciences have also failed that spirit.

From what we saw in the preceding chapter, the project of an all-encompassing science, or metaphysics, that originates in ancient Greece is not only a science of the *one* world—the world that encompasses all the relative worlds—but of one that, in order to secure access to this one world and to establish for it terms that are in principle intelligible to all, independently of their race, gender, customs, culture, religion, nationality, and so forth, presupposes an attitude critical of everything that is of the order of such particulars. This universal science embodies the ideal of a community freeing itself precisely from all traditions, and traditionalisms, and shaping itself freely according to insights of reason that are recognizable for their universality. However, the primal establishment of the new philosophy that characterizes the Renaissance, and that, according to Husserl, coincides with "the primal establishment of modern European humanity itself—humanity which seeks to renew itself radically, as against the foregoing medieval and ancient age, precisely and only through its new philosophy" (*C*, 12), lacked this critical attitude with respect to the Greek heritage. The Renaissance takes it over as "an *unquestioned tradition*" (*C*, 47), and it thus essentially misses what is so essential about the Greek project. Indeed, by its very nature the project and the task of a humanity that understands itself from the *one* world cannot be taken over slavishly. As *The Crisis* suggests, the ancient model of a universal rational science that implies the critical rejection of tradition precludes being appropriated in a traditionalist spirit. Husserl writes that the ancient model "was not to be taken over blindly from the tradition but must grow out of independent inquiry and criticism" (*C*, 8). The very spirit of the Greek conception of reason demanded a critical attitude toward the model in question as a heritage bequeathed to Europe, as well as a free and independent reactivation of this heritage. (This Husserlian caveat is important in many respects: it suggests, in particular, that the very attempt to found Europe on the Greek idea of philosophy as universal science, and in terms of a universal community, cannot take place in a merely historical fashion. To invoke the tradition in this context, without questioning it critically, is to go against what the very idea of philosophy requires.) But if the very idea of a universal and rational science radically excludes all uncritical acceptance of any received heritage (including that of itself), it is also the case, as Husserl notes, that the way in which ancient philosophy, in its first, original establishment, seeks to realize the universal task of philosophy is not without its own naivetés and inherent limits.[1] In fact, although this task is, as we have seen before, a remarkably strange task, Greek philosophy soon lost sight of the strangeness of this task in the very attempt to fulfill the task of developing an all-encompassing science. Furthermore, by conceiving of this task as self-evident, "the naive obviousness of this task [became] increasingly transformed . . . into unintelligibility," with the result that "reason itself and its [object], 'that which is,' became more and more enigmatic" (*C*, 13). If reason has become enigmatic, it is, Husserl suggests, because the wonders that mathematics and physics have accomplished, in particular, "the wonderful symbolic arts of the 'logical' construction of their truths and theories," have become "incomprehensible" to the extent that the reason or meaning for their existence is no longer evident.[2] As Husserl suggests, the Renaissance philosophers did not question what had been handed down from antiquity; therefore, "the first invention of the new idea [of a universal science in the Renaissance] and its method allowed elements of obscurity to flow into its meaning" (*C*, 47). These elements prevented the exact sciences from achieving "knowledge about the *world*," that is, about and for the world shared by all. Foregoing any reflective inquiry into the original meaning of the received conceptions, the new sciences adopted the universal insights of Greek geometry and mathematics without questioning their origin and proceeded to develop a kind of disengaged universality on the basis of the mathematization of nature and the formalization of mathematics. The abstraction and emptiness of the latter—though not altogether illegitimate, and above all highly successful—not only became increasingly severed from the concerns of humanity as such but also remained tied to one particular world, one particular humankind, and one particular horizon—to Europe as a particular ethnia. The reestablishment and modification of the Greek idea of a universal rational science by the modern sciences thus obfuscates the true spirit of the primal establishment of the idea of a universal science in Greece. It follows from this that "the spectacle of the Europeanization of all other civilizations" that begins with the Renaissance, rather than bearing witness "to the rule of an absolute meaning, one which is proper to the sense . . . of the world," may be, in Husserl's own words, for the time being at least, "a historical non-sense" (*C*, 16). Indeed, what is exported under the guise of the technosciences is a kind of universality that has no relation anymore to the *one* world, the one in which we all live.

If the modern age, an age characterized by its rediscovery of philosophy as a universal task, is "not merely a fragment of the greater historical phenomenon" constituted by the inaugural establishment of philosophy in Greece (*C*, 14), it is because this rediscovery is not a simple repetition of that event. Husserl writes that "as the reestablishment [*Neustiftung*] of philosophy with a new universal task and at the same time with the sense of a renaissance of ancient philosophy—it is at once a repetition and a universal transformation of meaning. In this it feels called to initiate a new age, completely sure of its idea of philosophy and its true method, and also certain of having overcome all previous naivetés, and thus all skepticism, through the radicalism of its new beginning" (*C*, 14). Indeed, the reestablishment of philosophy as universal rational science during the Renaissance marks a radically new beginning in that the modern age reshapes the universal task at the heart of philosophy and thus reshapes the very meaning of universality. But this reformulation of the universal task comes with its own naivetés, which are a function of the way the Renaissance relates to the Greek heritage.

Philosophy as "universal science, science of the universe, of the all-encompassing unity of all that is," which, according to the Vienna lecture, arises in Greece as a result of the *"new sort of attitude* of individuals toward their surrounding world" (*C*, 276)—that is, the radically critical attitude we have previously discussed—is the science of the *one* world, the world for everybody, that is, of humanity itself. The discovery of this *one* world enables the conception of a universal science in Greece—a science concerned with what is universal and that seeks to proceed according to principles and rules that are reconstructible by everyone. Now, the science that in Greece sustained this idea of universality, and served to flesh out the conception of the *one* intersubjectively shared world, is geometry, first and foremost. Its pure forms, its ideal shapes of space-time, which are constructed according to rules that are verifiable at all times, and that permit everyone to identically reproduce them, have absolute and universal value regarding the one and same world shared by everyone. Husserl writes:

> Out of the undetermined universal form of the life-world, space and time, and the manifold of empirical intuitable shapes that can be imagined into it, [geometry] made for the first time an objective world in the true sense—i.e., an infinite totality of ideal objects which are determinable univocally, methodically, and quite universally for everyone. Thus mathematics showed for the first time that an infinity of objects that are subjectively relative and are thought only in a vague, general representation is, through an a priori all-encompassing method, objectively determinable and can actually be thought as determined in itself or, more exactly, as an infinity which is determined, decided in advance, in itself, in respect to all its objects and their properties and relations. (*C*, 32)

As Husserl observes, "scientific acquisitions, . . . after their method of assured successful production has been attained, . . . are imperishable; repeated production . . . produces in any number of persons something identically the same, identical in sense and validity" (*C*, 277–78). What is thus found to be identical, and to obtain for all relative worlds—the pure forms of space and time—are imperishable idealities. Indeed, "what is acquired through scientific activity is not something real but something ideal," which itself, moreover, becomes "material for the production of idealities on a higher level, and so on again and again" (*C*, 278). This discovery of pure geometric shapes is not that of "mere spatiotemporal shapes" abstracted from bodies experienced in the intuitively given surrounding world. Nor are they arbitrarily imagined shapes, or shapes transformed by phantasy (*C*, 25). In distinction from the imaginary (hence, still sensible) idealities of pure morphological types, such as roundness, for example, which have never the perfection that allows for their absolute identical repetition, the pure forms of geometry—such as the circle—are, as Husserl writes, "limit-shapes," that is, identical, and invariant idealities obtained by way of a passage to the limit (*C*, 26).[3] These idealities arise from "a peculiar sort of mental accomplishment" (*C*, 348), which Husserl terms an "idealizing accomplishment," and thus possess "a rigorous identity" (*C*, 313), which submits to "the conception of the 'again and again' . . . *in infinitum*," a repetition that in nature differs from the open endlessness characteristic of abstract figures.[4] "The great invention of idealization" (*C*, 49) by geometry and mathematics, which provides "the pure shapes it can construct *idealiter*" (*C*, 24), and in such a manner that anyone can reconstruct them, is what permits an insight of universal sweep into the *one* objective world shared independently of all particularities.[5]

The universal science recast in the Renaissance, along with its distinctly new conception of universality, thus rests on a rediscovery of ancient geometry. It is a discovery, however, that dispenses with the task of reconstructing what had given birth to it in ancient Greece. The latter's accomplishments are taken for granted. As Husserl submits, geometrical methodology, which permits overcoming "the relativity of subjective interpretation" and attaining "something that truly is"—"an identical, nonrelative truth of which everyone who can understand and use this method can convince himself," is a given for Galileo, and he takes it over "with the sort of naiveté of a priori self-evidence that keeps every normal geometrical project in motion" (*C*, 29). Furthermore, this identical truth revealed by geometry is understood as the truth of nature. In fact, for him, "everything which pure geometry, and in general the mathematics of the pure form of space-time, teaches us, with the self-evidence of absolute, universal validity, about the pure shapes it can construct *idealiter,*" belongs to "true nature" (*C*, 24). It needs also to be said that the geometry that he inherited was "a relatively advanced geometry," one that had already become "a means for technology, a guide in conceiving and carrying out the task of systematically constructing a methodology of measurement for objectively determining shapes in constantly increasing 'approximation' to geometrical ideals, the limit-shapes" (*C*, 28–29). Its proven effectiveness was one more reason that exempted it from the need for questioning. According to *The Crisis*, Galileo received this heritage in such a way that "he, quite understandably, did not feel the need to go into the manner in which the accomplishment of idealization originally arose (i.e., how it grew on the underlying basis of the pregeometrical, sensitive world and its practical arts) or to occupy himself with questions about the origins of apodictic, mathematical self-evidence" (*C*, 29).[6] For Galileo the original strangeness of geometrical idealization, that is, the discovery of pure shapes and their universally reconstructible evidence, is gone. Geometry is for him an unquestioned cultural acquisition. Without having to reflect back on its genesis, the self-enclosed world of its pure forms can be manipulated like any other cultural tool. Geometry's evidences have become self-evident, in other words, rather than reflecting on the origin of geometry—a reflection that would have permitted him to link it to the universal and transcendental eidetic structures of the pre-geometrical life-world—it is taken over uncritically, as an abstract truth. It did not dawn on Galileo to make geometry, "as a branch of universal knowledge of what is (philosophy), [and] geometrical self-evidence—the 'how' of its origin—into a problem" (*C*, 29). However, Galileo in turn develops a conception of universal science that, even though it has become obvious for us today, was definitely *merkwürdig*, strange, or odd at the time. The notion of universality characteristic of the modern sciences that come into being with Galileo is a strange notion as well. But its oddity is distinct from the one that characterizes the universal in the primal establishment of the European spirit in Greece. The strangeness of the universality peculiar to the modern sciences derives, as we will see, from its alienation from the life-world. The strangeness of this new conception of universality is that of the merely abstract.[7] At any rate, since the Renaissance slavishly takes the truths of geometry as abstract givens, the radically novel conception of universality of the emerging natural sciences (which marks the inception of modernity), notwithstanding the fact that it will have been a clear advance over the Greek notion of a universal science, is tinged with naiveté. As Husserl holds, this naiveté is responsible for the current crisis of the sciences.

Of what, then, does the new idea of the universality of the sciences consist? According to Husserl, during the Renaissance the sciences that had been inherited from the ancients—"Euclidean geometry, and the rest of Greek mathematics, and then Greek natural science"—undergo "an immense change of meaning." This change, which primarily affects mathematics, that is, geometry and the formal-abstract theory of numbers and magnitude, sets new tasks for its disciplines, "tasks of a style which was *new in principle*, unknown to the ancients," not only "*universal* tasks" but infinite tasks (*C*, 21). Indeed, as Husserl holds, in spite of the Greeks' idealization of empirical numbers, units of measurement, empirical figures in space; their transformation in geometry of propositions and proofs into ideal-geometrical propositions and proofs; and, finally, their understanding of Euclidian geometry as "a totality of pure rationality, a totality whose unconditioned truth is available to insight and which consists exclusively of unconditioned truths recognized through immediate and mediate insights"—"Euclidian geometry, and ancient mathematics in general, knows only finite tasks, a finitely closed a priori" (*C*, 21). The Greek world is a finite world—a cosmos within natural limits whose unexceedable horizon encloses all the *pragmata* of the mortal beings. The discovery of infinite ideals, and hence infinite tasks, is, for Husserl, a positive achievement of modernity and represents a clear advantage that the modern sciences have over the ancient. Antiquity, Husserl notes in *The Crisis*, does not grasp "the possibility of the infinite task which, for us, is linked as a matter of course with the concept of geometrical space and with the concept of geometry as science belonging to it" (*C*, 21–22). As Jacques Derrida has argued, as a passage to the limit, geometric idealization is by definition the infinite transgression of the sensibly ideal morphological shapes of the life-world. Hence, the inaugural idealization that opened Greek geometry endows it already from the outset with infinite fecundity. Yet this infinitization "no less *first* limits the a priori system of the productivity. The very content of an infinite production will be confined within an a priori system which, for the Greeks, will always be *closed*."[8] In distinction from the Greeks, for whom the ideal and universal knowledge of geometry was limited to a finite number of forms or shapes for the whole of which it furnished a rational foundation, the moderns take geometry as a science capable of accounting for all possible forms. Husserl writes: "To ideal space belongs, for us, a universal, systematically coherent a priori, an infinite, and yet—in spite of its infinity—self-enclosed, coherent, systematic theory which, proceeding from axiomatic concepts and propositions, permits the deductively univocal construction of any conceivable shape which can be drawn in space" (*C*, 22). The very notion of ideal space to which the Greeks arrived by idealizing empirical figures, contains, for us, in ideal form, all possible spatial shapes. Compared to the Greek finite understanding, for us, ideal space is "a rational infinite totality of being," "an infinite world" of idealities whose ideal objects "become accessible to our knowledge [not] singly, imperfectly, and as it were accidentally, but as one which is attained by a rational, systematically coherent method. In the infinite progression of this method, every object is ultimately attained according to its full being-in-itself" (*C*, 22). With "the actual discovery and conquest of the infinite mathematical horizon," one that is not only limited to ideal space but is soon extended to numbers as well, the task of the sciences becomes infinite, one of infinite universal tasks. However, the radicality of this reconfiguration of the concept of universality does not come to a close with mathematics.

Indeed, as Husserl remarks, the latter's rationalism "soon overtakes natural science and creates for it the completely new idea of *mathematical natural science*—Galilean science" (*C*, 23). Posing "the radical *problem of the historical possibility of 'objective' science*, objectively scientific philosophy," it is not a matter merely, for Husserl, "of establishing science's historical, factual point of origin in terms of place, time, and actual circumstances, of tracing philosophy back to its founders, to the ancient physicists, to Ionia, etc.; rather, it must be understood through its original spiritual motives, i.e., in its most original *meaningfulness* [*Sinnhaftigkeit*] and in the original forward development of its meaningfulness" (*C*, 347). Only by following Husserl through his discussion of Galileo's mathematization of nature, and the genesis of modern natural sciences, will we be able to evaluate the full extent of the reformulation of the concept of universality in the Renaissance and its underlying unquestioned self-evidences.[9]

Even though the idea of the mathematization of nature is something that today is taken for granted, it was initially a rather strange idea, as Husserl contends. In my analysis of the underpinnings of this idea I will highlight this strangeness, not only because it is, as we saw in the previous chapter, a constitutive aspect of universality (one that has drawn little attention as far as I am able to judge), but also because the kind of strangeness that Husserl associates with the universality of the modern sciences differs in kind from the one we have discussed so far. It is perhaps not insignificant that while speaking of the Greek project of a universal rational science, Husserl uses the German term *merkwürdig*, remarkable, but also strange, or odd, whereas the modern sciences are described as a *befremdliche Konzeption*, that is, as a conception that appears strange, if not even displeasing or disconcerting (*C*, 37). Husserl begins his discussion of Galilean science by noting that for the Greeks, ideality, identity, and universality are primarily characteristics of the realm of the pure forms. For them "the real has [only] a more or less perfect methexis in the ideal." Husserl concludes that, therefore, all application of the pure forms of geometry to nature was only "a primitive application" (*C*, 23). Now, with Galileo, nature no longer participates in a realm of idealities distinct from it; it itself is idealized, and is shown to possess its own ideal substratum. Husserl writes that "through Galileo's *mathematization of nature, nature itself* is idealized under the guidance of the new mathematics; nature itself becomes—to express it in a modern way—a mathematical manifold" (*C*, 23). Needless to say, with this idealization of a domain initially foreign to the ideality of pure forms, nature becomes the object of universal insights. But what is it in the first place that allows pure mathematics and geometry to become the guide to the formation of exact physics? What is, Husserl asks, the "hidden, presupposed meaning" of Galileo's guiding model of mathematics, which "had to enter into his physics along with everything else," that is, with everything that consciously motivated him? (*C*, 24–25). If I am interested in Husserl's answer to this question, it is precisely because it will tell us something significant about the idealities and the universality peculiar to the modern sciences.

Even though the abstraction of mere spatiotemporal shapes from things intuited in the world of everyday life never leads all by itself to the formation of geometrically ideal, that is, absolutely identical shapes, the perfection of technical capabilities in the practical world allows for the experience of the progressive precision of these shapes and hence of "an open horizon of *conceivable* improvement" regarding them (*C*, 25). As Husserl remarks, "out of [this] praxis of perfecting, of freely pressing toward the horizons of *conceivable* perfecting 'again' and 'again,' *limit-shapes* [*Limes-Gestalten*] emerge toward which the particular series of perfecting tend, as toward invariant and never attainable poles" (*C*, 26). From the repetitive attempts aimed at perfecting, say, the measurements of shapes, the ideal limit-shapes, or pure shapes, which subsequently become the object of geometry, arise by way of acts of idealization, that is, acts that Husserl characterizes as distinctly different from acts of abstraction. Unlike the shapes abstracted from spatiotemporal bodies, these limit-shapes are pure idealities, that is identically repeatable forms that are "intersubjectively determinable, and communicable in [their] determinations, for everyone" (*C*, 27). Husserl writes: "If we are interested in these ideal shapes [for their sake] and are consistently engaged in determining them and in constructing new ones out of those already determined, we are 'geometers.' The same is true of the broader sphere which includes the dimension of time; we are mathematicians of the 'pure' shapes whose universal form is the coidealized form of space-time" (*C*, 26). Next to real practice, geometry and mathematics, whose objects are the pure limit-shapes, or spatiotemporal forms, that emerge in real praxis where they can only be infinitely approximated, thus give rise to "an *ideal* praxis of 'pure thinking' which remains exclusively within the realm of pure limit-shapes" (*C*, 26). What also sets this ideal praxis radically apart from empirical praxis, however, is the fact that in pure mathematics and geometry these shapes are no longer the object of graduation and approximation. In mathematical praxis exactness is attained, "for there is the possibility of determining the ideal shapes in absolute identity, of recognizing them as substrates of absolutely identical and methodologically, univocally determinable qualities" (C, 27). But besides the idealizations of all sensibly intuitable shapes (such as straight lines, triangles, and circles) that mathematics and geometry can carry out according "to an everywhere similar method," it also becomes possible to use "these elementary shapes, singled out in advance as universally available, and according to universal operations which can be carried out with them, to *construct* not only more and more shapes which, because of the method which produces them, are intersubjectively and univocally determined." Indeed, the discovery that characterizes modern geometry was that of the possibility of "producing constructively and univocally, through an a priori, all-encompassing systematic method, *all* possible *conceivable* ideal shapes" (C, 27), whether or not there are sensibly intuitable models for them in reality. With this, the ideal space has become infinite, as has the task, "which for us, is linked as a matter of course with the concept of geometrical space" (C, 21–22).

Yet, as Husserl notes, although geometry construes the entirety of all conceivable shapes in thought alone—and, seemingly, in complete abstraction from the practical world—geometrical methodology "points back to the methodology of determination by surveying and measuring in general, practiced first primitively and then as an art in the prescientific, intuitively given surrounding world" (C, 27). Since the shapes that are intuitively experienced, or that are merely conceived in general (through abstraction), blend into one another in the "open infinity" of the space-time continuum of the prescientific surrounding world, they are "without 'objectivity.'" They are not "intersubjectively determinable, and communicable in [their] determinations, for everyone—for every other one who does not at the same time factually see" them (C, 27). Now, the role of the art of measuring already consists in securing some intersubjective objectivity for these shapes. It serves to render each single shape that is experienced in the space-time continuum of shapes characteristic of everyday life univocally determinable according to a methodology that is intersubjectively grounded. By "picking out as [standard] measures certain empirical basic shapes, concretely fixed on empirically rigid bodies which are in fact generally available," and holding these against other bodies, the art of measuring becomes capable of determining the latter "intersubjectively and in practice univocally—at first within narrow spheres (as in the art of surveying land), then in new spheres where shape is involved" (*Gestaltsphären*) (*C*, 28). What Husserl seeks to bring into the open here is the ultimate rootedness of pure mathematics in the life-world. The purely geometrical way of thinking, and, hence, the strive for philosophical knowledge, that is, "knowledge which determines the 'true,' the objective being of the world," is the idealization of "the empirical art of measuring and its empirically, practically objectivizing function." As is made clear in the appendix titled "The Origin of Geometry," the art of measuring is "pregiven to the philosopher who did not yet know geometry but who should be conceivable as its inventor" (*C*, 376). Even though the "philosopher proceeding from the practical, finite surrounding world . . . to the theoretical world-view and world-knowledge . . . has the finitely known and unknown spaces and times as finite elements within the horizon of an open infinity," he has not yet, therefore, "geometrical space, mathematical time, and whatever else is to become a novel spiritual product out of these finite elements which serve as material; and with his manifold finite shapes in their space-time he does not yet have geometrical shapes" (*C*, 376). Undoubtedly, the philosopher becomes only the protogeometrician on the basis of a new sort of praxis, one that arises from pure thinking, but it is one that takes its clues from the praxis of the gradual perfection of the art of measuring. For Husserl, then, the art of measuring is clearly "the trail-blazer for the ultimately universal geometry and its 'world' of pure limit-shapes"; pure mathematics and geometry have their origin in this method for securing intersubjective truth, and it is this origin that provides them with their true meaning. This is the premise on the basis of which Husserl argues that, by taking the achievements of these disciplines for granted, Galileo had become oblivious to geometry's and mathematics' origin in the life-world that alone makes them meaningful for humankind. But something else becomes clear at this juncture as well, namely, that the rediscovery of ancient geometry in the Renaissance amounted not only to having recourse to "a tradition empty of meaning" (*C*, 366) but also that the prime (if not the sole) way of seeking to secure universal intersubjective validity in modern Europe takes place by way of spatiotemporal shapes and forms. Yet Husserl's prime concern is to demonstrate that the new sciences that have come into being by modeling themselves after ancient geometry are disconnected from the prescientific life in the given world, which represents the horizon of all meaningful inductions.[10] By highlighting only Galileo's obliviousness to geometry's origin in the life-world, and the ensuing consequences for the development of the modern sciences, the fact that universality is primarily ascribed to geometrical idealities, and that this priority of the universality of spatiotemporal shapes affects the very concept of universality itself, does not therefore receive, in Husserl's work, the attention it merits. Undoubtedly, geometry is the first philosophical science because it permits the establishment of the absolute identity of ideal shapes in such a way that they are the same for everyone at any time. But the possibility of universality thus becomes, first and foremost, a function of the shape of the *res extensa*, of things of nature, more precisely, of their idealized shapes, and this to such a degree that in the absence of such shapes it seems to be impossible to secure anything universal at all. The fate of "psychology," which, in the wake of the Cartesian dualism of nature and mind, has never been capable of achieving the status of a science comparable to that of the natural sciences, is a clear indication of the limitation of the modern concept of universality to the universality of the idealized shapes of spatiotemporal bodies.

In "The Origin of Geometry" Husserl argues that the persisting truth-meaning of geometry is a function of the possibility to produce for the spatiotemporal sphere of shapes invariant and apodictically general contents that can be idealized and can "be understood for all future time and by all coming generations of men and thus be capable of being handed down and reproduced with the identical intersubjective meaning." But universality is not equivalent to idealized spatiotemporal shape as the privilege accorded from the Greeks via the Renaissance to the present to what is extended in the world of bodies, would seem to suggest. When Husserl adds that "this condition is valid far beyond geometry for all spiritual structures which are to be unconditionally and generally capable of being handed down" (*C*, 377), he does not wish to imply that universality is predicated on ideal spatiotemporal shapes alone but rather that in order to achieve an intersubjectively recognizable universality, "the apodictically general content [alone of other than geometrical forms], invariant throughout all conceivable variation" (*C*, 377), is to be taken into account in the idealization. Indeed, the possibility of idealization and universality is not exclusively linked to geometrical form; hence the concept of universality itself is not intrinsically limited to shape in the spatiotemporal sense. As "The Origin of Geometry" points out, "'ideal' objectivity . . . is proper to a whole class of spiritual products of the cultural world, to which not only scientific constructions and the sciences themselves belong but also, for example, the constructions of fine literature" (*C*, 356–57). Language (that is, language in general) is particularly a domain from within which "ideal objects" and "ideal cognitive structures" arise (*C*, 357, 364). In spite of the preeminence that the ideal shapes of geometry have enjoyed in the sciences, and in a conception of philosophy *more geometrico*, that is, as Husserl points out, a conception that embraces the "methodological ideal of physicalism," they constitute only one of the possible formations capable of ideal objectivity and of "intersubjective being" (*C*, 359).[11] Yet the exemplarity of geometrical universal truth is not therefore diminished. Indeed, as Derrida has shown, a distinction made by Husserl in *Experience and Judgment* bears on these different types of ideality. Compared to the idealities of words or cultural products, which are "bound idealities"—in that they are dependent on an empirically determined temporality or factuality—the geometrical ideal objectivities are "free idealities" (though free only with respect to empirical subjectivity) and thus the only ones that can claim to be truly universal.[12]

Still, the intricate connection between spatiotemporal shapes and rational universal ideality will have to continue to interest us as we now turn to Galileo's mathematization of nature. In fact, as we will see, the very possibility of the modern exact sciences rests on this connection. Even though pure geometry and mathematics reveal identical and nonrelative truths, these truths pertain only to bodies in the world—to the bodily world. According to *The Crisis*, Galileo realized that all "*pure* mathematics has to do [solely] with bodies and the bodily world only through abstraction; that is, it has to do only with *abstract shapes* within space-time, and these, furthermore, as purely 'ideal' limit shapes" (*C*, 29). Galileo was thus fully aware of the fact that the universal truth of which pure mathematics is capable concerns exclusively an abstraction of the bodily world, its abstract shapes, and, in the end, only its ideal and fully identifiable limit-shapes. Pure mathematics derives its universal truths from the bodily world alone, more precisely from the idealized shapes of these very bodies. Yet there is much more in the physical world than just bodies. Or, differently put, the spatiality of bodies is only one of the eidetic components of bodies. Hence if there is to be a philosophical or scientific knowledge of the world, the specific qualities, or sensible plena that all actual shapes possess in empirical sense-intuition, as well as "the universal causal style" by which all experienced bodies are bound, must necessarily be accounted for. Needless to say, it is mathematics once again that shows Galileo the way to accomplish this task. The latter had not only shown that through idealization of subjectively relative objects one can arrive at objectively determinable entities but also that by descending again from the world of idealities to the empirically intuited world, as demonstrated by the contact between mathematics and the art of measuring, "one can universally obtain objectively true knowledge of a completely new sort about the things of the intuitively actual world, in respect to that aspect of them (which all things necessarily share) which alone interests the mathematics of shapes, i.e., a [type of] knowledge related in an approximating fashion to its own idealities" (*C*, 32). Indeed, by becoming "applied geometry," ideal geometry made it possible for the art of measuring to calculate, for everything in the world of bodies, "with compelling necessity, on the basis of given and measured events involving shapes, events which are unknown and were never accessible to direct measurement" (*C*, 33). Galileo thus concluded that it should be possible to do for all the other aspects of nature—the real properties and the real-causal relations of bodies in the intuitable world—what had been done for the sphere of shapes, namely, by extending "the method of measuring through approximations and constructive determinations" (*C*, 33), that is, a method developed exclusively with respect to shapes, to their altogether different realm. A difficulty arises at this point, however: how can a science or philosophy of the one and same world that binds us all be achieved if "the material plena—the 'specific' sense-qualities—which concretely fill out the spatiotemporal shape-aspects of the world of bodies *cannot*, in their own gradations, be *directly* treated as are the shapes themselves"? (*C*, 33). Exactitude is possible only with respect to idealities. Even though sensible qualities are subject to gradation, in their case, as well as in the case of everything that is of the order of the concrete sensibly intuited world, it is, as Husserl writes, "difficult for us to carry out the abstract isolation of the plena . . . through a universal abstraction opposed [*in universaler Gegenabstraktion*] to the one which gives rise to the universal world of shapes" (*C*, 34). As a result no precise measurement of them is possible nor "any growth of exactness or of the methods of measurements" (*C*, 34). If no direct mathematization of the plena is possible, it is because there seems to be no world of idealities specifically their own. In short there are no limit-plena, and, hence also no "geometry" of such idealities. As Husserl quite unambiguously remarks: "We have not two but only *one* universal form of the world; not two but only *one geometry*, i.e., one of shapes, without having a second for plena" (*C*, 34). What this means is that with respect to the objective world, or nature, we possess, as Jan Patočka formulates it, "only one rational and general form to whose ideal objectivity no parallel in the domain of quality exists" (*MNM*, 233–34). As far as the one and the same world is understood objectively, that is, as a bodily world, there is only one form of universality, and this form of universality is inherently thought from this one aspect that all bodies have in common, namely shape.

Motivated by the Greek idea of an all-embracing science, Galileo concluded that in order to account for the world of nature as the one and the same objective world that we all share, those aspects of it that (unlike the shapes of bodies) cannot directly be mathematized, and which, because they lack a mathematizable world-form, are heterogeneous to spatiotemporal forms, can nevertheless be mathematized, although in an oblique way. Indeed, since in every application to intuitively given nature, pure mathematics must renounce its abstraction from the intuited plena, without therefore having to give up what is idealized in the shapes, Galileo realized that "in one respect this involved the performance of coidealization of the sensible plena belonging to shape" (*C*, 38) and that, consequently, the intuited plena are capable of indirect mathematization. In short, the objective world as a whole "becomes attainable for our objective knowledge when those aspects which, like sensible qualities, are abstracted away in the pure mathematics of spatiotemporal form and its possible particular shapes, and are not themselves directly mathematizable, nevertheless become mathematizable *indirectly*" (*C*, 34). Now the indirect mathematization of that part of the world that has no mathematizable world-form is possible only if one assumes that the plena and the shapes of the bodies to which they belong are intertwined. Husserl notes that indirect mathematization is "thinkable only in the sense that the specifically sensible qualities ('plena') that can be experienced in the intuited bodies are closely related [*verschwistert*, that is, like brother and sister] in a quite peculiar and *regulated* way with the shapes that belong essentially to them" (*C*, 35).[13] According to this idea, or rather hypothesis, which founds Galileo's new physics, "every change of the specific qualities of intuited bodies which is experienced or is conceivable in actual or possible experience refers causally to occurrences in the abstract shape-substratum of the world, i.e., that every such change has, so to speak, a counterpart in the realm of shapes in such a way that any total change in the whole plenum has its causal counterpart in the sphere of shapes" (*C*, 36). Even though this conception has lost "its strangeness [*Befremdlichkeit*] for us and [has taken] on—thanks to our earlier scientific schooling—the character of something taken for granted" (*C*, 36), for Galileo this was not yet the case. We must, Husserl writes, "make clear to ourselves the *strangeness* of his basic conception in the situation of his time" (*C*, 37). If this idea with which the groundwork was laid for an all-encompassing science of the objective world is strange, it is not merely because of its novelty. Since it is a conception that in the meantime has become obvious to us, and is universally accepted, we can assume that its strangeness derives, first, from the fact that it permits the establishment of something that is universally valid and that, therefore, collides with held beliefs. Undoubtedly, the Renaissance had already opened itself to the general idea (which announces itself in everyday experience) that all occurrences in the intuitive world yield to universal induction. But the assumption that "everything which manifests itself as real through the specific sense-qualities must have its *mathematical index* in events belonging to the sphere of shapes" (*C*, 37), and that makes it possible to indirectly mathematize the plena, that is, the construction *ex datis*, and full determination, of all events in the realm of the plena (*C*, 37), is also strange in the sense that it is, and always remains, a mere hypothesis. More precisely, this assumption is remarkable and strange because, in spite of its verification in numerous instances, it remains a hypothesis that must endlessly be confirmed. Husserl writes: "the Galilean idea is a *hypothesis*, and a very remarkable one at that [*von einer höchst merkwürdigen Art*]; and the actual natural science throughout the centuries of its verification is a correspondingly remarkable sort of verification. It is remarkable because the hypothesis, in spite of the verification, continues to be and is always a hypothesis; its verification (the only kind conceivable for it) is an endless course of verifications" (*C*, 41–42). The idea that sustains Galileo's physics—the mathematical approach to nature and the universality that it establishes with respect to the plena and causality—remains forever hypothetical. Indeed, since the mathematization of the plena is based on a substruction in thought of a hypothetic relation between shapes and the qualities of spatiotemporal things, that is, on something that can never be experienced and verified as presenting itself as such, and hence in full self-evidence, the verification of such a relation needs to be repeated again and again. The truth of a connection between bodily shapes and plena cannot be acquired once and for all, and, consequently, it is never a given.[14]

What is strange about Galileo's founding hypothesis, and what puts it at odds not only with the natural attitude but also with the scientific spirit of Galileo's time, is that the universality that it establishes with respect to the one and same world of physics presupposes an infinite task. In spite of the repeated verification of this hypothesis in the praxis of the sciences, it must be continuously reasserted. Undoubtedly, this essential instability of the universal laws of the sensible qualities of intuitable things (and of the overall causal style of these things) derives from the indirect mathematization in which the plena are tied to ideal shapes, that is, essentially, to an order foreign to them. In conclusion, we can say that the infinite need to verify the hypothesis that supports the indirect mathematization of nature, by which the one and same physical world is rendered scientifically and universally intelligible, shows that the infinite task-character of the objective universal derives from this universal's intrinsic foreignness to its object. As Husserl emphasizes, the constant necessity to verify exact physics' founding hypothesis is not caused by possible error but because "in the total idea of physics as well as the idea of pure mathematics [there] is embedded the *in infinitum*, [as] the permanent form of that peculiar inductivity which first brought geometry into the historical world" (*C*, 42). It is rooted in the distinct foreignness of idealities predicated on spatiotemporal shapes—that is, idealities resulting from the objectification of "one abstract aspect of the world": the pure shapes of "ideal geometry, estranged from the world [*weltentfremdete*]" (*C*, 33)—to what even within the objective world is not of the order of the bodily. Furthermore, even though in the indirect mathematization of the plena "one always has to do with what is individual and factual," the whole method has from the outset "a *general* sense." Husserl writes: "From the very beginning, for example, one is not concerned with the free fall of *this* body; the individual fact is rather an *example*" (*C*, 41).

The factual success and inductive productivity of the approach in question is not in doubt. It infinitely surpasses the accomplishments of all everyday forms of prediction. Nevertheless this success, which remains meaningless as long as its method is not tied back to the concerns of the life-world, is also a function of an intrinsic foreignness of a universal derived from one aspect of the world of bodies to other aspects of the latter. Even though such foreignness is an intrinsic feature of universality as such, the particular way in which the idealized bodily shapes are brought to bear on the sensible qualities of the things of nature (those permitting of sensible experience), that is, the need to confirm infinitely the hypothesis of a link between spatiotemporal shape and sensible plena, indicates an intrinsic limit of this very concept of universality to its application to nonphysical, or "non-thingly," aspects of the world. Let us recall that for Husserl the idea of a universal philosophy, or science, that announces itself in Greece, one that is synonymous with what the name *Europe* stands for, is the idea of an all-embracing philosophy, or science. Such a philosophy cannot limit itself to an intersubjectively binding understanding of the objective world, the world of nature, or to a concept of universality that is only binding for the physical world. Furthermore, given that geometry has been the model for the sciences, the question arises as to the extent to which universality is linked to shape in the first place. In order to achieve an intersubjective consensus about the ideal objectivities of the spiritual products of the cultural world, to which Husserl calls attention in "The Origin of Geometry," it thus becomes necessary to uncouple universality from idealized shape, and to think the form of other ideal objectivities in terms that are no longer tributary to this feature of bodily things.[15]

As a result of the absence of a reflection back on the original meaning-giving achievement of the idealization of the spatiotemporal forms that gave rise to the geometrical ideal constructions, it appeared that geometry produced "a self-sufficient, absolute truth which, as such—'obviously'—could be applied without further ado" (*C*, 49). Rather than being understood as "indices of 'inductive' lawfulness of the actual givens of experience," the mathematical limes-formations arrived at through idealization were taken to correspond to the objectively true being of nature.[16] As early as Galileo, a "surreptitious substitution [*Unterschiebung*] [took place] of the mathematically substructed world of idealities for the only real world, the one that is actually given through perception, that is ever experienced and experienceable—our everyday life-world" (*C*, 48–49). Husserl submits that this substitution of idealized nature for the prescientifically intuited nature is of the order of a disguising or covering over and replacement of the life-world:

In geometrical and natural-scientific mathematization, in the open infinity of possible experiences, we measure the life-world—the world constantly given to us as actual in our concrete world-life—for a well-fitting *garb of ideas* [*Ideenkleid*], that of the so-called objectively scientific truths. . . . Mathematics and mathematical science, as a garb of ideas, or the garb of symbols of the symbolic mathematical theories, encompasses everything which, for scientists and the educated generally, *represents* [*vertritt*] the life-world, *dresses it up* [*verkleidet*] as "objectively actual and true" nature. It is through this garb of ideas that we take for *true being* what is actually a *method*—a method which is designed for the purpose of progressively improving, *in infinitum*, through "scientific" predictions, those rough predictions which are the only ones originally possible within the sphere of what is actually experienced and experienceable in the life-world. (*C*, 51–52)

If this is the case, if, indeed, the pregiven world provides the horizon within which and in relation to which the idealization of nature takes place, then the substitution of the objective world of nature for the life-word amounts to an ethicophilosophical error. By reflecting back on what in the life-world motivated the creation of geometry—and, by extension, the sciences that from the Renaissance modeled themselves after it—the accomplishments of geometry and the sciences are not only tied to purposes "which necessarily [lie] *in* this pre-scientific life and [are] related to its life-world" (*C*, 50); the idealized limit-shapes, in short, the spatiotemporal universals, also reveal themselves to be the products of acts of concrete intentional consciousnesses. In other words, by bringing into relief the life-world from which all idealizations and intersubjective identifications emerge, the geometrical universal exposes its historicity—that is, its production by a constituting consciousness. With this, the intersubjective accomplishments of geometric idealization that have given rise to the success of the European sciences are shown to be the product of a transcendental ego whose accomplishments are the very object of the new *episteme* of phenomenological philosophy, which understands itself as the critical renewal of the Greek idea of an all-embracing science. In part 3 of *The Crisis* Husserl pursues two distinct avenues to elaborate a transcendental phenomenology. Of these two ways—one of which starts out from prescientific life and its surrounding world, the other from psychology—we will only consider the one that inquires back into the pregiven life-world.[17]

§ 3   Universality in the Making

The idea of philosophy as a rational science that emerges in Greece and that, according to Husserl, coincides with the idea of Europe, is that of a truly universal science—a science concerned with what is universal and carried out in a universally reconstructible way. In the wake of the rediscovery of the Greek heritage at the beginning of the modern age, this idea found a powerful expression in "natural-scientific world-universality" (*C*, 246), which, basing itself on the spatiotemporal shapes of bodily things, made the objective world universally transparent. Yet, as Husserl points out, such objectifying accomplishment is also "limited to the mere spatiotemporal shapes or to the structure of space-time belonging universally to the world." He adds: "It can be seen that such an accomplishment was possible only through the essence of this structure and that, accordingly, exact objectification could have significance for the world, at least at first, only as a world of bodies, whereby everything about the things that was itself non-corporeal was abstracted" (*C*, 349). The question then is, how truly universal is a science whose "natural-scientific world-universality" does not apply to the realm of the souls? As Husserl argues in *The Crisis*, the repeated attempts to establish a scientific psychology modeled after the natural sciences have not only failed; the project itself is an absurdity. Even though "there is an immense difference between the essence of psychic subjectivity and the essence of a thing" (*C*, 327), it is, indeed, the attempt to objectify, that is, to treat what is of the order of subjectivity—acts of consciousness *and* phenomena—like corporeal things. According to Husserl, all "analogizing . . . does violence [to this difference]" (*C*, 327). Even the indirect mathematization applicable to objective qualities is bound to fail in the case of the psychic life. Husserl concludes that for a "world as the world which also contains spiritual beings . . . the idea of an ontology of the world, the idea of an objective, universal science of the world, having behind it a universal a priori according to which every possible factual world is knowable *more geometrico*—this idea which led even Leibniz astray—is a *nonsense*. For the realm of souls there is in principle no such ontology, no science corresponding to the physicalistic-mathematical ideal" (*C*, 265). Yet the impossibility of the sciences to objectify the realm of the souls, and thus to account for what is universal about it, not only demonstrates that the universal project of the sciences misses out on one essential aspect of the world but, primarily, that it is not universal to begin with. Husserl writes: "Philosophy as universal *objective* science—and this is what all philosophy of the ancient tradition was—together with all the objective sciences is not universal science at all. It brings into its sphere of inquiry only the constituted object-poles and remains blind to the full concrete being and life that constitutes them transcendentally" (*C*, 176). Now, for Husserl, who claims that "psychic being is investigatable in transcendental universality, in a fully systematic way, and in principle in essential generality in the form of an a priori science" (*C*, 265), in a way, in other words, that meets the demand of universality, the issue is not simply one of compensating for what the natural sciences cannot achieve by developing a rigorous science that would do justice to what is specific to the realm of souls. It is not merely a question of juxtaposing subjective universality to the natural-scientific world-universality. Indeed, what is at stake in the phenomenological turn to the subjective is the renewal of the task and the promise constitutive of the Greek idea of an all-embracing rational science—a truly universal science, one, incidentally, in which universal objectivity would be reinscribed and hence transformed. The realm of the subjective, Husserl holds, is one "which is completely closed off within itself, existing in its own way, functioning in all experiencing, all thinking, all life, thus everywhere inseparably involved" (*C*, 112). Yet, notwithstanding its existence in its own right, and subtending all other domains, including that of the objective sciences and the philosophies building on them, the realm of the subjective is thematic neither in everyday life nor in the sciences. But if philosophy is to be an all-encompassing science, how can it "fulfill the sense of its primal establishment as a universal and ultimately grounding science if it leaves this realm to its 'anonymity'"? (*C*, 112). Not only that, as Husserl will argue, the "anonymous subjectivity" is the "*one* single ground" on which all the objective sciences, the historical philosophies, and everyday thinking rest. It follows from this that only by taking this "constant substratum" (*C*, 113) into account can philosophy become the universal science that it promised to seek in its primal establishment.

Given that the universality of the natural sciences was predicated on the spatiotemporal shapes of corporeal things, it follows necessarily that the more encompassing universality sought through a turn to the sphere of the subjective can no longer be of the order of identifiable and identically iterable idealized shapes. Even though the mathematical and geometrical idealities are clearly universal in that they are free with respect to empirical subjectivity, they are only relative, or bound idealities, compared to those of the transcendental subjectivity that transcendental phenomenology explores in both of its approaches to the latter, whether inquiring back from the pregiven life-world, or from psychology.[1] The free idealities characteristic of transcendental subjectivity must necessarily be distinct in nature from those predicated on spatial and temporal shapes. Furthermore, philosophy as rigorous science, or transcendental phenomenology, rather than rendering the domain of the subjective accessible through indirect symbolic and mathematical methods, moves "in spheres of direct intuition" of the things themselves.[2] These things are, as we will see, the "essential forms" (*Wesensformen*) of both individual and collective consciousness. Whether inquiring back from the life-world or from psychology, transcendental phenomenology seeks to exhibit the genuinely free universal idealities in the realm of the subjective as the "essential forms" that universally shape the subjective and its world-constituting accomplishments, thus establishing phenomenology as the true realization of the Greek idea of a universal science. For the present purpose it will not be necessary to elaborate these forms—what Husserl, elsewhere, terms the noetic-noematic structures of the sense-constituting accomplishments of subjectivity—in full detail. It must suffice to establish the soundness of such a concept of subjective form and, furthermore, to show that, effectively, a universal science of the essential forms of consciousness is possible in a fully systematic way—in principle, in essential generality in the form of an a priori science. With this in mind I turn to the discussion of the life-world in section A of part 3 in *The Crisis*, where

Husserl sketches out the rudiments of transcendental phenomenology in programmatic fashion.

As is well known, Husserl's concern with the "life-world" in his last, and unfinished, work has drawn special attention from his interpreters. Notwithstanding the fact that he had already made sporadic use of the term (especially in his writings from the 1920s concerned with attempts to overcome the Cartesian dualism of body and soul), by making of the word *life-world* a philosophical category, they have declared it to be something of a turn in his work.[3] Even though what, in the conclusion of *Formal and Transcendental Logic*, is called the "world given in 'pure experience,'" or the "aesthetic world," is already in essence the "life-world," it is certainly true that the life-world becomes an explicit theme only in *The Crisis*.[4] However, its analysis is not conducted there for the sake of the life-world itself; its analysis is only staged to provide one way, however new, into transcendental phenomenology. As Paul Ricoeur has noted, "the return to the *life-world* is only a moment, an intermediary degree of a more fundamental 'return': the return to science as such, to reason as such, beyond its limitation in objective thought."[5]

If Husserl opens his investigation of the life-world by claiming that objective knowledge rests on "an unquestioned ground of presuppositions" (*C*, 104), and that this ground is that of the self-evidences characteristic of the life-world—such as the presupposition that the everyday surrounding world of life exists, that it is a world that constantly undergoes change, even though it is also the one and same world for all, and that in this world we are objects among objects, etc.—his objective is clear: to thematize and to explain "these manifold validities-in-advance, i.e., 'presuppositions,'" (*C*, 111) that permeate both prescientific and scientific life.[6] "Taken for granted, prior to all scientific thought and all philosophizing questioning," these ontic validities are, as Husserls puts it, "the most obvious of the obvious" (*C*, 110). But precisely because they are the "*constant presuppositions* of scientific and, at the highest level philosophical thinking" (*C*, 110), it becomes incumbent on philosophy—particularly in the wake of the crisis of the European sciences—to radically and systematically investigate the obvious that the sciences have never deigned worthy of exploring. The single most prominent presupposition of prescientific, as well as scientific, thought is "that the world is—always in advance—and that every correction of an opinion, whether an experiential or other opinion, presupposes the already existing world, namely, as a horizon of what in the given case is indubitably valid as existing" (*C*, 110). It is above all this one presupposition that motivates Husserl's interest in the life-world. If the aim of the sciences is to transform prescientific knowledge in and of the world into exact knowledge of the world, as a world "which in itself is fixed and determined," and which is to be achieved through an infinite process, the origin of the presupposition in question requires elucidation.[7]

As I have said already, the life-world is not, as such, the theme of Husserl's late work but only a new way into transcendental phenomenology. What is more, the life-world, as we will see, is not simply the everyday world that at all times surrounds us; it is not, therefore, something that is explicitly given (and there for everyone to see and experience) and that could be investigated without further ado.[8] Characterizing the life-world as the spatiotemporal world of everyday experience in prescientific life, a number of commentators have interpreted the life-world to be the everyday surrounding world in all its sociocultural concreteness and contingency. Therefore some cautionary remarks are warranted. From the start, it should be noted that even though Husserl repeatedly underlines the pregivenness of the life-world, this does not mean at all that it is explicitly given, and experienced as such, in actual everyday life. Such pregivenness of the life-world does not entail consciousness, and thematic givenness. As the hidden ground of both prescientific and scientific life and thought, the life-world requires a disclosure in order for it to come into view in the first place.[9] Indeed, without the suspension, or *epoche*, of the objective sciences, the life-world cannot become thematic at all.[10] For this reason alone the life-world cannot simply be identified with the actually lived everyday world in which the sciences are, undoubtedly, a powerful presence. Furthermore, the phenomenological investigation of the life-world in light of the latter's ground-function for all prescientific and scientific life, in which the sense-constructs (*Sinngebilde*) and the subjective achievements peculiar to the life-world become manifest, requires an additional *epoche*, a transcendental *epoche* of the natural attitude characteristic of both prescientific and scientific life. Indeed, as will become increasingly clear hereafter, if the life-world is in some way the everyday world that surrounds us, it is not simply this world in its empirical concreteness but this world above all in its makeup by the transcendental structures of experience. *Life* in "life-world" thus refers to the tight fabric of the subjective and intersubjective acts of our experience of the world and is therefore "life" in a transcendental sense. Let us not lose sight of these caveats as we attempt, while turning to Husserl's sometimes confusing and misleading descriptions of the life-world, to describe in broad strokes at least what it amounts to.

As Husserl writes, the life-world is "the only real world, the one that is actually given through perception, that is ever experienced and experienceable—our everyday life-world" (*C*, 49). It is thus the world we all have in common—the world common to us all (*allgemeinsam*). Pregiven, in both everyday and scientific life, it is a world whose basic structures are fixed at all times and for all time. Husserl writes: "the life-world was always there for mankind before science, then, just as it continues its manner of being in the epoch of science" (*C*, 123).[11] This world is "the obviously existing, ever intuitively pregiven world" (*C*, 111). The attitude that pervades it is the natural attitude, namely, the unquestioned assumption that things exist and that in their perception things present themselves as being there in person.

Husserl readily admits that inquiring into the life-world as the unthematized presupposition of the idea of objectivity that dominates the *universitas* of the positive sciences, is to take on "the most obvious of the obvious" (*C*, 110). But according to *The Crisis*, the investigation of what is taken for granted by both prescientific and scientific life opens up "a realm, indeed an infinite realm, of always ready and available but never questioned ontic validities," namely, "that the world is—always is in advance—and that every correction of an opinion, whether an experiential or other opinion, presupposes the already existing world" (*C*, 110). Theoretical praxis, Husserl observes, "is the art of theories, of discovering and securing truths with a certain new ideal sense which is foreign to prescientific life, the sense of a certain 'final validity,' 'universal validity'" (*C*, 111). As we saw in Chapter 2, the universal objective a priori of the natural sciences is a truth that, initially at least, was experienced as odd and detached from everyday life and its opinions. As Husserl repeatedly remarks, the new science that inquires into the "validities-in-advance" characteristic of the life-world is not only a very strange science because of the new type of questioning that it addresses to the sciences, but also because it belongs to "a new and immediately highly enigmatic dimension" (*C*, 111). As we will see, the strangeness of this new science and the truths that it exhibits are distinct in nature from the one characteristic of the exact sciences. Precisely because this new science's truths concern the subjective dimension, the strangeness of these truths must differ from those that relate to bodily things and that alienate the life of the soul. Given that the new science of the life-world (or, rather, the science that takes its starting point in the life-world) seeks to renew the Greek conception of a universal and all-embracing science, it is to be expected that its oddity is closer to the constitutive foreignness of the universal peculiar to the emerging philosophy in Greece.

As I have indicated, however, in spite of Husserl's claim that it is our everyday life-world, actually given through perception, the life-world as the soil of both prescientific and scientific life is not readily accessible. To bring it explicitly into view as an object of investigation in its own right, or in Husserlian parlance, to make it thematic, the new science field has to be secured through a method of access that "is articulated into a multiplicity of steps, each of which has, in a new way, the character of an epoche, a withholding of natural, naive validities and in general of validities already in effect" (C, 135). The first *epoche* suspends all the objective sciences, more precisely, the objective theoretical interests, aims, and activities of that kind of knowledge. Indeed, how could the life-world as constituted by the unquestioned presuppositions and naivetés on which the knowledge in prescientific life and in the objective sciences rests, be rendered accessible without such an *epoche*? Only by suspending the objective sciences is it possible to face these presuppositions to begin with and to reflect upon them in a thinking mode. Obviously, the fact that the world exists is not something that one could cease assuming, yet in suspending the natural attitude with its belief in the existence of the world, this assumption reveals itself as a subjective presupposition. Without putting the naturalizing perspective of the objective sciences out of play, this subjective dimension peculiar to the world (and to the things within it), that is, precisely its subjective character, remains hidden. But through this bracketing of the natural sciences (as a result of which the life-world becomes thematic as a realm of subjective presuppositions, in-advance-validities, or preformed meaning formations) the life-world is only brought to light in its manifold relativities and conflicting subjective truths. Indeed, as we saw in Chapter 1, from the standpoint of the objective sciences the life-world qualifies as "the 'merely subjective-relative,'" or mere opinion (*doxa*) (C, 125).

Obviously, not everything is relative in this "merely subjective-relative" realm.[12] To bring the nonrelative nature of this realm into focus, let me point out immediately that the characterization of the presuppositions and validities-in-advance unearthed by the first *epoche* as subjective, and as belonging to a subjective realm, is anything but a pejorative provision. As Husserl remarks, the questions concerning the manifold validities-in-advance taken for granted in everyday and scientific life are "questions, too, [that] concern the obviously existing, ever intuitively pregiven world; but they are not questions belonging to that professional praxis and *techne* which is called objective science . . . ; rather, they are questions of how the object, the prescientifically and then the scientifically true object, stands in relation to all the subjective elements which everywhere have a voice in what is taken for granted in advance" (*C*, 111). If the exploration of the life-world is called an inquiry into "the *enigma of subjectivity*" (*C*, 5)—an inquiry that will prove to be rich in unsettling and strange insights precisely because it devotes to the life-world a "universal and theoretical interest" (*C*, 112)—it is because subjectivity is understood here from its active, productive, or, as Husserl sometimes says, creative involvement in these presuppositions and validities and, hence, in the very constitution of the world as a form of meaning. Subjectivity is conceived here primarily from its act character—as an accomplishing, performative, and even "historical" activity. The "realm of subjective phenomena which have remained 'anonymous'" within prescientific and scientific life, thematized by the new science, is a realm of "purely subjective phenomena throughout [and] not merely facts involving psychological processes of sense data; rather, they are mental [*geistige*] processes which, as such, exercise with essential necessity the function of constituting forms of meaning [*Sinnesgestalten*]. But they constitute them in each case out of mental 'material' which [itself] proves in turn, with essential necessity, to be mental form [*geistige Gestalt*], i.e., to be constituted; just as any newly developed form [of meaning] is destined to become material, namely to function in the constitution of [some new] form" (*C*, 112). The new dimension of phenomena—the purely subjective phenomena—of the life-world that emerge once one begins to question the meaning- and validity-implications of the presuppositions of extrascientific and intrascientific life are subjective phenomena insofar as they are the result of mental processes through which they have come into existence. Now, the processes at the origin of the forms of meaning, or mental forms, are said to engender these forms according to "essential necessity," that is, in conformity with universal laws of essence. Therefore it is the establishment of the essential laws that govern the realm of the seemingly subjective-relative that will yield a subjective a priori, a universal dimension peculiar to this realm. As a consequence, another, and "a much greater task" (*C*, 142) than that of just mapping the life-world, and developing a science of how things are experienced in the life-world, awaits the phenomenologist. It is also a much greater task because the subjective a priori that is sought cannot be of the order of a truth in itself, which is the prerogative and ideal of all objective approach. According to Husserl, even to conceive of it "in analogy with the truth-in-itself of nature, is a nonsense."[13] The great task in question is that "of a pure theory of the essence [*reinen Wesenslehre*] of the life-world" (*C*, 141).

At this juncture a further clarification of Husserl's understanding of the life-world becomes necessary. On numerous occasions Husserl defines the life-world as the world of objects that in everyday life surround us. For example, the life-world is said to be "the spatiotemporal world of things as we experience them in our pre- and extrascientific life and as we know them to be experienceable beyond what is [actually] experienced. We have a world-horizon as a horizon of possible thing-experience. Things: that is, stones, animals, plants, even human beings and human products; but everything here is subjective and relative" (*C*, 138). If, according to Husserl, the life-world is "the obviously existing, ever intuitively pregiven world" (*C*, 111) of everyday life, it is, first of all, only in the sense of the subjectively lived world as a spatiotemporal framework as such, in advance of any conscious thematization of this world, and independently of its actual historical, social, or cultural, particularities. Furthermore, if the life-world is pregiven in all other worlds, and is shared by all as the one world we all have in common, it is only in the sense that the formal structures of experiencing the world as a spatiotemporal complex are universal. All inquiry into what is "formal and general, what remains invariant in the life-world throughout all alterations of the relative," that is, into the life-world a priori, takes its starting point from "what alone determines for us in life the sense of talking about the world," namely, that it is "the universe of things, which are distributed within the world-form of space and time and are 'positional' in two senses (according to spatial position and temporal position)—the spatiotemporal *onta*" (*C*, 142). What is at stake in the task faced by the new science about the life-world a priori, becomes tangible at this point. The formal and general structures that this science investigates concern nothing less than *world itself* (that is, first, the world of spatiotemporal things) as it is subjectively lived, that is, as the world that is valid and meaningful in the life-world. It is an inquiry into the essential subjective structures of the world not as an objective whole but as a meaning-construct (*Sinngebilde*), that is, in Husserl's parlance, of the world as a phenomenon. Conversely, qua meaning-construct, the world's—the *one* world's—universal or essential structures have their correlate in a "universal accomplishment [*Leistung*]" (C, 113), that is, the equally essential acts of consciousness. Husserl writes: "We shall come to understand that the world which constantly exists for us through the flowing alterations of manners of givenness is a universal mental acquisition, having developed as such and at the same time continuing to develop as the unity of a mental configuration, as a meaning-construct [*Sinngebilde*]—as the constant of a universal, ultimately functioning subjectivity" (C, 113). The passage through the life-world as a way toward the new science that is to renew the Greek project of a universal all-encompassing science serves to show how the hitherto anonymous sphere of subjectivity is made up of processes through which the universal sense of the one world presupposed by all the spiritual accomplishments of humankind is constituted according to essential laws. The one world, of which we are aware in the life-world, despite the fact that, or precisely because, we live in particular worlds, is to be shown to be a spiritual, mental, universal achievement, the product of intentional acts of consciousness—hence, a historical accomplishment, one that continues to develop and whose unity is constantly in the making. The one world, the total horizon of the world, as that which is shared by all, is thus not something to be taken for granted, or something positively given, and that exists once and for all independently of humankind. Rather, its universality is something that is secured, and is to be secured, by human beings in an infinite process.

As we have seen, what is invariant and general in the subjective-relative realm of the life-world is to be approached first by way of the world of spatiotemporal objects, because in the life-world, as "a world of sense intuition, [and] a sensible world of appearances, . . . everything that exhibits itself . . . as a concrete thing obviously has a bodily character, even if it is not a mere body, as, for example, an animal or a cultural object, i.e., even if it also has psychic or otherwise spiritual properties" (C, 106). Notwithstanding the fact that in the life-world one is aware of the world only in relation to objects and their content alterations and the changes in their perception, as well as through their relations to other objects, that is, as the horizon of existing objects, "'the' world, as existing in a unified way, persists throughout, being corrected only in its content" (*C*, 105). But as Husserl is quick to observe, the life-world is not only our everyday spatiotemporal world of bodily things; it is also the world of "straightforward [*schlichten*] intersubjective experiences" (*C*, 133). After having shown that in all sense-perception of objects my living-body (*Leib*) plays a constant role—in the sense that all the aspects of bodies appearing in perception are intimately linked to the kinesthetically functioning living body—he notes that as "full ego-subjects," we are not merely "ego[s] through the living body [*die leibliche Ichlichkeit*]," but each of us is, as well, a "full-fledged 'I-the-man'" (*C*, 108). I am an ego not only by virtue of a living body but also insofar as I am an individual human being, one together with others in the world. Husserl writes: "Thus in whatever way we may be conscious of the world as universal horizon, as coherent universe of existing objects, we, each 'I-the-man' and all of us together, belong to the world as living with one another in the world; and the world is our world, valid for our consciousness as existing precisely through this 'living together'" (*C*, 108). As a human subject, the ego is not only a living body that is constantly active "on the basis of [its] passive having-of-the-world [*passive Welthabe*]" (*C*, 108) of objects; this world, as the coherent universe of existing objects pregiven to the ego, is also the world of the others, the one world that the human beings share with one another. The world thus is not merely my world but always already *our* world, a world that is a function of living together. Now, in the life-world all our affections by and actions on objects, as well as all our dealings with others in the world, take place against the background of this passive having-of-the-world. In all of one's preoccupations one is aware of the world, but one is conscious of it always only "in terms of some object-content or other, in the alteration of the different ways of being conscious . . . and also in the alteration of affection and action . . . and such that the affecting objects are now thematic, now unthematic" (*C*, 109). The consciousness of the world in the life-world is thus a consciousness in constant motion. This is not only the case for me as an individual ego faced with the sensibly intuitable world of bodily things but also for me as a human being in the world with others. Although "we, in living together, have the world pregiven in this 'together,' as the world valid as existing for us and to which we, together, belong, the world as world for all, pregiven with this ontic meaning," this awareness of togetherness, and hence, of *the* world as *our* world, comes in the life-world always only "with a residuum which remains unthematic—remains, so to speak, anonymous" (*C*, 109). To elucidate this unthematic and anonymous residuum is the prime objective of phenomenology.

As we have seen, the *epoche* of the objective sciences makes the life-world explicitly thematic. But this suspension of the objectifying attitude and the accompanying awareness of the pregiven world is something that happens already in some form in what Husserl terms "waking life." "Waking life is always a directedness toward this or that, being directed toward it as an end or as a means, as relevant or irrelevant, toward the interesting or the indifferent, toward the private or public, toward what is daily required or intrusively new" (*C*, 281). In "normal, unbroken, coherent life," one wakingly lives in the life-world; that is, one is conscious of the fact that the life-world "is always already there, existing in advance for us, the 'ground' of all praxis whether theoretical or extratheoretical" (*C*, 142). One lives in the awareness of the fact that we always "live-in-certainty-of-the-world." Such waking life amounts to "be[ing] awake to the world, being constantly and directly 'conscious' of the world and of oneself as living *in* the world, actually experiencing and actually effecting the ontic certainty of the world. The world is pregiven thereby, in every case, in such a way that individual things are given" (*C*, 142–43). But, according to Husserl, one must distinguish the consistently reflective attitude from this still "naive and natural straightforward attitude" (*Geradeheinstellung*) in which one consciously experiences things or objects "*within the world-horizon,*" that is, as "'something of' the world."[14] The different attitudes of being conscious of the world rest on the "fundamental difference" between things within the world, and the world itself, which is not a thing. The world-horizon is irreducible to the things that appear within it, and therefore we must assume that the ways in which the being of an object within the world and the world itself are experienced "prescribe fundamentally different correlative types of consciousness for them" (*C*, 145). Now, rather than simply taking a conscious stand in the pregiven life-world, the reflective attitude makes the life-world thematic by reflecting on *how* it and the objects within it are given. Such inquiry into "the 'how' of the subjective manner of givenness of life-world and life-world-objects" (*C*, 143) no longer takes for granted the givenness of the life-world that the first *epoche* explicitly brought to light, and straightforwardly takes a stand within it, but inquires into the pregiving of the world. Indeed, to be given, Husserl explains, means "to be valid in a conscious fashion [*bewusstseinsmässig geltend*], and to be for us certain in its being with this or that content."[15] Whereas in normal, straightforwardly waking life, one lives toward the world-horizon (*in den Welthorizont Hineinleben*)—an attitude in which "all our interests have their goal in objects" (*C*, 144) and in which we "live in 'infatuation' [*lebt . . . verschossen auf die Einheitspole hin*]" (*C*, 176) with the things in the world—there is, Husserl ascertains, "a completely different [*ganz andere*] sort of waking life involved in the consciousness of having of the world" (*C*, 144). It "consists in a transformation of the thematic consciousness of the world which breaks through [*durchbrechende Wandlung*] the normality of straightforward living" (*C*, 144). This wholly other kind of thematization of the world, which violently shatters and transforms ordinary consciousness of the pregivenness of the world, arises with the realization that rather than simply having objects "as the substrates of their properties . . . we become conscious of them (and of everything ontically meant) through subjective manners of appearance, or manners of givenness" (*C*, 144). The violence and oddity of this completely different kind of waking life regarding the world rests with the subjective dimension of the world that takes us away from the infatuation with the objects themselves. With the awareness of the subjective modes in which objects—and hence the world—are pregiven to us, a "new universal direction of interest" emerges, an "interest exclusively and consistently directed toward *how* . . . the coherent, universal validity *world*—*the* world—comes into being for us; how, that is, there arises in us the constant consciousness of the existence, of the universal horizon, of real, actually existing objects, each of which we are conscious of only through the alterations of our relative conceptions of it, of its manners of appearing, its mode of validity, even when we are conscious of it in particularity as something simply being there" (*C*, 144–45). The "new universal interest" in the manifold ways in which the world and its objects appear to us in the life-world thus opens up the possibility of establishing how, subjectively speaking, *the* world, "the coherent, universal validity world," comes into being for us. In the subsequent analyses into the correlation of consciousness and world, "a great horizon of remarkable [*merkwürdige*] truths" comes into light, Husserl ascertains, that never before had been investigated and that do not fail to "evoke philosophical wonder" (*C*, 165). As we have seen, the reflective attitude that opens up this new interest arises in waking life from the life-world itself. The very oddity of these truths is not only owed to the recognition of a correlation between world and world-consciousness but results from the fact that this correlation reveals itself to have "an essential necessity" and that it allows for translation "into essential generalities, into an immense system of novel and highly astounding a priori truths" (*C*, 166). The strangeness of the truths in question only glimpsed in waking life in the life-world— a strangeness that evokes philosophical wonder, in other words, which causes philosophy to violently make a breakthrough in everyday life— stems from the recognition of the universality of the subjective a priori. The very universality of the subjective structures exhibited in the analyses of how things and the world appear to us shatters straightforward living toward things within the world in everyday waking life and opens up the task of the philosophical.

However, in spite of the fact that this new direction of interest is born in the life-world itself, to be carried out genuinely, it requires securing the new realm of inquiry and the development of a method of investigation cut to the size of this new field. Although the first *epoche* of objectifying knowledge has made the pregiven life-world manifest as one of manifold relativities, the investigation of the correlation of world and world-consciousness in light of the subjective universal a priori requires that the pregivenness of the life-world become manifest as such. A second *epoche*, in Husserl's parlance, a transcendental *epoche*, that is, a freeing of the inquiring gaze from the natural attitude, and its general thesis of the existence of the world, thus becomes necessary for the pregiving structures of subjectivity to surface. Needless to say, that the world is pregiven is not something one could cease assuming, but by suspending the belief in the existence of the world, one can come to see *how we produce* this (necessary) assumption, how subjectivity is involved in its assumed existence. Through the transcendental *epoche*, the world-constituting subjectivity, the transcendental primordiality of constituting life anterior to all constituted formations, becomes thematic as such. Finally, this second *epoche* also makes possible the "transcendental reduction," which itself opens up the dimension of the transcendental correlation between world and world-consciousness.

For our purposes, a very summary description of the findings of the correlation analyses must suffice. Once one begins to inquire into the modes in which objects are subjectively given within the life-world, that is, "into *how* an object . . . exhibits itself as being and being-such, we enter a realm of more and more involved and very remarkable exposition [*sich immer mehr verwickelnder und sehr merkwürdiger Aufweisungen*]. . . . [I]n reflection we recognize with astonishment [*Staunen*] that essential correlations obtain here which are the component parts of a farther-reaching, universal a priori" (*C*, 159). The first discovery made in scrutinizing the *how* of the appearance of things is that of "a fixed typology . . . [that] applies not only to perceiving, to bodies, and to the penetrable depths of immediate sensibility but to any and every entity within the spatiotemporal world, and to its subjective manners of givenness" (*C*, 166). While having, at first, the looks of a "confusingly manifold typology of correlations, comprising further differentiations at every turn," this typology proves itself to be a "total multiplicity," that is, a multiplicity that possesses ideality and essential generality (*C*, 166). Husserl observes that in centering on the subjective acts in which world and things appear to us, "a number of never thematically investigated types, not only of individual things but also of syntheses, in an inseparable synthetic totality which is constantly produced by intentionally overlapping horizon-validities" come into view (*C*, 145). This "synthetic totality," or "universe of synthetically connected accomplishments" (*C*, 145) of consciousness, is the totality of the world-constituting acts of subjectivity or, as Husserl also calls it, the "world-nucleus [*Weltkern*]" (*C*, 133), that is, the subjective correlate of the world as the world that has ontic meaning and ontic validity for us. The subjective universe of "universal accomplishing life in which the world comes to be as existing for us constantly in flowing particularity, constantly 'pregiven' to us" (*C*, 145), thus reveals itself as the constitutive correlate of the world and its own universal structures. That which in the natural attitude characteristic of both the prescientific life in the life-world and scientific life was taken for granted—the spatiotemporal existence of things in the world, their universal causal style, etc.—all this now appears to be a function of subjective accomplishments, whose universal structures are therefore more fundamental.

An additional implication of the discovery of the synthetic totality of the subjective accomplishments regarding things in the world requires mention here. As we have seen, the analyses of the correlation between things and the subjective modes of their givenness yield a multiplicity of acts that form a synthetic totality. As far as an individual entity is concerned, this is "an ideal set of actual and possible experiential manners of givenness, each of which is an appearance of this one entity." Consequently, any actual concrete experience of an object is merely a realization of one of the manners of givenness that make up the total multiplicity of the intentional acts in question. According to Husserl, the latter represents "a horizon of possibly realizable processes, as opposed to the actual process, and as such it belongs to each experience, or rather to the intention which is operative within it" (*C*, 167). The horizon of the possible ways in which things can be given—a horizon that is necessarily implied in any actual concrete way in which an entity is given—thus relativizes the originality of any singular experience of a thing and links it to the ideal and synthetic multiplicity of the manners of givenness that form the total horizon within which that experience occurs. Differently worded, the life-world a priori shows that any singular experience occurs against the background of a universal world-horizon implicit within any such experience. Husserl leaves no doubt regarding the "fact" that "no conceivable human being, no matter how different we imagine him to be, could ever experience a world in manners of givenness which differ from the incessantly mobile relativity" of the world pregiven to him and the "great horizon of remarkable truths" about this pregiven world that the correlation analyses have brought to light (*C*, 165).

From these analyses of the modes in which things are perceived in the life-world, and from which it becomes clear that "anything that is—whatever its meaning and to whatever region it belongs—is an index of a subjective system of correlations" (*C*, 165), it follows that the total intentional accomplishment of subjectivity involved in the constitution of the world as a formation of meaning cannot be that of the "isolated subject." Husserl advances that "we are dealing, rather, with the entirety of the accomplishment of communalized intersubjectivity" (*C*, 167; trans. mod.). As we have already seen, the life-world is not only that of everyday surrounding spatiotemporal things; within the life-world we are also with others. Apart from the phenomena that affect the ways in which things are subjectively perceived in the individual ego's perception of things—kinesthetics, alteration of validity, horizon-consciousness, and so forth—there is also "the fact that in our continuously flowing world-perceiving we are not isolated but rather have, within it, contact with other human beings" (*C*, 163). Since in "*living with one another* each one [has not only his or her perceptions, presentifications, devaluations of his or her certainties, etc., but] can take part in the life of others"; straightforward, or individual, perception is from the outset communalized from within. In a way analogous to what happens in individual perception and experiences where the individual series of experiences within my own experiential life enter into contact, and mutually correct each other, my experiential acquisitions also enter into contact with those of others, with the effect that, "for the most part, intersubjective harmony of validity occurs, [establishing what is] 'normal' in respect to particular details, and thus an intersubjective unity also comes about in the multiplicity of validities and of what is valid through them" (*C*, 163). By way of this reciprocal correction—or, as Husserl also describes it, "critique" (*C*, 163)—of individual validity claims, the world as one and the same world is engendered in a communalized subjectivity that "continuously maintains constant validity as the world which is in part already experienced and in part the open horizon of possible experiences for all; it is the world as the universal horizon, common to all man, of actually existing things" (*C*, 164).[16] Even though each one has his or her experienced things, "each individual 'knows' himself to be living within the horizon of his fellow human beings.... He knows that he and his fellows, in their actual contact, are related to the same experienced things in such a way that each individual has different aspects, different sides, perspectives, etc., of them but that in each case these are taken from the same total system of multiplicities of which each individual is constantly conscious (in the actual experience of the same thing) as the horizon of possible experience of this thing" (*C*, 164).

The unifying multiplicities exhibited in the investigation of individual object-perception are themselves relativized by the deeper-lying multiplicities of communalized life within which individual object-perception is inscribed. What all of this proves is not only that the total synthesis of intentional subjectivity has multiple levels but also that this synthetic accomplishment is that of a communalized intersubjectivity (*vergemeinschafteten Intersubjectivität*). As Husserl points out, "all the levels and strata through which the syntheses, intentionally overlapping as they are from subject to subject, are interwoven form a universal unity of synthesis; through it the objective [*gegenständliche*] universe comes to be—the world which is and *as* it is concretely and vividly given (and pregiven for all possible praxis)" (*C*, 168). The "obscure horizon" (*C*, 167) of the formation of the world as objective universe is none other than that of the syntheses of communalized intersubjectivity. It is in "intersubjective constitution" that "the world, meaning by this the total system of manners of givenness, however hidden, also of modes of validity for egos" (*C*, 168), comes into being. The world thus formed through intersubjective constitution is the world as a "structure of meaning [*Sinngebilde*]." Husserl writes: "Through this constitution, if we systematically uncover it, the world as it is for us becomes understandable as the structure of meaning formed out of elementary intentionalities" (*C*, 168). The *one* world shared by all is a product of elementary subjective accomplishments, not something objectively given but something whose unity is constantly generated through critical acts of correction by which individual validity claims become relativized. In uncovering and opening up the "obscure horizon" of its constitution "through methodical regressive inquiry" (*C*, 167), the world as a structure of meaning reveals itself as the correlate of the world-constituting transcendental ego. For the accomplishment of this task, the transcendental *epoche* is instrumental.

From everything we have seen so far, it should be clear that the transcendental ego is not the individual ego but the ego of communalized intersubjectivity. As Husserl also notes, however, by suspending the natural attitude with respect to the world in the transcendental *epoche*, not only the world is reduced to a phenomenon, but humankind is reduced, as well, "to the phenomenon 'mankind.'" While the reduction of world to the transcendental phenomenon "world" permits one to understand it as a meaning-formation, the reduction of humankind to the phenomenon "mankind" "makes it possible to recognize mankind as a self-objectivation of transcendental subjectivity which is always functioning ultimately and is thus 'absolute'" (*C*, 153). Before discussing the phenomenon "mankind" any further, let us recall that bracketing the natural attitude, the radical, or transcendental, *epoche* reduces everything objective to the unitary multiplicity of its subjective modes of givenness, that is, to the status of something intended or meant (*Gemeintes*). In this inquiry into the subjective, however, the objective is not transformed into "a psychic occurrence in men through which they gain experience of the world, everyday or scientific opinion about the world" (*C*, 179). Qua *epoche* of everything objective, the subjective in the sense of psychic process has been put out of play as well, precisely because the subjective in this sense presupposes the givenness of the world. Undoubtedly, in "the pure attitude focused upon correlations, created by the epoche, the world, the objective, becomes itself something subjective," but since "even the 'subjective' is relativized"

(*C*, 179) by the *epoche*, subjectivity refers here to something other than the psychological subjectivity of the "I." Husserl explains: "The world (called 'transcendental phenomenon' in the transformed attitude) is from the start taken only as a correlate of subjective appearances, views, subjective acts and capacities through which it constantly has, and ever attains anew, its changeable [but] unitary sense" (*C*, 179). These appearances of the world reduced to its phenomenal essence, are construed as its subjective manners of givenness. If, consequently, "the ego-poles and everything about them of a specifically ego-character become the subject of essential inquiry, they . . . become, in a new and still higher sense, the subjective aspect of the world and also of its manners of appearing." In contrast to the psychological concept of subjectivity, which presupposes the over-againstness of the objective world, as well as its pregivenness and unquestioned existence independent from it, the concept of subjectivity in the *epoche* "encompass[es] everything: ego-poles and the universe of ego-poles, multiplicities of appearance or object-poles and the universe of object-poles" (*C*, 179). As Husserl avers, for the sense-constituting transcendental ego the assumption of a being exterior to it makes no sense.[17] Indeed, it is not to be thought as an inside opposed to something outside. It follows already from this unheard of concept of subjectivity that the transcendental ego constitutive of the world is not human subjectivity, nor the collective subject of humankind insofar as the latter remains part of the world that it is supposed to constitute. As a real entity, the *we* in the sense of "we human beings" has become a phenomenon in the *epoche*, that is, an "object-pole and [hence] subject-matter for inquiry back into the correlative intentionalities" of which it is the pole, and through whose function the *we* has attained its ontic meaning. Husserl, therefore, can ask: "are the transcendental subjects, i.e. those *functioning* in the constitution of the world, human beings? After all, the epoche has made them into 'phenomena,' so that the philosopher within the epoche has neither himself nor others naively and straightforwardly valid as *human beings* but precisely only as 'phenomena,' as poles for transcendental regressive inquiries" (*C*, 183). As a consequence, the transcendental subject is not human if human is to refer to "real psychophysical beings" whether individual or collective (*C*, 183). The world-constituting ego is the ego not of humankind as a sociohistorical reality but of its phenomenon in the shape of communalized intersubjectivity. The transcendentally accomplishing subjectivity highlighted by the radical *epoche* and whose total essential form becomes available through eidetic reduction is an ahuman subjectivity. But what becomes clear at this point as well is that the subject-pole constitutive of the *one* world is, like the *one* world itself, not a static idea but an Idea in the Kantian sense, ever unfinished and thus the object of an infinite task. This, then, is the new universal truth unearthed by the new science that renews the Greek project of a rational and all-encompassing science. It is, indeed, a very odd universality that binds all humans, precisely because it is ahuman, but its ahumanity, that is, its aloofness with respect to all particular humanities, is also what secures its universally binding value for human beings. Anything human, would be too human, in order to be truly binding. But the ahumanity of this new universal truth is not, unlike the objective a priori, an alienating form. Husserl argues that "each human being 'bears within himself a transcendental "I"'—not as a real part or a stratum of his soul (which would be absurd) but rather insofar as he is the self-objectification, as exhibited through phenomenological self-reflection, of the corresponding transcendental 'I'" (*C*, 186). Furthermore, as is obvious from the elaborations on the transcendental ego in section B of part 3 in *The Crisis*, where Husserl pursues a way into phenomenological philosophy from psychology, the transcendental ego, although in one sense radically different from the empirical psychological ego, is, in a different sense, still the same. It is, therefore, that the intrinsic alterity of the subjective a priori's universality is distinctly different from the alienness of the objective universal.

Before further elaborating on this new, more all-embracing, universal, it is necessary to recall Husserl's contention that his conclusion that the world-constituting intersubjective ego is nothing human was a bit premature given that it is always "I" "who performs the epoche, and even if there are others, and even if they practice the epoche in direct community with me, [they and] all other human beings with their entire act-life are included, for me, within my epoche, in the world-phenomenon which, in my epoche, is exclusively mine" (*C*, 184). The point Husserl wishes to bring home here is that the discovery of transcendental subjectivity always rests on what he calls "the primal 'I' [*Ur-Ich*], the ego of my epoche, which can never lose its uniqueness and personal indeclinability" (*C*, 185). But there is no mistaking this primal "I," which performs the radical *epoche* in "a unique sort of philosophical solitude" (*C*, 184), for one "I," that is, in the sense of an "I" that would have cut itself off from all the others, and to which it thus continues to belong. As Husserl avers, the

"I" that performs the epoche is "actually called 'I' only by equivocation though it is an essential equivocation since, when I name it in reflection, I can say nothing other than: it is I who practice the epoche, I who interrogate, as phenomenon, the world which is now valid for me according to its being and being-such, with all its human beings, of whom I am so fully conscious" (C, 184). Because the "I" who focuses on transcendental intersubjectivity is not the "I" of the single, concrete individual, the role that Husserl attributes to the "primal 'I'" does not contradict the preceding claim "of a transcendental intersubjectivity constituting the world as 'world for all,' in which I again appear, this time as 'one' transcendental 'I' among others, whereby 'we all' are taken as functioning transcendentally" (C, 184).[18] Yet this emphasis on the primal "I" as one that "starting from itself and in itself . . . constitutes transcendental intersubjectivity, to which it then adds itself as a merely privileged member, namely, as 'I' among the transcendental others [als Ich der transzendentalen Andern]" (C, 185), has frequently been denounced as indicative of an essential Husserlian solipsism. Taking its starting point in this primal "I," however transcendental, is certainly further evidence of Husserlian phenomenology's continuing indebtedness to the metaphysics of subjectivity. Be that as it may, the central position attributed to the "I" in the constitution of intersubjectivity is paradoxically what endows Husserl's concept of universality with a set of features that radically distinguish it from the objective conception of universality, whether in the natural sciences or in philosophies modeled after the latter. Indeed, by insisting on the fact that transcendental intersubjectivity is constituted, first and foremost, by the "I" who practices the *epoche* (which then makes itself declinable, for itself, transcendentally), Husserl highlights his understanding of universal intersubjectivity and its correlate, the world-horizon, as products of intentional acts. He also shows that rather than being preformed ideas in some *topos ouraneos*, intersubjectivity and world-horizonality are dependent on subjective acts of consciousness. Transcendental community is not a given; rather, it is something that is being produced, that, therefore, is also historical in the sense that one has never finished bringing it to life by a communalized subject that itself needs constant work.[19] Both communalized intersubjectivity and the world-for-all are tasks precisely insofar as they are sense-formations constituted by an ego. They are Ideas in the Kantian sense. Finally, by highlighting the primordiality of the "primal 'I,'" Husserl may also suggest that in the face of communalized intersubjectivity, the singularity of the "I" who constitutes this very same intersubjectivity is not a given either. It itself is something that can only be achieved in a radical act, that is, in the act in which "I" perform the *epoche*. Husserl's insistence on the "primal 'I'" is thus also an attempt to secure the singularity and uniqueness of an "I" that at the same time appears as one transcendental "I" among others in constituted intersubjectivity, by turning it into the objective of an infinite task. Undoubtedly, as Husserl acknowledges, as products of an ahuman subjectivity, these Ideas appear strange and contrary to everyday opinions. But insofar as these Ideas are products of a consciousness practicing the *epoche*, they are, unlike objective universality, absolutely binding.

The universals that have made the natural sciences so successful in mathematizing nature are, as we have seen, a function of the spatiotemporal shape of bodily things. Universality for the sciences, and the philosophies that have taken their lead, is predicated on geometric form. According to Husserl, all attempts to map the realm of the psyche in a way similar to the explication of nature by the sciences must therefore fail. Now, the life-world, as the ground to which the objective sciences must be traced back, is the spatiotemporal world of things experienced in pre- and extrascientific life. The science of the life-world—a science inquiring into transcendental subjectivity—shows that "natural, objective world-life is only a particular mode of the transcendental life which forever constitutes the world, [though] in such a way that transcendental subjectivity, while living on in this mode, has not become conscious of the constituting horizons and never can be aware of them" (C, 175–76). However, once transcendental subjectivity reflects on its infatuation with the objects in the world, "the full and true ontic meaning of objective being, and thus of all objective truth, is set forth" (C, 176). It thus becomes clear that objective science and its universal truths are not truly universal but are inscribed, as it were, in the universal structures exhibited by the inquiry into the life-world. The science of transcendental subjectivity is the only science that can claim the title of a universal science. What makes it universal is thus not the spatiotemporal forms of the bodily things in the world but the structures of the elementary intentionalities that form the structures of meaning, including those of the spatiotemporal form. Rather than being predicated on shape, the universality of the new science of the accomplishing life of transcendental subjectivity is predicated on what Husserl calls "the essential form [*Wesensform*] of the transcendental accomplishments in all their types of individual and intersubjective accomplishments, that is, the total essential form [*die gesamte Wesensform*] of transcendentally accomplishing subjectivity in all its social forms" (*C*, 178). What is universal in the endless flow of subjective constituting life are the essential forms, or forms of essence, as well as the totality of these forms disclosed through the method of eidetic reduction. If these forms, which are forms in a new sense, in that they constitute subjectivity in its innermost elementary acts and intentionalities, are universal, it is also because every "I" can practice the radical *epoche* of the natural attitude, perform the eidetic reduction, and reconstruct the procedures by which the universals in question have been laid bare.[20] In short, they can be established intersubjectively in the strictest way and made apodictically evident.

At one point, while evoking "the endless array" of problems and discoveries made in the wake of the reoriented interest of the *epoche*, and the subsequent recognition of "the purely subjective in its own self-enclosed pure context as intentionality," one wonders whether the correlation-analyses will ever hit rock bottom. But Husserl remarks that, although,

> indeed, every "ground" that is reached points to further grounds, every horizon opened up awakens new horizons, and yet the endless whole, in its infinity of flowing movement, is oriented toward the unity of one meaning; not, of course, in such a way that we could ever simply grasp and understand the whole; rather, as soon as one has fairly well mastered the universal form of meaning formation, the breadths and depths of this total meaning, in its infinite totality, take on valuative [*axiotische*] dimensions: there arise problems of the totality as that of a universal reason. (*C*, 170)

In spite of the daunting complexity of the analyses of the world-constituting processes of subjectivity, each newly disclosed level of sense-formation reveals itself also to be interwoven with deeper lying syntheses, thus suggesting a universal unity of synthesis. If the one, infinite totality of meaning intimated by the universal form of meaning-formation cannot simply be grasped and understood as a whole, is it not precisely because, rather than simply a hidden ground, this ground is a ground still to be constituted in an infinite process, or progress? The infinite totality in question here is the horizon with respect to which a particular meaning-formation acquires meaning to begin with, but this horizon also temporalizes it, defining it as one moment in the infinite task of accomplishing the total meaning. The infinite totality presupposed and aimed at by all subjective and intersubjective acts of consciousness takes on valuative dimensions, Husserl holds. Indeed, the one total meaning—toward which the universal forms structuring all the acts of intentional meaning-formation, particularly, to the extent that they are acts of a communalized intersubjectivity, point—has the status of a value, a norm, or principle of axiology. With this valuative quality, that is, the idea (in a Kantian sense) of a totality of meaning of all acts of consciousness, Husserl, as we have seen, invokes the question of a universal reason.

This question, which had been broached in the first part of *The Crisis* (and in the Vienna lecture), is not further developed in the remaining part of the existing body of the work. Yet in the manuscript appended as chapter 73 by Walter Biemel to the unfinished manuscript in the first complete edition of *The Crisis* as volume 6 of the *Husserliana*, this question is taken up at some length. To conclude, I turn to a commentary of some of these pages, whose unquestionable ponderousness should not distract from their indisputable significance regarding that with which we have been concerned, and which the English translation of *The Crisis* features as appendix 4. The idea of a truth in itself, and its correlate, being itself, on which the project of a universal science of the world rests, that is, the project of philosophy as it emerges in ancient Greece, may well be "a philosophical invention [*Erfindung*]," Husserl admits. But he is also quick to note that it is "not a dispensable invention without significance, but one which raises—or is called to raise—man to a new level in a new historical development of human life [*in einer neuen Historizität menschheitlichen Lebens*], a historical development whose entelechy is the new idea and the philosophical or scientific praxis belonging to it, the method of a new sort of scientific thinking" (*C*, 336). Even though as a thinking being, "the man of everyday life . . . has the *katalon*" (i.e., the notion of the general, or universal, in everyday life), he achieves only relative truths. Yet the very "invention," or discovery, of the idea of a truth in itself—a universal truth—submits everyday life to the very strange demand of an altogether different kind of life and historicity—a life in view of the nonrelative and its universally binding truths. Although from the Renaissance on, this new standard for shaping human life has taken root in Europe under the form of the objective sciences, the Greek idea of a life refashioned in light of universal truths by Husserl's elaborations on the intersubjective constitution of the world is now conceived of in more fundamental terms than those of the natural sciences and their type of universally binding truth. Explaining that his use of the term *transcendental* to characterize phenomenological philosophy as the new science that renews the Greek idea of an all-embracing rational science, and, hence, the idea that animates "Europe," pays tribute to idealism as the only philosophy that has provided something of a bulwark against the objectifying thrust of the natural sciences, Husserl invokes Kant's *Critique of Pure Reason*, ascertaining that "*reason* is the specific characteristic of man" and that, therefore, human life "is a constant becoming through a constant intentionality of development" (*C*, 338). Indeed, reason induces human beings to seize "in consciousness . . . the idea of autonomy, the idea of a resolve of the will to shape one's whole personal life into the synthetic unity of a life of universal self-responsibility." For the human being, to possess reason amounts to having a telos, a goal toward which to develop, and thus to be able, in such development, "to be true to himself . . . to remain identical with himself." Needless to say, to have reason in no way means to be reasonable. It only means to have an innate goal, and with it a task to accomplish, one that, as Husserl emphasizes, is inextricably linked to the will of the community of humans as a whole to shape its life according to principles of reason as well.

Philosophy, as a rational and universal science, is the highest means toward attaining the goal inherent in the human being of becoming an autonomous and self-responsible being. Philosophy, as rigorous science, not only articulates this goal but does so in a manner congruent with the goal itself, in other words, in an apodictically grounding way, one that thus can be understood or reconstructed by anyone. Husserl writes: "The universally, apodictically grounded and grounding science arises now as the necessarily highest function of mankind . . . namely, as making possible mankind's development into a personal autonomy and into an all-encompassing autonomy for mankind—the idea which represents the driving force of life for the highest stage of mankind" (*C*, 338). Philosophy consequently has an imminently practical or ethical purpose. But that is not all! Qua rational science it is an intrinsically historical science in the sense that at no stage of its development is its apodictically grounded articulation of reason as the telos of humanity completed. "Philosophy is nothing other than [rationalism], through and through, but it is rationalism differentiated within itself according to the different stages of the movement of intention and fulfillment; it is *ratio in the constant movement of self-elucidation* [*Selbsterhellung*], begun with the first breakthrough of philosophy into mankind, whose innate reason was previously in a state of concealment, of nocturnal obscurity" (*C*, 338). Rather than the definite and polished presentation of what is universal, the idea of a universal science that irrupts for the first time in Greece, and that constitutes the idea of "Europe," is a rational science in that in setting reason as a goal, this very goal impels it to critically overcome each one of its historical elaborations by seeking greater and greater clarity about itself. Philosophy, as rational and universal science, is intrinsically historical, not merely because it develops differentially in response to the various stages in which its goal is intended and finds fulfillment but precisely because it is driven by the rational task of achieving increasing self-elucidation. This defining quality of critical self-elucidation—one that sets it apart from religion and mythical constructs—is what makes philosophy rational and has caused it to be in constant movement since its dawn in Greece. Although from the outside philosophy may appear as just one cultural—or, I add, ethnic—formation among others, and its history, merely, "a causal process occurring in the world, in the world's space and time," "seen from the inside," it is "the constant struggle of 'awakened' reason to come to itself, to an understanding of itself, to a reason which concretely understands itself in understanding the existing world, existing in its whole universal truth" (*C*, 339). According to Husserl's poignant expression, *rationality* means to be "on the way to a higher rationality." It is not a title that one—Europe, for instance—can claim to effectively possess, for rationality is equivalent to the awareness "again and again [of] its unsatisfying relativity . . . [and] is driven on in its toils, in its will to attain the true and full rationality." It is not a title that Greece can simply be credited with, since the struggle of reason to come to itself has led to the discovery that reason, or rationality, is "an idea residing in the infinite." As Husserl observes, with this discovery that reason is an Idea in the Kantian sense, a "final form [*Endgestalt*]" is discovered, which itself becomes "the beginning form [*Anfangsgestalt*] of a new sort of infinity and relativity" (*C*, 339). Distinct from the infinity (and relativity) of the objective, or spatiotemporal, universal world, this new form of infinity characterizes the infinite tasks of critically and intersubjectively working toward a rational humankind.[21]

The demand of apodicticity, together with universality and absolute self-responsibility—the founding ideas of "Europe"—is the first of these new infinite tasks. Although this discovery is, as we have seen before, made for the first time by Descartes, thereby opening up the period of modernity, and thus precedes Husserl's own attempt to radically renew its genuine sense, Descartes' discovery is a discovery of "what, in the transcendental understanding, outlines the primal ground and the primal method of all philosophy" (C, 340), namely the demand of absolute self-responsibility and universal reconstructibility. By foregrounding the idea of apodicticity, not only a new beginning is made—one of newly infinite tasks—but also a new beginning in philosophizing and of what philosophy means. For, indeed, by making apodicticity into the fundamental problem of philosophy, to philosophize is to implicate not only all other philosophers, but it is to implicate humankind as a whole. Rediscovering apodicticity, that is, the demand to think responsibly and in respect of others, in conformity with the goal of making any claim one makes universally reconstructible, is to acknowledge that as a bearer of reason one is intersubjectively tied up with all others. If apodicticity is the ultimate meaning of philosophy, then philosophy is necessarily about intersubjectivity, and the infinite process and progress of self-elucidation without which there can be no such thing. As Husserl remarks, with the rediscovery within phenomenology of apodicticity as the ultimate meaning and task of philosophy, "there begins a philosophy with the deepest and most universal self-understanding of the philosophizing ego as the bearer of absolute reason coming to itself, of the same ego as implicating, in his apodictic being-for-himself, his fellow subjects and all possible fellow philosophers; [this is] the discovery of absolute intersubjectivity (objectified in the world as the whole of mankind), as that in which reason, in obscurity, in elucidation, in the movement of lucid self-understanding, is in infinite progress" (C, 340).

The new sense of philosophy, accruing from apodicticity as its fundamental problem, entails a new sense, as well, of what it means to be human. The new meaning given to human existence in the wake of the philosophical discovery, or rediscovery, of apodicticity is that of "the ultimate self-understanding of man as being responsible for his own human being: his *self-understanding as being in being called to a life of apodicticity*, not only in abstractly practicing apodictic science in the usual sense but [as being mankind] which realizes its whole concrete being in apodictic freedom by becoming apodictic mankind in the whole active life of its reason—through which it is human" (C, 340). This is the infinite task of a humanity striving to live a life according to the idea of reason, a task that Husserl has identified as the essential meaning of "Europe" as an idea. The realization of this idea is not only an infinite task; it is also a realization that, rather than fulfilling a pregiven and programmatic notion of what rationality means, it consists in the will to be rational, and hence also in the call to intersubjectively establish what is universal, and this in a process that itself is infinite. Husserl remarks that "mankind understanding itself as rational, understanding that it is rational in seeking to be rational . . . signifies an infinity of living and striving toward reason; . . . reason is precisely that which man *qua* man, in his innermost being, is aiming for" (*C*, 340–41). In what is clearly a critical reference to Kant, Husserl concludes that such understanding of reason as the will to be rational, and thus to be true to oneself insofar as the human is capable of the odd demands that come with having reason, "allows for no differentiation into 'theoretical,' 'practical,' 'aesthetics,' or whatever." Being human, that is, living according to the goal set by the idea of something universal—an idea that violently irrupts in Greece and has shaped what "Europe" as an idea means—"is teleological being and an ought-to-be, and . . . this teleology holds sway in each and every activity and project of an ego." It is meant to hold sway, as Husserl concludes, because the human being "through self-understanding . . . can know the apodictic *telos*; and . . . this knowing, the ultimate self-understanding, has no other form than self-understanding according to a priori principles as self-understanding in the form of philosophy" (*C*, 341).

PART II

Martin Heidegger

§ 4 Singular Essence

Terms such as the *Occident* or the *West* have long been used interchangeably with the term *Europe*. Apart from being highly questionable synonyms within a given language, this interchangeability encounters additional limits with the translation of these terms into other languages. The term *Occident*, for example, commonly used to translate the German *Abendland*, contains no reference to the *Abend* (evening) in the word *Abendland*, the "land of evening," coined by Caspar Hedio in 1552 in response to Martin Luther's evocation of *Morgenland* in his translation of the New Testament. In the same way that the *Occident* implies its opposite, *Orient*, *Abendland* is supplied with an antonym, the "land of morning." Although in German both *Abendland* and *Occident* are often used synonymously (English leaving one no other option but to translate *Abendland* as "Occident"), they are not, as the long and intricate history of the terms demonstrates, simply equivalent in meaning.[1] This is not the place, however, to rehearse this history; in the following we will only be interested in Martin Heidegger's understanding of the notion of *Abendland*, which itself, as we will see, is primarily indebted to Friedrich Hölderlin and the very peculiar and unique way he used this term. Suffice it therefore to say very schematically that, unlike the notion of the Occident, in which a relation of tension with the Orient dominates (whether the Orient is endowed with the promise of salvation or is that from which the Occident has to emancipate itself), the word *Abendland* is dominated by the sense of evening, being the land of the evening, as the Greek term *Hesperia*, the "west country," the land of the setting sun—a term to which Hölderlin consistently resorts in his poetry—even more clearly suggests.

Like *Europe*, the words *Occident* and *West* (*Abendland*) have no particular prominence in Martin Heidegger's early work. It is in his 1935 *Introduction to Metaphysics* that the notion of "Europe" first acquires an exemplary significance in that it is explicitly linked to Heidegger's main philosophical concern, namely, the question of Being. Even though the term *Abendland* or *Occident* features in the *Inaugural Address* (1933), it too becomes a much more pronounced notion only after 1935. Indeed, Heidegger's use of the terms *Occident* and *occidental* originates unmistakably in the work he began in the 1930s on Friedrich Hölderlin. Before elaborating, however succinctly, on the way Heidegger thinks with Hölderlin about the Occident and Europe, we must first remind ourselves that, as with Husserl, these names (including the reference to the Orient, or *Morgenland*) do not rest on geographical distinctions. Furthermore, as one of the interlocutors remarks in "Das abendländische Gespräch" (1943), the erroneous belief that "the Occidental signifies something *Völkisches* or even national, and, hence, that it contains a restriction to something that one knows and compares in historical fashion," must be emphatically rejected.[2] Apart from the fact that the Occident is not to be understood as a region and, moreover, that this concept, since it also includes both Americas, does not simply coincide with "Europe"—whose specificity thus needs clarification as well—Heidegger's rejection in "Letter on Humanism" of a contrasting relation between the Occident and the Orient as two distinct regions of the world also indicates the need to begin thinking of what he terms "the mysterious relations to the East which found expression in Hölderlin's poetry" (*BW*, 218; trans. mod.).[3] In a short commentary in "Letter on Humanism" on Hölderlin's elegy, "Homecoming," Heidegger argues that for the poet "the West is not thought regionally as the Occident in contrast to the Orient, nor merely as Europe, but rather worldhistorically out of nearness to the origin [*Ursprung*]." Considering that Heidegger's thought is an attempt to foreground philosophy as metaphysics in the question of Being, the notions of the "Occident," "Orient," and "Europe" are thus to be understood "worldhistorically out of nearness to the origin"—in other words, as embedded in the conception of a history of Being. They become meaningful only from the relation of proximity or distance to the origin that, in particular, the terms *Orient* and *Occident* suggest. The Occident would seem to refer to the present time and is, compared with the Orient, a late phenomenon within the history of Being. In a sentence reminiscent of Hegel's speculations on the relation of the Occident to the Orient, Heidegger remarks that destiny (*Geschick*), or rather, that which was sent on its way at the beginning, "guides the spirit on its way [*Wanderung*] from the Orient to the Occident."[4] On the one hand, the Occident, as the land of evening, the land of the setting sun, is marked by a decline (*Untergang*) of that which arose or was sent on its way in the Orient.[5] Yet what irrupted in the Orient (which for Heidegger, following Hölderlin, means Greece) is the thought of Being. If the Orient thus names what emerged in Greece, it also follows that the Orient is not the "Asian" (*das Asiatische*). Unlike Heidegger's later references to the "Eastasian" (*ostasiatisch*), in, for example, "A Dialogue on Language," which already implies other great beginnings besides the Greek one, the Asian names that kind of other that the Greeks had to confront and overcome to come into their own. Heidegger writes that rather than coming into their own by isolating themselves within their own space, it is "only thanks to the most fierce, but also the most creative confrontation [*Auseinandersetzung*] with what was most foreign to them and most difficult—the Asian—that this people rose into the brief orbit of its historical uniqueness and grandeur."[6] Needless to say, the place of the Asian other is occupied in paradigmatic fashion by the Persians, whom the Greeks defeated in a series of confrontations, especially the famous sea battle of Salamis.[7] In any case, in "Das abendländische Gespräch" Heidegger recalls that "Hölderlin thinks of Hellas in an oriental fashion (*morgenländisch*), that is, as a (*ein*) land of the rise (*Aufgang*) of the heavenly fire," and adds that "Greece—a land, rather than the land—is, therefore, the age in which, rather than the first rise and beginning, the passage of the first beginning of the fire of the heavens, that is, the transition of the Oriental to the Occidental occurred."[8]

At this point a note on how one is to understand the decline of the Orient in (or more precisely, as) the Occident—that is, of the thought of Being that arose in Greece—is certainly warranted. Indeed, the issue is not that owing to a pathological hypertrophism of reason that supposedly happened to the Occident, it is threatened by extinction as all the theoreticians of decline argued; nor, as one of these theoreticians, Oswald Spengler, held in "The Decline of the Occident," by a loss of its former grandeur, but rather that the Occident is defined by the decline of what arose in the commencement.[9] Notwithstanding Heidegger's contention that such a decline does not exclude grandeur (indeed, the forgetfulness of the commencement that characterizes the Occident, rather than being a lack, is "the richest and most prodigious event: in it the history of the Western world comes to be borne out," namely, the event of metaphysics), does one not also have to face the paradoxical possibility that because it is essentially declining, the Occident never achieved any *originary* greatness and that at the limit it never existed but is still to come? (*EGT,* 141). Just as modern science, as it has developed in Europe, is not, according to Husserl, the realization of what promised itself under the title of a universal rational science in Greece, Greek philosophy, which attained dominance in Occidental-European philosophical thought, is, according to Heidegger, only the inceptive end—that is, a fall away from—of the originary inception of the Greek conception of Being (see *IM,* 202). If metaphysics characterizes thought in the West, the *West,* or the *Occident,* are names for the forgetting of the inceptive question of Being. In "Letter on Humanism" Heidegger notes that the forgetfulness of Being, peculiar to all of Western philosophical thought (hence its metaphysical framework), is neither the result of a negligence or weakness of thinking in the West nor of "a lesser capacity of early Western [*abendländischen*] thinking" (*BW,* 208). The possibility, if not the necessity, of the forgetfulness of Being—that is, of the difference between Being and beings—is intrinsically intertwined with the destiny of Being itself. In "The Anaximander Fragment" Heidegger observes that oblivion to Being belongs to the self-veiling essence of Being. It belongs so essentially to the destiny of being that the dawn of this destiny rises as the unveiling of what is present in its presencing. This means that the history of Being begins with the oblivion of Being, since Being—together with its essence, its distinction from beings—keeps to itself (*EGT,* 50).

Since one of the fundamental traits of that which at the dawn of thinking emerges in Greece is Being in its unconcealedness, forgetfulness or oblivion is intimately tied to what happens at the commencement. Heidegger writes that "Greek antiquity, Christendom, modern times, global affairs, and the West interpreted as the land of evening—we are thinking all these on the basis of a fundamental characteristic of Being which is more concealed in *Lethe* than it is revealed in *Aletheia.* Yet this concealing of its essence and of its essential origin is characteristic of Being's primordial self-illumination, so much so that thinking simply does *not* pursue it" (*EGT,* 25–26). The essential provenance of the forgetting of Being, that is, its foundation in *Lethe* as a fundamental characteristic of Being itself, which "completely dominates the destiny (*Geschick*) of Western history and of all history determined by Europe," is thus a *Seinsgeschick*—a specific way in which Being has sent, or posted, itself in the history of Western thought (*BW*, 208). Indeed, without this forgetfulness, and per extension the errancy that comes with it, there would be no history. The decline that characterizes the Occident is therefore nothing simply negative. Decline (*Untergang*), Heidegger writes, is to be understood in the same way we speak of the setting of the sun, which disappears behind the mountains or sinks into the sea; in other words, decline is "a going down in the sense of an entering into a concealment."[10] In the Occident that which arose at the beginning disappears in oblivion. In short, then, the failure of Western thought to reflect on Being itself is not just any failure but a necessary or inevitable failure, linked to the trait of *Lethe* that characterizes Being, and thus constitutive of the West as a whole and of Europe in particular. Rooted in the forgetting of Being, and in an omission of thinking Being, the Occident and Europe are therefore, as we have already seen, not geographical entities, not even geopolitical entities, but in Heidegger's words, "epochs" understood in light of the history, destiny, or sending of Being (*EGT*, 27). For this same reason Europe and the West can no longer simply be determined as spiritual projects in the sense Husserl still conceived of them. Both the West and the Occident, along with Europe, are from the beginning historical figures of the forgetfulness of Being, which has made other "powers" than those of Being preeminent in the very history illustrated by these names, which, paradoxically, are the cause of the Occident's so-called greatness.

But the Occident is not merely the place and time of the decline of the sending that occurred in Greece—of "a sending which always concerns the Spirit," as Heidegger remarks; simultaneously "the land of the place and the evening as the time of destiny," the Occident, as "the proper time-space of destiny," is also something waiting to happen, something "still to come."[11] According to the 1942–43 lectures on *Parmenides*, Greece, as "*the event* of the history of the Occident," is the interruptive disclosure and subsequent reconcealment of the essence of truth. Heidegger writes: "According to this essential origination of *aletheia*, the Occident (*Abendland*) is the not yet decided or delimited landscape of the earth upon which an evening (*Abend*) is descending, which as evening essentially takes its beginning from the dawn and therefore harbors in itself the morning of this landscape" (*P*, 147). If, as Heidegger submits, the Greeks "alone are the custodians of the beginning of the Occident," it is precisely because in the transition of this beginning to the Occidental, what began in Greece became the destiny of the Occident, in that this beginning became concealed again (*P*, 147–48). But for this very reason the destiny of the Occident is twofold; in terms of the history of Being, the Occident also contains within itself the possibility of being the place and time in which what was sent in Greece could experience a new, or more precisely another, beginning. Rather than merely being the land of decline, in the sense of being an "abyss of decay," the Occident, as Heidegger remarks in his essay on Georg Trakl, is "the land of descent," as the land of "the transition into the beginning of the dawn (*Frühe*) concealed within it."[12] The Occident, insofar as it is decline and descent, also harbors the possibility of becoming "perhaps and in a wholly other mode, a land of dawn, an Orient."[13] This is also the reason Heidegger can open his inquiry in "The Anaximander Fragment" into what entitles antiquity to continue to address the most recent latecomers to philosophy, with the following questions:

> Do we stand in the very twilight of the most monstrous [*ungeheuersten*] transformation our planet has ever undergone, the twilight of that epoch in which earth itself hangs suspended? Do we confront the evening of a night which heralds another dawn? Are we to strike off on a journey to this historic region of earth's evening? Is the land of evening only now emerging? Will this land of evening overwhelm Occident and Orient alike, transcending whatever is merely European [*durch das Europäische hindurch*] to become the location of a new but primordially fated history [*anfänglicher geschickten Geschichte*]? (*EGT*, 17)

Notwithstanding the insufferable pathos of this passage, it is made clear here that by thinking the essence of the West in terms of what the early saying of Anaximander says, in other words, by breaking with the forgetfulness of what speaks out at the commencement, the Occident, to which this forgetting gave rise, can for the first time become an Occident—a land of evening—that prepares a new dawn, as well as an Orient distinct from the previous one that, to paraphrase Jacques Derrida, posted a missive that never arrived at its destination (*EGT*, 16). But equally important is the suggestion that, although Europe is the transitory site toward such a land of evening, the new dawn would also imply the end of Europe. By harking back to the Greek beginning, Europe is to be superseded by the site of a new history that has been sent on its way in a more primordial fashion. Indeed, as the following quote from Friedrich Nietzsche (with which Heidegger rounds off his questions before proceeding to an interpretation of Anaximander's fragment) demonstrates, with the undoing of the forgetfulness of the commencement of the Occident and Europe, a certain Europe, no doubt, can be forgotten. Nietzsche writes: "A higher situation for mankind is possible, in which the Europe of nations will be obscured and forgotten, but in which Europe will live on in thirty very ancient but never antiquated books."[14]

Undoubtedly, the passage beyond Europe thus advocated in no way coincides with the impending threat of Europe's destruction that Heidegger diagnoses first in his 1935 *Introduction to Metaphysics* and again in 1942 in *Hölderlin's Hymn "The Ister."* Caught, according to the 1935 lectures, in the pincers between America and Russia, Europe is threatened with extinction. In the 1942 work America is singled out for seeking the destruction of Europe as the beginning of the Occident. In the lectures on "The Ister" Heidegger remarks that "we know today that the Anglo-Saxon world of Americanism has resolved to annihilate Europe, that is, the homeland (*Heimat*), and that means: the commencement of the Western world. . . . This act is the renunciation of commencement, and a decision in favor of that which is without commencement" (*HHI*, 54–55). America, then, by seeking the destruction of Europe, is intent on forgetting the commencement by destroying it, thus taking itself out of the Western or occidental world and into the ahistorical. Forgetting the commencement by destroying Europe is not, of course, the overcoming of Europe that Heidegger has in mind. On the contrary, it is in the name of the commencement, and what has been sent on its way by the event in question, that a certain Europe—a Europe that is the beginning of the Occident insofar as it is forgetful of the commencement—must make room for the event of a new epoch of Being and site of history.

If it is true that America and Russia are also part of the Occident to which Europe belongs, is it not then also necessary to distinguish Europe from the Occidental? Heidegger refers occasionally to the "Occidental-European" tradition of thought or philosophy, the hyphen linking and separating both the Occident and Europe. But what, then, is specifically European, apart from the Occident to which Europe inevitably belongs? Europe is the beginning of the Occident in the sense that, however forgetful of what began in Greece, it is whatever it is only in relation to this first commencement. By contrast, America, though part and parcel of the Occident, seeks its oblivion through destruction. Now, even though Europe is what it is only in relation to the commencement, it too, as Heidegger contends in *Introduction to Metaphysics*, is threatened by inner self-destruction and, consequently, by a forgetting of its commencement as the Occident in Greece. This is the backdrop against which the somewhat enigmatic remark in *What Is Called Thinking?*—that "for the time being the Occidental is sunk into [*versunken*] what is European"—occurs.[15] The same holds for the question and statement in "Hölderlin's Earth and Heaven": "Does the occidental still exist? It has become Europe" (*EHP*, 200). First of all, the two statements are, geopolitically speaking at least, counterintuitive, since it would seem more accurate to hold, as Jean-Luc Nancy does, for example, that "Europe has dissolved into the 'Occident' whose *subject* it once had been, and [furthermore] that the Occident itself has become dissolved in the 'occidentalized' world, which in turn is in the process of remodeling itself in terms of new 'transnational spaces'" (*PEF*, 13). What Heidegger means, however, is not only that the Occident is sunk into, lost, and forgotten in what is European. Rather, the Occident (in other words, the ambiguous, because twofold, fate of the decline of Greece as the Orient, at once decay of the originary conception of Being *and* "the great beginning that may possibly come") has come to coincide entirely with what Europe has turned out to be, from the perspective of the history of Being. At least since the triumph of method (which began in Europe in the seventeenth century with Galileo and Newton, the founders of the modern sciences—as a result of which the world became calculable and hence available as an objectified reserve everywhere and at all moments for the human being understood as a subject), Europe *is* the world-historical happening of technology as the acme of the forgetting of Being. Europe, or more precisely, modern Europe is, indeed, the name for the technical-industrial mastery of the earth—that is, always the "world" as inhabited by the living—a mastery whose calculating making-available of everything does not come to a stop at the borders of "Europe" itself. Heidegger writes: "Europe's technological-industrial domination has already covered the entire earth. On the other hand, the earth, as a planet, has already been included in the interstellar-cosmic space which is placed at man's disposal by the planned projects of man" (*EHP*, 200). Europe, in other words, stands for the complete

Europeanization of the earth and of man, a process that not only "attacks at the source everything that is of an essential nature" but also deprives the other of conceiving of his or her otherness in terms different from those borrowed from the West.[16] In terms of the history of Being, Europe as the planetary domination of technology is the culmination of the forgetting of what announced itself in Greece—the commencement of the Occident. In Françoise Dastur's words: "Europe is merely what has become of the Occident, that is to say, the technical, planetary order, which is nothing other than completed, or accomplished, metaphysics. . . . The whole planet becomes European today."[17] Although Europe as the planetary domination of technology is the conclusion of the decline that began with the transition from the Orient to the Occident, it needs to be rigorously distinguished from what we have said about the Occident so far. If the Occident is entirely sunk into Europe, then its fate is entirely tied to that of Europe, especially to Europe's Europeanization of the world, more precisely, to Europe as standing for the planetary domination of technology. Yet if Europe is indistinguishable from a completely Europeanized world, is the fate of the Occident not also dependent on the whole world as well? Or, to put it differently, could it be that the fate of the Occident is not only no longer in the hands of Europeans but that as the promise of a new land of morning it also rests in the hands of the rest of the world? But sunk into Europe, the Occident is also that which has become lost in Europe, Europe being the figure not only of the completion of the forgetting of Being in metaphysics but also the forgetting of this forgetting itself. Consequently, Europe designates the forgetfulness of the Occident, of that in which what promised itself in Greece decays but in which Europe may also experience a new morning. Indistinguishable from the planetwide forgetting of the Occident, does not "Europe" also become the name for the possibility of a resurgence of the promise of another beginning, wherever it may take place—that is, the promise of the final occurrence of an Occident that would be another morning not merely for Europe but for the earth as a whole? These are questions, however, that we will have to leave in abeyance for the moment.

To sum up then, terms like the *Occident*, the *West*, the *Orient*, and *Europe* need to be understood from the turn that Heidegger takes around 1935 away from fundamental ontology and to the history of Being. In the text by Heidegger that will concern us in this chapter, *Europe* and the *West* often seem to be used synonymously; in other words, *Europe* stands here as that which has become of the Occident. Later in this book, when we take up Heidegger's interpretation, in the context of his lectures on Hölderlin, of the relation of the Occident to the Orient (*Morgenland*), we will also have an opportunity to clarify with greater precision the notion of the "Orient," in particular how Orient and Occident are interconnected.

In *Being and Time* Heidegger made his first attempt to overcome Western metaphysics as an ontology oblivious to the question of Being (and, as he would later show, responsible for the domination of technology in the West) by returning to the Greeks. But the attempt in *Introduction to Metaphysics* to tackle the then current European situation—and to ward off the looming catastrophe by way of a return to the origins of Europe and the West in Greece—has been judged by some as highly inappropriate, if not ludicrous. Undoubtedly, since Heidegger also seeks in the *Introduction to Metaphysics* to come to grips with what in the *Spiegel* interview he called "the greatest stupidity of his life," it must be admitted that by distancing himself from Nazism through a recourse to the Greek origins of the West, Heidegger, whatever concepts or values he opposes to the dominant ideology, is booby-trapped by many ambiguities![18] Not only that, Heidegger's returning to the Greeks in order to confront the contemporary situation in Germany and Europe also has something untimely about it. But rather than a merely untimely naiveté, Heidegger's is a reflected, that is, self-conscious, untimeliness in which Greece, rather than conforming to its traditional—that is, aestheticist and humanist—exemplarity, is characterized in terms that reveal a completely recast conception of it, endowing it as the origin of the West with traits that are strange and intrinsically foreign to its classicist and romantic portrayal. If the very "untimeliness" of Heidegger's undertaking is also, as Manfred Riedel has pointed out, what makes his endeavor a "thought-worthy attempt," it is mainly, I would hold, for confronting contemporary Europe and the West with a demand that does not compare with any other.[19] Indeed, if we concentrate on Heidegger's reflections on Europe, the West, and Greece after Husserl's elaboration of the idea of Europe as the Greek idea of a universal rational science, it is not exclusively for reasons of continuity regarding the history of the idea or concept of "Europe" but because Heidegger's understanding of precisely what the Greek legacy of Europe consists in displaces in a significant manner a number of the central features that, according to Husserl, characterize this idea. As we will see, as a result of Heidegger's reinterpretation of the Greek legacy, the task that this heritage represents for Europe becomes even more unsettling and demanding than this heritage appeared to us in the case of Husserl. Indeed, what constitutes "Europe" for Heidegger is far stranger and more foreign to Europe as a geographical and historical entity than universality in all its Husserlian oddity. Although I will not elaborate on Heidegger's involvement with the Nazi regime, the strangeness of what, according to Heidegger, Greece has bequeathed to Europe should, at least implicitly, make the distance between Heideggerian phenomenology—at least after the turn (1934–35), at which point he begins to distance himself from the regime—and the ideology of National Socialism, if not fully obvious, then at least tangible.[20]

Let me begin by pointing out that if the *Introduction to Metaphysics* seeks to retrieve the originary foundations of Europe in Greece, it is not because Europe or the West would suffer a crisis. Even though what Heidegger diagnoses as the "darkening of the world" (*IM*, 52) (a situation without precedent and that concerns the world in its entirety, where the resources of the tradition as a whole are no longer of any avail) has undoubtedly, at first sight, the look of a crisis, the absence of the term *crisis* in his analysis is significant.[21] Indeed, as Jacques Derrida has noted, in spite of "many non-fortuitous analogies, in spite of the temporal coincidence (1935)," the *Introduction to Metaphysics* is "radically heterogeneous with respect to the *Crisis of European Sciences and Transcendental Phenomenology* or the *Crisis of European Humanity and Philosophy*."[22] For Husserl, as we have seen, the crisis is a crisis of reason, a crisis that divides reason, but that reason is able to diagnose, and for which it can offer a critical solution. From a Heideggerian perspective one could say that the notion of crisis is a concept of calculating ratio, something that reason calculates and predicts in advance and with which it reckons. Husserl's notion of crisis remains tributary to his unquestioned Cartesianism, that is, to his understanding of subjectivity, and in particular transcendental subjectivity. The crisis does not affect subjectivity itself or its inherent rationality. Yet rather than being the result of the sciences' methodology and ensuing loss of relation to the life-world (of their inability to provide a meaningful understanding of exigencies that are binding for humanity as a whole), the "darkening of the world" of which Heidegger speaks derives, on the contrary, from Western thought's self-completion in calculating technological thought. This destitution is not something brought about by outside factors but by that which endangers Western thought from within. Even though in *Rogues* Derrida has demonstrated that the crisis of modern rationalism as construed by Husserl in the Vienna lecture implies a form of rationalism that originates in reason itself, it is only in Heidegger, as we will later see, that this internal relation to the spirit itself of what leads to its own destitution is explicitly recognized and its consequences drawn.[23] Heidegger's avoidance of the notion of crisis, his preference for the expression "the darkening of the world," rests on the insight that this darkening is the effect—or more precisely, the completion—of Western metaphysical thought and that therefore nothing from within this thought can serve to diagnose or to supply a cure for the disaster.[24] Hence Heidegger's recourse to the commencement in Greece, that is, to thinking the unthought of metaphysical thought (an unthought that even Greek philosophy *qua* philosophy was unable to think through) in order to prepare the conditions for an awakening, not of reason and rationality but of "Spirit, and thus for an originary world of historical Dasein, and thus for subduing the danger of the darkening of the world" (*IM*, 52).

For Husserl, the modern sciences that arose in Europe and that have come to dominate the world do not accomplish per se the universality promised by the idea of a rational science that arose in early Greece. Nor does, for Heidegger, the very fact that Western philosophy has its origins in Greek philosophy necessarily make it the realization of that which came into view for the first time early in Greek thought. In fact, that aspect of Greek thought that came to universally dominate Western thinking and the latter's search for what is universal is nothing but the very end of Greek thought, an end that had already begun in Greece itself. By contrast, the question and the thought of Being that opened up in early Greece only to be soon forgotten in Greece itself—a forgetting that led to the development in the West of metaphysics as the science of all sciences, as the universal science of what is universal—is a question and a way of thinking that promises genuine "universality." Undoubtedly, one of the reasons why Heidegger does not qualify the thought of Being in terms of universality is that he views universality as a metaphysical concept. Heidegger is critical of Husserl's conception of a universal humankind because for him "the universal humanity [*die allgemeine Menschheit*] of modern man" is, in the same way as the state or nation, a mode in which "man wills to be and must be to be the subject that in his modern essence he *already* is."²⁵ The notion of a universal humankind thus remains tributary to the metaphysics of subjectivity. But there is at least one other reason why Heidegger avoids the notion of universality: the great beginning of Greece, according to Heidegger, concerns (at least at first) only Europe and the West, and within Europe—according to *Introduction to Metaphysics*—the German people first and foremost.²⁶ In contrast to Husserl, for whom the idea of a universal rational science that breaks forth in ancient Greece is, metalinguistically speaking, neutral, the thought of Being is linked by Heidegger to the specificity of a language, more precisely to the Greek and German languages—that is, to communities or peoples.²⁷ If this is so, it is because of Heidegger's concern with the finitude of Dasein (and not the other way around), of Dasein's ineradicable involvement in the world. By linking the thought of Being specifically—and, as may seem, exclusively—to the fate of Europe and the West (and within Europe, to the Germans first of all), Heidegger draws radical consequences from Husserl's claim that the universal *episteme*—which is built on *doxa*—not only frees itself from *doxa* but also merely radicalizes and continues *doxa* itself. Therefore, in the *Introduction to Metaphysics*, what is by right "universal"—Being—is construed from a people (the Germans) and this people's language.²⁸ Whereas the idea of a universal rational science bears immediately on all cultures and peoples, European and non-European alike, the beginning in Greece at first claims only Europeans, and within Europe (according to the *Introduction to Metaphysics*) the people of the middle in particular—the Germans. But the thought of Being, although anchored in a particular language and a people (as a result of which the universal loses its abstraction and acquires a hold on what is), does not in principle preclude the possibility of other incarnations. In fact, linking philosophy and the concern with the universal to the idiomatic singularity of a language is not only a way of overcoming the lack of a binding power by an abstract notion of universality; it is also, as we will see, that which secures an openness for a plurality of ways of philosophizing and, above all, for the possibility of an entirely different, not yet foreseeable, way of thinking. In his later work at least, Heidegger acknowledges the existence of other great beginnings apart from the Greek one. In his 1959 lecture "Hölderlin's Earth and Heaven" he remarks that, in addition to the beginning of the West, there are other beginnings and that the great beginning of Europe, as a beginning still to come (rather than to be reactivated, as would be the case in Husserl), must open itself up "to those few other great beginnings which with their own character, belong in the sameness of the beginning of the in-finite relation in which the earth is contained" (*EHP*, 201). I defer an in-depth discussion of this line of thinking to later. For the time being, let me only emphasize that in spite of their differences and specific character, all these other great beginnings have, in the same way as the Greek beginning, opened themselves up to what Heidegger, avoiding here the term *Being*, now refers to as the in-finite relation. What is called "sameness" in this context is, rather than being the universally identical—Being as the in-finite relation—something to which all the beginnings with their own character belong.[29]

For Heidegger Europe's fate does not descend from the idea of an all-embracing rational science. Rather, it is the irruption in Greece of the question of Being that determines Europe and the West. Even though in the Vienna lecture Husserl alludes to the idea of Europe in terms of a feeling, as an idea of an all-embracing universal science "Europe" is primarily a rational conception that calls on the powers of reason shared by all human beings. It is therefore not surprising that to what Husserl characterizes as a change of attitude or orientation (*Umstellung*) necessary to gain access to what transcends the particular, Heidegger opposes an *Umstimmung*—that is, a "transformation" of the mood or state of mind—for a thinking experience of Being to be possible (*EHP*, 176–77). If the thought and the question of Being are tied to the fate of Europe, it is not, for Heidegger, in the quality of a rational conception but rather of a *Stimmung*, more precisely a *Grundstimmung*, required to ask this "question [that] is the broadest in scope" (*IM*, 2) and that "cannot be compared to any other" (*IM*, 6). Let me also add that the cardinal role attributed by Husserl to unrelenting criticism and self-criticism in attaining a universal truth, which for him amounts to the exercise of reason itself, is replaced in Heidegger by the theme and practice of the question—of questionableness (*Fraglichkeit*)—and its implication for the questioning subject.[30]

The founding event with which Western philosophy commences is the event of the question—not just any question but, in its Leibnizean wording, the question, "Why are there beings at all instead of nothing?" This question is the broadest in scope because it is not a question that centers on any particular, individual being. Rather, it is a question about beings as such and as a whole. Unlike any other question, this question directed at "beings as a whole and as such" (*IM*, 3) inquires into the ground from which—or the opening within which—what is comes into being. But although "the why-question challenges beings as a whole, so to speak, [and] outstrips them," it never completely departs from them (*Die Warum-Frage tritt dem Seienden im Ganzen gleichsam gegenüber, tritt aus ihm heraus, wenngleich nie völlig*) (*IM*, 5). The why-question not only remains anchored in what is; it also challenges the questioner. Indeed, the questioner (whether an individual or a people, like the Greeks) is one of the beings addressed by this question. As a consequence, the question that brings itself into opposition with beings as a whole in order to face them as such recoils back on the questioner and on questioning itself. "Why the why? What is the ground of this why-question itself, a question that presumes to establish the ground of beings as a whole?" (*IM*, 5). Just as in Husserl, for whom *theoria* as the concern with what is universal is eminently practical, the question of Being is a question of immediate concern to the human being. It is a question that bears on what it means to be human to begin with.[31] In short, because the question of Being not only presupposes an exit from beings as a whole, in order to set them over and against itself, but also recoils on the questioner, "questioning is not some arbitrary process but rather a distinctive occurrence that we call a *happening* [*Geschehnis*]" (*IM*, 6). Questioning opens up all that is to itself as such—to its Being, that is, a Being that, rather than an abstract entity, always remains the Being of what is—while simultaneously affecting the questioning itself through this dimension, the question and its questioning representing a distinct and unique occurrence in the world: a "provocative happening" (*erregendes Geschehnis*), that is, a happening pregnant with history, one by which history opens up, more precisely, the history of the West or Europe.

By asking the why-question, everything familiar about the world is made to stand in the strange light of Being. But because the question also extends to the questioner and the questioning itself, an additional estrangement occurs. When the question recoils back into its own Why, "we discover [Heidegger writes] that this distinctive why-question has its ground in a leap by which human beings leap away from all the previous safety [*Geborgenheit*] of their Dasein, be it genuine or presumed. The asking of this question happens only in the leap and as the leap, and otherwise not at all" (*IM*, 6). Questioning beings as a whole and as such in view of Being takes place in a double leap away from what is and from oneself. If it is also a provocative happening, it is because it implies a radical break with all the safety and security of the human being regarding what is and with respect to oneself. This break with, and leap beyond, everything that provides shelter is precisely what makes the question of Being—the question that opens up the history of the West and of Europe—such a distinct question, linking the West and Europe from the beginning to a radical rupture with the customary, the familiar, and the homely. Not only does this question require the performance of an essential transcending, or breaking away from homeliness, but what it inquires into—the questionworthy, that is Being—is also, as we will see, something extraordinarily strange, foreign, alienating, as it were.[32] Rather than endowing the questioner with a "lightness of being," this question, as the philosophical question par excellence, makes everything "only more difficult" (*IM*, 12): indeed, it is a burden of sorts.

If this question happens only in the leap, and as the leap away from all previous safety, the "subject" of this question cannot be the (metaphysical) subject. Before further exploring the alienating violence of the question of Being, let us inquire into *who* asks this question, or, more precisely, into the who or what becomes constituted in the leap that this question accomplishes. After claiming that the task of philosophy is never to make things easier, but instead more difficult, Heidegger remarks:

> The burdening [*Erschwerung*] of historical Dasein, and thereby at bottom of Being itself, is rather the genuine sense of what philosophy can achieve. Burdening gives back to things, to beings, their weight (Being). And why? Because burdening is one of the essential and fundamental conditions for the arising of everything great, among which we include above all else the fate [*Schicksal*] of a historical people and its works. But fate is there only where a true knowing about things rules over Dasein. And the avenues and views of such a knowing are opened up by philosophy. (*IM*, 12)

If philosophy and, in particular, its founding question weighs down on its subject by giving back to things their weight, then the burden in question is that of the *as such* of what is itself, that is, of Being; it is the burden of having to *be* in the constant awareness of the *as such* of beings as a whole and to measure what is against this ground. But as the reference to fate also suggests, the question of Being is a burden, not in the sense of a happening that befalls one fatally and with iron necessity but in the sense that without heeding this question, Dasein—whether as singular Dasein or as the Dasein of a people—could not be a historical Dasein. Thus it is also the burden of a task. Indeed, by presupposing the knowledge of the avenues and vistas opened up by the philosophical question of Being, "fate" amounts to a way of being shaped by precisely these paths and trajectories and the direction or the sense in which they point. Heidegger's avoidance, in this context, of terms such as *teleological beginning* or *entelechy* to refer to the horizon that is opened up by the question of Being is motivated, it seems, by the fact that no subject whatsoever (whether individual or of humanity as a whole) could ask such a question without ceasing to be a subject. In contrast to the subject, Dasein is an essentially finite being. The questioner of the question, that is, the one who is at once claimed by Being—from the future, as it were—is "historical Dasein" or, as the *Introduction* holds, the "historical-spiritual" Dasein of a people (*IM*, 11).[33] This emphasis on the Dasein of a people is clear evidence that what constitutes a people (*Volk*), according to Heidegger's understanding of this notion, is not of the order of natural, biological, genetic, or racial characteristics. Such a nonnaturalist concept of a people, that is, one conceived in terms of Dasein, is a direct consequence of anchoring the thought of Being in the particular. Indeed, such anchoring is necessarily accompanied by a radical transformation of the instance selected; this also incarnates the universal. If the later Heidegger explicitly dismisses the notion of a people or nation as notions still tributary to the metaphysics of subjectivity, it is because from the beginning the notion of a "people" had already been thought in terms of the fundamental structures of Dasein: that is, the structures of thrownness, of being ahead of oneself, and never identical to, or with and within oneself.[34] The additional consequences of conceiving of a people in terms of Dasein will be taken up in a moment.

According to the lectures on metaphysics, the happening of the inaugural question of philosophy is "the authentic happening [*das eigentliche Geschehen*] in the history of a people" (*IM*, 9). In contrast with Husserl, for whom the emergence of the idea of a rational and universal science in early Greece is essentially the breakthrough of the concept of humanity itself—and is therefore a challenge to humankind as a whole to live up to a possible history of humanity as such—for Heidegger the irruption of the question of Being concerns a people and its historical-spiritual fate. More precisely, it makes a people a people to begin with, in that it provides that people with a historical horizon.[35] But, of course, as the philosophical question par excellence, the question of Being is, above all, the inaugurating event of the West. The word *Being*, Heidegger notes, is linked first and foremost to "the spiritual fate of the West [*Abendland*]" (*IM*, 40), that is, according to the *Introduction of Metaphysics*, to the spiritual fate of Europe. Yet if for Husserl Europe is a spiritual figure or form (rather than a geographical entity), for Heidegger it is linked to a spiritual strength or force, a force constituted by the exigencies that accompany the question of Being but that now is threatened by decline. If Europe is indeed depicted by Heidegger as "bustling and chasing after beings" (*IM*, 39), it is precisely because the beginning of Europe is determined by the question of Being. Only because it has fallen out of Being could it turn to "bustling and chasing after beings." The exclusive concern with beings (which for Heidegger is not a merely modern phenomenon but is linked to the West from the start, and whose problematization does not therefore derive from some predisposition or worldview such as cultural criticism, for instance, but from a meditation on the Being of beings) is possible only against the backdrop of the event of the question and the subsequent oblivion of Being. No doubt Europe failed to attend to the demand and promise of that to which it owes its birth from the beginning. But if Europe has always been inattentive to itself, even to the point of virtual self-destruction, today, according to Heidegger, it faces still another threat: "This Europe, in its unholy blindness always on the point of cutting its own throat, lies today in the great pincers between Russia on the one side and America on the other. Russia and America, seen metaphysically, are both the same: the same hopeless frenzy of unchained technology and of the rootless organization of the average man" (*IM*, 40).[36] Thoroughly singular and unique, Europe has from its inception put its very singularity in danger; now it finds itself in the pincers (which may also be forceps) between the powers, Russia and America. In addition to the exclusive concern with beings, which is as old as Europe itself insofar as it is born from the forgetting of the question of Being, what is new in Europe (including Germany of course) is that, squeezed between Russia and America, it faces total extinction. Although seemingly located geographically outside Europe, these powers (which, as we will see, also haunt Europe from within) are metaphysical powers, which derive from a misprision of the essence of *techne*.[37] They are the very powers of nihilism. Owing to unchained technology, on the one hand, and to the "rootless organization of the average man," on the other, both of which

Heidegger associates with Russia and America, the ensuing threat of full effacement—not only of Being but even of the phenomenon of oblivion to Being—threatens Europe with annihilation.[38] But Europe is not alone in being brought to ruin as a result of such Americanization and Bolshevikization—the whole earth is said to be affected by these trends: "The spiritual decline of the earth has progressed so far that peoples are in danger of losing their last spiritual strength, the strength that makes it possible even to see the decline [which is meant in relation to the fate of 'Being'] and to appraise it as such" (*IM*, 40). As a consequence, no real help in assessing or possibly reversing the current development can come from outside Europe.[39] If there is to be a realization at all of what is happening as a result of unleashed technology and the mass organization of men, namely, the loss of even the possibility of experiencing it as a decline—a loss that Heidegger refers to as the "darkening of the world"—it can arise only from within Europe itself, specifically from within Germany, which, as Leibniz already argued, is the middle of Europe.[40]

Although in the heart of Europe the German people—now Nazified, that is (if one listens carefully to what Heidegger is saying), both Americanized (when, indeed, "a boxer counts as a great man of a people") and Bolshevikized (i.e., mass-organized)—may indulge in the knowledge of their vocation, this knowledge and certainty is historically insignificant as long as the Germans have not created within themselves an ear, not yet for what as a metaphysical people they could be capable of but an ear, first of all, for the *possibility* of a resonance of such a vocation and for grasping its tradition creatively. Heidegger avers: "We lie in the pincers. Our people, as standing in the center, suffers the most intense pressure—our people, the richest in neighbors and hence the most endangered people, and for all that, the metaphysical people. We are sure of this vocation; but this people will gain a fate from its vocation [*Bestimmung*] only when it creates *in itself* [*erst*, that is, first of all] a resonance, a possibility of resonance for this vocation, and grasps its tradition creatively" (*IM*, 41). Unlike Husserl, who still believed that a direct appeal to reason was a possible means of overcoming the crisis of Europe, and of realizing the idea of a universal humankind in an infinite process, Heidegger faces what he believes to be a situation where there is not even a resonance in the German people for its responsibilities toward itself and Europe. His discourse is thus geared toward elucidating and realizing the conditions of possibility under which, alone, a "political" and "ethical" transformation of this people's fate could take place. Undoubtedly modeled after what presumably happened in Greece, the German people's ascendance to the status of a *Volk* would seek to accomplish this transformation in the process of pure and originary self-formation. According to Philippe Lacoue-Labarthe's compelling argument in *Heidegger, Art and Politics*, the self-formation of a people (and of what a people *ought* to be) is conceived by National Socialism in terms of a craftsman's paradigm and is thus technicist in nature, which leads Lacoue-Labarthe to characterize National Socialism's understanding of politics—if not that of modernity in general—as a national aestheticism. But whether therefore the exigencies proper to such a pure emergence (as Heidegger, at least, defines them) also constitute the people as a work of art is not so certain. In fact, as we will see, if Greece is a model for the becoming of a historical people, it is a model precisely insofar as it gives nothing to imitate. For the moment let me only point out that for Heidegger the self-formation of a historical people cannot consist of realizing some *eidos* that would be its own.[41] He spells out the conditions under which the German people can become a people to begin with, that is, a people with a history: "All this implies that this people, as a historical people, must transpose itself [*hinausstellt*]—and with it the history of the West—from the center of their future happening into the originary realm of the powers of Being. Precisely if the great decision regarding Europe is not to go down the path of annihilation—precisely then can this decision come about only through the development of new, historically *spiritual* forces from the center [*Mitte*]" (*IM*, 41).

The German people are thus not yet a people. Nothing of the order of the natural, the biological, or the genetic predisposes them to become a people. In a clear rebuttal of "the naturalist neopagan National-Socialist ideology that negates the transcendence of spirit"—in particular by Alfred Rosenberg—Heidegger links the possibility of becoming a people to an exclusive recourse to spiritual forces.[42] As a people, the Germans' destiny lies exclusively with the spiritual forces still to be developed from the middle of Europe, that is, through a creative appropriation of their (Greek) tradition and in resistance to what from both sides endangers their ability to reconnect with the question of Being, whose forgetting endangers the very recollection of such forgetting itself. This responsibility of the German people (people, not in the sense of a genetically homogeneous race or nation but as the people of the *Dichter und Denker*) for Europe as a spiritual entity (and implicitly, for the spiritual strength of the entire earth): this is Germany's fate, a clearly spiritual fate based on a spiritual strength. But let us see in greater detail precisely what it would take for the German people to become a people, and thus to become ready to assume this task. The German people can only become responsible for Europe as a whole, and by extension become a European people to begin with, if this people transposes itself from the center or middle (*sich selbst . . . aus der Mitte . . . hinausstellt*) into the originary realm of Being. In other words, to achieve its vocation, this people needs to go outside of itself, leap beyond itself, and open itself so to speak to the outside and, ultimately, to the originary realm of the powers of Being. To put this differently, the German people will rise to the status of a historical people responsible for itself and the West only on the condition that this people of the middle become capable of decentering itself, turning eccentric, and exposing itself to the powers of Being—to what it means to *be*. Indeed, "the definite [*massgebende*] form of history" does not consist in a people's regression to former times or in the continuation of what is familiar from its past by simply imitating it. On the contrary, a people, according to Heidegger, rises to the level of the historical only if this people repeats and retrieves (*wieder-holen*) "the inception of [its] historical-spiritual Dasein, in order to transform it into the other inception [*in den anderen Anfang*]" (*IM*, 41). Rather than retrieving former times, only the fundamental happening (*Grundgeschehnis*)—that is, the nondatable event (one that does not cease to happen) of the laying of a ground—prior to a people's past and present can ground the history of a people, but again, only on the condition that this beginning is transformed into another, more originary beginning. What is to be retrieved, repeated, and transformed in order for a people to be a historical people is not something that belongs to a constituted past, something that would only have to be reactualized; rather, it is "the inception of [a peoples'] historical-spiritual Dasein," in other words, of the specific ways in which Being has disclosed itself to a people in the shape of specific avenues and vistas within which it understands itself. We know from the analytic of Dasein in *Being and Time* that for Dasein to be is to *be with*, to be expropriated by what is foreign and alien to it—that is, the world, as well as the beings within it, including other Dasein. Furthermore, as we will see in greater detail, a beginning is a beginning only if that to which it gives rise is thoroughly unfamiliar, unknown, even unpredictable. Hence, to retrieve and repeat this beginning implies assuming its strangeness in an even more radical and more originary fashion—not as the original strangeness of the beginning but as the strangeness of the beginning to come. Heidegger writes: "An inception is not repeated when one shrinks back to it as something that once was, something that by now is familiar and is simply to be imitated, but rather when the inception is begun again *more originally*, and with all the strangeness, darkness, insecurity that a genuine inception brings with it" (*IM*, 41). To begin again by repeating the beginning in a more originary fashion is to reinvent this beginning by stripping it of everything that could be imitated, of everything that would thus diminish its radicality and strangeness. To pose the question of Being, according to Heidegger, is to attempt to "restore [*zurückzufügen*] the historical Dasein of human beings—and this always means our ownmost future [*künftiges*] Dasein, in the whole of the history that is allotted to us—back to the power of Being that is to be opened up originally; all this, to be sure, only within the limits of philosophy's capability" (*IM*, 44). From what we have seen so far, such a restoration, whatever its urgency in the face of the increasing "darkening of the world," has nothing reassuring about it. On the contrary, the question of Being is not only a strange question; it is also one that demands that an individual, or for that matter, a people, depart from oneself—from understanding oneself in the self-referential terms of, for instance, the natural, the biological, the native, the ethnic—and face the strangeness, darkness, and insecurity of the to-come, in order to have a historical-spiritual fate to begin with.

If the question of Being—a question that stands in "connection with the fate of Europe, where the fate of the Earth is being decided"—is asked from the position of the German people, it is because, as Heidegger holds, "for Europe itself [the German people's] historical Dasein proves to be the center" (*IM*, 44). The eminently historical question that is the question of Being—*historical* understood here as what is to come rather than as what has been (and which, therefore, is no longer happening) or from the present (which instead of happening, passes) (see *IM*, 46–47)—is therefore neither a merely academic nor abstract question. At first sight, linking the question of Being to the fate of the German people seems to be motivated by the fact that the German people occupy a central position in Europe *qua* geographical entity. But this centrality is not simply geographical. As we will see in a moment, caught between the pincers of America and Russia, the centrality of the German people is seen to derive from the fact that they suffer the most severe darkening of the world, not only on account of the onslaught of the demonic (America and Russia) but even more so because of the disempowering or destitution of spirit that the Germans have brought on themselves. Philosophically more important, therefore, is the fact that although the question of Being concerns the spiritual fate of the West, this question—as one that concerns the Dasein of the West—can always only be asked on the basis of the inception of the historical-spiritual Dasein of a people, from and in view of this particular people's ownmost future Dasein. It follows from this that the European people who pose the question of Being, whoever they may be, are necessarily, and in principle, the people of the middle— this time, however, no longer in a merely factual sense. The center is essentially to be thought with respect to the history of Being. In each case, furthermore, the question of Being "intrinsically belongs to the world history of the earth" (*IM*, 47). As should now be clear, in the question of Being, it is historical-spiritual Dasein that is at stake and thus also the very possibility of a world. When Heidegger invokes the terms *Europe, people of the middle,* or *earth,* it is never in a geographical or planetary sense but in a historical-spiritual sense, that is, in terms of "world."

If the question of Being has become such an urgent question for a Europe caught in the pincers between Russia and America, it is because of the threat that both of these metaphysical powers pose to Europe's world and spiritual character. The darkening of the world of which Heidegger speaks contains within itself a disempowering of the spirit, resulting from the onslaught of what he calls "the demonic," that is, "the predominance [in Russia and America] of a cross-section [*Durchschnitt*] of the indifferent ... which aggressively destroys all rank and all that is world-spiritual [*welthaft Geistige,* that is, a spirituality that has world-character]" (*IM*, 48–49). "World," Heidegger explains, "is always *spiritual* world" (*IM*, 47). The darkening of the world does not mean, of course, that human beings would be completely bereft of a world and would thus become like the animals, which, as Heidegger contends, have no world. In Russia and America, and, as a result of their assault, in Europe, too, the world that human beings as human beings possess has (only) become dimmer and murkier. But the dissolution of light—and, as a consequence, of the world—in Europe (and throughout the earth as well) is not only attributable to the two powers in question. What makes Europe's situation all the more dire is that "the disempowering of the spirit comes from Europe itself" (*IM*, 48). As we have seen, from its inception on, Europe has been in the process of self-annihilation. At this juncture, however, Heidegger points to another, more recent cause, one that concerns Germany more specifically: the dissolution, in the first half of the nineteenth century, of the spiritual strength and power required to stand up to the "originary questioning about grounds and the bonding to such grounds" achieved in German Idealism. As a result of this dissolution, covered up by the phrase "the collapse of German Idealism," "Dasein began to slide into a world that lacked that depth from which the essential always comes and returns to human beings, thereby forcing them to superiority and allowing them to act on the basis of rank. All things sank to the same level" and became objects of calculation (*IM*, 48). At this point the disempowering of the spirit (and the subsequent darkening of the world) that began in Europe itself, and in particular, in its middle, quantitatively intensified in Russia and America, achieving a certain quality in its own right: that of the measureless, the gigantic, "the demonic [in the sense of the destructively evil]" (*IM*, 49). Caught between the pincers of Russia and America, Europe is thus haunted by none other than what it itself has given birth to, that which, cut off from its origin in Europe's historical-spiritual world, has turned into a power of its own, destructive of world and spirit. The relation to Being itself harbors the possibility not only of a loss of strength to stand up to what Being demands but also that such loss of strength can turn into a wholly independent power, the power of the mediocre or the indifferent, which then becomes a power that turns against all that is world-spiritual. What this shows is that what brings Europe into its own—the relation to Being—is also that which can possibly destroy it and that, again, the question of Being is thus anything but a reassuring question.

Let us then inquire into what Heidegger opposes to the multiple misinterpretations of spirit (*Geist*) that have caused its destitution: spirit as intelligence, spirit as a tool serviceable for goals, spirit as culture, and, finally, spirit as a showpiece or spectacle. What, indeed, is spirit in the first place? In the *Introduction to Metaphysics* Heidegger draws on the infamous 1933 Rectorship Address to provide a succinct definition of *spirit*: "'spirit [*Geist*] is originally attuned, knowing resolution to the essence of Being [*Geist ist ursprünglich gestimmte, wissende Entschlossenheit zum Wesen des Seins*]'" (*IM*, 52). Let us bear in mind that in the analytic of Dasein in *Being and Time*, Heidegger sought to avoid the term *spirit*, primarily because of its subjectivist determination, its opposition to matter and body. If nevertheless all the basic terms that make up this definition of *spirit* refer back to *Being and Time*, this is only proof of Heidegger's effort to develop a concept of spirit that is no longer subjectivist, one that is thought in terms of the fundamental characteristics of Dasein. Indeed, the definition in question suggests that spirit is not something of the order of the intellect but a state of mind in which Being is disclosed to Dasein (*erschlossen*, that is, in which Dasein recognizes Being, in the sense that it is *gewiss* or certain of it) in such a way that Dasein is concerned by Being, taking Being resolutely (*entschlossen*) upon itself. But rather than eliciting this definition with the help of *Being and Time*, we will limit ourselves to the consideration of only Heidegger's explicatory comments in the *Introduction to Metaphysics* to the definition in question: "Spirit is the empowering of the powers of Being as such and as a whole. Where spirit rules, beings as such always and in each case come more into being (*wird . . . seiender*). Asking about beings as such and as a whole, asking the question of Being, is then one of the essential fundamental conditions for awakening the spirit, and thus for an originary world of historical Dasein, and thus for subduing the danger of the darkening of the world, and thus for taking over the historical mission [*Sendung*] of our people, the people of the center of the West" (*IM*, 52).[43]

The question of Being is a question that concerns beings as such and as a whole. It is a question about Being itself within the opening of which all beings come to the fore and to a stand. The question of Being keeps that opening open and holds everything that is into this opening. It is a question by which what is comes to stand into the light from which it emerges into the form of an appearance. Spirit, then, is the name for this refolding of all that is into Being, as a result of which all beings come "more into being." It is a linkage that takes place as a knowing attunement and by which what is becomes meaningful in the sense that it forms a world. To ask the question of Being (which, as I have already indicated, is an eminently "practical" question) is the condition for accomplishing, to begin with, the restoration of a world, as well as the reawakening of a spirituality that has world-character and the retrieval of Dasein's historical destiny. To ask the question of Being is therefore to ask the question that concerns the fate of Europe and the West, insofar as Europe and the West, at their inception, are determined by these goals—which goals they abandoned early on by busying themselves with beings alone, finally ending up caught between the pincers of "demonic" powers. The question of Being is the only means to uphold—as a *kat-echon*, as it were—the darkening of the world, if not to subdue this danger.

Yet if Europe and the earth as a whole are threatened by a darkening of the world, it is because the question of Being is no longer experienced as meaningful. Heidegger notes: "The question loses its rank [as the broadest and most fundamental, that is, universal question] at once in the sphere of a human-historical Dasein to whom *questioning* [rather than theorizing and critiquing] as an originary power remains foreign [*fremd bleibt*]" (*IM*, 7). Indeed, as Heidegger ceaselessly argues, Being has become an empty word. But if so much depends on asking this question, the fact that we no longer understand Being is not to be recognized as "something alien and other [*wovor wir stehen als einem fremden Anderen*]" but as something that in its very alienness concerns us directly, given that we stand within this inability of knowing what Being means (*IM*, 53). As we have already seen, the question of Being is the strangest of all questions, since it requires a leaping away from all that is familiar. If the originary power of the question has presently become foreign to Dasein, the goal can no longer consist in making it a familiar question again, since this question is itself a thoroughly unfamiliar one. However much Dasein is concerned by this question, it will never become ordinary. Evoking Nietzsche, Heidegger argues in *Introduction to Metaphysics* that the questioning of this question, as the philosophical question par excellence, "is out-of-order [*ausser der Ordnung*]," and he concludes: "Philosophizing . . . is extra-ordinary questioning about the extra-ordinary" (*IM*, 14). In the *Introduction to Metaphysics*, ordinary everydayness, apart from being conceived in view of the "urgent concerns and the satisfactions of dominant needs," is, significantly enough, understood in terms of "requirements or even regulations" (*IM*, 14). As a consequence, the questioning of the extraordinary appears as something out-of-order, as a break with order. The question is, so to speak, an unruly one. In any event, rather than dispelling the oddity of the question of Being, it will have to be confronted in its very strangeness and with all the insecurity that it comports.

Until now we have only spoken of the *question* of Being as an extraordinary questioning of the extraordinary, that is, of beings as such and as a whole, or Being itself. But what is it that is so extraordinary—so outside of the ordinary but also so exciting (*erregend*), marvelous, astonishing—about Being? What is it that makes the "subject matter" of the question that is properly the constituting question of the West or Europe so strange, alien, or foreign? As Heidegger recalls, "in the age of the first and definitive unfolding of Western philosophy among the Greeks, when questioning about beings as such and as a whole received its true inception, beings were called *phusis*" (*IM*, 14). In an effort "to win back intact the naming force" of this Greek word and to thus ward off the narrowing of its meaning (one that occurred already in Greece itself) to *ta physika*—not to mention its translation into Latin as *natura*—Heidegger claims that this word "says what emerges from itself (for example, the emergence, the blossoming, of a rose), the unfolding that opens itself up, the coming-into-appearance in such unfolding, and holding itself and persisting in appearance—in short, the emerging-abiding sway [*das aufgehende-verweilende Walten*]" (*IM*, 15). As such a happening, that is, as the coming-forth-into-an-appearance, and of beings holding themselves therein, *phusis* is the Greek name for "what is, as such and as a whole": in short, for the Being of beings (*IM*, 17). Let us acknowledge that it is not easy to see from this originary Greek determination of Being as the emerging-abiding-sway what is supposedly so odd about it. To get a first hint of this strangeness, it is necessary to return to the question itself. Indeed, by reflecting on the "instead of nothing" in the philosophical question "Why are there beings at all instead of nothing?"—not only does the question itself become increasingly odd, but so does that which is being asked about. With the addition of the words "instead of nothing" to the question of why there are beings at all, the question of Being is no longer simply a question about the ground of beings. The addition turns the inquiry into Being into the search for a ground "that is supposed to ground the dominance of beings as an overcoming of Nothing" (*IM*, 30–31). Beings, including the human being, now no longer appear in their self-evidence as beings but as "torn from the possibility of not-Being [*der Möglichkeit des Nichtseins entrissen*]" (*IM*, 30). It now appears that beings *are* only insofar as they have been wrested from the Nothing and that their being amounts to nothing less than a resistance to the possibility of not being. Heidegger continues: "Insofar as beings stand up [*widersteht*] against the extreme possibility of not-Being, they themselves stand in Being, and yet they have never thereby overtaken and overcome the possibility of not-Being" (*IM*, 32–33). As a result, not only does "the question itself lose every secure foothold. Our Dasein, too, as it questions, comes into suspense, and nevertheless maintains itself, by itself, in this suspense" (*IM*, 31). Indeed, not only does this question forfeit its secure foothold in a presumed self-evident existence of what is, but since it is one that also recoils upon the questioner, the latter is likewise stripped of the security of belonging completely to him- or herself. As a consequence, "*this* questioning ... pushes us into the open, provided that it itself, as a questioning, transforms itself (as does every genuine questioning), and casts a new space over and through everything" (*IM*, 32). With this emphasis on the Nothing from which Being and beings are wrested without ever coming into the security of self-evident being within themselves, the defining question of Western philosophy—as well as the Being it inquires into—reveal themselves as unsettling, in every sense of the word. If, furthermore, the thought of Being is construed as inaugurating the destiny of the West, Europe, and the German people as the people of the center, this thought does nothing less than tie the fate of the West, Europe, and the German people to a radical breaking away from all sheltering assumptions (i.e., race, ethnicity, nationality), opening the West, Europe, and the German people up to the foreign, the strange, the alien. The West, Europe, and the German people will only be what their names promise on the condition that they live up to the "avenues and vistas [*Bahnen und Sichtweiten*]" (*IM*, 11) opened up in the originary happening of the question of Being. They are thus not yet what they are; their being is futural; it is still to come.

Yet we have only caught a glimpse of the strangeness of Being and so must ask ourselves again why Being is something so extraordinarily odd, so foreign. Why, in Heidegger, is it associated with a loss of familiarity, security, and transparency? Let us note at this point that if Being appears strange, it is because it affects, claims, and disappropriates the human being. The notion of the strangeness of Being has no meaning except with respect to Dasein. From the outset the lectures on metaphysics have made it clear that the question of Being is a happening, insofar as it is the result of this question's recoil back upon the questioner. What follows from this is that in order to grasp what is so exceedingly strange about Being, we must turn to the questioner and inquire into what happens in the recoil. I recall that the fundamental ontological inquiry into the meaning of Being in *Being and Time* takes place by way of an analytic of Dasein rather than directly. Something similar takes place in the *Introduction to Metaphysics*, where the powers of Being are exposed and expanded on mainly through an exposition of their effects on Dasein. But there is a difference, as well. We recall that when contrasting Being with Nothing in order to begin highlighting the intrinsic strangeness of Being, Heidegger declared not only that "the true talk of Nothing always remains unfamiliar [and] does not allow itself to be made common" (*IM*, 28) but also that such true talk occurs only in thinking and in poetry. It is above all in poetry that Heidegger, in the *Introduction to Metaphysics*, locates "true talk" of Nothing and of Being in all its oddity. Indeed, the tragic figure of Antigone in Sophocles' play of the same name is here the starting point for an analysis of Being's intrinsic strangeness, in which the key word will be *uncanny*. Before we can proceed, however, to a discussion of Heidegger's interpretation of this tragic figure, we must first return to the question of what a beginning is.

§ 5 The Strangeness of Beginnings

According to *Introduction to Metaphysics*, the thought of Being that irrupts in ancient Greece is a prodigiously strange thought; for Heidegger the birth of this thinking coincides with the advent of Europe and the West. It is strange because—implicating Dasein and, in particular, historical Dasein—this beginning throws Dasein out of everything that is familiar to it and within which it is sheltered. But if this thought at the inception of Europe or the West is odd, this is not only because it unseats Dasein's home world and with it the understanding of what "human" means but, above all, because this thought is a beginning. A beginning (*Anfang*), if it is one, is exceedingly strange because, first of all, it is not an "outset" (*Beginn*). In *Parmenides* Heidegger notes that, with respect to the early thinking in the Occident with which Western thought begins, "outset refers to the coming forth of this thinking at a definite 'time'" and, let me add, in a distinct place, as well as among an ethnically determined people (*P*, 7). A beginning is different from the emergence during that age of the thinking that founds a site for truth among the historical people that are the Greeks in that it concerns that which such thinking thinks. Heidegger writes: "The 'beginning' is what, in this early thinking, is to be thought and what is thought. . . . The thinking of thinkers is the *thinking of Being*. Their thinking is a *retreating in face of Being*. We name what is thought in the thinking of the thinkers the beginning. Which hence now means: Being is the beginning" (*P*, 7). Consequently, a beginning is not of the order of the past; as a beginning (*das Anfängliche*) it is rather what "lies in advance of what is to come," that which, having been sent on its way, turns itself again and again into a gift that can be received or ignored (*P*, 1). If what begins in Greece stands at the inception of Europe and the West, it is because the latter are not only far-removed from the outset of thinking in Greece (and far-removed, as well, from the beginning to the point of complete oblivion to the thought of Being) but because Europe and the West could also name the possibility for a renewed openness to the beginning.[1]

Indeed, if a beginning, rather than referring to that with which something starts, names that which springs forth from what has made a debut and has emerged (and, consequently, is something that comes last, since "it only comes out in what is occurring and is only fully there at its end"), it also follows that, in all rigor, a beginning is only a beginning on the condition that it is an opening up to something entirely new that could not have been anticipated by what preceded it and hence is mitigated in its radical novelty (*HHGR*, 3). For the same reason that a beginning has no history itself in that nothing in advance of its event makes its occurrence likely or necessary (rather a beginning is the possible advent of a history), it also excludes that it be the response to a situation that preceded it and by which it would have been called forth. Furthermore, if Heidegger's analyses concerning the fate of Europe or the West avoid, as we have seen, the term *crisis*, it is also because the thought of Being, as a beginning to which Europe and the West must reach back in order to overcome the impending "darkening of the world," can in no way be understood as a response to a crisis. This thought, and by extension Europe and the West, is a beginning in the strictest and strongest sense—a "great beginning"—and as such is thus something quite extraordinary. As a true beginning it would be unique: not only uncanny but, indeed, the uncanniest (*das Unheimlichste*). Heidegger writes:

> The inception [*Anfang*] is what is most uncanny and mightiest. What follows is not a development but flattening down as mere widening out; it is the inability to hold on to the inception, it makes the inception innocuous and exaggerates it into a perversion of what is great, into greatness and extension purely in the sense of numbers and mass. The uncanniest *is* what it is *because* it harbors such an inception in which, from overabundance, everything breaks out at once into what is overwhelming and is to be surmounted [*das Überwältigende, Zubewältigende*]. (*IM*, 165–66)

If a beginning that is truly a beginning is the most uncanny, this is not simply because it is overpowering and terrifying on the basis of the expectations that come with the novelty of the start but because as a beginning it brings with it a fundamental unhomeliness. Indeed, a genuine inception implies a loss of everything familiar. Furthermore, the "strangeness, darkness, insecurity" (*IM*, 41) that accompanies the beginning characterizes that which is promised in such a start and links it to the ever-present possibility that this promise could turn into unmitigated disaster. There is no beginning that does not also contain this risk of a radical betrayal of its promise. If in the thought of Being that irrupts in early Greece the inception of Europe and the West is at its most uncanny, this is because of the inevitable unhomeliness that accompanies it, which can lead to the worst, rather than initiating something universal to be held on to and in which one could become at home. This turn for the worse comes by way of the forgetfulness of "the character of this inception as a mystery" (166)—and of its fundamental ambiguity.

In the same way as Husserl, Heidegger traces Europe or the West back to Greece, not, however, to the emergence in Greece of the idea of a rational science but to the breakthrough in Greece of the question of Being, and hence to the emergence of philosophy as an attentiveness and exposedness to Being. From the start I wish to point out that Heidegger's Greece is a truly strange Greece, one that Western metaphysics has lost sight of, since, according to Heidegger, it cannot think of Greece except in a non-Greek manner (*P*, 96).[2] What follows from this is also that Heidegger's conception of Greece as the great beginning of Europe and of the West cannot be retraced to the classical and romantic nostalgic turn to Greece. Even though Heidegger occasionally called for a debate, or *Auseinandersetzung*, with the beginning of modern philosophy in France, it is well known, that non-German thinkers—in particular, French thinkers, with the exception of Descartes—are barely acknowledged in Heidegger's reflections on the modern contributions to the thought of Being and hence to what constitutes Europe or the West. In Heidegger's work this is clearly a blindness, if not quite an ideological blind spot in his thought.[3] In what follows, however, I would like to briefly allude to an omission that, in spite of its perplexity and disturbance, is perhaps not so easily accounted for. Indeed, like Husserl, Heidegger pays little to no tribute to the role of the Jewish, Christian, or even Islamic heritages in shaping the idea of Europe. Paul Ricoeur, for one, has expressed his deep consternation with the fact that Heidegger "has systematically eluded the confrontation with [what he calls] the bloc of Hebraic thought" or, even more poignantly, "the Hebraic massif."[4] The question of such a neglect is all the more disturbing given that European culture has turned Judaism, in particular, into a foreign element and manifested a will to eliminate it on the presumption of Europe's primarily Greek or, eventually, Greek and Latin origin. All things considered, something similar may obtain in the case of Islam as well. But a cautionary remark is warranted before I take up later in this work the criticism that has been directed from within the phenomenological tradition against the privilege that both Husserl and Heidegger accord to the Greek inaugural event—especially by Patočka and Derrida. Indeed, however significant and illuminating the historical contributions of Rome and Jerusalem have been to the shaping of Europe, factual evidence may in no way shake Heidegger's privileging of the Greek moment in the conception of Europe to the exclusion of its Jewish, Christian, and Islamic elements.[5] Historical and cultural arguments miss the mark here since the reasons for this exclusion may rest on philosophical necessities—on necessities of thought, in short—rather than on empirical or ideological grounds.[6] Consequently, any discussion or critique of the exclusion by Heidegger—who by this exclusion participates in a philosophical tradition that stretches at least from Leibniz to Nietzsche and beyond—of Jewish, Christian, and Islamic elements from what supposedly constitutes Europe or the West must be carried out on the level of principle itself: in short, it must be transcendental in nature and address the structural reasons on the basis of which an originary Greek beginning can dismiss all other, non-Greek elements.[7] Even though it may be the case that one of Heidegger's reasons for crediting Greece alone with being the origin of Europe is related to a Lutherean rejection of Rome, this should not encroach on the principal reason for the exclusions in question. In advance of any discussion or possible critique of the privilege assigned to Greece on the basis of philosophical, rather than historical or cultural, arguments, let me put forth the following question: does Heidegger not, by conceiving of "beginning" in the way that we have seen—namely, as what is most uncanny—turn "beginning" into an extremely rare occurrence in the first place, precisely insofar as it requires a startling, unexpected, and complete break with what precedes it? Indeed, even when in "Hölderlin's Earth and Heaven" he acknowledges other great beginnings, it is only a question of a "few other great beginnings."[8] Must a "beginning," in order to be one, not be something that is radically new and unexpected—perhaps even so singular as to admit for structural reasons of no antecedents, influences, borrowings, imitations, or appropriations whatsoever? To put it differently, defining Greece as the beginning of Europe is precisely to emphasize the absence of any indebtedness, or, to use a Husserlian term, to affirm the presuppositionlessness of what is European or Occidental, in other words, their autonomous rise from reason. By extension, Europe or the West would only merit being so called if they were truly free of any liabilities and influences (not only from the outside but from the inside as well).[9] As a beginning in the genuine sense, the inception of the exceedingly strange thought of Being—in other words, of philosophical thought—cannot by right be indebted to, or mixed up with, anything like Jewish, Roman-Christian, or Islamic traces, particularly since, as one can safely assume, these elements are also essentially religious for Heidegger. To conceive of the "Hebraic cluster [*massif*]" only as a "religion" (as is clearly the case with Heidegger, rather than, as Zarader, as "a founding text [the Bible], the tradition derived from it, the coherent universe that it composes, and the place that a certain number of questions like language, thought, or history, occupy in this universe") is, of course, highly problematic, all the more so if Zarader's hypothesis that Heidegger "uses categories of thought inherited from the Jews, to think a question-content [*teneur-de-question*] he inherited from the Greeks," should prove to be correct.[10] But having reduced the "Hebraic cluster [*massif*]" to the dimension of faith that for Heidegger is foreign to thought (and as regards the reduction of the Jewish concern with God to a question of ontotheology, which, rather than being original, has therefore its equivalent in Greek thought), Judaism cannot for him claim the status of a beginning, in a strict sense, in the history of Europe and the West. Needless to say, in the flattening down of the Greek beginning, all of these additional sources have their role to play. But if, according to Heidegger, the beginning of Europe is Greek— that is, philosophical—"Greek" names an event rather than referring to a geographical, ethnic, religious, or historical entity, and it points to a conception so uncanny, so unfamiliar, so strange that it implies a bracketing of all established customs, beliefs, institutions, and, above all, anything "religious." It would be tempting to say that the beginning Heidegger has in mind is an absolutely secular beginning, in advance of the religious/secular divide, had Heidegger not, in *Nietzsche* (in a passage that, as Giacomo Marramao has pointed out, has received little attention until now), delivered a drastic critique of the concept of secularization. Heidegger readily admits that since the history of modern humankind "was *mediately* prepared by Christian man, who was oriented toward the *certitude* of salvation," "one can interpret certain phenomena of the modern age as 'secularization' of Christianity." Any talk of secularization, however, "is a thoughtless deception, because a world toward which and in which one is made worldly already belongs to 'secularization' and 'becoming-worldly.' The *saeculum*, the 'world' through which something is 'secularized' in the celebrated 'secularization,' does not exist in itself or in such a way that it can be realized simply by stepping out of the Christian world."[11] In any event, "the 'religious,'" Heidegger writes, "is not only something Roman as far as the name is concerned. The Greeks had no 'religion' because they were, and still are, those who are looked upon by the gods [*die von den Göttern Angeblickten*]."[12] As an indisputably Latin concept, "religion" refers to the whole of the cult and the rituals that gather and bind a community. The attempt to think the Greek beginning as a philosophical beginning, free of all traces of religion, is therefore to conceive of it as anterior to all possible institutionalization of the relation of the mortals to the gods in the shape of rites and ceremonies.[13] Heidegger's consistent efforts to dechristianize the conceptuality of philosophy—i.e., in *Being and Time*, which is Heidegger's first major attempt to repeat and renew Greek thought—are further evidence of his attempt to retrieve a beginning of philosophical thought in advance of the various historical denominations (Judaism, Christianity, Islam) and free of any traces of the religious in philosophy.[14]

As I have already intimated, the thought of Being, as that thought which is the genuine commencement of Europe, is equiprimordial with a conception of what or who is human. This determination of the human being, which is definite for the West, presupposes an equally definite understanding of Being. In *Introduction to Metaphysics*, rather than elaborating directly on what Being means, Heidegger can therefore proceed to highlight the strangeness of the thought of Being by first investigating how the Greek thinkers conceived of the human being. Heidegger approaches this Greek conception of Being-human, one that, as he remarks, "strikes us as strange" (*IM*, 156), by focusing on the beginning of philosophical thought in Greece—that is, the poetic thinking (*dichterisches Denken*) of Heraclitus and Parmenides. Let us bear in mind that this discussion of the pre-Socratics' understanding of Being and Being-human occurs in the context of an elucidation of the most prominent division and opposition in Western metaphysics—namely, the division between Being and thinking on which the Western understanding of Being rests. Since Heraclitus highlighted the conjugate belonging-together of *physis* (as the emerging sway from which beings emerge) and *logos* (as gathering, and that which holds beings gathered in Being) at the inception of Western philosophy, it is difficult, as Heidegger notes, to see how both *physis* and *logos* could enter into the relation of disjunction that is characteristic of Western thought. Yet, as the metaphysical distinction between Being and thinking demonstrates, something within the unity of *physis* and *logos* must make this distinction possible. The determinateness of the metaphysical opposition between Being and thinking is conceivable only from a more fundamental rift that is already at work in the originary belonging-together of Being and thinking postulated by the pre-Socratic thinkers. To make visible this process of disjunction, it is necessary, Heidegger contends, to first comprehend the essential belonging-together of *physis* and *logos* still more clearly, and "in a purely Greek way" (*IM*, 144)—that is, not merely without recourse to later conceptual developments but first and foremost from "the dawn of that destiny in which Being illuminates itself in beings and so propounds a certain essence of man; that essence unfolds historically as something fateful [*als geschichtliches*], preserved in Being and dispensed by Being, without ever being separated from Being," and thus without conceiving of the Greek as "a particular people [*völkische*] or nation, nor as a cultural and anthropological group" (*EGT*, 25). Heidegger, therefore, turns to Parmenides, for whom thinking—or rather apprehension (*noein*)—and Being are united to the point of being the same (*to auto*). Indeed, Being necessarily implies apprehension "because it holds sway and insofar as it holds sway and appears" (*IM*, 148). But, Heidegger continues, such an intimate unity between *noein* as "the receptive bringing to a stand of what appears" and what shows itself (Being) is not "merely indifferent all-the-sameness" but a unity of that which contends (*IM*, 147). With this, however, the possibility of division and Being and thinking's setting themselves apart are inscribed in the originary unity. According to Heidegger, *noein* as apprehension (and, similarly, *logos* as gathering in Heraclitus) is not something primarily human. *Noein* and *logos* are, within Being as the opening for the appearing of beings, the "objective" correlates, as it were, of such coming into appearance. Consequently, if human beings are to be capable of being involved in such appearing and apprehension, it is, primarily, because they belong to Being. It follows from this that "the essence and the manner of Being-human can be determined on the basis of the essence of Being" (*IM*, 148). But "in this belonging-together of Being and the human essence, their disjunction comes to light" as well (*IM*, 150). Indeed, apprehension, which occurs simultaneously with the appearing of beings, is the happening within which the human being comes to stand in a disjunctive face-to-face relation to Being (*ins Angesicht tritt*) and is destined to be the recipient (and preserver) of the shining forth of Being. The opposition that thus occurs in spite (or because) of the intimate belonging-together of Being and Being-human is a unique opposition in that it destines the human being to be a historical being. Rather than a human activity, apprehension (and gathering) is "a happening [*Geschehen*] in which the human being itself happens, and in which he thus first enters history [*Geschichte*] as a being, first appears—that is [in the literal sense], itself comes to Being" (*IM*, 150; trans. mod.). The happening of the human being "is the knowing entrance-into-appearance of the human being as historical" (150–51); it is a happening in which Being and the human come to stand in a relation of opposition because they intimately belong together.

According to Heidegger, Parmenides' saying that thinking and Being are the same contains the "determination of Being-human that is definite [*massgebend*] for the West, and just as decisively it contains an essential characterization of Being" (*IM*, 150). This very strange determination, compared to which all subsequent definitions of the human being are forms of decline, determines Being-human by way of Being understood as the emerging sway. The human, consequently, is, on the one hand, one of the beings that have come into an appearance; it is, on the other hand, a being that comes face to face with Being, in the double sense of an opponent and a preserver. Yet, even though Parmenides' saying provides a determination of the human being and of Being that is decisive for the West, we still do not know, Heidegger asserts, exactly how the essence of Being-human is determined here. Parmenides' poetizing thinking gives us no more specific clues than does Heraclitus's fragments as to *what*, and particularly *who*, the human being is. Undoubtedly: "Who is the human being—we do not learn this through a scholarly definition but only when the human being steps into the confrontation with beings by attempting to bring them into their Being—that is, sets beings into limits and forms, projects something new (not yet present), originally poetizes, grounds poetically [*ursprünglich dichtet, dichterisch gründet*]" (*IM*, 153–54; trans. mod.). Although, in a thinking mode, Heraclitus and Parmenides expand on who the human being is, theirs is perhaps not such an originally poetic grounding of the human being. Therefore, to better understand their determination of Being-human—especially Parmenides' saying, and by the same token, the setting apart of that which for Parmenides is united, Heidegger must turn to Greek thinking poetry (*denkerisches Dichten*), more precisely to tragedy, and especially to the figure of Antigone.[15]

Heidegger writes that "because the thoughtful determination of Being-human that Parmenides accomplishes is difficult to approach directly and strikes us as strange, we will first seek help and instruction by listening to a poetic projection of Being-human among the Greeks" (*IM*, 155–56). But what is it, precisely, that is so strange about Parmenides' determination of the essence of Being-human and from which we have obviously become estranged? What is it that requires this recourse to Greek tragedy and its conception of the essence of the human, which is paradoxically even stranger than Parmenides' thoughtful determination of the human in relation to beings qua beings? Why is this determination, which is definite for the West (in that all later determinations of the essence of what is human presuppose it as that of which they have lost sight), in need of a detour through a poetical elaboration of that very same determination? What is unique and also strange about the Greek understanding of the human being (which constitutes the grounding conception of Europe and the West) is that it defines human essence on the basis of the challenge inherent in the human being's head-on confrontation with beings—and the inevitable risk of perdition that comes with such a confrontation, in which beings can be encountered either in relation to Being or in a complete disregard of it. This determination is neither a thesis nor an answer to the philosophical question of *what* the human being is. The determination in question does not legislate on the essence of the human being by fixing it in a substantialist or essentialist way; rather, it establishes the way of being (*das Wesen*) of Being-human—that is, its temporal mode. Questioning Being, and thus determining Being-human on the basis of the temporal mode (*Wesen*) of Being itself, is to determine it from the human being's confrontation with what is—that is, in view of the concomitant risk of ruin that such confrontation implies. To say, as Heidegger does, that by venturing into this confrontation, the human Being faces the necessity to decide is to say as well that it is this very necessity that makes the human being a historical being. Heidegger writes: "Only where Being opens itself up in questioning does history happen, and with it that Being of *the human being* by virtue of which the human being ventures [*wagt*] the confrontation with beings as such" (*IM*, 153). The questioning relation to Being, on which the determination of the human being that is definite for Europe and the West rests, entails that the confrontation with beings inevitably includes the risk of a turn away from Being, rather than merely giving rise to a preserving apprehension of Being. From this inscription of failure as a necessary possibility into the relation of man to Being, it also follows that this determination of the essence of man that decides about the essence of Europe and the West is an essence that has nothing properly its own. It is precisely this question of venturing forth into a confrontation with what is and the necessary risk that comes with this venturing forth—the question of *Wagnis* and *wagen*, a question that does not allow us to settle the matters of what or who the human being is once and for all by way of a predetermined answer—that Heidegger seeks to deepen by turning to Greek thinking poetry.

To get a better grasp on the determination of Being-human that is implicit in Parmenides' saying that thinking and Being are the same, an intimation of Greek Dasein is required. Heidegger, therefore, turns to Greek poetry, more precisely, to the Sophoclean tragedy *Antigone*. He writes: "The thinking of Parmenides and Heraclitus is still poetic, and here this means philosophical, not scientific. But because in this poetizing thinking, thinking has precedence, thinking about human Being also acquires its own direction and measure. In order to clarify this poetic thinking sufficiently in terms of its proper counterpart, we now interrogate a thinking poetry of the Greeks. This poetry is tragedy—the poetry in which Greek Being and Dasein [a Dasein belonging to Being] were authentically founded" (*IM*, 154).[16] Parmenides' thinking is poetic in that it provides a draft, or projection, of the Being of beings in a poetic mode; such a poetizing thinking is philosophical. It is a mode of thinking that has its own specific way of proceeding, a "direction and measure" that is exclusively its own, precisely because, in this unique way of setting Being-human into limits and form, thinking, rather than poetizing, dominates. In order to grasp the specificity of this way of conceiving of Being-human, Heidegger seeks an encounter with its "proper counterpart [*ihm zugehörige Gegenseite*]"—the thinking poetry of the early Greeks. His aim in this recourse to Greek tragedy is to clarify the proper way in which Being-human is determined in poetizing thinking by confronting the latter with a determination that—although it is distinct—is its proper counterpart and has a direction and a measure of its own. In no way does Heidegger want to simply conflate the tragic determination of the human being highlighted in his discussion with its philosophical determination. The recourse in *Introduction to Metaphysics* is warranted because the philosophical definition of the human being, admittedly, "strikes us as strange," but only in order to cast the poetically thinking determination of what and who is human into sharper relief. Furthermore, by way of the clarification in question, Heidegger seeks to reenter into a relation with the genuine possibility of philosophical thought—that is, with that which gives it its chance and constitutes both its promise and its danger.

As we have seen, the beginning of Europe and the West, which is shaped by poetizing thinking and thinking poetry in Greece, both of which center around the question of Being, is a beginning in the genuine sense because, in principle, it is free of all traces of the religious. In *Introduction to Metaphysics* this beginning, admittedly the most uncanny and mighty, is characterized as primal history, as *Ur-geschichte*. The context of this observation occurs in a digression or a "remark" inserted into Heidegger's discussion of the first antistrophe of Sophocles' second choral ode in *Antigone*, in which the human being is shown to be the uncanniest "thing" because he forces nature under his yoke. The remark aims to hold the description of Being-human in the ode at safe distance from any archaeological or anthropological interpretation vying with the natural sciences. What is described here is not, Heidegger holds, the beginning of history in a primitive state but the ontological reasons why the human being is a historical being. *Ur-geschichte*, as the hyphenization of the term suggests, refers to the uncanny beginning of historicity, of being-historical. Now, knowledge of this primal history, which is knowledge of the inception of the historical and hence no positivistic archaeology, is, Heidegger adds, "neither half nor whole natural science, but, if it is anything at all, it is mythology" (*IM*, 166). This reference to mythology, although not unique in Heidegger's work, is one of the rare occasions on which he alludes to it; it is also a disturbing reference considering the dominating ideology of the times, from which Heidegger, in the *Introduction*, has, with the exception of his assumption of the uniqueness and singularity of its beginning, consistently sought to distance himself.[17] Notwithstanding the fact that he does not elaborate further on how he wishes this notion of mythology to be understood, it is clear that we should not take it as a reference to a particular myth or to the entirety of all myths. Nor does *mythos*, for Heidegger, resonate with the fascist opposition of *mythos* to *logos*. It is only since Plato that *mythos* has been associated with the gods and that it has entered into an opposition to *logos*, a hierarchical and value-positing opposition that various fascists ideologues sought to overturn. By contrast, Heidegger's understanding of *mythos* as *Sage*—either poetical Saying or Saying in the thinking mode, of Being—reaches back to Homer and the Poets, who understood the term as speech, tale, story, or fiction. In the essay "Moira," which is devoted to Parmenides' fragment 8, in which he elaborates on the relation between Being and thinking, Heidegger, after having recalled that the poem opens with an invocation of the goddess *Aletheia*, notes that "thought has scarcely touched upon the essence of the mythical, especially with regard to the fact that the *mythos* is the saying [*Sage*], while saying is the calling bringing-into-appearance" (*EGT*, 94). *What Is Called Thinking?* is even more explicit on this point:

> Myth [*Mythos*] means the telling word [*das sagende Wort*]. For the Greeks, to tell is to lay bare and make appear—both the appearance and that which has its essence in the appearance, its epiphany. *Mythos* is what has its essence in its telling—what is apparent in the unconcealedness of its appeal. The *mythos* is that appeal of foremost and radical concern to all human beings which makes man think of what appears, what is in being. *Logos* says the same; *mythos* and *logos* are not . . . placed into opposition by philosophy as such; on the contrary, the early Greek thinkers (Parmenides, fragment 8) are precisely the ones to use *mythos* and *logos* in the same sense.[18]

Undoubtedly, the title "mythology" is ambiguous and confusing because for us "the words *mythos* and *logos* are connected in such a way that both forfeit their primordial essence," so as to designate a doctrine of the gods, which, according to the Enlightenment, human beings invented in the absence of the exact sciences (*P*, 70). By contrast, Heidegger's understanding of the term refers to the saying and thinking of Being in advance of the metaphysical *mythos/logos* divide. In *Hölderlin's Hymn "The Ister"* Heidegger notes that "mythology is that historical 'process' in which Being itself comes to appear poetically." Thinking, in turn, as essential thinking, that is, the thinking of Being, "stands in an originary relation to poetizing," which brings Being into appearance (*HHI*, 111).

Although equiprimordial—yet for this very reason also fundamentally distinct from one another—"mythology" names the originary belonging together of both *mythos* and *logos*, poetizing and thinking.

It follows from all of this that the notion of mythology, understood as knowledge concerning the origin or *Ur-Geschichte* at the inception of Europe and the West, must be exempt from any religious connotations, that is, regarding the Greek gods of which myth commonly speaks. The beginning of the West can only be a genuine beginning, or a beginning in the first place, if *ab initio* it is anterior to any particular religion, that of the Greeks and their "mythology" included. Myth, then, must be understood in such a way that, from the outset, it excludes any religious implications. In the context of Heidegger's thought, the mythic is therefore to be conceived as a mode of Saying—that is, of letting Being, as the opening in which beings come into an appearance, shine forth. Furthermore, since Being itself is anterior to the godhead and to mortals, Being is necessarily older than anything that is of the order of the religious, and, consequently, the Saying that occurs in or as myth is older than religion and the religious as well.

We still cannot ignore the fact, however, that myths are often about gods and the relation of human beings to the gods. This cannot be overlooked, especially when Heidegger, in order to clarify the determination of Being-human that is definite for the West, finds himself compelled to resort to a Greek tragedy that, in the same way as all other Greek tragedies, is generally seen to stage the conflict of the ancient and the new gods. Furthermore, even though Heidegger claimed that the Greeks had no religion, on one occasion at least he seems to link the mythical to the religious. In *What Is Called Thinking?* for instance, after having stated that the assumption that *mythos* has been destroyed by *logos* is a misconception, Heidegger adds: "But nothing religious is ever destroyed by logic; it is destroyed only by the God's withdrawal."[19] And finally, as Lacoue-Labarthe has pointed out, a "'religious' overdetermination," owing to a certain type of Christianity, pervades much of Heidegger's work. To put it differently, something of the order of Christian revelation (which remains intelligible only because it was once an article of faith), and perhaps even something of the order of Judaism, as Zarader intimates, permeates all of his work.[20] Hence, if indeed Heidegger resorts to a Greek tragedy to shed light on Parmenides' saying, and thus to retrieve the pure beginning of the thinking of Being that constitutes the West, the question of the religious implications of tragedy reemerges.[21] It is more precisely a question concerning the purity of the philosophical thought of Being, that is, of its indebtedness to the religious—a question, hence, regarding the possibility of a beginning that by right would be a beginning in the first place. In spite of these difficulties, let us not lose sight of the fact that, even though, as Heidegger himself acknowledges, "'myth' does of course have to do with the gods" and "'mythology' is about 'the gods,'" the gods in question are the Greek gods. And so Heidegger adds: "Yet it is not sufficient to use the single God of Christianity as the measure and then point out that the Greeks practiced a polytheism of gods that are comparatively less 'spiritual' and altogether of a lesser nature. As long as we make no attempt to think the Greek gods in the Greek way, i.e., on the basis of *aletheia*, we have no right to say a word about these gods, whether in favor of them or against them" (*P*, 60–61).

Even before proceeding to elucidate Parmenides' saying through the lens of *Antigone*, Heidegger invokes, in *Introduction to Metaphysics*, Greek tragic poetry, especially *Oedipus Rex*, as the highest and purest portrayal of the Greek philosophical insight into "the unity and antagonism of Being and seeming [*Sein und Schein*]" (*IM*, 111–12). If I briefly linger on this reference to *Oedipus Rex*, it is because it puts already his recourse to *Antigone* into perspective. What he highlights in *Oedipus Rex* is not so much the story of one who is first "in the brilliance and grace of the gods" and is then hurled from this state of grace by these same divinities; it is rather the "unique struggle between seeming (concealment and distortion) and unconcealment (Being)" through which, in the figure of Oedipus, Greek Dasein "ventures [*vorwagt*] into what is wildest and most far-flung: the passion for the unveiling of Being—that is, the struggle over Being itself" (*IM*, 112). In the same way as Greek philosophical thinking, Greek tragic poetry is thus understood by way of a problematic that, by right, is older than the sacred and, moreover, than the religious. A careful reading of Heidegger's analysis of the choral ode of Sophocles' *Antigone* would arrive at the same conclusion. For the time being, and in order to reach a provisional conclusion, I should opt for a more economical position, arguing that Heidegger's recourse to tragedy in elucidating Parmenides' saying and his intent on thus recovering the beginning of the thought of Being—hence, of Europe and the West—in all the purity of its uncanniness, is a recourse to a kind of poetry in which he forcefully seeks to foreground the relation between humans and the gods by way of the question of Being.

We have not yet fully developed the uncanny nature of the thought of Being, but it should be clear from what has been said so far that it is a thought that, once heeded, throws Dasein out of the ordinary and makes it a homeless being. The characterization of the figure of Antigone in the 1942 lectures in *Hölderlin's Hymn "The Ister"* gives us perhaps the most explicit description of how Heidegger conceives not only of the recoil of the questioning of Being on the questioner but also of tragedy as an instance of thinking poetry. In these lectures, which offer a much more extensive reading of the tragedy in question than do the Freiburg lectures of 1935, the depiction in the first choral ode of the uncanniness and unhomeliness of human Dasein—to which the analysis of the earlier lectures were limited—appears as that of the ordinary human condition. It is against the backdrop of this ordinary human condition that Antigone is singled out to exemplify Greek Being-human in its extreme uncanniness and unhomeliness, as it responds to the call of Being. Particularly since Hegel's influential interpretation of this tragedy, we tend to think of Antigone's struggle with the law of the state and her subsequent self-sacrifice as deriving from her unflinching will to uphold the other law—that is, the law of the underworld, the bonds of blood, and the family. In his *Sophokles* (1933), Karl Reinhardt—whom Heidegger credits with having come "essentially closer to Greek Dasein and Being than all previous attempts, because Reinhardt sees and questions tragic happenings according to the fundamental connections among Being, unconcealment and seeming" (*IM*, 113)—convincingly argued that "the usual concepts and categories with which one has sought to approach the essence of *Antigone* since Hegel . . . have been abstracted from classical and postclassical aesthetics." However, by subscribing to the belief that the unifying concept of the manifold conflicts present in *Antigone* is that of a conflict of ideas, that is, "a conflict between two equally valid principles," one assumes that "Sophocles is a tragic poet in the same way as Schiller, Kleist, and Goethe." In Reinhardt's view *Antigone* is not at all a conflict of norms or laws that would mutually imply one another, with the result that the pursuit of one would demand the sacrifice of the other. Rather, that which in the figures of Antigone and Creon stands in a way of opposition is "in itself without conflict. It remains in itself uncontested by the other, and does not convert the other way, the other law, idea, or morality, into its own way, law, or idea—like Tasso, Prince von Homburg, Wallenstein." Rather, for Reinhardt, the tragedy of *Antigone* is based on a conflict "between two human centers, including their equally eccentric worlds [i.e., two types of hubris], which move around the same invisible middle, and in which each one is bereaved of equilibrium and measure, and thrown from its route." He concludes: "According to its idea, *Antigone* is not a conflict of norms, but the tragedy of two human downfalls which are, insofar as their essence is concerned, separate, but demonically connected in the sense of counter-images that follow one another."[22] In the lectures from 1942 Heidegger proposes an interpretation of the tragedy that is indebted not only to Reinhardt's anticlassicist stance but also to the latter's account of Antigone's reasons for laying her brother to rest. Invoking the polar laws of Zeus and Dike, Heidegger holds that "in her words Antigone speaks of neither of these" (*HHI*, 116). Reinhardt had already pointed out that "by situating herself in the divine and the eternal totality, being obedient both to Zeus in the heavens and to Dike in the depths, Antigone fulfills the unwritten law" of the divine as such.[23] He adds: "Antigone is not only bound to the chthonic, she is absolutely bound to the divine as a whole."[24] Heidegger bases his reading of the tragedy, which pivots on his singular interpretation of "the unwritten law" of the divine, on Antigone's words addressed to Creon:

> It was no Zeus that bade me this,
> Nor was it Dike, at home amongst the gods below,
> who ordained this law for humans,
> And your command seemed not so powerful to me,
> that it could ever override by human wit
> the immutable, unwritten edict divine.
> Not just now, nor since yesterday, but ever steadfast
> this prevails [*doch ständig je west dies*]. And no one knows from whence it once appeared. (*HHI*, 116).

According to Jacques Taminiaux, Hegel's and Heidegger's interpretations of Greek tragedy converge in that both link Antigone to an ontological *theoria* of which she is the highest and purest expression.[25] As Heidegger notes in *Hölderlin's Hymn "The Ister,"* however, instead of being theoretical or philosophical, the "knowledge," or rather intimating, of the thinking poetry of Sophocles regarding Being is of the order of *phronein*—"a pondering and meditating that comes from *phrone*, that is, from the 'heart,' from the innermost middle of human essence itself" (*HHI*, 107).[26] Furthermore, in a conclusion that clearly undercuts Hegel's interpretation of tragedy according to which Antigone acts in conformity with the "prevailing or ancient cult of the dead, or the familial blood-relatedness," Heidegger writes: "That which is determinative, that which determines Antigone in her being, is beyond the upper and the lower gods. And yet it is something that pervasively attunes human beings as human beings." Already from the dialogue between Antigone and Ismene in which Antigone hints at the reasons why she refuses to obey Creon's order, it is clear that Antigone takes as "the point of departure governing all [her] actions . . . that against which nothing can avail [*tamekhana*]." What she takes "into her ownmost essence" is something "which resists that entire *mechanoen* that is named explicitly in the second antistrophe of the choral ode as the work of the human being who ventures forth in all directions" and against which nothing can prevail, precisely because "it is that which is destined to us and is fitting" (*HHI*, 101–2).[27] Yet that against which no machinations whatsoever can in the end be successful is the uncanny, the unhomely—in Heidegger's terminology—Being itself. Basing himself on Antigone's words to Creon, Heidegger holds that the essence of Antigone is determined by that which "ever steadfast . . . prevails," and which, in spite of the fact that it is not to "be encountered anywhere as something first posited" either through human or divine ordinance, is of the order of the unconcealed (although no one knows whence it appeared)—that is, of Being.[28] Antigone, then, is the uncanniest because she is at home neither in the upper nor in the underworld, determined in her action neither by Zeus nor by Dike alone (*HHI*, 116–17). She obeys the unwritten law, of which Aristotle in *Rhetoric*, and in an explicit reference to Sophocles' *Antigone*, said that in distinction from the written law it alone fulfills the task of a law in the first place because it represents the universal and immutable law.[29] It is to Being that Antigone responds first and foremost, and, if she is a tragic figure, it is because of the risk of perdition that comes with such faithfulness to its unwritten law. Thus understood, tragedy is the poetic, mythic mode of Saying Being: of spelling out, in a poetic way, how the questioning of Being recoils on the questioner, "unhoming" him or her, as it were, from the order of both the worldly and the religious. Only such a mode of Saying Being, precisely because it is free from all traces of the religious, is on par with the poetic thinking of Parmenides' saying. Only through this mode of saying can a Greek tragedy such as *Antigone* serve to illuminate a conception of Being that, owing to its strange purity alone, can claim to be *the* exceedingly strange beginning of Europe or the West.

Before I turn to Heidegger's interpretation of the Sophoclean tragedy both in *Introduction to Metaphysics* and in *Hölderlin's Hymn "The Ister,"* this, then, is the moment at which we need to provide a first account of the question of Being itself and of that into which it inquires. As the beginning of Western thought and poetry, this question, which alone inquires into what is questionworthy insofar as it concerns the West, is thus "the question to come [*die künftige Frage*]." To pose this question, Heidegger says in the lectures on Hölderlin from 1934–35 that preceded his lectures on metaphysics, is "to venture forth into the strangeness [*Befremdlichkeit*] of the questionworthy" (*HHGR*, 270). The thought of Being is strange because what it demands of those whom it concerns— Western humanity, first and foremost—is a way of being that itself is strange. Heidegger writes: "Being as destiny is the uncanny, the outsized, that which at all times remains an annoyance to everything that is petty and calculating" (*HHGR*, 229). While commenting in the 1942–43 Parmenides lectures on a statement by Aristotle from the *Nicomachean Ethics*, according to which thinkers know things that are effusive, admirable, and therefore difficult—in short, demonic (*daimonia*), Heidegger notes that this word *daimonia*, which he translates as "das Un-geheure"—the terrible, tremendous, prodigious, and so forth, but above all, the unfamiliar, the odd—names everything that from the perspective of ordinary persons goes beyond what is *geheuer*, namely, that which does not remain "within the limits of beings, of the real, of the 'facts.'" Indeed, that which shines into, and shows itself in the thought of thinkers and poets, is Being, and where "Being comes into focus, there the extraordinary [*das Nicht-Geheure*, that is, also the un-canny], the uncanny [*Ungeheure*], literally understood," announces itself (*P*, 101). Reflecting on the word, Heidegger emphasizes that "'uncanny,' as used here, has nothing at all in common with its banal sense of 'impressive' and 'moving'" (*P*, 106). The word must—as its hyphenation demonstrates—be taken literally: it refers to what is not familiar, not, however, to an exceptional and spectacular oddity. The *Un-geheure*, which is not of the order of "the exception, in principle explainable, to the ordinary [*Geheuren*]," is "in its essence . . . the inconspicuous [*Un-auffällige*], the simple, the insignificant [*Un-scheinbare*], which nevertheless shines in all beings" (*P*, 102,

105). Rather than being juxtaposed with what is ordinary, and hence understood as the nonordinary, the *Un-geheure* and that which is *Geheuer* are thus intimately interlaced: "The uncanny is that out of which all that is ordinary emerges, that in which all that is ordinary is suspended without surmising it ever in the least, and that into which everything ordinary falls back. *To daimonion* is the essence and essential ground of the uncanny" (*P*, 102). With this recollection of the Greek expression *to daimonion*, which Heidegger translates as "the divine," he gives us a first hint at what it is that shines into the familiar. "That which looks into all that is ordinary, the uncanny as showing itself in advance, is the originally looking one in the eminent sense: *to theaon*, i.e., *to theion*. We translate 'correctly,' though without thinking in the Greek manner, 'the divine'" (*P*, 104). According to Heidegger, the gods, insofar as they shine forth while looking into the existent, are "Being itself as looking into being" (*P*, 111). In a passage from the "Letter on Humanism" devoted to Heraclitus's response to some foreigners who found him warming himself at the stove, that "here too the gods are present," Heidegger avers: "*Kai entautha*, 'even here,' at the stove, in that ordinary place where every thing and every condition, each deed and thought is intimate and commonplace, that is, familiar [*geheuer*], 'even there' in the sphere of the familiar, *einai theous*, it is the case that 'the gods are present.'" Even in the most familiar place, or rather, precisely within what is most familiar, that which is not familiar—the *Un-geheure*—abides. Citing Heraclitus: "*ethos anthropoi daimon*, 'The (familiar) abode is for man the open region for the presencing of god (the unfamiliar one),'" Heidegger argues that in the neighborhood of the most familiar [*im Umkreis des Geheuren*], that is, precisely within man's ethos or abode—where the stove or the hearth is located—that which is most unfamiliar, *to daimonion*, the *Un-geheure* presences (*BW*, 234). In its very secludedness, the home and the homely is also an openness to the unfamiliar, the unhomely, and only as such is the home the home of man. In other words, only to the extent that Being shines forth into the familiar exposing it to the wholly unfamiliar, and hence unsettling the very homeliness of the home, is the human abode a home to begin with.

Heidegger writes: "The uncanny [is] the Being that shines into everything ordinary, i.e., into beings" (*P*, 101). The thought of Being that marks the beginning of the West is the thought of the *Un-geheure* that on every occasion is of the order of an *irruption*, whether it takes place in the shape of the presencing of the gods or in philosophical wonder, that is, by way of the "astounding, visible in the astonishing, namely, the uncanny, which pertains so immediately to the ordinary that it can never be explained on the basis of the ordinary" (*P*, 101; trans. mod.). In all its occurrences, this originary thought, which unsettles what is in all its familiarity, is nothing less than the movement of *thaumazein*, which Heidegger translates as *Ent-setzen*.[30] The dislocating thought of Being is a unique irruption, *Ein-fall*, and this irruption occurs suddenly so as to preclude all refuge and shelter. This thought, which is also the founding thought of the West, is therefore, from the beginning, a leap into the abyss of the groundless (*P*, 149–50).

§ 6 The Originary World of Tragedy

In his search for a universality that—in distinction from the mathematically subtracted world of idealities characteristic of the objective universe of the natural sciences—would also encompass the subjective activities of the human being (and hence be a true universality), Edmund Husserl, in the late 1930s, drafted the outlines for an analysis of the life-world. According to *The Crisis of European Sciences and Transcendental Phenomenology*, the life-world is the spatiotemporal world of things as we experience them in prescientific and extrascientific life—that is, everyday life—and thus is the world as we live it, or the lived world. Through an analysis of how the world and its things are actually given to an ego—in other words, through an analysis of the various intentional or meaning-giving acts that are constitutive of the world as lived and experienced—Husserl sought to establish the essential forms of the innermost elementary acts of all subjective and intersubjective life, that is, life involved in the formation of the world shared by human beings. The total essential form of transcendentally accomplishing subjectivity—an essentially dynamically open totality, always modifiable because of new intentional acts, and hence constantly in the making—was finally to furnish the absolutely binding universality that the idea of a universal rational science had promised at the dawn of philosophy in Greece but that the objective world of the sciences restricted to the world of idealities predicated on spatial form alone. In short, the inquiry into the transcendental structures of constituting subjectivity was to realize for the first time in full the Greek idea of a universal and apodictic science that Husserl construes as the life project characteristic of Europe.

Martin Heidegger's analyses of Dasein's everydayness and being-in-the-world would seem to have anticipated in some way Husserl's inquiry into the life-world in *The Crisis of European Sciences*, not the least because the latter is also, as is commonly admitted, Husserl's own response to Heidegger's investigations in *Being and Time*. But precisely because they take place in view of a fundamental ontology, Heidegger's analyses of human Dasein exclude from the start, as the Czech phenomenologist Jan Patočka has pointed out, all concern with what the early Husserl (and Patočka as well), terms the "natural world" or the life-world. Heidegger's analyses in *Being and Time* do not focus on Dasein's lived experiences (perceptions, thought, or sensibility) in order to convert them by means of a phenomenological reduction to the reality of the noetic, or subjective, realm.[1] Indeed, according to Patočka, "Heidegger reverses the situation: the event of Being, the opening up of the phenomenal realm, the 'temporalization' of time, and the clearing of the world (world = light) are what makes humanity, that is, the birth of the human being [as a subjective agent], possible [in the first place]. The event of Being which, although inexplicable, illuminates everything, is contemporaneous with the 'birth' of man" (*MNM*, 99). Seen from the perspective of fundamental ontology, the natural world or life-world is a world of beings closed upon themselves without the interruption of the event of Being in the light of which they could manifest themselves *as* beings. For Heidegger, according to Patočka,

> such a "natural world" [or life-world] could not be the object of a phenomenological description. The analysis of its structures would always only grasp already existing results independently of the originary event of Being which makes them possible and conditions them in their entirety. [According to Heidegger, Patočka argues,] one can grasp the originary world only in the cipher [*chiffre*] of a mythical story about the nuptials of the world and the sky, the gathering of the inhabitants of the world and those of the heavens, of heaven and earth. (*MNM*, 99)

As opposed to Husserl's conception of the life-world, only an originary world opened up by Being—by Being's luminous withdrawal—is susceptible to phenomenological description. Unlike Husserl's life-world, which, although it is never completed, is the object of an infinite process of approximation to the idea of genuine universality, Heidegger's originary world (distinct also from the world as an interrelatedness of references [*Verweisungszusammenhang*] in which, according to *Being and Time*, Dasein always already finds itself) is never given, and always remains to be unfolded in all its originarity. Undoubtedly, by evoking the term *originary world* in order to distinguish Heidegger's reflections on Being and world from the Husserlian life-world, Patočka is thinking of *Introduction to Metaphysics*, in which Heidegger indeed introduces the notion of "an originary world of historical Dasein" (*IM*, 52). Since *originary*, in the expression *originary world* is a translation of the German *ursprünglich*, an originary world is the essence of what *world* means, a world that is found and established through a leap from out of what is into the opening in which everything comes into appearance. In conformity with what he has established with regard to the notion of beginning, an originary world (*ursprünglich* and *anfänglich* are intimately related) is thus a world that is a beginning, a beginning world, a world as a beginning. In contrast to the already constituted structures grasped in the analyses of the subjective accomplishments in the life-world, what is *anfänglich* lies, as Heidegger notes in the 1942–43 Freiburg lectures on Parmenides, "in advance of what is to come" (*P*, 1). Indeed, for Heidegger it is not the natural or life-world that is at issue in fundamental ontology but "the originary world," in which the event of Being, by bringing beings forth into their shining forth *as* beings, opens up a historical world.

If, however, such an originary world can only be grasped "in the cipher of a mythical story about the nuptials of the world and the sky, the gathering of the inhabitants of the world and those of the heavens, of heaven and earth," in short, in "mythology," it follows that it is to be found in the works solely of those who, like Homer, gave a historical people its gods and, hence, a world.[2] It is the poets and the thinkers, according to Heidegger, who inaugurate or found an originary world—that is, who articulate Being in a form that encompasses all the domains of what is. Like painting, the aim of which is "essentially to project (*hypothesis*) the one aspect [*des einen Anblicks*] in whose unity *beauty* is shown," poetry *brings together* everything that is with the result that Being appears in all dimensions of the visible, unifying them, and thus opening up a world (*EHP*, 156). In an "Addition" to *Parmenides* Heidegger notes that "Being and the truth of Being are essentially beyond men and humanities [*über alle Menschen und Menschentümer hinweg*]" (*P*, 166). In the originary world opened up by thoughtful poeticizing, Being is thus what concerns everyone and everything. But because, as *Being and Time* already established, Being is not a genus (if genus is understood in a logical sense of the universal and the all-encompassing, that is, as summum genus, or the highest class that subsumes all beings as particular cases); "its 'universality' is, therefore, to be sought higher up" than, say, the universality of the total form of the life-world.[3] Commenting on a line from Hölderlin's poem "Remembrance"—"But what remains is founded by the poets"—Heidegger submits that "the poet is the founder of Being [*Seyn*]" and adds: "Being thus inaugurated in poetry encompasses beings in their totality: the gods, the earth, the human beings, and the latter in their history—as history, i.e. as a people" (*HHGR*, 214–15). Being and the originary world as they are founded in great poetry are not of the order of a universal that applies without distinction to everything particular and that thus ignores the singular way in which responsibility for and to Being, and the originary world that it opens up, is granted to Dasein. Rather, the universal in the sense of the general is, in Heidegger's words, "equally valid for every particular instance, [and] always proves to be something neutral or indifferent [*Gleichgültige*]" (*EHP*, 52). A universality that indiscriminately applies to all possible particulars is something that can never become essential in any essential way for a particular Dasein. Unlike the universal as something general, the "universality" of an originary world is never something that is already given or present at hand. If the poets must found an originary world, it is precisely because such a world and its higher universality is not something ageless but must be brought about by gathering all that is into the one unifying aspect in which Being historically shines forth. It follows from this that the originary world opened up by the poets is not binding for humanity as such and as a whole, as is the case with the universality of the structures of the Husserlian life-world but (at first) only for a singular and concrete people. What distinguishes the "universality" that constitutes the originary world to be found in the works of the poets (who poetize—in a thinking manner—Being in a particular language) from the universality of the fundamental structures of the life-world, is that it "only" provides "the unity of a world" for a particular people (*HHGR*, 223). "Only" here is not to be understood as a limitation but rather as that which alone, and uniquely, determines the ground from which all other essential consequences derive. Furthermore, the poetic projection of an originary world that "only" binds a particular people is not, therefore, a merely relative world, since this poetic projection, rather than being a projection in accordance with an already existing world, is the founding of such a world in the first place. The originary world's intimate connection to a particular people and its language does not make it less universal. As we will henceforth see, the world in question is indeed one in which a people becomes a people to begin with by shedding everything that is of the order of the natural, the ethnic, and the racial, that is, all particular determinations. As a consequence, such a world, which structurally implies self-transcendence, although irreducible to abstract universality, is by definition a world open to the other. Yet however singular this openness to the other is (and such a world requires this openness for a people to be a people), it can in no way be restricted to what is particular about this world. For what follows, it is thus crucial to stress that the kind of "facts" from which universality is gained in both Husserlian and Heideggerian conceptions is not without implications for how "universality" must be understood in each of them. Whereas transcendental phenomenology derives the constituting eidetic structures of subjectivity by way of phenomenological reduction from the open totality of all human acts through which the world is given, the poetic projection of the originary world, and hence its corresponding humanity, occurs *not* on the basis of an analysis of a "manner of Being, that is . . . the everyday one," but rather through a confrontation of the human being's "extreme possibilities and limits," in other words, of "the most extreme limits and the most abrupt abysses" of his or her being (*IM*, 175, 165, 159).[4] However, the privileged place for such a confrontation of the human being in his or her extreme possibilities is, according to Heidegger, primarily great poetry.

Since the originary world, rather than always already given, only comes into being as a result of a grounding act by the poet, a succinct digression regarding thinking and poetizing—*Dichten* and *Denken*—is warranted at this point. Indeed, although poetizing and thinking belong together in an originary fashion, and are concerned with the same thing—that is, the saying of Being—what needs to be clarified is whether such saying occurs in a conjoined fashion or whether one could have priority over the other. Undoubtedly, Heidegger's parlance of "thinking poetry" and "poetizing thought" is indicative of the intimate belonging together of poetizing and thinking. But the allusion in *Hölderlin's Hymn "The Ister,"* that thinking poetry names and poetizing thinking unfolds, could also suggest distinct tasks and hence perhaps the possibility of a specific time for each one of them, that is, of times in which one may prevail over the other (*HHI*, 91). According to "Was heisst Denken?" "the essence of poetry rests in thinking"—insofar as thinking is the gathering remembrance of that which is to the thought—but Heidegger also holds that thinking in its most originary sense is a poetizing.[5] Let us turn now to considering the following passage from "The Anaximander Fragment":

> Thinking is poetizing, and indeed more than one kind of poetizing, more than poetry and song. Thinking of Being is the original way of poetizing. Language first comes to language, i.e. into its essence, in thinking. Thinking says what the truth of Being dictates; it is the original *dictare*. Thinking is primordial poetry [*Urdichtung*], prior to all poesy, but also prior to the poetics of art, since art shapes its work within the realm of language. All poetizing, in this broader sense, and also in the narrower sense of the poetic, is in its ground a thinking. The poetizing essence of thinking preserves the sway of the truth of Being. (*EGT*, 19)

Drawn from a context in which Heidegger seeks to translate and elucidate a saying about Being by one of the earliest Greek thinkers, this passage is, it would seem, at first primarily concerned with thought. But precisely insofar as thinking is the thinking of Being, it is primordial poetry, in that by thinking, Being thought brings language to speak in language, which by the same token thus also comes into its essence (*Wesen*); in short, it becomes manifest as the projection of Being. It follows from this that by the same right primordial poetry is thinking in a primordial sense as well, that is, the thinking of Being, since thought as primordial poetry, or poetry as primordial thought—both making language speak in language, in other words, projecting an understanding of Being—both (as the same) lay the foundation for an originary world for historical Dasein. Thus, to say that one founds, whereas the other unfolds the founded, does, at the limit, not make sense. Yet since thinking and poetry are both, in a primordial sense, about Being, and are therefore the same, they must also differ, because the unity of both is anterior to all poetry in the sense of poesy and to all thought in the sense of philosophical thought. This difference, rooted in the different ways in which thought and poetry relate to Being, however slight it may be, is, as we will see in what follows, at the same time also abyssal, and therefore justifies the distinction between thinking and poetizing in the first place, as well as the different tasks that at different times may become incumbent on them.

Undoubtedly, Heidegger's typically conjoined use of *Dichten* and *Denken*, both of which are in very different ways "about" the originary world, suggests a parallelism between both and hence the absence of preeminence of one over the other. Such parallelism, however, not only in no way diminishes their difference—which in *Elucidations of Hölderlin's Poetry* is even said to be "abyssal [*abgründig davon verschieden*]"—but is also, as Heidegger points out in "The Nature of Language" (where the notion of parallelism explicitly serves to describe the relation between poetry and thinking), that which incites each one in its fashion to excel and surpass the other.[6] Furthermore, *Elucidations of Hölderlin's Poetry* also hints at a temporal divergence between poetizing and thinking insofar as each occurs "in its time" (*EHP*, 126). Without yet engaging the difference between poetry and thinking, let me only point out for the moment that it is this parallelism between both that explains why the *Introduction to Metaphysics* can, at one point, turn to a poetic projection of Being—and hence of an originary world—to Sophocles' *Antigone* in order to illuminate the thinking projection of Being by Heraclitus and Parmenides. Since the philosophers' thoughtful determination of the essence of Being-human is said to be "difficult to approach directly, and [to] strike us as strange [*schwer zugänglich und befremdlich*]," Heidegger seeks "help and instruction by listening to a poetic projection of Being-human among the Greeks," despite the fact, as he will later admit, that this poetic projection is no less strange than its thoughtful determination by the pre-Socratic thinkers (*IM*, 156). If, in the more exhaustive interpretation of the tragedy provided by the 1942 lectures on *Hölderlin's Hymn "The Ister,"* thinking in turn provides help for understanding Sophocles' tragedy, as well as Hölderlin's hymn, it is seemingly for the same reason that both are parallel ways in which the saying of an originary world occurs.

Before further considering the difference and reciprocity of thinking and poetry, however, we need to attend to the fact that although the 1935 lectures on metaphysics interpret Sophocles' *Antigone* without any explicit reference to Hölderlin's poetry, the lectures in *Hölderlins Hymnen "Germanien" und "Der Rhein"* from the preceding winter semester (1934–35) are crucial to understanding the deep motive for the turn to a poetic work—moreover, to a work of tragedy—in order to illuminate works of thought. In fact, what becomes obvious from these lectures is that the turn to a poetic work to elucidate a philosophical one is more complex than what the parallelism between poetry and thinking seemed at first to suggest. Indeed, in these lectures one witnesses an intriguing deference of thought to poetry that hints at differences between both—differences that concern their tasks but also their times—that will be significant for everything that will follow. For the time being, however, I limit myself to underscoring that even though Heidegger neither follows Hölderlin in the details, nor even in the overall thrust of the latter's interpretation of *Antigone*, without an acknowledgment of how Hölderlin's poetry already bears on Heidegger's understanding of Sophocles' tragedy in *Introduction to Metaphysics* it is difficult, if not impossible, to truly make sense of his interpretation of *Antigone* in the first place. After having wondered whether "Sophocles still speaks at all in Heidegger's translation" of the first choral ode, Otto Pöggeler remarks that "Hölderlin's relation to Greek poetry was more important to Heidegger than two hundred years of philological work!"[7] The meaning of Heidegger's interpretation of the tragedy can only be truly gleaned if what Karl Reinhardt describes as "the chasm—a chasm that could not be deeper—between Hölderlin and the classical conception of the tragedy," which has been determinant for Heidegger's approach, is fully taken into consideration.[8] If Hölderlin's poetry and his understanding of *Antigone* mediate Heidegger's reading of this tragedy, it is not least because the poet, in Reinhardt's words, also "projected [*hineindeuten*] characteristics of the present into the *Antigone*."[9]

Now, the lectures in *Hölderlins Hymnen "Germanien" und "Der Rhein"* forcefully make the point that poetry is "the originary language of a people [*Ursprache eines Volkes*]," in other words, that "which carries from the ground up the setup of Being [*Seinsgefüge*] of the human being as historical Dasein within the whole of beings" (*HHGR*, 64, 36). Whereas the thinker opens up—that is, thinks and structures (*gefügt*) the way of being of a people, and the statesman brings "a people to itself as a people," the poet is the one who first founds and discloses "the truth of a people" (*HHGR*, 144). Echoing Hölderlin's words from the Böhlendorff letter of December 4, 1801, Heidegger submits that for a people to be a people, that is, a historical Dasein, such historical being must "first be affected [*Betroffenwerden*] by Being as a whole, and second, must be able to formulate [*Fassenkönnen*] Being through the effective presentation of beings that brings them forth and puts them to work [*erwirkenden*]" (*HHGR*, 291). However, only the poet, if he is a true beginner, opens up and founds the originary world for a people in a poetry that thinks

Being [*Wesensdenken*] in "a creative projection—creative, in so far as the essence of beings does not lie at the roadside, and would only need to be picked up like the respective beings themselves" (*HHGR*, 164). Insofar as "poetry is the fundamental event of Being as such," the poet alone founds and discloses Being in relation to whose overpowering sway a people can find itself "in the extreme open of naked exposure [*das äusserste Draussen der nackten Ausgesetztheit*]" and thus be a historical Dasein— if indeed "Dasein is nothing other than the exposure to the overpowering sway of Being [*Ausgesetztheit in die Uebermacht des Seyns*]" (*HHGR*, 257, 30–31). According to Heidegger, "for occidental thought this foundation of Being took place in Homer, whom Hölderlin calls the 'poet of all poets'" (*HHGR*, 184). Yet even though "one cannot imagine occidental [*abendländische*] history without the Greeks, which as a people set the standards and ranks, . . . contemporary historical Dasein can nonetheless not return to them" (*HHGR*, 205). A repetition or reproduction of "the first beginning in the sense of a renewal of Greek world and its transformation into the here and now" is an "impossible task," Heidegger contends (*P*, 166). In the aftermath of the Greeks, contemporary historical Dasein must found its destiny in an originary world of its own—one that is not Greek yet one that, as we will see, is not without a complex relation of confrontation and dialogue with it. Without yet broaching the relations between Greece (the Orient) and the Occident that arise from what Heidegger terms "the Greek-German sending [*Sendung*]" of philosophy—and of poetry as well—the task that the contemporary world (and, especially, "the people between the peoples"—i.e., the Germans) faces is, according to the 1934–35 lectures, to fully acknowledge that the Germans as a historical people have been abandoned by their gods and are torn apart (*HHGR*, 151, 56, 80). Hölderlin is not only the poet who "is the first to experience poetically, that is, to say poetically, the German need [*Not*] of being unhomely," but he is also the poet who adamantly sought to hold out in the face of "the absence [*Fehl*] of the God" as long as it would take until the coming of an originary world that would name the God to be granted to the Germans—one that would be the home for this people still to come (*HHI*, 12; *EHP*, 46). Following Stefan George, who, after having become acquainted with Norbert von Hellingrath's edition of Hölderlin's late hymns at the beginning of the twentieth century, characterized the poet as a visionary of the future of the German people, Hölderlin—the poet of poetry—is also for Heidegger "the poet, who first poetized what is German to begin with [*die Deutschen erst erdichtet*]" and consequently the poet of (*genetivus objectivus*) the Germans (*HHGR*, 220). In this, Hölderlin, who, as Heidegger emphasizes, "is not Greek, but the future of the Germans," is "originarily a beginner [*anfänglich ein Anfänger*] ... a beginner of that beginning, which even today, but already for a long time, waits without even having begun to be empowered" (*HHGR*, 255, 269). Precisely to the extent that Hölderlin is the poet of the Germans as a historical people still to come, he has not yet become a (or rather, *the*) power in the history of the German people. In Heidegger's words, his work "stands almost like a petrified projection [*Vorsprung*] into the Dasein of our people, as a veiled poetic foundation of our Being" (*HHGR*, 184). Now, this still veiled projection in Hölderlin's poetry of the historical Being or originary world of the Germans as a people, kindles the task of the philosopher: namely, to "conquer in a thinking manner [denkerische *Eroberung*]" this poetry by grasping "conceptually" that which the poet poetizes (*HHGR*, 5). As opposed to the task of thinking that arises in a debate with Greek thought (in which thought has to seek help from poetry and the originary world that it projects for the Greeks in order to illuminate early Greek philosophy), the current task of philosophy is to elucidate in a thinking mode the only great poetry in which the destiny of a people—the Germans—is sketched out and that, considering their position within Europe, concerns the destiny of Europe in its entirety. The thinkers, "heeding the spoken word and thinking of it, so that it may be properly interpreted and preserved ... help the poet" in his task as a beginner, by unfolding conceptually the originary world that he has founded (*HHGR*, 49). This task of assisting the poet derives, as we have seen, from the fact that the German people have not yet recognized in Hölderlin the poet who founded their historical and future Dasein. Until such recognition Hölderlin remains, as it were, a foreigner to the Germans.[10] If philosophy can set itself this task of assisting the poet, it is, first of all, because Hölderlin's poetry is not just any poetry but a thinking poetry (*denkende Dichtung*). However, as a task *of* philosophy, as a philosophical task, first and foremost, this turn to a poetry like that of Hölderlin must also have its grounds in philosophical thinking. Heidegger therefore writes: "If here there is a task for philosophy, then this task can only be determined by philosophy's own necessities, that is, from the Greek-German sending, according to which thinking enters on the basis of its own origin into the originary dialog with poetry and its distress" (*HHGR*, 151). Within the framework of its Greek-German sending, philosophy must enter into a dialogue with poetry, because Being, which philosophy thinks, is first founded in originary poetry and the originary language that emerges with it. But to the extent that thinking is not philosophy in the traditional, metaphysical sense but is in itself poetic, and, hence, poetizing thought (*dichtendes Denken*), thinking not only has its own necessities but a foundational role as well. This foundational role concerns, as we will see, the specific ways in which thinking thinks the originary world that the poet founds as the home of a people.

Since in *Introduction to Metaphysics* Heidegger leans on a work of thinking poetry that is a tragedy—Sophocles' *Antigone*—in order to illuminate pre-Socratic thinking of Being, a question imposes itself here: does the task of thinking Being as it has been founded in originary poetry not have the further goal of showing that, independently of genres, originary poetry is essentially tragic poetry? And consequently, does the task that characterizes thinking in the present age—a task that, according to Heidegger, derives from the still veiled foundation of another history for the German people in Hölderlin's poetry—not also consist in grasping the thus to be revealed beginning as one of "tragic Being [*tragisches Seyn*]"? Although the reference to a "heroism of reason" in the Vienna lecture provides the context for an occasional reference by Husserl to the tragic (as, for instance, when in a text from 1936 he alludes to "the tragedy of the vocation [*Tragik der Berufung*]" for "the great and genuine ethos" of a philosophical thinking that is radically self-responsible and, as I have shown, is the essence of the European *telos*), only in Heidegger does the tragic become an essential dimension of the task of a thinking and poetizing that concerns the founding and unfolding of the thought of Being that since Parmenides is the philosophical "idea" par excellence of the West (*C*, 299).[11] The expression "tragic Being" occurs with reference to Hölderlin's essay, "The Ground for Empedocles," where, according to Heidegger, the poet " speaks not only of his own poem on Empedocles, but of tragic poetry in general, and that means, of tragic Being" (*HHGR*, 118). In "The Anaximander Fragment" the experience of Being is explicitly linked to the tragic, on the condition, however, that *tragic* be understood in a specifically Greek way. Heidegger contends here that "the experience of beings in their Being which . . . comes to language [in this early fragment of Greek thought] is neither pessimistic nor nihilistic; nor is it optimistic. It is tragic. That is a presumptuous thing to say. However, we discover a trace of the essence of tragedy, not when we explain it psychologically or aesthetically, but rather when we consider its essential form, the Being of beings" (*EGT*, 44). If indeed "'the tragic' is not to be measured, as modern human beings think, according to the passion of which we can have a psychological 'lived experience' and that belongs to the person of genius, but rather according to the truth of being as a whole and in keeping with the simplicity in which it appears," then the dramatic action in a Greek tragedy is based on an experience of Being in which the truth of Being is taken to its end, i.e., experienced in all its extreme consequences (*HHI*, 103). In the lectures on Parmenides, Heidegger can therefore also submit that "there is only *Greek* tragedy and no other besides it. Only the essence of Being as experienced by the Greeks has this primordial character [*Anfänglichkeit*] that 'the tragic' becomes a necessity there" (*P*, 90). Strictly speaking, then, no modern tragedy is conceivable; but does this also exclude all "tragic" dimensions in Hölderlin's poetry, if indeed the latter poetically projects an originary world that would be binding for contemporary humanity? Needless to say, since the "tragic" is to be understood ontologically, rather than in contemporary, i.e., aesthetic or psychological terms, *tragic* would first have to refer to an experience of beings as a whole. Such an experience, however, whose presence in Hölderlin is, for Heidegger, beyond doubt, would not necessarily have to mean that the tragic nature of the originary world founded by Hölderlin's originary poetry would, even it could not be tragic in a modern sense, be necessarily tragic in a strict Greek sense: it could be tragic in an other, equally originary way. In any event, the turn in *Introduction to Metaphysics* to Sophocles' *Antigone* in order to clarify the thought of Being in Heraclitus and Parmenides serves first of all to bring to light the primarily historical character of Being in that Being is always the Being of a people as it has been founded by great poetry; but this turn by thought to *Antigone* serves also to drive home the idea that the Greek conception of Being is necessarily "tragic Being" and that any other projection of Being and of an originary world must in some sense be "tragic" as well.[12]

Insofar as poetry founds the Being of a people, poetry (and in privileged manner, tragedy) lays out an originary world—a world, indeed, that encompasses all the realms of what is: the heavens and the earth, gods and humans. In the lectures preceding his discussion of *Antigone* in the *Introduction to Metaphysics*, Heidegger holds that "the poetry by

Sophocles called *Antigone* is as poetry a founding of the whole of Greek Dasein since poetry as projection (rootage and salvation) of Being grounds the Dasein of human beings on the earth in sight of the gods. As a founding, poetry brings forth and sets into work the ground of the possibility for the human being to settle on the earth, between her and the gods—that is, to become historical, in other words, to be a people" (*HHGR*, 216). However, before I turn to the pages devoted to *Antigone* in the *Introduction to Metaphysics* in order to thread out the major articulations of this originary world, that is, how Being's irruption into all the domains of beings opens up the structures of a world that is the binding beginning for the Greeks as a people, one more brief glance at Hölderlin's leverage over Heidegger's interpretation of *Antigone* is needed.

In a 1939 essay entitled "'Andenken' und 'Mnemosyne'" Heidegger claims that "disguised by the Romanticism of 'Blut,' 'Boden,' 'Volkstum,' and 'Reich,'" Germans are unable to get a view of Hölderlin's poetry. He then highlights the strangeness (*Befremdlichkeit*) of this poetry, which—just like the "friends" in the poem "Remembrance," who leave the homely and the protected place of residence—"goes to the source" and "thinks ahead [*Vor-denken*]" into that which frightens (*schreckt*) ordinary human beings, namely, Being.[13] Heidegger adds: "The Saying of this 'thinking' as poetizing thinking denies us all evasion into anything known or comparable."[14] Indeed, within the history of Being, Hölderlin's poetry, even though it projects an originary world in which the Germans could be at home, represents a "*vor-zeitig-einziger Wendepunkt*," that is, a unique untimely turning point of "the exposure to, and into Being, an exposure that frees from beings." More precisely, this poetry is a turning point in which Being, or the true, becomes "*das Ent-setzende*," that which dislocates and throws one out of the ordinary and homely.[15] If Heidegger's interpretation of *Antigone* strikes us as strange, perhaps even horrifying the classical philologist, it is not least because of the ascendency of his Hölderlin commentaries over the interpretation in question. Indeed, Heidegger will argue not only that Sophocles' tragedy strikes us as strange but also that it represents the poetry of a relation between the Being-human and Being in which the human undergoes a radical dislocation from the realm of beings through his or her relation to Being—and, as a result of which, the human being that this poetry projects is the strangest of all beings, the most uncanny, in truth.

The section in *Introduction to Metaphysics* that Heidegger devotes to Sophocles' *Antigone*, more precisely, to the first choral ode, is not, as I have already pointed out, the sole occasion in which Heidegger discusses the tragedy in question.[16] Another crucial treatment of this tragedy occurs in the 1942 lectures in *Hölderlin's Hymn "The Ister."* Among the differences between the two treatments—some of which are listed here, first, in a very schematic way, before we return to them later—the most obvious is that compared to the earlier interpretation, the 1942 interpretation more or less takes the whole tragedy into account. If the recourse to poetry in the 1935 lectures serves to illuminate the pre-Socratic philosopher's conception of Being, and is thus primarily at the service of philosophical thinking, in the 1942 commentary philosophical interpretation seeks above all to tease out and articulate the grounding conception of Being in great poetry. By limiting itself now to "laying apart in a thinking manner [*denkerisch auseinandergelegt*]" what has been poetically said, philosophical interpretation retreats, it would seem, before what the poet says (*EHP*, 65; trans. mod.). A further important distinction concerns the scope of the two interpretations. Whereas the 1935 interpretation seeks to respond to the question of what and who Man is, according to the Greeks—Greek man, of course, but also the human being in general—in 1942 the focus is primarily on the singular figure of Antigone, who, as Heidegger remarks, is not only the eponymous heroine of the poem but "the purest poem herself [*das reinste Gedicht selbst*]" (*HHI*, 119; trans. mod.). Whereas in the *Introduction to Metaphysics* the human being is shown to be the most uncanny, now Antigone is said to be the uncanniest of the most uncanny in that she is authentically uncanny and thus represents the deepest understanding of humanity and of its destiny for the ancient Greeks. This distinction between inauthentic and authentic uncanniness, made by Heidegger in the discussion of *Antigone* in *Hölderlin's Hymn "The Ister,"* also shapes the outlines of the originary world that emerges from the readings of the tragedy in both interpretations. For this reason it will be necessary in the following delineation of the contours of the originary world as it is described in *Introduction to Metaphysics* to take also the complementary features—or, perhaps, the counterturning aspects—that emerge from the later interpretation into account.

Yet before we can turn to Heidegger's commentary of the first choral ode, in which the basic features of the originary world opened up by the poet for Greek humanity are to be found, a cautionary remark is warranted: contrary to what some critics have suggested, this world is in no way a whole, hale (*heile*), or wholesome world. In the conclusion to his commentary on the first choral ode Heidegger remarks that "in the unique urgency [*Not*] of their Dasein, [the Greeks] alone used only violence, and by doing so did not abolish the urgency but only augmented it; thus they won for themselves the fundamental condition of true historical greatness," but this is not to celebrate some unadulterated, healthy world (*IM*, 174–75). Even though, according to Heidegger, Hölderlin surpassed Friedrich Nietzsche in reconceiving the great age of the inception of Greek Dasein (*IM*, 133), as we proceed in the discussion of this world, the originary world opened up by the Greek poets for this Dasein, we might do well to remember Nietzsche's observation in "Homer's Contest" that to understand this world in "Greek fashion" means to shudder.[17] As Heidegger emphasizes in the lectures in *Hölderlin's Hymn "The Ister,"* the choral ode's depiction of the human being appears to keep itself "in general everywhere . . . merely to telling of the un-homely" (*HHI*, 109). Indeed, what the chorus explicitly says about the human being is that by venturing forth in all directions within the realms of beings, the human being comes to nothing and remains utterly homeless. All of the human's machinations by means of which he or she seeks to master beings only serve to encapsulate him or her in a world that "begets in itself its own un-essence, the versatility of many twists and turns, which in itself is the lack of ways out" (*IM*, 168). The world that thus emerges from the song is a world of seeming—one that is marked by a forgetting of Being. Such oblivion to Being shapes the originary world, if it does not even bring it about in the first place. Indeed, "The Anaximander Fragment" makes it quite clear that a world is based on the withdrawal of Being. Heidegger writes: "When Being keeps to itself in its destining, world suddenly and unexpectedly comes to pass." Without luminously holding to itself, that is, without an "*epoche* of Being"—*epoche* now understood in an ontological sense, and as a function of the history of Being, rather than as a phenomenological attitude—no world comes forth (*EGT*, 26–27). While the commentary of the ode in *Introduction to Metaphysics* is largely limited to depicting this rather bleak world of Greek humanity, the possibility of authentic unhomeliness that *Hölderlin's Hymn "The Ister"* evokes in the figure of Antigone is, at first sight at least, no less bleak since such authentic unhomeliness is "merely" an athomeness in the unhomely originary world of Greek humanity, one that has to be paid by death, as well.

Nevertheless, such authentic unhomeliness within this desolate world is its counterturning redeeming trait, that which thus completes the projection of the originary world occurring in the first choral ode.

The chorus's description of the human being and his or her relations to beings does not, according to Heidegger, amount to a primitive history of the beginning of humankind; hence it is not of the order of an anthropology. By contrast, Heidegger claims that "if [it is] anything at all, it is mythology" (*IM*, 166). In this song, he remarks, no determination of the human being as such—that is, in and from him- or herself alone—occurs. Nor are the various activities of humans of which the ode speaks to be understood as "an application of faculties that the human being has" (*IM*, 167). Rather, the human being is depicted in all his or her elementary relations to and within the basic dimensions of what is—that is, by way of all his or her doings or "machinations" through which that which is becomes mastered and is at the same time revealed as what it is. Furthermore, if the chorus reaches the conclusion that the human being is *to deinotaton*, the most uncanny, it is not only on the basis of his or her ways of relating to particular beings, and by extension, to beings as a whole, but above all because the chorus singles out the human being's most exorbitant and transgressive actions within the different realms of what is. In other words, the "poetic projection of Being and of the human essence" (*IM*, 169) that occurs in the first choral ode, by depicting the human being's most extreme relations (and that therefore reveal his or her essence, or way of being, within the various dimensions of what is) amounts to laying out the fundamental relational structures of the originary world granted by Being to one particular people—the Greeks. In contradistinction to the Husserlian conception of the life-world, whose structures pertain to humanity as such, the originary world that emerges from the chorus's intimate interlinking of beings and human being pertains, first and foremost, to the Greeks and only "mediately" to other humanities—in particular, the German people—who in order to find what is proper to them must, as we will see, first come to grips with this Greek conception of Being and being human that is essentially foreign to them.

According to the first of the three interpretive phases through which Heidegger seeks to establish in different respects what the whole ode is about, three decisive words draw his attention, since, according to his interpretation, they sustain the ode as a whole from within. The first key word is that "the human being is *to deinotaton*, the uncanniest of the uncanny [*das Unheimlichste des Unheimlichen*]" (*IM*, 159). Grasping the human being's humanity "from the most extreme limits and the most abrupt abysses of its Being," this characterization of man within the whole of the existent in which everything is uncanny (*deinon*), highlights, from the start, the human being's eccentricity within what is. Yet as Heidegger notes, uncanniness here is not to be understood "in the sense of an impression made on our emotional states" (*IM*, 161). Rather, devolving from the human being's fundamental ways of relating to what is, it is ontological in nature and concerns his or her essence or way of being.[18] But since "the uncanniest" can also be understood merely as a modification, that is, as a superlative form of uncanniness, Heidegger remarks that "the uncanniest is not the augmentation of the uncanny to the highest degree. It is what is one of a kind, within the uncanny [*der Artung nach das Einzigartige am Unheimlichen*]" (*IM*, 173). Only the human being is capable of being the uncanniest, that is, unique within the uncanny in terms of genre, because only the human being comports toward beings as such. Such comportment implies an understanding of Being, and thereby also the possibility of forgetting being, as a result of which the human being achieves, as we will see, what is the hallmark of the uncanniest, his homelessness. Heidegger concludes in *Hölderlin's Hymn "The Ister"* that "whatever is unhomely in its essence ... exceeds infinitely, that is, in essence, everything uncanny" (*HHI*, 84). For this same reason he characterizes the human being as being in essence "a *katastrophe*—a reversal that turns them away from their own essence" (*HHI*, 77). Indeed, the assertion that all beings are uncanny, and that the human being, however, is the most uncanny, rests on what is termed "the opposed confrontations of Being [*die gegenwendigen Aus-einander-setzungen des Seins*]" (*IM*, 159). These confrontational relations between Being and the human being are explicitly discussed in Heidegger's commentary on the final strophe of the song in terms of a confrontation of *dike* and *techne*. For the time being, let us only mention that the Greek word *deinon*'s own "uncanny ambiguity," which names, on the one hand, "the terrible in the sense of the overwhelming sway [*überwältigenden Waltens*]"—that is, "the violent [*das Gewaltige*], the overwhelming [being] the essential character of sway"— and, on the other hand, "the violent in the sense of the one who needs to use violence" evidences all by itself this confrontation between what is insofar as it *is*, and the human being (*IM*, 159–60). Whereas all that *is* is uncanny because in it the "overwhelming power" of "beings as a whole" or Being itself holds sway, the human being, who in one respect is part and parcel of the uncanny manifold of beings, also violently confronts it and hence is not only doubly uncanny but the uncanniest (*IM*, 160). "The human being is violence-doing not in addition to and aside from other qualities but solely in the sense that from the ground up and in his doing violence, he uses violence against the overwhelming" (*IM*, 160; trans. mod.). Heidegger concludes that "using violence is the basic trait not just of his doing but his Dasein"—it is the way of his Being, of being the there (*Da*), that is, the openness for Being to disclose itself (*IM*, 160). As will become clear from the second phase of Heidegger's interpretation of the choral ode, where the violent acts of the human being are spelled out in greater detail, "violence-doing [*Gewalt-tätigkeit*]" here is not to be taken in the usual sense of the expression but "in an essential sense" (*IM*, 160).

Although "violence" is a correct translation of the German word *Gewalt*, it misses all the connotations of *walten* gathered together by the prefix *Ge-*, especially the meaning of "to be at work," "to rule," or better, "to hold sway." The overwhelming violence of Being derives from its all-pervasiveness. Elaborating on what is said in the final strophe of the ode regarding the unifying trait of the two senses of *deinon* (the violence of the overwhelming sway of Being and the one of the violence-doer that is directed at Being), Heidegger has recourse to the fundamental Greek word *dike*—which he renders by "fittingness" (*Fug*) rather than, as is commonly the case, by "justice" or "norm"—to put the *deinon* as the overwhelming into relief. If Being overawes and does so violently, it is because it fits everything that is into a fitting arrangement according to determined directions.[19] "In all its domains and powers, the overwhelming, as regards its powerfulness, is fittingness" (*IM*, 171). Put differently, Being is violent and overwhelming because it gathers everything that is into a fitted and fitting whole. It follows from this that Being is violent as well because it is Being itself that, as we will see, urges the human being into violence-doing. In this commentary on the last strophe of the choral ode, Heidegger explains why all the human being's activities in the various domains of beings are in essence violent: "Violence, the violent, within which the doing of the violence-doer moves, is the whole circuit of the machination [*Machenschaft*], *to machanoen*, that is delivered over to him. We are not taking the word 'machination' in a derogatory sense.

With this word we are thinking something essential that announces itself in the Greek word *techne*" (*IM*, 169). Human activities, or doings, within all the domains of beings that make up the originary world drawn up by the choral song, are violent because they are "machinations." "Machinations" translates the Greek *to machanoen*, a word that refers in particular to strife and to skill in battle. Consequently, to understand the human being's doings within the various realms of beings and with regard to the overwhelming sway of Being as machinations is to suggest that these doings are forms of a violent struggle against the overwhelming. Machinations, however, presuppose the knowledge of *techne* and, hence, suggest the violent nature of that knowledge as well: "*Techne* means neither art nor skill, and it means nothing like technology in the modern sense. We translate *techne* as 'knowing'" (*IM*, 169). Machination as violence-doing is thus inherent to *techne* in its "genuine sense," that is, as the knowing it takes to master and to render subservient the beings that make up all the domains of the originary world by setting Being into work. Such knowing is violent in essence because it is constituted by a "looking out beyond [*Hinaussehen*] that which, in each case, is directly present at hand. In different ways and on different routes and in different domains, the Being-out-beyond [*Hinaussein*] sets to work in advance that which first gives to what is already present at hand its relative justification, its possible determinateness, and thus its limit. Knowing is the ability to set Being into work as something that in each case *is* in such and such a way" (*IM*, 169–70). Knowing in the sense of *techne* is violent as well because it arrests what transcends the present at hand, that is, Being, in particular beings, turning Being into the Being of those particular beings. As a creator (a *Schaffender* rather than a *Schöpfer*, or a genius in the image of a creator-god, whose activities are therefore not limited to the *polis* but include those on land and sea, as well as in the heavens), the human being's machinations render Being manifest by violently bringing it to stand in particular beings, in beings, consequently, that *are* (*als das seiende Sein*), in short, in works—the work of art being only the most eminent because the most immediate expression of such knowing.[20] Heidegger can thus conclude his elaboration on violence-doing: "Thus *techne* characterizes the *deinon*, the violence-doing, in its decisive basic trait; for to do violence is to need to use violence against the overwhelming: the knowing struggle [*das wissende Erkämpfen*] to set Being, which was formerly closed off, into what appears as beings" (*IM*, 170–71).

As Heidegger readily acknowledges, the translation of *deinon* as "uncanny" (*un-heimlich*) appears alien, and violent, and is, moreover, philologically speaking, wrong. But what nonetheless justifies such a translation is that this term *un-canny* permits an unraveling of that which, according to Heidegger, are the essential implications of the Greek characterization of Being and Being-human (which, however, the Greeks themselves did not articulate in explicit fashion). More precisely, if, as he argues in *Hölderlin's Hymn "The Ister,"* the semantic realm of *to deinon* is triple, signifying "the fearful, the powerful, the inhabitual," the German word *unheimlich* has the distinct privilege of rendering "the concealed ground of the unity of the manifold meanings of *deinon*, thus grasping *to deinon* itself in its concealed essence" (*HHI*, 64). The German word is thus able to name and think that for which the Greeks—who, as *Hölderlin's Hymn "The Ister"* emphasizes, "thought and spoke from out of the unsaid"—had no word, and which thus remained unthought (*HHI*, 107). Furthermore, by hyphenating *un-canny*, Heidegger does several things. First, he demarcates his use of the term from its familiar meanings, in particular, in romantic literature and, most likely, also in psychoanalysis. The "un-canny" is not of the order of an impression; it is not an inner or subjective affect caused by something inexplicable, such as the powerful or extraordinary. By hyphenating the word, he distinguishes his understanding of the term from that of Rudolf Otto as well, who, in *The Sacred*, had already translated the Greek word *deinos* as "the *uncanny*—in a word, the numinous."[21] Second, by writing the word in this manner, the un-canny, in the same way as all the hyphenated constructs in *Being and Time*, designates a total phenomenon, "what the *deinon* is, as it is in itself"; in particular, as the ontological condition of human Dasein as a being that from the outset is in-the-world, in other words, in an openness (*IM*, 161). Finally, and above all, the hyphen serves to highlight the privative character of the *un-* in *unheimlich*. Privation here is not negation in a metaphysical sense, for indeed, as Heidegger remarks in *Hölderlin's Hymn "The Ister,"* "the 'un-' in the un-homely does not express a mere lack or simply a shortcoming." "Whatever belongs to the 'un-' in the uncanny is of an essence other than that which we could ever grasp with the aid of negations that slide back and forth" (*HHI*, 85–86, 78). In a discussion in *Parmenides* of the word *lathon*, counter to the Greek word for truth, *aletheia*, it is significant that Heidegger translates *lathon* as that which is concealed and is secret, in German, *heimlich* (*P*,

22). As a consequence, *un-heimlich* must be understood from concealedness, thus referring to a privation of *Heimlichkeit*, that is, the secrecy and concealedness of athomeness, and hence as an exposure within an openness that, however, is meaningful only with respect to the athomeness of which it is stripped. Like the term *un-geheuer* or *das Un-geheuere*, which we discussed in the previous chapter and which Heidegger uses to indicate that "where . . . Being comes into focus, there the extra-ordinary [*das Nicht-Geheure*] announces itself," *un-heimlich*, too, has to be understood literally, that is, as being deprived, or depriving, of a home—in short, in the sense of being unhomely, *a-topos*, *a-oikos*—to which, however, the privativum *un-* inexorably continues to link it (*P*, 101). Hyphenating the word thus allows Heidegger to link "uncanny" (more incisively than he had already done in chapter 40 of *Being and Time*) to "not-being-at-home [*das Nicht-zu-Hause-sein*]," that is, to being "unhomely."[22] To sum up: by translating *deinon* as *un-heimlich*, Heidegger seeks to name what he believes the Greeks implicitly connected with this word but did not articulate as such, namely, a radical defamiliarization or "unhoming." Here is what Heidegger himself has to say about the term: "We understand the un-canny as that which throws one out of the 'canny,' that is, the homely [*Heimische*], the accustomed, the usual, the unendangered. The unhomely [*Unheimische*] does not allow us to be at home [*heimisch*]. Therein lies the overwhelming" (*IM*, 161).[23] If everything that *is* is uncanny, it is because it is not at home and does not offer a secure abode in which to be with itself. What renders the manifold un-canny in the sense of unhomely is Being, which holds sway in what is, and hence deprives it of any homeliness with itself. What is overwhelming with respect to the manifold of what is is precisely this un-homing that results from the Being of beings. Heidegger continues: "But human beings are the uncanniest, not only because they spend their lives essentially in the midst of the un-canny understood in this sense [that is, as the unhomely], but also because they step out, move out of the limits that at first and for the most part are accustomed and homely, because as those who do violence, they overstep the limits of the homely, precisely in the direction of the uncanny in the sense of the overwhelming" (*IM*, 161). In addition to existing among beings that are themselves uncanny, and in which one cannot be at home because of the overwhelming sway of Being, human beings *themselves* leave whatever may seem homely and familiar to them for the sake of the overwhelming, that is, ultimately, for the sake of unhomeliness. But when Heidegger adds that as a violence-doer he also oversteps (*überschreitet*) the limits of the homely, he also hints at the human being's capacity for *hubris*, insolence, excessive pride, and eccentric deeds. Such "presumptuousness [*Vermessenheit*] towards beings" is one more reason why he is *to deinotaton* (*HHI*, 115). To be *to deinotaton*, in the sense of having no home within what is, of moving violently out of everything homely, and even of overstepping all limits, is "the basic trait of the human essence" according to the Greeks, "the authentic *Greek* definition of humanity" (*IM*, 161).[24]

Two further key words in the ode, which Heidegger adopts from Hölderlin's translation of *Antigone* (whose own rendering of these words in German, as Pöggeler and others have pointed out, was based on the punctuation from an old translation of Sophocles' tragedies in which the two components of the words in question, rather than being opposed, are apposed to one another), namely, the oxymoronic compounds *pantoporos aporos* and *hupsipolos apolis*, serve to draw out the basic implications of the human being's stated un-canniness.[25] According to the second keyword, or statement, which pertains to one dimension of beings within which humans dwell—nature, in short—the human being is *pantoporos aporos*. Commenting on a line from the middle of the second strophe—"Everything trying out, underway; untried, with no way out he comes to Nothing [*Ueberall hinausfahrend unterwegs, erfahrungslos ohne Ausweg kommt er zum Nichts*]"—Heidegger observes: "Everywhere the human being makes routes for himself; in all the domains of beings, of the overwhelming sway, he ventures forth [*wagt er sich vor*], and in this very way he is flung from every route" (*IM*, 162; trans. mod.). Let us bear in mind that *poros* names the passage, or passage through, to something. Indeed, the human being's violent response to the unhoming sway of Being is to venture forth into all the distinct realms of beings by (violently) fraying, or clearing, paths for oneself into or through all these realms in order to get power over them and to establish therein a home. In the interpretation of the first choral ode in *Hölderlin's Hymn "The Ister"* Heidegger puts much greater weight on the fact that by autonomously venturing forth and being everywhere under way, human beings are seeking to become homely among beings. Skillfully transforming and making all the realms of beings their own, they seek "to find their own vicinity through such realms. The homely is sought after and striven for in the violent activity of passing through that which is inhabitual with respect to sea and earth, and yet in such passage the homely is precisely not attained" (*HHI*, 73). Thus, rather than achieving "entry into their own essence," all the human being's attempts to reach everywhere, notwithstanding the fact that they seem to "'come to something,'" end up coming "to nothing, because they remain stuck with particular beings, and fail to grasp their being or essence in such beings. The 'nothing' to which they come is that which, turning counter to being, directly excludes human beings altogether from being." Breaking into all the realms of what is, and thus being "'at home' on every passageway through beings," human beings not only leave anything homely behind, but they are thoroughly unhomely (*HHI*, 75–76). The human being becomes routeless, wayless, hence also without a way out from any of the ways in which he or she is under way—*aporos*, without a way out. If human beings are said to be the uncanniest, it is neither because they "tr[y] what is" in the entirety of its un-canniness nor because, in venturing forth into all the domains of what is, they unhome themselves, but above all because in venturing forth to the point of becoming radically homeless, they are "thrown out of all relation to the homely" as such and, consequently, face the risk of ruin, or Nothing (*IM*, 162).

Whereas the second keyword of the ode refers to the human being's relations to all the domains of beings, the third prominent word speaks of his or her doings within "the ground and place of human Dasein itself ... the *polis*" (*IM*, 162). The human being is not only the uncanniest because he or she violently frays paths into all the domains of beings (with the result that the human being runs the risk of losing all relation to the homely); his or her actions within the domain that seemingly is his or her own, and which is the site in which all the routes that he or she cuts into the realms of beings cross—namely, the *polis*—expose him or her to the risk of becoming *apolis*, without a site of his or her own. The third fundamental word that the third strophe of the choral ode evokes is thus that the human being is also *hupsipolis apolis*. Now the *polis*, in Heidegger's interpretation, is not, in addition to the regions called up in the first strophe and counterstrophe of the ode, merely another region of beings; nor is it the state or the city state, as the term is commonly translated. The *polis* is nothing as historically determinate as what the Romans called *res publica*, or the "state" familiar to the moderns. In *Parmenides* Heidegger explains: "The *polis* is neither city nor state and definitely not the fatal mixture of these two inappropriate characterizations. Hence the *polis* is not the notorious 'city state' but is, rather, the settling of the place of the history of Greek humanity [*die Ortschaft des Ortes der Geschichte des Griechentums*], neither city nor state, but indeed the abode [*Stätte*] of the essence of this humanity" (*P*, 89–90). It is "the ground and place of human Dasein itself" (*IM*, 162). According to the *Parmenides* lectures, the *polis* refers to that "in which the humanity of the Greeks has the center of its Being [*die Mitte seines Seins*]." It is "the pole, the place around which everything appearing to the Greeks as a being turns in a peculiar way," hence, "the abode, gathered into itself, of the unconcealedness of beings" (*P*, 89–90). Heidegger's rendering of *polis* by "site" (*Stätte*) calls for a remark. In *Hölderlin's Hymn "The Ister"* he observes that one should not presume that the Greeks, even though they lived in the *polis*, "were also in the clear as to the essence of the *polis*." Consequently, to understand what the *polis* is in a Greek sense, it is necessary "to think more Greek than the Greeks themselves"—that is, in a way distinct from late reflections on the *polis* and politics by Plato and Aristotle, in other words, at the end of the great Greek era, whose thought, according to Heidegger, may not be adequate at all to the question of the *polis*. To do justice to the essence of the *polis*, and to think this essence in the Greek sense by thinking "more Greek than the Greeks themselves," "we ourselves must, in relation to ourselves, think more German than all Germans hitherto," Heidegger declares (*HHI*, 80–81). Only the German word *Stätte* (site) renders the essence of the *polis*, whose meaning the Greeks themselves genuinely mistook, in an adequate fashion. What, then, is the *polis* as the site—as the ground and place of historical Dasein? The *polis* is the open site, "the site of the abode [*Aufenthaltes*] of human history that belongs to humans in the midst of beings" (*HHI*, 82)—the *there*, the *Da* (of historical Dasein)—from within which the assignment of what the domains of beings, through which the human being cuts roads, are *as such*, and from which, and with respect to which, the cutting of the roads into these domains occurs. The *polis* is the stand that human beings (as a historical people) occupy in the middle of beings insofar as human beings understand Being; it thus represents the particular way in which they are amidst beings. Linking *polis* to *polos*, Heidegger holds that the *polis* is perhaps "that realm and locale around which everything question-worthy and uncanny turns in an exceptional sense. The *polis* is *polos*, that is, the pole, the swirl in which and around which everything turns" (*HHI*, 81). As the site "in which all beings and all relational comportment towards beings is gathered," from whose "stead there springs forth whatever is granted [*gestattet*] and whatever is not, what is order and what is disorder, what is fitting and [what] is unfitting," the *polis* is not only not to be understood from the political in a modern sense; it is, as we have seen, neither state nor city (*HHI*, 86, 82). Indeed, the *polis* extends well beyond the limits of a city or state; it reaches as far as all human beings' violent attempts to cut roads through the various domains of beings go. "The *polis* is the site within whose expansive realm every *poros* moves," and it therefore extends to the limits of what a historical people experiences as world (*HHI*, 89). As the site from which and with respect to which all beings—as well as the whole of a historical people's relational comportments to beings— becomes decided, the *polis* is indeed, as Heidegger repeatedly suggests, the question-worthy (*das Frag-würdige selbst*) par excellence (*HHI*, 81). To be within this site is first of all to use violence in creating this site and what belongs to it. By *only* being thinkers, poets, priests, or rulers (*only*, that is, by uniquely and in an originary fashion grounding the thinking, poetry, relation to the gods, and rule that opens the site for the historical Dasein of a people), thinkers, poets, priests, and rulers are violence-doers who "use violence . . . and become those who rise high in historical Being as creators, as doers" (*IM*, 163). But because, as Heidegger remarks in his lectures on "The Ister," "the *polis* is the site of beings, it also contains the most far-ranging extremes in terms of the possibilities of all human comportment towards beings, and thus of being unhomely" (*HHI*, 95). If the *polis* is the questionworthy par excellence, it is also because it is the site of daring, venturing, or inevitable risk. In his commentary on the final strophe of the choral song, Heidegger writes: "The knower fares into the midst of fittingness, draws Being into beings [in the 'draft'], and yet can never surmount the overwhelming. Thus the knower is thrown this way and that between fittingness and un-fittingness [*Unfug*], between the wretched and the noble. Every violent taming of the violent is either victory or defeat. Both throw one out of the homely, each in a different way, and they first unfold, each in a different way, the dangerousness of the being that he has won or lost" (*IM*, 171–72). Violence-doing can never hope to surmount the violence of the overwhelming because the human being as a being in the midst of what is is part and parcel of it. But whether violence-doing is victorious to the extent that it fits fittingness, or whether it is defeated by the unfittingness produced by hubristic acts, in both cases what violence-doing accomplishes is dangerous. Both of these extremes lead to the un-homing of the human being, although in different ways. Both are "menaced by perdition" (*IM*, 172). In his commentary on the last strophe Heidegger does not linger on the perdition that strikes the one who engages in hubristic action (probably because, in an overweening and audacious way, this person has already forfeited the overwhelming from the outset). Instead, Heidegger proceeds immediately to a discussion of the perdition that awaits the creator, or rather, the doer (*der Schaffende*):

> The one who is violence-doing, the creative one, who sets out into the unsaid, who breaks into the un-thought, who compels what has never happened and makes appear what is unseen, this violence-doing one stands at all times in daring [*tolma*]. Insofar as he dares the surmounting of Being, he must risk the assault of un-beings, the *me kalon*, dis-integration, un-constancy, unstructure, and unfittingness. The higher the peak of historical Dasein rises, the more gaping is the abyss for the sudden plunge into the unhistorical, which then only flails around in a confusion that has no way out and at the same time has no site. (*IM*, 172)

Even the doer whose violence-doing fits Being, and is used by it, runs the inevitable risk of perdition, since the beings in which he sets Being to work (and thus surmounts Being)—with respect to which everything else increases in its being—cannot but provoke the assault of nonbeing, which triggers the disintegration of the world thus created. Furthermore, by rising high in the *polis*, such elevation necessarily causes a gaping abyss to open that only grows deeper the higher the creators rise. Indeed, rising high in the site of human Dasein, the creators, precisely to the extent that they ground the very site of historical Dasein, throw themselves out of this site: "Rising high in the site of history, they also become *apolis*, without city and site, lonesome, un-canny, with no way out amidst beings as a whole, and at the same time without ordinance and limit, without structure and fittingness [*Fug*], because they *as* creators [*Schaffende*] must first ground all this in each case" (*IM*, 163). As a matter of fact, "the *polis* is . . . not some indifferent space that in turn admits of the empty possibilities of 'towering high' and of downfall; rather, it is the essence of the *polis* to thrust one into excess and to tear one into downfall, and in such a way that the human being is destined and fitted into both these counterturning possibilities and must be these two possibilities themselves" (*HHI*, 86). It follows from this that the originary world projected by Sophocles' tragedy for Greek Dasein, a world in which the human being frays paths through all the domains of what is, intent on making it a habitable home for him- or herself, and in which poets, thinkers, statesmen, and so forth seek to master Being by setting it into works that open up a world in which every being is more in being (in that it here appears as what it is as such), the human being either comes to nothing and/or plunges into "site-less confusion [*stättelosen Wirniss*]" (*IM*, 172; trans. mod.), in short, into disastrous unhomeliness and chaos. Furthermore, when Heidegger submits that "human beings do not 'have' the[se] possibilities in addition and extrinsic to themselves, rather their essence consists in being those who, in ascending within the site of their essence, are at the same time without site," the implication is that the creators of the *polis*, who as *Schaffende* (i.e., doers or workers), are not the only ones determined in essence by the unhomely but that rather everyone who participates in the site in question is (*HHI*, 86). Although human beings cut themselves off from the historical site of human dwelling precisely insofar as they dwell in it—rather than on account of some impious deeds or sacrilegious acts of daring that would only put the safe abode they have secured for themselves at risk—the danger of hubristic transgression, although Heidegger does not explicitly allude to it here, is clearly part and parcel of the human being's extreme un-canniness.

Within the framework in which we approach Heidegger's commentary on the first choral ode—namely, regarding the outlines of the originary world that emerge from the song—the second phase of his interpretation of the un-canniness of the human being, in which he seeks to demonstrate how the poem "unfolds" or specifies the domains into which the human being ventures forth, as well as what these activities within the site of historical dwelling amount to, is especially important. According to Heidegger, the entire poem is not engrossed in an exhaustive description and clarification of the domains and behavior of human beings. Nor is it, I would add, a phenomenological description of the elemental domains and activities pertaining to humans that would make up the primitive core of the life-world that then could serve to establish the pure, ideal, and universal structures of these domains and activities. Rather, as Heidegger asserts, "this is a poetic projection of human Being on the basis of its extreme possibilities and limits" (*IM*, 165). By sketching out the elemental features of Being-human from humanity's extreme possibilities and limits, these domains and respective activities appear as the constituents of a poetic or mythological figuration of an originary world that outlines the relations between Being and Being-human, relations that are, according to the Greeks, decisive and binding for human beings. Furthermore, since this understanding of the human on the basis that the individual *is* (that is, in relation to Being, a conception that shows the human being to be the un-canniest of all beings insofar as he or she is homeless to the point of putting the very relation to what is homely at risk) is a historical definition of the human (in that, apart from having been binding for Greek self-understanding, it is also the forgotten matrix of Europe and the West), the thoughtful poetic staging of the structures of this originary world is something that continues to speak to Europe and the West, to whose originarity (*Anfänglichkeit*) both must respond in order to find a world that will be binding for them.

The first domains into which man ventures forth are, according to the choral ode, the sea and the earth. The sea is described in its overwhelming elemental nature, and the "breakaway" of the human who gives up firm land and ventures forth into the "superior power of the sea's placeless flood" is called "a breaking forth upon the groundless waves" (*IM*, 164). The human being's relation to the earth is portrayed as a "restless break-in to the indestructible sway of the earth" into "the calm (*Ruhe*) of [its] growth" and the tireless dispensation of its riches, a violent breaking up of the earth with plows (*IM*, 164). Finally, into "life which revolves within itself," "the humans cast their snares and nets; they tear this life away from its own order, enclose it in their paddocks and pens, and force it beneath the yoke" (*IM*, 165). Breaking forth and breaking up, capturing and subjugating, these are the actions by which the violence-doer confronts the overwhelming power of the sea, the earth, and the animal. But Heidegger also calls attention to the fact that by doing violence to the sea, the earth, and the animal, the violence-doer allows what is overwhelming about these things "to break into openness in all its excessive violence" (*IM*, 166). In other words, within this openness they become what they are—regions and beings within a world in the first place.

If this first domain into which the human being frays routes is that of the overwhelming that *surrounds* (*umwaltet*) him or her, the second domain, which the second strophe elicits, *pervades* the human beings in its sway (*durchwaltet*). This second realm of beings, which human beings have "to take over expressly as the beings that they themselves are," concerns the overwhelming violence of language, understanding, passion, and building (*IM*, 166). Even though language, understanding, passion, and building seem to be mere human attributes or powers that the human being takes up and uses, they belong to the overwhelming in the same way as the sea, the earth, and the animal. Indeed, rather than being the inventor of language, understanding, mood, and building, the human being must discipline and surmount the violent forces of this kind of overwhelming by doing violence as well—that is, by way of "the violence-doing of poetic saying, of thoughtful projection, of constructive building, of state-creating action" (*IM*, 167). If the breaking forth, breaking up, capturing, and subjugating of which the first strophe speaks amounts "in itself [to] the first opening of beings *as* sea, *as* earth, *as* animal," this is so because "a breaking-forth and breakup happen only insofar as the powers of language, of understanding, of mood, and of building are themselves surmounted in doing violence" (*IM*, 167). The violence to which human beings resort in language, understanding, constructing, and building is intrinsically tied into the violent acts of laying out paths into the beings that envelop humanity in their sway. Indeed, the violence-doing in the domain that overwhelms the human being by pervading him or her allows him or her to discipline and shape "the violent forces by virtue of which beings disclose themselves as such, insofar as the human being enters into them. This disclosedness of beings is the violence that the human being has to surmount in order to be himself first of all—that is, to be historical in doing violence in the midst of beings" (*IM*, 167).

Before further elaborating on the originary world whose essential dimensions are progressively coming into view, let us bear in mind that this world is the world of the Being of the un-canniest, that is, the human being. In the second phase of his commentary, Heidegger seeks to build up this Being in its essential forms. The un-canniness of violence-doing—that is, its lack of a way out—can only be fully grasped in light of the intimate connection that exists between using violence in language, understanding, constructing, and building, and the violence of laying out paths into the beings that surround the human in their sway. Heidegger notes that human beings "not having a way out . . . are continually thrown back on the paths that they themselves have laid out; they get bogged down in their routes, get stuck in ruts, and by getting stuck they draw in the circle of their world, get enmeshed in seeming, and thus shut themselves out of Being. In this way they turn around and around within their own circle" (*IM*, 168). The human beings' hopelessness, or lack of having a way out of the ways they fray themselves through all the realms of what is, is consolidated by the fact that the human being, insofar as he or she deems to master these activities, is a violence-doer in language, understanding, constructing, and building. As a consequence, "what [these powers] yield to humans immediately is merely the inessential, and thus they drive humans out and keep them out of their own essence" (*IM*, 166–67). If the use of violence in language, understanding, constructing, and building cocreates the paths that humans lay out into the elementary realms of beings, and if, furthermore, this violence brings the beings into which the human breaks forth, and which he or she breaks up, or which he or she captures and subjugates, into what they are, then this is an openness that is predicated on seeming. Consequently, the world that the human being begets is one in which he or she is stuck, as if in an imprisoning circle. In his or her own circle, the human being who, according to the chorus, "is not at home [*uneinheimisch*] in his own essence" (*IM*, 167) and hence uncanny, "turn[s] around and around," and "turn[s] aside everything that threatens this circuit. . . . The violence-doing, which originally creates the routes, begets in itself its own un-essence, the versatility of many twists and turns, which in itself is the lack of ways out, so much so that it shuts itself out from the way of meditation on the seeming within which it drifts around" (*IM*, 168). The only thing at which the human being's violence-doing shatters is death. In the face of death it becomes unmistakably clear that ultimately, the human being has no way out. Death is "this un-canny thing, which sets us simply and suddenly out from everything homely once and for all," because it "over-ends [*über-endet*] all completion, and over-limits [*über-grenzt*] all limits" (*IM*, 168–69; trans. mod.) in that, from the beginning, death outdoes all ends and all enclosing limits, including that of the circle of the human being's own making in which he or she turns around and around. Because the human being is incapable of mastering the undoing that characterizes the Nothing, or death, "being-here (Da-sein) is the happening of uncanniness [*die geschehende Un-heimlichkeit selbst*]" as such (*IM*, 169).

At this point in his commentary, Heidegger makes the following observation: "With the naming of *this* violent and uncanny thing, the poetic projection of Being and of the human essence sets its own limits for itself" (*IM*, 169). In other words, in the concluding strophe of the ode no further powers will be summoned. Instead, the final strophe merely takes back the whole of what has been said so far into its basic trait, namely, "the unitary, reciprocal relation between the two senses of *deinon*" (*IM*, 169). But by evoking death, the poetic projection of Being and Being-human—that is, of the originary world—sets itself into limits in still another sense, since the poetic projection shows itself to be that of a world of human un-canniness and unhomeliness, one that finds its limits in death as that un-canniness that overends the intrinsic circularity of being without a way out or an end. The world of seeming inscribed within the originary world projected by the choral ode, and in which the human is shut out from Being is, from the start, overended and overlimited by the Nothing. The originary world is in no way simply a whole or hale (*heile*) world, since it comports a world of seeming fraught by unhomeliness and hopelessness. But this world finds its limits in death, which at the same time also opens up a possibility for a meditation on the seeming in which man drifts around, and hence on Being and Being-human—by which, contrapuntally, another dimension of this originary world comes into view.

While discussing the way man catches and subjugates "the flock of birds in the air, the animal life in the water, the bull and stallion in the mountains," Heidegger, in passing as it were, makes an observation about living creatures that warrants our attention: "The living thing, lightly dreaming, whose cycle of life reverberates in itself and in its environs, constantly renews itself, streaming out over itself in ever new forms, and yet it remains in its own *single* route, it is familiar with the place where it spends the night and roams" (*IM*, 164–65). Let us remind ourselves that after having argued, in "Letter on Humanism," that although they knew neither of a logic nor of a physics, the thinkers before the school of Plato thought "*phusis* in a depth and breath that no subsequent 'physics' was ever again able to attain," Heidegger adds that "the tragedies of Sophocles—provided such a comparison is at all permissible—preserve [*bergen*] the *ethos* in their sagas more primordially than Aristotle's lectures on 'ethics.'" The "Letter on Humanism" recalls that in Greek, "*Ethos* means abode, dwelling place. The word names the open region in which man dwells" (*BW*, 232–33). Its oldest meaning is that of the haunts or abodes of animals; in Homer, for example, it is the accustomed place in which the horses spent the night. According to the choral ode, the human being, who is permanently under way, with no way that is his or her own, destroys the habitat—the *ethos*—of the animal with "snares and nets," "tear[ing] this life away from its own order, [and] enclos[ing] it in their paddocks and pens, and forc[ing] it beneath the yoke," thus throwing the living things out from the "single route" that is their own (*IM*, 165). The human being thus destroys the *ethos* of living things, and he or she, who is permanently under way with no way out, having no place of his or her own, is also obviously without an abode, without an *ethos*. As a violence-doer in the face of the overwhelming power of Being, the human being who constantly breaks away from any place of his or her own—and who as a result is a thoroughly homeless being—is in the strict sense of the word without an *ethos*. Even as the creator of the site from which, and in view of which, all his or her actions of breaking forth and breaking up, of capturing and of subjugating, take place, the human being becomes *a-polis*, without a site.

This Greek sense of Being-human, which arises in early Greece and sets the stage for Europe and the West, is itself uncanny, precisely in that it shows that to *be* is to be homeless. Let me also emphasize that ultimately, the un-canniness of Greek Being cuts all the ties of this conception of Being to its factual Greek foundation. It is therefore a conception that not only has a fundamentally universal appeal, although not in the sense of being abstractly applicable to everyone but in the sense that the very un-canniness of this conception is what allows a particular people (such as the Germans) to relate to it as the other in a confrontation with which this people can possibly accomplish a mode of Being of its own. But before we can show that this concept of what and who the human is insofar as he or she *is*—that is, insofar as he or she stands in a relation to Being—namely, as a being without an *ethos*, is not yet—as the reference to the limits that death imposes on the human beings' world of seeming suggests—the whole story of what began in Greece and thus became the legacy of the West, we have first to return to the site in which all the routes frayed by human beings into the domains of beings cross—the *polis*.

As we have already seen, by eliciting the *polis*, and the human being's doings within it, Sophocles does not just add one more realm to the domains of being into which the uncanniest cuts his roads. The activities that characterize the *polis* do not form "a special or isolated region of human activity" (*HHI*, 94). But by evoking the *polis* subsequently to the portrayal of the sea and the earth, the choral ode also implies that it does "not intend the things it names in a merely geographical or geological way," that is, as what we would today call "natural phenomena" (*IM*,

163–64). Nor are all the roads that the human being frays into these various domains to be understood as merely biologically and anthropologically determined activities. Indeed, the entirety of the activities and occasionings undertaken by human beings, whether they concern so-called natural phenomena or more specifically political activities, is historical, and has "in every respect the *polis* as its site, as the locale to which it belongs" (*HHI*, 94). Indeed, as Heidegger's commentary of Aristotle's *Politics* demonstrates, only "Being-in-the-*polis*" (and the coimplicated Being-with-others) represents "the human being's authentic life" insofar as such being realizes "*the* human potentiality for being [*Seinsmöglichkeit*]" without which he or she would not be properly human.[26] As the "the essential abode [*Wesensstätte*] of historical man," that is, as "the 'where' [*das Wo*]" "wherein the Being of man in its relation to beings as a whole has gathered itself," the *polis* is the site of the historical unconcealment and concealment of the world destined to the Greeks as a people (*P*, 95–96). All the domains into which the human being ventures forth, and all of one's activities—all the machinations (*techne*) that the chorus attributes to the human being—are determined from within and with respect to the *polis*, that is, the site of concealment and unconcealment, in short, of the happening of truth. In other words, all these activities are primarily activities by which what is is brought into the open of the world as precisely this or that. Heidegger's remark that in the choral ode "the 'sea' is said as if for the first time" (*IM*, 164) equally obtains for earth and sky. By breaking forth and breaking into these domains, by capturing and subjugating all that lives, the un-canny allows the overwhelming nature of all these domains—as well as of the living things—to break into openness, to appear within the historical site of the polis as what they are as such.

Debating the myth of *Er* in *Politeia* by which Plato concludes his elaborations on the *polis*, Heidegger, in *Parmenides*, takes up the concept of *politeia*—a concept commonly translated as "constitution" (*Verfassung*) of the state. However, consistent with the Greek understanding of *politeia* as the political form of life (*bios politikos*) and the rights enjoyed by the *polites*, Heidegger defines *politeia* as the way of being of the *polis* (*wie die* polis *west*), that is, as that which the *polis* properly is considering the totality of its essential relations (*Wesensbezüge*). He writes that "*politeia* means first, in the language of everydayness, the 'life' belonging to a *polis* and determined by it, the dealings in it, and then correspondingly means the very structure [*Fassung*] of the polis in general, from which can then be discerned something like a 'constitution' [*Verfassung*]" (*P*, 95). Although in the language of everydayness *politeia* is said to mean at first "the 'life' belonging to a polis and determined by it," let me emphasize the word *life*, which, by being placed between quotation marks, is also set aside for something more essential. The *polis* that the first choral ode evokes is not, for Heidegger, the space of politics in the modern sense, according to which the political "is experienced in a 'technical' manner" in that it represents "the technical and historiographical fundamental certainty of all action" and consciousness (*HHI*, 94). Nor is it simply the public space of interaction and interlocution of free people. Rather, as should be evident from what we have seen so far, the *polis* is the originary world itself, from which all relations to the powers of the overwhelming emerge, a world anterior even to the public space of the *vita activa* that Hannah Arendt associated with the *polis*. Furthermore, since the *polis*, thus understood, belongs to a poetic projection, the "life" that belongs to this originary world is of an order other than that of the life of the life-world in the Husserlian sense. Indeed, *politeia*, as the way the *polis* exists, represents, qua site of unconcealment and concealment of what is, the originary world or, what amounts to the same thing, the *Da* of historical Dasein as it arises in the poetic projection of the historical being of Greek humanity. The life that characterizes it is thus that of the *being* of a historical Dasein.[27] As the site of unconcealment and concealment, "all the most extreme counter-essences, and, therein all excesses, to the unconcealed and to beings, i.e., counter-beings in the multiplicity of their counter-essence" as well must therefore also hold sway in the essential site of being that is the *polis*. Therein lies hidden the primordial ground, Heidegger remarks in *Parmenides*, "of that feature Jacob Burckhardt presented for the first time in its full bearing and manifoldness: the frightfulness, the horribleness, the atrociousness [which is part and parcel] of the Greek *polis*. Such is the rise and the fall of man in his historical abode of essence—*hupsipolis*—*apolis*—far exceeding abodes, homeless, as Sophocles (*Antigone*) calls man. It is not by chance that man is spoken of in this way in Greek tragedy" (*P*, 90).

At this juncture, let us again remind ourselves of Heidegger's contention that the thinker unfolds what has been founded by the thinking poet—namely, a poetic conception of Being, and with it an originary world for a historical people. Undoubtedly, Heidegger has been engaged in such an unfolding throughout the two phases of his interpretation of the first choral ode of *Antigone*. If a third phase of interpretation is warranted, however, it is clearly because unfolding the poetized in a thinking manner is not the only task of thinking. Heidegger remarks, especially in his second reading of the tragedy in *Hölderlin's Hymn "The Ister,"* that the Greek poets leave much unsaid: Being is not named as such in *Antigone*; it remains unsaid, or what is more, the saying of the choral ode "first poetizes [Being] into the unsaid" (*HHI*, 118). If in fact Sophocles' tragedy (and Hölderlin's hymn "The Ister" as well) describes the human being's attempt to become at home and to find a world for him- or herself by violently cutting paths through all domains of beings (an attempt that comes to nothing since he is merely pursuing beings), the *deinon*, or rather, the *to deinotaton*, may lend itself to still another interpretation, a thinking interpretation, one that spells out explicitly what in the poetic saying remained unsaid. After the explication in the first two phases of the interpretation of "what is directly said in the poetry," the interpretation, Heidegger claims, rather than being at its end, "stands for the first time at the inception. The authentic interpretation must show what does not stand there in the words and which is nevertheless said" (*IM*, 173). Although such an authentic interpretation must admittedly have recourse to violence, since it exceeds philological exegesis and therefore appears "unscientific," the third phase of authentic interpretation is far from arbitrary. As is evident, especially from the 1942 lectures, to show in a thinking manner "what does not stand there in the words and which is nevertheless said" is justified by what Heidegger calls the knowledge of the chorus—the *phronein* from out of which everything that the choral song says about the uncanny and the human being as the uncanniest is spoken.

At the risk of repeating what has been established so far, let me turn to the third phase of the interpretation of the choral song and follow its argument step by step. Circling back to the point made at the end of the second phase, namely, that the uncanniness of the uncanny—that is, its uniqueness in kind—lies in the counterturning movement of the overwhelming sway of Being and the human being's violence-doing, or more precisely, "in the oppositional [*gegenwendigen*] relation of *dike* and *techne*," Heidegger again recalls that "the possibility [that] arises of plunging into what has no way out and no site: perdition" (*IM*, 173) is intrinsically linked to this opposition or counterturning. Such perdition is not accidental, that is, merely the result of the violence-doer's failure to succeed in a particular act of violence. "Instead, this perdition holds sway and lies in wait fundamentally in the opposition between the overwhelming and doing violence" (*IM*, 173). In fact, such perdition is not only unsparing; it is even necessary. In Heidegger's words: "Doing violence *must* shatter against the excessive violence [*Übergewalt*] of Being, as long as Being holds sway in its essence, as *physis*, as emerging sway," for indeed, the violence-doer is one being among beings (*IM*, 173). Undoubtedly, if the chorus in the song in question unfolds a poetic projection of an originary world, this very world, in which the human being only comes to perdition, is definitely a dismal one. Not only is it not a hale or wholesome world, but it is, to again summon Burckhardt's words, a thoroughly frightful, horrible, and atrocious world. However, Heidegger's emphasis on the verb *must* in the statement "doing violence *must* shatter against the excessive violence of Being" indicates that this atrociously dismal world may be much more complex than it appears at first sight. Indeed, apart from signifying the inexorable nature of shattering, the italicized verb suggests yet another meaning—a counterturning meaning, as it were—of this necessity. This other meaning of the necessity of shattering comes to view in Heidegger's remark that it "can subsist only insofar as what must shatter is urged [*genötigt wird*] into Being-here [*Dasein*]. But the human being is urged into such Being-here, thrown into the urgency of such Being, because the overwhelming as such, in order to appear as such, in order to appear in its sway, requires [*braucht*] the site of openness for itself" (*IM*, 173–74). To put it another way, the necessity for Dasein to shatter derives from its fundamental role as the site of openness for Being. The inevitability of this shattering is not only because all machinations ultimately fail in the face of the overwhelming but because the human being is urged into violence-doing by Being itself, since Being needs such violence in order to come into an appearance. Historical Dasein, or, according to *Introduction to Metaphysics*, historical humanity, is determined as the "the breach [*Bresche*] into which the excessive violence of Being breaks in its appearing, so that this breach shatters against Being" (*IM*, 174). From the outset Dasein is the breach or "*in-cident* [*Zwischen-fall*]" (*IM*, 174) within which the lighting or clearing of Being occurs but that also causes Dasein, necessarily, to break. The human being's shattering, although inevitable, is thus not meaningless, an inescapable iron fate; rather, it is a shattering in which that which has sent itself on the way toward Dasein as Dasein's historical destiny—namely, Being—is at stake.

This inevitable shattering is the price, as it were, Dasein has to pay for attending to Being and, hence, of being the lighted openness of Being in which beings can come into an appearance. Everything homely or familiar is ontologically significant to the human being; only insofar as by breaking with it can the overwhelming sway of Being break into and come to stand within it. More precisely, if the homely is only to be dealt with in order for Being to irrupt within it, and thus to impart Being to all beings, the shattering of the human being is the pitiless result of being the addressee of what has sent itself on its way toward him or her to open up an originary world. World occurs only where the human being is torn away from everything homely, including being with himself, so that he can become the breach for Being to shine forth within the whole of beings that he holds open: "The uncanniest (the human being) is what it is because from the ground up it deals with and conserves the familiar [*Einheimische*] only in order to break out of it and to let what overwhelms it break in. Being itself throws humanity into the course of this tearing-away, which forces humanity beyond itself [*ihn über ihn selbst hinweg*], as the one who moves out to Being, in order to set Being to work and thus to hold open beings as a whole" (*IM*, 174). Now, if the human being's certain shattering—ultimately, his or her tragic death—is indeed the price to be paid for the opening of a world in the first place (that is, for the whole of earth and heaven, men and gods, to interrelate), it also follows that no psychological or aesthetic understanding of this "fate" can adequately grasp what its significance is. The "fate" suffered by the shattering human being is neither simply fateful, nor is it any longer to be thought of as merely dismal. Moreover, it is a "fate" that human beings take on themselves, in all its implacability. This is what the following, although undoubtedly bombastic, statement establishes: "Therefore the violence-doer knows no kindness and conciliation (in the ordinary sense), no appeasement and mollification by success or prestige and by their confirmation. In all this the violence-doer as creator sees only a seeming fulfillment, which is to be despised. In willing the unprecedented [*Unerhörten*], the violence-doer casts aside all help. For such [a] one, disaster [*Untergang*] is the deepest and broadest Yes to the overwhelming" (*IM*, 174). If the human being as violence-doer says Yes to the overwhelming, and by extension to his or her own downfall, it is for the sake of the world opened up in which everything is more in being thanks to the excessive violence (*Übermacht*) of Being. The affirmation of perdition by the creator is a Yes to being used by the overwhelming for it to shine forth in the world that has thus been opened up, however ephemeral it may be. For indeed, the downfall of the doer occurs in the shape of "the shattering of wrought work," by means of which Being has been brought to a stand amidst beings, fitting them together into what is a historical world. Yet, arrested in the work, Being also withdraws, undoing at the same time the work and the world to which it gave rise. The human being's Yes to this shattering of what he or she has violently wrought, by bringing Being to a stand in a work, is thus also the acknowledgment that the work and the world opened up by it is at the same time unfit (*Unfug*), leaving, therefore, "the overwhelming to its fittingness [*Fug*]" (*IM*, 174).

In his commentary on Sophocles' tragedy in *Hölderlin's Hymn "The Ister,"* Heidegger singles out the figure of Antigone as the one character in which the poet poetizes such unconditional exposure to, and affirmation of, the uncanniness of Being. Antigone here appears as the highest embodiment of the Greek human condition, urged as she is by Being itself into an unhesitatingly affirmed perdition. But before we can follow Heidegger through his elaborations on the figure of Antigone, whom he characterized as being "the purest poem herself" (*HHI*, 119; trans. mod.), we need to return to the question of uncanniness and unhomeliness. In his 1942 lectures, Heidegger reminds us that "Sophocles' word, which speaks of the human being as the most uncanny being, says that human beings are, in a singular sense, not homely, and that their care is to become homely" (*HHI*, 71). Although, "not 'at home,' not homely within whatever is homely," the human being is not, therefore, merely "wandering around" (*HHI*, 74) like the adventurer for whom "wilderness becomes the absolute itself," since the distinction between the homely and the unhomely no longer pertains to such a one (*HHI*, 75). The singular sense in which the uncanniest is unhomely is a function of one's search for an unattainable home. Heidegger writes: "Being unhomely is no mere deviance from the homely, but rather the converse: a seeking and searching out the homely, a seeking that at times does not know itself" (*HHI*, 74). The specific way in which the uncanniest is unhomely is determined by this relation to the homely from which the human being is barred. Unable as he or she is to be at home in his or her own essence, the human being seeks and searches out a home in all the directions in which he or she is under way. "The adventurer is merely not-homely; the *deinotaton*, by contrast, is the most uncanny being in a specific manner of being homely, namely that which, within its own essence, finds no entry to this essence, remains excluded from it and without any way out that could allow it to enter the center of its own essence. The one who is properly unhomely relates back precisely to the homely, and to this alone, yet does so in the manner of not attaining it" (*HHI*, 74–75). In short, the singular manner in which the uncanniest is unhomely rests on his or her negative possession of the homely, a possession "in the manner of an absencing" or, more precisely, in the paradoxical sense that "whatever is homely possesses the unhomely one" (*HHI*, 75). In any event, if the unhomeliness of the uncanniest is to be understood in relation to homeliness, it follows that one can and must distinguish between proper and improper unhomeliness: the first being an unhomeliness in which the uncanniest takes the relation to the homely upon him- or herself, and another in which this relation remains unacknowledged and forgotten. Distinct from the unhomeliness characteristic of the adventurer, who is at home in the foreign (more precisely, for whom the distinction between the homely and the unhomely no longer exists), the uncanny one who blinds him- or herself to the intimate relation between homelessness and athomeness seeks a way out of this fundamental unhomeliness by busying him- or herself with beings. The very delusion of this unhomely one, "of being truly among beings, without this being the case" (*HHI*, 109), shows to what extent even this kind of unhomeliness, in which one lets him- or herself be driven about amidst beings, is still linked to the homely. The unhomeliness is enacted "in a mere presumptuousness toward beings in order to forcibly contrive from beings in each case a way out and a site. This presumptuousness towards beings and within beings, however, only is what it is from out of a forgottenness of the hearth, that is, of being" (*HHI*, 115). The relation of this uncanny one to beings is one "of forgetting and blindness, as a result of which he or she is unable to have being in view or in thoughtful remembrance" (*HHI*, 109). This is the kind of unhomeliness of the uncanniest described by the chorus of elders in the first choral ode; it pertains to the ordinary, everyday condition of the human being. Yet according to Heidegger, it is also this uncanny one who, in the closing words of the ode, is expelled by the elders from the hearth and denied any genuine knowledge because his or her unhomeliness is improperly unhomely. By contrast, Antigone's unhomeliness is of a different kind.

Just as authenticity had been shown, in *Being and Time*, to be a possibility of Dasein that arises from within Dasein's everyday inauthentic way of being—namely, the possibility of being free for its ownmost potentiality for being—in the same way, the possibility of proper or authentic unhomeliness is rooted as a potentiality for being in improper unhomeliness. Rather than an original pristine condition from which Dasein would have fallen, authenticity and proper unhomeliness are above all "only" essential possibilities of Dasein, modifications that Dasein *can* take upon itself. Especially, in *Hölderlin's Hymn "The Ister,"* the relation between the two ways of being the uncanniest—that is, the unhomely one—is conceptualized in terms of a counterturning (*Gegenwendigkeit*), which not only shows that both these ways imply one another but also that they are interconnected in a unitary fashion. Insofar as the human being is the uncanniest of all beings, the human being is this twofold possibility at once. "The human being is destined and fitted into both these counterturning possibilities and thus must be these two possibilities themselves . . . To be in such a way, however, means to be determined in essence by the unhomely, to be counterturning" (*HHI*, 86–87). If the figure of Antigone can be characterized as being "the purest poem herself," it is because she carries to full fruition this essential possibility of being properly unhomely. Not only is she thrust into excess and torn into downfall, but her intrinsic unhomeliness is such that she becomes at home within it.

According to Heidegger's 1942 commentary on the Sophoclean tragedy, the uncanniness of the human being, and the unhomeliness in which it is grounded, "is named poetically in the choral ode by the word *deinon* but is not thoughtfully unfolded." Heidegger makes the additional remark that "even within this poetic telling, the unhomely essence of uncanniness comes to light, although decisively, only by way of intimation [*nur ahnungsweise*]" (*HHI*, 91; trans. mod.), with the result that this essence of the human being has scarcely been acknowledged within the Western tradition. Nor, finally, does the poet elaborate on the specificity of the knowing, or, rather, the "proper knowing," about the home and the homely from which everything spoken by the chorus concerning the human being's uncanniness has from the outset been determined, and on the basis of which the chorus is seen to exclude the improperly uncanny and his or her delusions from the hearth. Undoubtedly, this is a kind of intimation (*Ahnen*) that, although fundamentally different from calculating reason—that is, from theoretical knowledge, including even philosophical knowledge—has its own rigor and clarity. Heidegger translates the chorus's *phronein* by which the elders appeal to their knowing as a "poetizing knowing" (*HHI*, 111), but where this "poetizing knowing" comes from, and to what it belongs, is not spelled out by the poet. This knowing that knows about the hearth as the site of athomeness leaves the essence of homeliness that this "poetic word" (*HHI*, 111) evokes unsaid as well. Let us also take notice of the fact that what ultimately motivates Antigone, or more precisely, that of which "Antigone tells of where she belongs, tells of whence she knows herself to be greeted" (*HHI*, 115) and counseled (*HHI*, 103), "Antigone, and that also means the poet, leaves without a name" (*HHI*, 117). In the exchange with her sister she refers to it only as that against which no human contrivance can avail, since it appears of its own accord; to Creon she speaks of it as that which prevails beyond the laws of Zeus and Dike. A thoughtful unfolding and saying, if not naming, of what the poetic rendering of uncanniness left unsaid thus becomes necessary. Certainly, it is safe to assume that knowledge of this unsaid has, from the start, informed Heidegger's translation and interpretation of the poetic words in question. But in the extensive elaboration on the chorus's final words in *Hölderlin's Hymn "The Ister,"* Heidegger also explicitly takes on that which in the poem remained unsaid, naming it in terms of the saying characteristic of poetizing's counterpart—that is, of thinking.[28]

In her response to Ismene's admonition not to undertake the dangerous and difficult task of burying their brother, Antigone tells her sister to "*pathein to deinon touto*," to let her, in Heidegger's translation, "take up into [her] own essence the uncanny that here and now appears" (*HHI*, 99). Antigone, he argues, is "the supreme uncanny" (*HHI*, 102) because, rather than making herself uncanny, she experiences and endures the uncanny, letting the uncanny itself make her what she is and who she can be. Yet

> what is the "uncanny," in which Antigone knows she has been ultimately counseled, acquainted as she is with the foreboding, the perilousness, and the gravity of this counsel? The uncanny is nothing other than this: the fact that she takes as her all-determinative point of departure that against which nothing can avail, because it is that appearing that is destined for her . . . , and of which no one knows whence it has arisen. In fittingly accommodating herself [*pathein*] to this, Antigone comes to be removed from all human

possibilities and placed into direct conflict over the site of all beings and into a sublation of the subsistence of her own life. (*HHI*, 103)

The uncanny that falls to Antigone, and that she takes into and upon herself, is, in her own words, a "supreme necessity" against which no machinations whatsoever are of any use and which, consequently, removes her from the site of all human possibilities, insofar as these are precisely of the order of the machinations attended to mastering Being, and brings her into a direct confrontation with that site—that is, the *polis* and, mutatis mutandis, the very world that it represents. Responding to the injunction of this "supreme necessity," Antigone becomes unhomely "in a way that exceeds every other being unhomely. She looms over the site of all beings not merely like Creon, who in his way also looms high therein. Rather, Antigone even steps out of this site altogether. She is utterly [*schlechthin*] unhomely" (*HHI*, 103). If, according to the Greeks, "supreme uncanniness" belongs to the essence of all human beings, it is because they alone comport themselves toward Being. In everything in which they get involved they are on a path toward Being, seeking to become homely within it as the open abode in which beings, and they themselves, come into an appearance, and this always in the shape of a particular site. Yet in

> undertaking the risk of becoming homely, [human beings] must place everything at stake in such play and therefore encounter *this*: the fact that the homely refuses itself to them. Constantly on the path toward the homely site, and at the same time placed at stake in the play that repudiates the homely, human beings in their innermost essence are those who are unhomely. And because only human beings, on account of that relation toward beings that distinguishes humans alone, can be unhomely in this way, supreme uncanniness belongs to their essence. (*HHI*, 90)

Distinct from those who are the uncanniest amidst all uncanny beings, Antigone is the "supreme uncanny" in that in her figure the "supreme uncanniness" that belongs as a possibility to the essence of Being-human becomes enacted. Although "intrinsically unhomely," the human beings' unhomeliness "bears further intrinsic possibilities of 'intensification'" (*HHI*, 104). Heidegger asks: "What if that which were most intrinsically unhomely, thus remote from all that is homely, were that which in itself simultaneously preserved the most intimate belonging to the homely?

What if this alone, of all things, could be unhomely in the proper sense?" (*HHI*, 104). Antigone is "within the most uncanny . . . the supreme uncanny," since she becomes "homely within and from out of such being unhomely" (*HHI*, 104). By retaining in her unhomeliness the relation to the homely, she is properly unhomely. And vice-versa: she becomes unhomely precisely by taking that to which she belongs, the homely, upon herself. In Heidegger's words: "She makes the pursuit of that which is of no avail the origin of her essence. She chooses destiny as that which alone is fitting. She thereby takes it upon herself to be unhomely. This experience and undertaking is the supreme action and proper history of the humankind she belongs to, the *tolma* of her very essence" (*HHI*, 109).

What Antigone's being unhomely consists in, and the sense in which she preserves the relation to the homely in her unhomeliness, still remains unclear. Nor is it obvious why Heidegger makes a distinction between a proper and an improper way of being homeless. Above all, we do not yet fully understand in what kind of home the uncanniest of the uncanniest can be at home, in short, what a home genuinely is, a home distinct from a supposedly sheltering place amidst beings. However, Heidegger's thoughtful interpretation of the closing words of the ode hints at how "home" is to be understood in a Greek sense and how, paradoxically, "unhomeliness" can derive from belonging to the home. The knowing of the elders' of the hearth itself, which, according to Heidegger, explains the expulsion of the uncanniest from the hearth—that is, from "the homestead in which everything homely is grounded" (*HHI*, 115)—is a knowing that, in order to be genuinely a *phronein*, "must spring from a belonging to the hearth and thus stem from a kind of being homely" (*HHI*, 110). According to Heidegger, from the perspective of pre-Socratic thought, the poetic word *hearth* refers to "the middle of beings, to which all beings, because and insofar as they are beings, are drawn in the commencement." And he adds: "This hearth of the middle of beings is being. Being is the hearth. For the essence of being for the Greeks is *physis*—that illumination that emerges of its own accord and is mediated by nothing else, but is itself the middle. This middle is that which remains as commencement, that which gathers everything around it—that wherein all beings have their site and are at home as beings" (*HHI*, 112–13).[29] In short, then, even though the closing words of the choral song speak nowhere of Being, the homely from which Antigone's unhomeliness is to be understood, and to which she refers as that which appears of its own accord—of which no one knows from where it comes, and against which nothing can be of any assistance—is Being itself as it emerged in the inaugurating conception of early Greek thought, itself the forgotten commencement of the West.

As is shown by the rejection of the uncanny from the hearth, "the uncanny one has an essential relation to the hearth, but it is that of forgetting and blindness, as a result of which he or she is unable to have being in view or in thoughtful remembrance" (*HHI*, 109). The unhomeliness of the uncanny is thus oblivious to "the homestead in which everything homely is grounded" (*HHI*, 115). The uncanny, therefore, has not yet roused itself to the essence of unhomeliness and is thus unable to become at home in it. Of this homelessness that is cut off from its ground, Heidegger writes:

> Being unhomely shows itself as a not yet awakened, not yet decided, not yet assumed potential for being homely and becoming homely. It is precisely this being unhomely that Antigone takes upon herself. Her suffering the *deinon* is her supreme action. This action is the movement and "drama" of becoming homely. In becoming homely, being unhomely is accomplished. And this not merely in the sense that, in becoming homely, being unhomely finds its conclusion; rather, Antigone's becoming homely first brings to light the essence of being unhomely. Becoming homely makes manifest the essential ambiguity of being unhomely. (*HHI*, 115)

As opposed to the merely unhomely one, who, rather than answering for and to the homely from which his way of being is to be understood, indulges in unhomeliness by way of forcibly contriving from beings a way out and a site, Antigone breaks with the "forgottenness of the hearth, that is, of being . . . through 'thoughtful remembrance' ['*Andenken*'] of being and through a belonging to the hearth" (*HHI*, 115). She takes unhomeliness explicitly upon herself, thus heeding the ground of unhomeliness, and becomes homely within it. Bringing the essence of unhomeliness to light as a way of being in which athomeness has not yet been realized, Antigone, in taking unhomeliness upon herself, thus accomplishes and realizes it in the first place. If Antigone's unhomeliness is of a different kind, it is because in taking it upon herself "she is 'properly' unhomely" (*HHI*, 117).

The properly unhomely one is the one who is at home in that which radically defamiliarizes human existence in all its sheltering ordinariness and in the pursuit of beings and that unhomes all being-with-oneself—in short, Being in all its uncanniness. Homeliness and the home is to be thought from the perspective of Being, which determines the essence of the human being. In its most primordial sense, the home is not a place where one is common, a stable place where, secluded and protected, one can be in and for oneself. According to Heidegger's affirmation in "Letter on Humanism" that the thought of Being is "at home on the path of silence," it appears that a home, rather than being a refuge, is more precisely a path toward Being. Being on the path toward Being, belonging to Being as something that can never be recovered as an essence or a substance but that instead unsettles all fixations in grounding essences or substances, one becomes homely (*BW*, 223). In conformity with Heraclitus's saying that *ethos anthropo daimon*, Heidegger holds that "the (familiar) abode for man [is] the open region for the presencing of god (the unfamiliar one)" (*BW*, 234). Consequently, the home or abode in which humans dwell—in other words, the *ethos* of humanity—is the site in which that which unsettles everything ordinary shines forth—the god, for Heraclitus; Being, for Heidegger. In it the human being is at home insofar as he or she comports toward this otherness, which in turn unhomes him or her. In contradistinction to the ordinary condition of the human being's uncanniness (the one who, in pursuit of beings and by his or her search for a home amidst beings forfeits all *ethos*), Antigone finds an abode and thus an *ethos* in becoming the very openness for the presencing of Being in all its overwhelming othering. However, to find a proper ethos, and hence a home in which to belong, *one must take unhomeliness upon oneself* rather than being blind to it by seeking to make oneself at home in the midst of beings.

If, according to Heidegger, the closing words of the ode are themselves "of an uncanny ambiguity," it is because they concern being unhomely itself (*HHI*, 117). In order to mark off the precise difference between proper and improper unhomeliness, let us consider exactly what it means to take unhomeliness upon oneself. For Heidegger, Antigone's becoming homely "makes manifest the essential ambiguity of being unhomely" (*HHI*, 115). This ambiguity of the essential unhomeliness of humanity, which devolves from the very fact that humans belong to Being insofar as they *are*, implies that unhomeliness is truly what it is on condition only of being fully assumed by Dasein. Certainly, obliviousness to the unhoming home that is Being, and the violent pursuit of a site within beings, does not make one less unhomely. In fact, as Heidegger remarks, "homelessness is the symptom [*Zeichen*] of oblivion to Being" (*BW*, 218). But to take unhomeliness upon oneself so as to become at home within it does not overcome it either, since in this case unhomeliness becomes precisely the true home of the human being. To take it upon herself to become homely within Being means for Antigone to take into her essence the full essence of Being—that is, of never being at home within herself, and ultimately to belong to death as that which is unmasterable by whoever merely ventures out amidst beings without a way out. To belong to Being, and to be in one's being essentially concerned with Being, is to be unhomely rather than being with, and resting within, oneself. Heidegger avers: "Being is not something that is actual, but that which determines what is actual in its potential for being, and determines especially the potential for human beings to be; that potentiality for being in which the being of human beings is fulfilled: being unhomely in becoming homely. Such is our belonging to being itself" (*HHI*, 120). Since, furthermore, Antigone already belongs to death insofar as she knows that to be is inevitably to be-toward-death, "she is the most unhomely one amid beings" (*HHI*, 120). Now, to take the full essence of what it means to be into or upon oneself entails nothing less than a decision regarding the essential ambiguity of unhomeliness. Yet because it concerns the very ambiguity of unhomeliness, this decision necessarily involves a risk; its outcome, furthermore, is unpredictable. Indeed, the knowledge of the proper essence of the unhomely, which subtends the chorus's rejection of the merely uncanny one, conceals within itself a pointer toward the risk (*Wagnis*) that Antigone must take, namely, of "distinguishing and deciding between that being unhomely proper to human beings and a being unhomely that is inappropriate" (*HHI*, 117). This risk, which is "the most uncanny risk that risks nothing less than the essence of uncanniness itself," is the risk "accomplished in the tragedy as a whole"—it is, indeed, coextensive with the tragic itself. The Sophoclean tragedy not only shows Antigone as assuming the risk of deciding between proper and improper unhomeliness; tragedy as such is the poetized form of deciding that which remains undecided. Heidegger remarks: "What is worthy of poetizing in this poetic work is nothing other than becoming homely in being unhomely" (*HHI*, 121). If "Antigone herself *is* the poem of becoming homely in being unhomely . . . in the proper and supreme sense" (*HHI*, 121), as Heidegger suggests, this is so because she "herself is this supreme risk within the *deinon*. To be this risk is her essence" (*HHI*, 117). To *be* this risk of a decision concerning unhomeliness, which rather than athomeness in Being can produce its complete opposite as well, this is, precisely, to take Being into one's essence.

Let us recall Heidegger's contention that Antigone's pursuit of Being—making it into the origin of her essence, and taking it upon herself to be unhomely in an authentic sense—"is the supreme action and proper history of the humankind she belongs to, the *tolma* of her very essence" (*HHI*, 109). Antigone is the purest poem herself of the being unhomely-homely of the human being that emerges with Greek humanity—a humanity that still bears on Western humanity and Europe as its determining ground. Heidegger remarks that "such being of human beings, their being unhomely-homely in the midst of beings, is said poetically, because it always remains only a potential for being that pertains to risk [*Seinkönnen der Wagnis*]—as something to be poetized and poetically decidable. Perhaps what is essentially and only to be poetized in this way, namely, the potential of human beings for being homely, is even the highest thing that the poet must poetize" (*HHI*, 121). The originary world Sophocles' choral ode poetizes—a world determined by the human being's relation to the Being of beings—culminates in Antigone's supreme action, in which she raises herself to being the risk of deciding between proper and improper unhomeliness. This potential for risk, which is not only the highest form of being opened by the world grounded by the poet, is also that with respect to which all of the human's ordinary doings within this world are determined. This potential for being that pertains to risk is, Heidegger contends, "what is supremely worthy of poetizing." Not only that, it is something that—perhaps—can only be poetized and poetically decided, if indeed it is the case that only poetry founds a world for a people. The thinker's task, then, is to come to the aid of the poet "by interpreting and grasping conceptually the relations" that constitute such poetic dwelling (*HHI*, 122; trans. mod.). Whereas the poet poetizes homecoming to the hearth, the thinker shows that this hearth, to which the human being is destined to find his or her way—although usually he or she is on the way to nothing—is Being, that is, unhomeliness as a home itself. The thinker's task consists not only of spelling out what the poet left unsaid but also of illuminating through a lucidly conceptual presentation this Greek conception of the human, which is thoroughly foreign to Western thought precisely because it is what concerns it most.

The Originary World of Tragedy 191

Heidegger concludes this reading of *Antigone*, which in the lectures in *Hölderlin's Hymn "The Ister"* was framed by an inquiry into Hölderlin's "poetizing of the rivers (i.e., of the locality and journeying of human beings as historical)," by asserting that if the "choral ode is the supreme poetic work of what is supremely worthy of poetizing, then this might well be the reason why this choral ode came to speak ever anew to the poet Hölderlin during the period of his poetizing of the hymns" (*HHI*, 121–22). Since for Heidegger the "poetic and historical dialogue [*Zwiesprache*] between Sophocles and Hölderlin" (*HHI*, 123) is paradigmatic of the way Europe must reach back to its Greek origins in order to discover what is properly its own, we will have to raise in the following the question of Hölderlin's relation to the originary world that Greek poetry projected for Greek humanity. Both Sophocles and Hölderlin "poetize the Same," Heidegger contends. Both poets poetize homecoming—Sophocles, as we have seen, the becoming homely of Greek humanity within Being, and Hölderlin "the becoming homely of the historical humankind of the Germans within the history of the West" (*HHI*, 124) as the hitherto "only perceptible phase [*bisher allein übersehbare*] of the history of Being" (*BW*, 220). Hereafter, then, I will seek to sketch out, however schematically, what Heidegger calls "the fundamental law of becoming homely" (*HHI*, 60).

First, however, we must return to Heidegger's characterization of Hölderlin as a poet of homecoming. In his lectures devoted to the poet's late hymns, he writes: "If . . . the historicality of any humankind resides in being homely, and if being homely is a becoming homely in being unhomely; and if, furthermore, such being homely can be determined only poetically and must be said poetically, then Hölderlin is the first to experience poetically, that is, to say poetically, the German need [*Not*] of being unhomely" (*HHI*, 125). In the face of the German distress of having no home or homeland (*Heimat*)—the term *Heimat* stands out in Heidegger's *Elucidations of Hölderlin's Poetry*—the poet not only names this distress, but he is also said to enunciate the law of homecoming in the first Böhlendorff letter to which Heidegger's lectures from the winter semester of 1941–42 on *Hölderlins Hymne "Andenken"* explicitly refer. In the lectures on the hymn "The Ister," Heidegger states that "that poetry of Hölderlin that has taken on the form of the hymn has taken into its singular core the becoming homely in one's own. . . . This *coming to be at home in one's own in itself entails that human beings are initially,* and for a long time, and sometimes forever, not at home" (*HHI*, 49). Consequently, the home of a historical people—the Germans, in this case—is not a given: it is no existing geographical or cultural entity, and if, therefore, such a home has in principle first to be found and won, the home in which a historical people can come to be at home cannot be of a territorial order to begin with. Moreover, the fact that human beings are not initially at home in their own "entails that human beings fail to recognize, that they deny, and perhaps even have to deny and flee what belongs to the home" (*HHI*, 49). Indeed, confusing their home with a geographical or historico-political—that is, empirical—locality, human beings are not only oblivious to what is their own, but they even flee any insight into their essence because such insight is exceedingly demanding and unsettling. As Heidegger emphasizes, "finding one's own, and appropriating what one has found as one's own, is not that which is most self-evident or easiest but remains what is most difficult" (*HHI*, 49). Now, in the same way as Sophocles and Pindar, with whose poetry he stands in a dialogue, Hölderlin, in his later hymns, takes into poetic care what is thus most difficult—that is, such a discovery of what is one's own; therefore, his poetry is also, and primarily so, a poetry of homecoming.

However, even though Hölderlin and Sophocles are poetizing the Same, this does not mean that they poetize something identical, for the Same implies difference. For Heidegger, "the Same is truly the Same only in that which is different" (*HHI*, 123). According to the lectures on "The Ister," the difference between Sophocles and Hölderlin is above all a difference between "the historical humankind of the Greeks and the Germans as other in each respective case" (*HHI*, 123). Heidegger remarks that "the grounds for the historical difference between these two humankinds lies in the fact that they are in each case historical in a different way, that is, must become homely in a different way. This is why they are unhomely in different ways in the beginning. Yet they are so for the singular reason that, being in the midst of beings in different ways, they comport themselves toward these beings and maintain themselves in them" (*HHI*, 123). Although no explanation is given as to the precise reason or ground for this difference of "being homely-unhomely in beings" in each respective case, nor what this difference "properly eventuates from [*sich ereignet*]" (*HHI*, 123), the difference between Greek and German humanity is such that they are respective projects of becoming homely on the basis of clearly different types of unhomeliness and that the projects exclude repetition or imitation on the basis of an underlying continuity. Heidegger's conception of the relation between the founding poetries of respective worlds for their humanities by the Greeks and the Germans, or by the Orient and the Occident, will now be our concern.

As a poetry of homecoming Hölderlin's poetry is primarily about finding what is one's own. In *Hölderlins Hymne "Andenken"* Heidegger, echoing the letter to Böhlendorff, writes that "what is one's own, and in which one is at home, the native [*heimatliche*] earth, is that which it is most difficult to achieve" (*HHA*, 135). When, furthermore, he asserts of Hölderlin's poetry that it never ever contains any certainty and satisfaction but "that all is task [*alles ist Aufgabe*]," it becomes manifest again that what is one's own, rather then being given, is something that needs to be found and won, if not produced (*HHA*, 142). Yet what is it that is properly German, and to which the Germans belong?[30] To retrieve what is properly one's own, a passage through Greece proves inevitable. However, if in fact Hölderlin's late poetry enters into a dialogue with the poets of Greece, it is first of all because "something having the character of a commencement [*etwas Anfängliches*] once occurred in the Greek world, and that which has the character of a commencement alone grounds history" (*HHI*, 56). What commences (but "only" commences) in Greece concerns the possibility of becoming homely, and the decision regarding athomeness or homelessness that such a possibility contains is also that of the historicality of human Dasein (as a possibility). Insofar as it is the unique commencement for a way of becoming at home (in homelessness)—for a way of having something that is properly one's own—the Germans have to reflect back on what happened in Greece for them to become a historical people in the first place. It is not a model to be imitated but a beginning to relate to according to a law still to be spelled out—"the fundamental law of becoming homely"—in order for the Germans to themselves become a beginning by finding a way of being at home that is specifically their own.[31]

To find one's own and to appropriate it is, as Hölderlin remarks in the Böhlendorff letter, that which is most difficult. This is because that which is one's own is what is most distant, if not even genuinely foreign to oneself. Consequently, "coming to be at home is . . . a passage through the foreign" (*HHI*, 49). Without an encounter, and a passage through the foreign, that which is one's own cannot be won. And vice versa: what is one's own can only be found through a coming home, through a return from the foreign. Yet such a return can only be achieved "as a journey out into what is foreign" (*EHP*, 118). Speaking of Hölderlin's poetry, Heidegger remarks that "the journey abroad to the foreign land remains essential for the return home into the law of his own poetic song" about homecoming (*EHP*, 108). Even a "love for what is not like home [*Liebe zum Unheimischsein*], purely for the sake of becoming at home in what is one's own, is the essential law of destiny by which the poet is sent into the foundation of the history of the 'fatherland,'" that is, the land of the commencement, the foreign land—that is, to Greece—which Hölderlin also refers to as the Orient [*Morgenland*] (*EHP*, 111–12). Here one can already clearly recognize that, according to "the law by which the poet, by means of the poetic passage away from home to the foreign land, becomes at home in what is proper to him," the foreign that must be traversed for a homecoming to be possible cannot be just any arbitrary foreign (*EHP*, 112). The foreign in question cannot "merely [be] the indeterminate or manifold other of one's own" (*HHI*, 49);[32] instead the foreign to be traversed must be prescribed by what is one's own. If to become homely requires a passage through and encounter with the foreign, it must be a "*foreign* that relates to the return home, that is, one with it [*mit ihr einige Fremde*], the *provenance* [*Herkunft*] of such return, and that which has been at the commencement with regard to what is one's own and the homely. For Hölderlin, the Greek world is what is foreign with respect to the historical humankind of the Germans" (*HHI*, 54). As the commencement of what is possibly to be one's own, the foreign with which the Germans must enter into a confrontational encounter or *Auseinandersetzung* to become homely in what is their own can only be something that, although different from it, also relates to it and is thus united with it. This foreignness is the Greek world, forgotten, and even denied, by the Germans. Yet Heidegger is quick to warn against confusing the Greek world that must be confronted if one is to acquire a home of one's own with classical antiquity as a model to be emulated or with the object of "a romantic desire to return" (*HHI*, 54). Above all it is not the Greece of the young Nietzsche. All of these representations of Greece disregard the uniqueness of Greece as a commencement. If the Greeks can be held to have once been a commencement, it is, as Heidegger argues in his commentary on the Böhlendorff letter in *Elucidations of Hölderlin's Poetry*, because what was proper to the Greeks is that they were the first to pass through what is foreign to them in order to "first come into possession of their proper element" (*EHP*, 112). How radical such passage through the unhomely is, and to what extent it determines becoming at home, is perhaps not fully articulated in Heidegger's commentary on the Böhlendorff letter. By contrast, the foreignness and strangeness of that kind of Greece that indeed represents a commencement for what is one's own can be truly gauged through the originary Greek world we have seen to emerge from Heidegger's interpretation of the first choral ode in *Antigone*. The statement at the end of *Elucidations of Hölderlin's Poetry*, namely that, in the encounter with the foreign, "what is merely strange in the foreign" is to be overlooked, "so that only that foreignness that is to be transformed through what is proper to one is preserved" and remembered (*andenken*), is another clear hint at the distinct strangeness of Greece as a commencement (*EHP*, 164). As Heidegger notes, "the historical relation between Greek and German humankind can tolerate neither assimilation nor equalization" (*HHI*, 124); in other words, the Greece that is the commencement of what is proper to the Germans is one that is thoroughly distinct from its common representations in classicism and romanticism, including the Hellenizing dreams of the Third Reich.

Hölderlin's conception of Greece differs from all classical and romantic, namely metaphysical, concerns with Greece, since, although intrinsically related to what is proper to the Germans, Greece is also (or, rather, therefore) what is most foreign to them. Hölderlin has a more "intimate" relation to Greece than the one that characterizes all Grecian delusions in that he acknowledges Greece's radical otherness. Once what is foreign about Greece becomes annihilated, "what necessarily gets lost is the possibility of a passage through the foreign, and thereby the possibility of a return home into one's own, and thereby that which is one's own itself" (*HHI*, 54). The very possibility of homecoming, that is, of a return into one's own, presupposes a passage to something in opposition to oneself, something that is the opposite of oneself and that, by the same token, is both intimately linked to and radically different from oneself. As I have already emphasized, the essence of one's own is not a given; it is not constituted in advance. Heidegger's reference in the lectures on "The Ister" to "the mystery [*Geheimnis*] of the coming to be at home of human beings as historical" (*HHI*, 55) is predicated precisely on this assumption that one's ownmost essential wealth becomes unfolded only through a passage through what is thoroughly foreign to oneself. What is more, such a passage not only requires that the Other be thoroughly different and foreign to oneself; it must also be superior to oneself for it to be encountered as an Other that can bring one into one's own. In order for what is one's own to unfold its own essential riches, the foreign must be the object of a "supremely thoughtful acknowledgment [*überlegenen Anerkennung des Fremden*]" (*HHI*, 55), that is, of an acknowledgment of the foreign that outclasses all other approaches to it by recognizing it—Greece, as a commencement, in particular—as superior. Consequently, one can say that the only kind of "Greece" that matters is that which stands in the sharpest opposition to oneself and can therefore be the object of a genuine encounter. Heidegger avers: "For only where the foreign is known and acknowledged in its quintessential oppositional character does there exist the possibility of a genuine relationship, that is, of a uniting that is not a confused mixing but a conjoining in distinction" (*HHI*, 125). With this reference to "a conjoining in distinction," the fundamental law of homecoming (that is, of making good on what from the beginning, in a certain Greece—one that Hölderlin, rejecting classicism, conceives from its oriental archaic past, and refers to as the Orient [*Morgenland*]—has been bequeathed to what he calls Hesperia, the land of the setting sun [*Abendland*]), namely, becoming at home in unhomeliness, begins to come into view.

Hölderlin's poetizing is about the becoming homely of the historical humankind of the Germans within the history to which they belong, and it seeks therefore a dialogue with the Greek founding poetry of becoming homely in the unhomely, not, however, because the Greeks are anterior to the Germans nor in order to repeat or imitate a venerable model. Heidegger asserts:

> Rather, Hölderlin recognizes that the historicality of these two humankinds is intrinsically different, insofar as what is proper to the Greeks and what is foreign to them is other than what is proper and what is foreign to the Germans. And from Hölderlin's perspective, the difference between these two humankinds shows itself in the fact that they are different in a reciprocal [*entgegengesetzt*] manner, which essentially means: They encounter one another and are thus related to one another. What for the Greeks is their own is what is foreign to the Germans; and what is foreign to the Germans is what is proper to the Greeks. (*HHI*, 124)

It is plain from the first Böhlendorff letter, which Heidegger paraphrases in the passage cited above, that for Hölderlin the relation between

Germans and Greeks is not just any relation but a relation of opposition to an other that matters in that it concerns one's very own essence. It is, moreover, a chiasmatic relation in which what is proper to the Greeks is foreign to the Germans and vice versa—a relation, consequently, in which the opponents are linked in an evermore intimate unity. What is properly one's own must be learned just as well as the foreign, Hölderlin tells his friend; but as we have seen, to find oneself and to appropriate what is one's own is what is most difficult. In *Hölderlins Hymne "Andenken,"* one reads: "Finding-oneself is never the stubborn insistence-on-oneself-alone, but a crossing over from what is one's own to the foreignness of the others, and a returning from this recognized foreignness into one's own" (*HHA*, 86). If to learn what is proper to oneself is what is most difficult, then to learn that which, of that foreignness of others, stands in the service of the appropriation of what is one's own is certainly much easier. Furthermore: "That which is easier [learning that which is foreign to oneself] lets one more readily excel" (*HHI*, 124). For instance, according the Böhlendorff letter, the Greeks excel in the gift of presentation and Junonian sobriety precisely because it is what is foreign to them, yet this gift of "the clarity of presentation" is precisely what is the Germans' ownmost own. But to develop what is properly their own, the Germans must learn it from the Greeks. By contrast, since "the fire from the heavens" is that which, according to Hölderlin, is the Greeks' innermost own, yet foreign to the Germans,

> it could also be that the Germans—granted that they learn to use freely what is their own and do not evade the conditions required for such learning—might, in what is foreign to them (the "fire from the heavens"), come to excel in what is proper to the Greeks. If, that is, they have become more open, so that "what illuminates" (the heavens) is "open to our view" . . . it could be that a "guest-house" . . . and establishment might be founded and built for the gods, one with which the Greek temples can no longer keep up [*nicht mehr nachkommen*]. (*HHI*, 124; trans. mod.)

What is most proper to oneself is thus best learned from the other, who "surpasses us in what is our own" and to whom that which is most proper to oneself therefore remains deeply indebted. At the same time, the "fire of the heavens," that is, the Greeks' openness to the foreign, which does not come naturally to the Germans but is proper to the Greeks, is something in which the Germans, precisely because it is foreign to them, could surpass the Greeks. Yet what precisely is it that is thus foreign to the Germans, but by which they could possibly surpass even the Greeks? It is, indeed, nothing less than this very openness to the foreign itself. In the second Böhlendorff letter, of November 1802, Hölderlin defines the specific essence of the Greeks as a "tenderness [*Zärtlichkeit*]" that consists in "their habit to assume [and accept] foreign characters and communicate themselves to them [*fremde Naturen anzunehmen und sich ihnen mitzuteilen*]." This openness to the foreign, then, is what is most specifically Greek, an openness that, needless to say, also required protection against such infinite tenderness by a principle foreign to the Greeks, the principle of presentational differentiation, in which they finally become masters.[33] In light of the foregoing interpretation of *Antigone*, to excel in what is specifically oriental about the Greeks would not mean that the West would become a new commencement; instead, it would signify another (or an other) commencement—another Orient, so to speak. Within the framework of the interpretation of the Sophoclean tragedy, in which Heidegger developed the law of becoming homely in unhomeliness, such another commencement would not only represent a response to what has been sent on its way by "Greece" (precisely insofar as it is characterized by an openness to the foreign); this law would also be that of another originary world of athomeness in a constitutive exposure to the other—of a world that not only never closes on itself but is essentially always only to come.

In a line from a late hymn Hölderlin holds that "thoughts of communal spirit are." In conformity with his consistent attempt to demarcate the poet from the metaphysical tradition of thought—although acknowledging as well that the poet maintains a close relationship to this tradition—Heidegger argues that *spirit* is here to be taken in a poetic sense and to refer to the destining and assignment of what is fitting for human beings. In reference to this line, Heidegger explains that it

> ponders poetically the fact that spirit is, and, in being, thinks for all beings what is fitting [*das Schickliche*] to their being. Yet insofar as human beings have a distinctive relationship towards beings, the human being is the one who is open for what is fitting and the one who, in being human, is pointed toward what is fittingly destined [*das Geschick*]. Because, and insofar as, human beings are open to what is fittingly destined and fit themselves to what is destined and thus take over and unfold, dismiss and confuse what is fit-

ting, but also what is unfitting, as the essential ground and non-ground of being human, human beings are historical. (*HHI*, 127)

In the thoughtful poetizing of Hölderlin, the term *spirit* names that which assigns (*zudenkt*) what is fitting to human beings. Open to what is destined to them, human beings, rather than assuming what has been sent on its way to them, can also blind themselves to this assignment and err as regards the nature of what is fitting for them. Because of this very duplicity of simultaneously being those who take what spirit destines to them upon themselves, and being those who reject the burden of this task, human beings are in essence in a situation of decision and are hence historical beings. From our discussion of Heidegger's account of Sophocles' *Antigone*, we have seen that to take on oneself what is destined to the human being—namely Being in all its uncanniness—or, to put it another way, to find what is fitting in being unhomely, is to become homely. Heidegger writes: "Preserving [*die Bewahrung*] such becoming is that being historical that attains its essential fullness when it comes to know what has been fittingly destined for it [*das Zugeschickte*] as that which has already been [*das schon Gewesene*]. That which is fittingly destined for human beings is what 'spirit' thinks, and thinks as directed toward human beings, so that it is 'spirit' in historical human beings that determines historicality" (*HHI*, 128). To become homely in unhomeliness is not only to be open to what "spirit" (or Being) has destined to the human being but also to preserve this injunction of being at home in unhomeliness. But this preservation of the demand of an unreserved openness to the other, of relentlessly venturing forth into the foreign so as to return into one's own, or more precisely, becoming homely in unhomeliness, is also to be historical. If this being historical attains its "essential fullness" when it recognizes that what has been sent on its way toward it is "that which has already been," this means that historicality is precisely the relation not to a constituted past but "only" to a commencement that, having been forgotten, demands not to be the beginning of something that follows from it but to be begun anew and to be preserved in its very nature as a commencement. By the same token,

> what is fitting and fittingly destined for them always remains for human beings that which is coming toward them, that which is futural [*das auf ihn Zukommende, Zukünftige*]. What is fittingly destined for us is never something that has been decided; it remains full of destinings [*Schickungen*] and

only is from out of them. What is fittingly destined for us sends its destining in one way and another and always remains in coming. In such coming, however, it can be thought only in being taken up and preserved as what is coming. (*HHI*, 128)

Since what is destined to the human being from the commencement on—athomeness in homelessness—is not something already established or positively decided, it is only something that by its very foreignness lies in wait for him or her in that it is only in coming. Being foreign as the beginning of what is one's own, that which is futural in the beginning is the sending on its way of what speaks directly to one's essence. That which is to come, and which one must await and guard in its address to oneself, comes from the foreign that, as one's opposite, is "that which has been at the commencement with regard to what is one's own and the homely" (*HHI*, 54). It "remains in coming," and only insofar as it is something that *is* only in coming can human beings take it on themselves in their essential homelessness, and so become homely. Taking what is destined to them upon themselves as that which is always only in coming, human beings—like Antigone—that open themselves up to what is destined to them *are*—"are" in the sense of a *becoming* homely in homelessness. In the same way as becoming homely does not annul homelessness, becoming at home within it is a permanent condition, or rather, an infinite process or an infinite task without even a regulative idea as a horizon.

~

In the same way as Husserl, Heidegger considers Greece to be the sole origin of Europe and the West. However, saving the West from the imminent threat that it faces by way of an originary recreation of its history not only requires the people of the middle—the German people—to reflect on what is their own by reaching back to the one singular other—Greece—that concerns it most immediately, but, as Heidegger suggests in "Wege zur Aussprache" (1937), this task is also a task incumbent on all other European peoples. They as well are to understand what is proper to themselves from within this framework that is the salvation of the Occident (*Rettung des Abendlandes*). Furthermore, this task requires a dialogue, or *Auseinandersetzung*, between the different European peoples, one that is based on "the superior courage of recognizing what is specifically proper about the other out of an overriding necessity." Such a dialogue of a "reciprocal self-questioning founded on the care about common historical tasks" is said to mutually transform all the partners of the dialogue and thus to bring them closer to what is their own.[34] Needless to say, broadening the reflection on what is one's own by expanding it to all European others as well leaves not only the central focus on Greece intact but also the basic forms and rules of the fundamental law of homecoming.

However, in a 1959 lecture entitled "Hölderlin's Earth and Heaven" on the poem that bears the title "Greece," written after the poet's return from Bordeaux and signed, significantly enough, "Scardanelli" (that is, as Heidegger remarks in conclusion to his lecture, by "a foreign name, just as if the poet had to reconcile himself and his ownmost self, i.e., had to submit and resign himself, to something foreign [*gleich als müsste der Dichter sich und sein Eigenstes in ein Fremdes schicken, d.h. bringen und fügen*]") (*EHP*, 205), the Western relation to the foreign is opened up to other others and to other shores than those of Greece and the European peoples. In concluding this chapter, I will take up this "strange" turn by Heidegger to a kind of foreignness that, although radically different from one's own, can perhaps no longer be conceived as an opposite. Yet, as Heidegger leaves no doubt in his lecture, without relating to the foreignness of other such shores the salvation of the Occident is no longer possible.

Let us take our starting point in Hölderlin's verse from "Greece," which claims that "a great beginning can come even to the humble." However great the dawning of Greece—that is, in Hölderlin's terms, the Orient—may be, the addressee of this beginning must not in advance be something equally great; it can however be something humble, namely, "the native land" of Hölderlin—in other words, Hesperia, or the Occidental. Hence the Occident is the humble in that, unlike the great beginning in Greece, it is not great in terms of originariness. Heidegger writes: "The humble is the occidental. Greece, however, the oriental, is the great beginning that may possibly come. The humble *is*, however, only insofar as it *becomes* that to which the great beginning can come" (*EHP*, 200). As the humble, the Occidental, rather than the culmination of an epiphanic process, is that to which the great beginning can come, and to which it may come if the Occident readies itself and becomes that, in the first instance, to which such a beginning can possibly come. As is evident from the extensive commentary in "Hölderlin's Earth and Heaven," in the second letter to Böhlendorff, the humble *becomes* the humble only on the condition of a return to it as one's native land, now, however, "'more familiar with the authentic essence of the Greeks'" and capable of looking in "'philosophical light'"—that is, in a light that "is 'philosophical,' [and that] arises out of Greece, as its name *philosophia* discloses, [at what is one's own]. There the truth of being originally opened itself up as the shining revelation of what comes to presence" (*EHP*, 186). Now, what is it precisely that in the context of "Hölderlin's Earth and Heaven" is said to come into presence and in the light of which the Occident can become ready for the great beginning to come? As Heidegger remarks, "Greece itself approaches [the poet] in the shining of earth and heaven, in the holy which conceals the god, in the poetizing-thinking being of man" (*EHP*, 187). What the poet preserves in remembrance after his return to the native land is, in particular, "the richer relation," "the more tender relation," or "the whole relation" that interconnects the shining forth of the four dimensions that make up what Heidegger elsewhere called the fourfold, making them belong to one another in what Hölderlin, using the term in its eighteenth-century sense characterizes as "tenderness [*Zärtlichkeit*]." "Tenderness," Heidegger comments, "constitutes the fundamental characteristic of the 'popularity' of the Greeks—that is, their native [*einheimische*] essence" (*EHP*, 185; trans. mod.). How is one to understand this richer relation characterized as one in which heaven and earth, gods and men belong together and, obviously, form a whole, that is, a world in tenderness, which Hölderlin, back in his native land, preserves in remembrance? On the basis of a philosophical fragment from the poet's first Homburg period, in which he speaks of "the more tender infinite relation," Heidegger shows the poet to draw on Schelling's and Hegel's speculative conception of the "in-finite" in order to thoughtfully poetize what has been sent on its way in Greece as the destiny of the Occident. Heidegger writes:

> In-finite means that the ends and the sides, the regions of the relation, do not stand by themselves cut-off and one-sidedly; rather freed of one-sidedness and finitude, they belong *in*-finitely to one another in the relation which "thoroughly" holds them from its center [*Mitte*]. The center, so called because it centers [*mittelt*], that is, mediates, is neither earth nor heaven, God nor man. The in-finity that is to be thought here is abysmally different from that which is merely without end, which, because of its uniformity, allows no growth. (*EHP*, 188)

In contrast to spurious infinity, but perhaps also to the dialectical and speculative conception of infinity itself, where, after all, the process of mediation takes place in view of a sublating end, "the 'more tender relation' of heaven and earth, God and man, can become more intimate" (*EHP*, 188). Most likely, a hint of how specifically "the more tender in-finite relation" differs from the Idealist conception of in-finity can be gleaned from the precise meaning of *tenderness* in this in-finite relation.

Drawing on some of Hölderlin's poems and drafts, Heidegger defines the richer, more tender, relation of which heaven and earth are a part as a relation of voices of destiny (*Stimmen des Geschicks*), that is, voices that are sent on their way, destined to other voices, and that in their response to one another find their "right disposition," or more accurately, their right determination [*Bestimmung*]. The sense in which these voices' relations to one another can be characterized as "tender" is suggested when Heidegger speaks of "the directions [*Weisungen*] of the great destiny which points and sends everyone to where he is needed according to his being," that is, in its proper place with respect to his or her other or others (*EHP*, 191). Tenderness is but an openness to the other and to the foreign from which everything comes into its own, its proper place. Such tenderness is a specific characteristic of the Greeks, and it concerns, as Heidegger submits, their "capacity for the highest affection [*Zuneigung*] for, and the utmost intimation [*Mitteilung*] of, what a people in their native character fatefully encounters as the foreign. . . . Tenderness, with its gladdening-bestowing and at the same time simply-receiving essence . . . holds the earth open to the heaven" (*EHP*, 192). In tenderness the native bends toward the other, or foreign, which in turn leans toward it, thus making one and the other communicate, each one dividing itself within itself, each one finding, in the process, its own proper place. The richer, more in-finite, relation between the native and the foreign, then, is that of a whole in which everything is held open to its other, in which nothing remains isolated and finite but infinitely reverberates with its other.

Of Hölderlin's poetry Heidegger asserts that "there are four voices which ring out: heaven, earth, man, and god. Destiny gathers the whole infinite relation in these four voices. Yet none of the four stays and goes one-sidedly by itself. In this sense, none is finite. None is without the others. *In*-finite, they hold themselves to each other, they are what they are from the *in*-finite relation, they are this whole relation itself" (*EHP*,

194). The whole relation is the relation in which what is native and one's own and what is foreign becomes determined in the first place, insofar as without a submitting (*fügt*) to the foreign, and a leaning toward it so as to become transposed into it (*bringt sich in ein Fremdes*), no propriety is conceivable. At the same time, this in-finite relation is the richer relation because it also allows the foreign to be the foreign to begin with and, by the same token, to have a constitutive role to play with respect to the native, which, without opening itself up to it, would never be what it is and would remain stuck in its isolation and finitude.

That which gathers together the four moments of the whole relation from its center, or rather, middle, is "the sending of destiny." "As the center of the whole relation, destiny is the all-gathering beginning. As the ringing out of the great destiny, the center is the great beginning" (*EHP*, 195). Seen as the destiny (as the sending on its way of the call for openness to the foreign) that gathers earth and heaven, man and god intimately together by making each one stretch toward the other (thus dividing and communicating itself, so as to be addressed by it), the beginning is not a punctual happening that, once it has taken place, would make room for things to follow from it. Heidegger, responding to the question of the manner in which a beginning *is* a beginning, remarks that "a beginning is present, insofar as it remains in its coming. For the mediation that gathers the four into the center of their intimacy is a first coming. Beginning remains as advent. The beginning remains all the more, the closer it keeps itself within the possibility that it can come, and in its coming brings and sends that which it keeps itself: the in-finite relation" (*EHP*, 195). Destiny as a sending is thus the incitation of the native and the foreign, the Occident and the Orient, to open themselves up in intimacy to exteriority, to an irreducible foreign and other. As a commencement, destiny is nothing but the enduring demand of such a relation as a relation to come. As the great beginning that emerged in Greece or the Orient, this beginning can, as we have seen, come to the humble—in short, the Occident.

At first sight, the very evocation by Heidegger of a commencement in Greece that bears on the Occident without linking it to the question of Being as the fundamental philosophical question of the West since Parmenides is surprising. Our task will consist in teasing out at least some of the stakes that come with this omission for precisely what is to be thought here—the in-finite relation that Greece has bequeathed to the Occident.

But first, let us return to "Hölderlin's Earth and Heaven," where Heidegger poses the question, "Does the occidental still exist?" He answers: "It has become Europe": the implication being that the occidental has been replaced by the planetary expansion of a world civilization shaped by technology, science, and industry, and which not only has its origin in Europe but has become synonymous with it (*EHP*, 200). Covering the entire earth as a planet, Europe's industrial-technological domination, which, by means of its "planetary-interstellar calculation," has done away with heaven and earth, and by extension, the in-finite relation, is no longer the Occident to which an Orient—a certain Greece—could come and speak (*EHP*, 201). As Heidegger claims, however, "the present-interstellar world condition is thoroughly european-occidental-grecian" in that the calculating relation to what exists only as a standing reserve is solely intelligible from the forgotten destiny that has been sent on its way at the commencement (*EHP*, 201). After having cited Paul Valéry's questions, in "The Crisis of the Spirit" (1919), of whether Europe is to become merely "a small cape of the asiatic continent" or to remain the brain of the entire terrestrial body, Heidegger proposes a third question that, rather than "pass over and beyond Europe," inquires back into its beginning (*EHP*, 201).[35] He asks: "Must Europe, as this cape and brain, first become a land of an evening from which another morning of the world-destiny prepares its rise?" (*EHP*, 201). In other words, since the in-finite relation has, as Heidegger suggests, "never yet appeared within our history as this *in*-finite relation, purely joined together by the gathering of the voices of destiny, never yet become present, never yet been founded as a whole within what is highest in art," Europe has never ever been the Occident as that which could prepare another morning (*EHP*, 200). Europe can only become the Occident if it opens itself up to this other, this foreign voice that comes from its great, but reserved, commencement and to which, so far, it has been oblivious. Only by thus becoming the Occident could Europe also become another morning, from which another beginning, and another Orient, could arise. This other morning would be that of the in-finite relation, in short, of a relating without compromise to the foreign, and ultimately without any closure upon itself in some kind of self-identity. Change can come in Europe, and that is, in the present world condition, only from the great commencement in Greece to which all return is excluded, but which, awaiting Europe, is that which can still come to Europe. At this juncture of his lecture, however, Heidegger makes a surprising observation: "The great beginning becomes present, as that which awaits us, only in its coming to the humble. But the humble can no longer abide in its occidental isolation. It is opening itself up to those few other great beginnings which, with their own character, belong in the sameness of the beginning of the in-finite relation in which the earth is contained" (*EHP*, 201). No explicit indication is given as to what these few other great beginnings could be, although one can safely assume that Heidegger must be thinking of Lao Tzu's and Chuang Tzu's Taoism or perhaps also of Japanese thought, as he had become acquainted with it through Count Kuki and other interlocutors. Nor does Heidegger elaborate on why "the humble can no longer abide in its occidental isolation," in other words, no longer link its fate to the Greek commencement alone. Let me first emphasize that by acknowledging other great beginnings, however few they may be, the hitherto claimed uniqueness and privilege of Greece seems to have become questionable not only in general but also in relation to the West itself. But a more nuanced appraisal of this acknowledgment of other great beginnings is warranted here. Undoubtedly, the change that must come to a world that has been thoroughly Europeanized through its technological and industrial domination can come first only from the forgotten commencement in Greece, which itself, in being forgotten, is responsible for what the Occident has become. But if, furthermore, the need for change demands an overcoming of the West's "occidental isolation," it is precisely because of the in-finite relation that itself demands that everything, including the Occident, open itself up to the foreign. What distinguishes the great commencement that is Greece is that as the in-finite relation it opens itself not only to the other and the foreign but, more important, is itself an openness to other great beginnings. This, then, is also the point at which we may broach the question of what is at stake in Heidegger's relinquishment of the notion of Being in the context of his understanding of the greatness of the Greek commencement. Initially, the Greek commencement was conceived by Heidegger as the emergence of the thought of Being as such. Is not the later abandonment of Being, or even its explicit crossing out, indicative of the recognition that Being qua Being can never be present *as* such and that hence it can (and must) manifest itself in founding events other than the Greek or the Occidental? Indeed, does not Heidegger's talk in "Letter on Humanism" of the history of metaphysics (i.e., of Western thought) as "a distinctive and up to now the only perceptible [*die bisher allein übersehbare*] phase of the history of Being"—in other words, as a phase that, because it has completed itself in modernity and come to an end in the "form of truth" of technology, can be grasped at one glance—not suggest that the history of Being may not be limited to the West and that nonmetaphysical histories of Being may have to be envisaged? But in what some have described as a second *Kehre*—the turn away from Being *as* the fundamental and founding conception of the commencement—Heidegger seems to go one step beyond merely acknowledging other great beginnings on the basis that they articulate the same, only differently, namely Being as it has been thought initially in Greece. Although Being implies, as we have seen, the uncompromising openness to otherness and to what is foreign, the notion of an in-finite relation alone would, in the first place, seem to permit a relation to *other* great beginnings. Certainly, as Heidegger notes, these other great beginnings, "with their own character, belong in the sameness of the beginning of the in-finite relation in which the earth is contained" (*EHP*, 201). But understood as different ways of projecting world in terms of an in-finite relation, Europe, as one such way (a way, moreover, that as metaphysical and technological also spells the end of Europe), can no longer ignore them and must enter into a dialogue with them. More important, the recognition of other great beginnings calls on Europe to cease to be Europe and to become the Occident for the first time by listening to the in-finite relation that has been sent on its way and thus to become a new morning for a world radically open to other beginnings, beginnings that, possibly, are no longer beginnings of the same. Undoubtedly, these commencements of the in-finite relation are other beginnings and irreducibly foreign to the West. Whether they still fit the characterization of opposites, others that are the others *of* Europe, would need to be seen. In addition, whether the encounter of these other great commencements would still abide by the rules of the fundamental law of becoming homely in the unhomely—a law developed in the context of the problematic of Being—or whether becoming homely in the unhomeliness of other beginnings would not rather call forth a different law: this is a question that would also need to be considered.

PART III

Jan Patočka

§ 7 Care of the Soul

In the same way as for Husserl and, all differences considered, for Heidegger, "Europe," for Jan Patočka, is not primarily a geographical or purely political concept. In fact, according to Patočka, if we talk about Europe solely as a political formation, "the question of what it really is, and what it grows out of, is neglected" because such talk pays no regard to the concept's *"spiritual* foundation" (*PE*, 179). But if it is necessary to understand that Europe is a concept that lies on spiritual grounds, this is not merely for conceptual reasons. Indeed, like Husserl and Heidegger, Patočka aims to come to terms with the present situation of Europe, and the world, and it is in the context of this urgent practical concern that the recollection of the concept's "spiritual origins" (*HE*, 80) takes place. The attempt to retrieve the spiritual origin of the concept of Europe, and, above all, the emphasis on the spiritual foundation of this concept, is a function of Patočka's concern with the present-day situation of Europe and the world. From the outset, let me therefore underline the intrinsic linkage in Patočka of the question of present Europe to the memory of, and responsibility to, the European heritage, even though, as we will see, Patočka will show himself to be quite selective in determining the ultimate origin of Europe that merits the title "spiritual."

In an essay from the 1950s entitled "Over-Civilization and Its Internal Conflict," Patočka, in a style clearly reminiscent of Husserl's *The Crisis of European Sciences*, characterizes the situation of modern and contemporary Europe as a crisis of rational civilization.[1] The same is also the case in the manuscript "Reflections on Europe," dating from the 1970s, in which Patočka, after having credited Husserl's *Crisis* for being of "capital importance for the problems of a post-European humanity," asks the question of whether "the Husserlian project of deepening the foundations of European rationality is capable of putting humanity onto a new road, and of overcoming the crisis of the principle of Europe" (*LS*, 181).[2] Although the notion of crisis is still frequently used in the *Heretical Essays*, in the private seminar from the summer of 1973, which preceded the drafting of the *Essays* and which has been published under the title *Plato and Europe*, the term *crisis* recedes and is replaced by notions of decay, decadence, decline, and so forth. Undoubtedly, if contemporary Europe with its technological civilization, or such civilization in general, is judged to be decadent, it is because it has nothing to oppose to its decline, and because of this, it still could be said to be in crisis. But a crisis that arises from an inability to overcome a decline is, perhaps, also indicative of a diagnosis of the current state of Europe (as well as of the world) for which the concept of Europe is no longer primarily associated with the Husserlian idea of a universal rational science, or the thought of Being, which, according to Heidegger, is the inaugural meaning of *philosophia*. Yet if the spiritual foundations of Europe are, for Patočka, also those of Greek philosophy, it follows from this that he must understand *philosophia* in a different sense from that of Husserl and Heidegger.

Let me point out that in the 1939 article "Czech Culture in Europe," in which Patočka inquires into the reasons by which Europe's universal mission has been altered by recent developments, the idea of Europe that he opposes to the threat faced by Europe in the 1930s, in particular by the multiplication of nationalist regimes, their entrenchment within cultural frontiers, and their refusal of universality, is essentially the idea of rationality. By its very nature, this idea implies, as Marc Crépon has argued in an essay devoted to Patočka's article, "a non-coincidence [of Europe] with its history and even geography," because what thus defines Europe, namely its rationality, does not, by definition, belong to it as its peculiar property. Crépon writes: "What is proper to Europe is in the end to have no property, to disavow, in the very movement of universalization, all forms of appropriation."[3] To participate in what Patočka conceives as European humanism—by Europeans and non-Europeans alike—thus implies overcoming the particularity of national cultures, which become meaningful only within the horizon of their disappropriation, given that each singular culture can only acquire universal signification by surrendering everything that is particular about it. Crépon adds: "If rationality belongs to the European heritage (Greece and the Enlightenment), it is also what frees from this heritage since, by its universal vocation, rationality is no longer what is Europe's most own. The paradox of rationalism is that it not only liberates "the others," but what also liberates the Europeans from themselves—in short, what makes them the object in turn of a rationality directed toward them, and which de-possesses them of their privilege. The universality of rationalism is synonymous with its decentering."[4] The idea of Europe upheld in Patočka's essay from 1939, rather than being that of a project intent on integrating singular nationalities into a European Culture, consists in the challenge of disappropriation addressed to all cultures, namely, "to open themselves," as Crépon puts it, "to the encounter of other foundations and other horizons."[5] Obviously, this is an understanding of the idea of Europe still very much in line with its Husserlian conception in the Vienna lecture and, above all, in the *Crisis*, which dates from approximately the same period. Even in some of his later work Patočka continues his effort to come to task with what Crépon calls "the excess of rationality" in a way similar to that of Husserl, by inquiring into the exact place of *ratio* in the life-world, and to balance it out by way of a principle of negativity.[6]

But in *Heretical Essays* and *Plato and Europe* a truly new, and original, conception of what is European emerges. In distinction from Husserl's conception that the origin and telos of Europe is a genuinely universal rational science, and from Heidegger's claim that Europe or the West is grounded in the oblivion of the thought of Being, Patočka holds that "Europe as Europe arose . . . from . . . the motive of the care of the soul" (*PE*, 70). "*Europe*, especially Western Europe, but even that other one [namely, Eastern Europe], arose out of *the care of the soul—tes psyches epimeleisthai*. This is the embryo out of which arose what Europe used to be" (*PE*, 89). According to Patočka, "the care of the soul [as] the central theme around which . . . the life plan of Europe crystallized" (*PE*, 15) is the theme that forms the core of Greek philosophy. "*The soul forms the center of philosophy. Philosophy is the care of the soul* in its own essence and in its own element" (*PE*, 91). Even though the motive itself appears only explicitly in Plato, Patočka contends that the idea of the care of the soul is the concern of Greek philosophy as such.[7] Thus if the specificity of Europe is owed to its spiritual origin in the heritage of Greek philosophy, this is because philosophy in Greece is to be understood from this fundamental concern with the soul. Yet, what is meant by the care, or tendance, of the soul? How is the soul determined, and in what sense is it to be cared for? Furthermore, considering that it replaces both the Husserlian and Heideggerian conceptions of what is European, what does it have in common with, and how does it differ from, the latter versions of what Europe is?

However, before elaborating in some detail on this claim that the Platonic motif of the care of the soul is the central theme of what Europe means, I need to clarify how this theme is intertwined with the Czech thinker's allegiance to phenomenological thought and his critical debate, in particular, with the philosophy of Husserl. More precisely, what is required is an—at least, very succinct—elucidation of how the motive of the care of the soul is connected in Patočka's thought to his critical reevaluation of Husserl's notion of the life-world. Such an elucidation is necessary all the more since Patočka himself does not seem (to my knowledge at least) to have explicitly drawn, and elaborated on, the connection. In 1936 Patočka published a book-length study entitled *The Natural World as a Philosophical Problem*—a study on the world pregiven in any acts of consciousness and to any subjective acts of intentionality, in short, on what Husserl first called "natural world" and, only subsequently," life-world."[8] Whereas the analysis of the "natural world" in this work, which seeks to provide a synthetic exposition of Husserl's various analyses on this subject, is still deeply indebted to Husserl's conceptualization of the life-world, thirty-three years later, particularly in the collection of essays published in *Le monde naturel et le mouvement de l'existence humaine* but also in manuscripts from the beginning of the 1970s, one of which the French translator entitled "Réflexion sur l'Europe," Patočka proposes a radically revised conception of the natural world.[9] Patočka's recast life-world is the result of the effort to fully break with Cartesianism and its presuppositions and to achieve what he refers to as an "asubjective phenomenology," distinct from the modern Cartesianists' philosophies, especially Husserlian phenomenology. More precisely, this novel understanding of the life-world is directed, first and foremost, against Husserl's subjectivization of the world, or the ultimate horizon, as well as against his understanding of the life-world from the perspective of the exact sciences—that is, exclusively, as the hidden ground of the formalization and objectification that they accomplish. Indeed, as Paul Ricoeur has also noted, for the Husserl of *The Crisis of the European Sciences and Transcendental Philosophy*, "the natural world remains a question of theoretical reason."[10] Contrary to Husserl, for whom, as a Cartesianist, subjectivity understood in purity is an absolute given—that is, given in absolute evidence as an absolute being—and according to whom the horizon of the world and its objects is (only) the correlate of the various intentionalities of this pure consciousness, in Patočka's later work the world is not "a part of interiority, but, on the contrary, an extreme outside which alone provides the framework for all exteriority, for each spatial thing and to space as such" (*LS*, 194–95). Rather than the constitutive agent of the world, the ego, or subject, whether transcendental or not, is led to be an intraworldly entity, similar in this to other objects within the world. As Patočka remarks, "the subject is simply a species of objectivity" (*LS*, 161). Taken in its broadest sense—that is, as "world" in an originary sense—the world is determined by its capacity to make everything appear, both subject and object. As will become clear hereafter, the natural pregiven world is the structure of appearing itself, one that is more universal, and more encompassing, than the universality characteristic not only of the laws that pertain to the objects of the world but also of the universality pertaining to the world-constituting acts of consciousness as they have been analyzed by Husserl. Compared to the world in this originary phenomenal sense, Husserl's "life-world (or natural world) is a secondary concept of world notwithstanding all the intuitive concretion that it pretends to reunite" (*LS*, 196). Even though Husserl sought to deepen the foundation of scientific rationality and formalism by demonstrating that its roots are to be found in the life-world, he was right, Patočka remarks, to characterize the latter as "the world of *doxa*—that is, of [mere] appearance" (*LS*, 196). Not only that, by conceiving of the life-world primarily as the ground of scientific ratio—that is, in view of something that, rather than a commonality, is something specifically European although it pretends to be universal, the life-world, thus understood, cannot lay claim to being something that is truly common to all forms of humanity (*LS*, 212). Patočka, therefore, concludes that "the *life-world* as Husserl understands it remains an abstraction, one which is regulated [*régie*] by the special function of science. Consequently, the *life-world* is not the world in the proper sense. The Husserlian conception [of the life-world] obfuscates [*escamotte*], does not thematize, and forgets the world as the properly phenomenal plane" (*LS*, 212). But in the same way as Husserl considered a reflection on the life-world to be the condition for overcoming the European crisis, for Patočka, too, a clarification of the world as the asubjective phenomenal foundation of both subject and object is required, if Europe, according to Patočka's more modest project, is to be given another chance (*LS*, 211).

For us to gain access to the natural world that constitutes the common foundation of humanity, the "world as world" needs to manifest itself as such. Such manifestation presupposes the discovery of that which "in man is independent of the historical consequences of his evolution"—independent, for example, of the development of the rational sciences, and, hence, of the specific version of metaphysics that the natural sciences represent (*MNM*, 24, 52). Patočka writes: "The problem of the natural world, conceived in depth as the restitution of the originary character of the world and of its components, is linked to the question of a revision of metaphysics" (*MNM*, 52). Indeed, since "the being of man is not like that of a stone, an animal, or a divinity, something that is already completed and which he receives passively," the natural world as that which is common to both prehistoric and historic man, it is not to be conceived as an essence that would be given once and for all (*MNM*, 24–25). Indeed, on one occasion at least, Patočka speaks of the natural world as an idea (*MNM*, 86). The discovery of the natural world as the common ground of all humanities presupposes a revision of metaphysics, because this ground to be brought to light is the source of all the human being's possibilities. In other words, for the later Patočka, whose indebtedness to Heidegger's fundamental ontology thus comes into relief, the natural world and its ontological characters are to be understood primarily in terms of, and in relation to, Being, and the sense of Being, in short, in a temporal perspective.[11] Human life, according to Patočka is *dunamis*—the realization of possibilities—and as such is characterized by movement in an originary temporal sense.[12] As a consequence, the natural world—that is, the world in advance of the human being's theoretical life, is not, at first, "the world that we contemplate, but the world in which we *move*, in which we are active" (*MNM*, 46). Distinct from Husserl's conception of the life-world as the realm of originary evidences, Patočka's conception of the originary foundation of being human shows that the life-world discloses itself only insofar as humans are continuously involved in movements in the world in which the world and human beings are interrelated.[13] The revised conception of the natural world provided by Patočka is a world in which human existence is primarily understood in terms of movement that therefore also implies a revision, more precisely, a radicalization and a new conception of the Aristotelean notion of *kinesis* itself, hence, a whole new ontology. Understood in an originary sense, movement is "originary life"—that is, "life that does not receive its unity from a conserved substrate but which creates itself its peculiar unity as well as that of the thing in movement" (*MNM*, 103).[14] Patočka writes: "The natural world is the world of movement; its key is to be found in the movement characteristic in the world, of the movement of a being that belongs to the world" (*MNM*, 47). Now, the phenomena analyzed by a "hermeneutics of the fundamental phenomena of human life," understood in terms of movement in this originary ontological sense, can, "in the same way as the intentional structures of Husserl, claim a universally accessible and demonstrable character" (*MNM*, 64). Taking "its departure in a comprehension of the three fundamental ecstasies of temporality and of the movements of existence that proceed from them," the reflexive method adopted to analyze the natural world shows that the latter is constituted by three movements that derive from the threefold structure of temporality analyzed by Heidegger in *Being and Time* and that are the realizations of "three fundamental possibilities of the human being" (*MNM*, 64, 106). These are "the movement of taking root [*enracinement*], of extending the self by way of an expropriation [*désaisissement*], and finally, of finding oneself through devotion.[15] This [threefold] movement is movement in the most originary and strongest sense. Each one of our 'physical movements' is in truth part of this total and all-embracing movement that we are" (*MNM*, 46).[16]

Before I elaborate on these three distinct movements that constitute the natural world, a further remark about how to understand the sweep of the concept of "natural world" may be warranted. Indeed, as Paul Ricoeur has argued in his preface to Patočka's *Heretical Essays*, Patočka's heresy with respect to the conception of the natural world in the classical versions of phenomenology consists in defining "the natural world as the world of prehistory" (*HE*, ix). Ricoeur adds: "the natural world is not the prescientific world, but the prehistorical world; that is, the non-problematic world" (*HE*, xi). It is true that Patočka, after having defined "the natural world, the world of human life . . . as the totality of the fundamental modes of human comportment, of their presuppositions and sedimentations," and shown that it "breaks up into various partial movements" (*HE*, 10), notes that "we could also speak of the natural world in a somewhat different sense if we were to understand by it the world prior to the discovery of its problematic character." Understood as the "world of a pregiven meaning," the natural world would thus come to designate the prehistorical world (*HE*, 12).[17] Yet although, admittedly, a reflection on the natural world in this sense might help us to understand what history is, Patočka also emphasizes that the natural world thus conceived is only "*one* mode of the natural world" (*HE*, 14; trans. mod.), that is, of the natural world in the sense of the totality of all human modes of comportment. As will become clear hereafter, the natural world, in the sense of the prehistorical world of humankind, corresponds to one of the fundamental movements that constitute the natural world, or life-world, as such. Not only that: however discrete, these movements are not without including one another even though in each world to which one movement gives rise, it is this movement that predominates. As a result, the natural world in the sense of the prehistoric world participates as well in the other two movements, particularly in the third movement of human life—that is, the movement of truth (*HE*, 33). It follows from this that even the prehistorical worlds are historical. Patočka concludes: "All the historical worlds are 'naturel.'" (*HE*, 12).

The three intimately interrelated temporal movements thus make up the total movement that we are and constitute the three fundamental ways in which we relate to the world. They constitute the natural world as a totality in which humans live their lives in a relation to this totality without, however, ever being able to dominate it by way of an objective intuition. Yet it is important to recognize that even though the three fundamental movements in question make up the natural world as a total, all-embracing, movement, they are not of equal stature. They are not situated on the same plane. Very succinctly: the movement of taking root is the primordial movement, since by acknowledging and accepting the priority of *physis*, or the earth, over our lives, this movement realizes the solid point to lean on, the resting place, required for any movement in the first place. This movement (together with the following) is at the heart of the human beings' prehistorical world. The second movement of self-extension by way of expropriation (of oneself but above all of the other, and his or her pragmatic manipulation), or of reproduction of oneself, occurs with respect to, and within, what is present and given (things and others in the world). This movement consists in transforming what is present and given in the name of life itself, turning what is, others and things, into utensils for the benefit of the prolongation of life, thus chaining life to itself. Let me also emphasize that if the first movement consists in a total relation to what already exists, whose aim is not only to secure a solid foundation for all movements but also the "ecstatic appeasement, and fascination by what has thus been reached"—which Patočka—in *Heretical Essays*—refers to as the dimension of the sacred and orgiastic, the second movement, which is all tied up with the usefulness of things for the benefit of individuation (and in which the primary domain of *phusis* has been repressed, or pushed back into darkness), in short, the movement of labor, culminates in the flight into anonymity, alienation, and inauthenticity (*MNM*, 114). The difference between these two movements is also the ground for another important difference, the one between the exceptional (the feast) and everydayness that plays such a crucial role within the problematic of the care of the soul, in particular, as it is elaborated in *Heretical Essays*.

Within the differentiation of the total movement, the third movement, entitled "movement of the breakthrough [*percée*], or of true self-comprehension"—or, according to the "Afterword" in *Le monde naturel comme problème philosophique*, "the movement of truth [*mouvement véritatif*]"—is "the most important, and, from the point of view of the human, the most significant" (*MNM*, 118; *MNPH*, 178). In distinction from the movement in which life is lived in the rapture of the feast, and on which "rests a reflection of the superhuman, and the divine," but especially from the life of labor in which we turn away from ourselves and fall prey to things in the world, "the third aspect of the movement of life is characterized as an approach to self-conquering one's self through self-sacrifice by claiming and taking upon ourselves our own finitude" (*MNM*, 119, 10). Indeed, this movement of life—the movement specific to an existence that explicitly embraces the problematicity of human life—is about "an encounter, not with a foreign being [as in the world of things], but with true being." Here, in the historical world opened by the movement of truth, it is a question of "seeing myself in my human essence and in my ownmost possibility—in what makes me an inhabitant of the earth, and which, at the same time, consists of a relation to being and the universe" (*MNM*, 118). In other words, in this third aspect of the movement of life, whose ontological structure is the foundation of philosophy, myth, religion, and art, "the possibility of [realizing] an explication with what we are, precisely in totality, takes place—namely, the possibility of either scattering ourselves [in the foundation of life] and losing ourselves in the singular [of the world of things], or of finding and realizing ourselves in our specifically human nature" (*MNM*, 119).

In distinction from what Patočka describes as Husserl's intellectualism in the latter's approach to the life-world, the approach of mapping the natural world according to the temporal aspects of movement underscores the primacy of practical involvement and of an understanding of being that, rather than thematic, is, in Husserlian terms, only instinctive, if not corporeal.[18] Needless to say, this primacy of the practical is also a determining element of the third movement of life. For the kind of reflection on the natural world that Patočka practices, the issue is not simply one of establishing in immanent intuition and pure donation an absolute being, since the awareness of that in terms of which we have to perceive ourselves if we are to accomplish the transition from our factical possibilities to our authentic possibility involves "a responsibility toward what we have been until now and toward what we plan to be in the future" (*MNM*, 56). With the third aspect of the global movement, the question is one of the responsibility toward life's ownmost destiny, which pits the human being against the factical possibilities—fusion with the divine, or self-alienation—that are incompatible with the possibility of freedom and, hence, authenticity. Looking down on the flight from its intrinsic finitude, facing its mortality rather than fusing with the sacred, or losing sight of one's mortality in the everyday routine of the sphere of work by relating everything that is encountered to one's own being understood as a self, the true, or ownmost mode of being consists in taking upon oneself the fundamental possibility for the human being of being authentic. The third movement within the global movement of the natural world is the breakthrough to authenticity in that here the acceptance of finitude takes the form of a mode of being of exposedness to others and of a life outside of one's own self-enclosed self. In contrast to what obtains in the individualized world of everydayness, "the confrontation of finitude takes on now the meaning of devotion. My being is no longer defined as a being for me, but as a being in devotion, a being that opens up to being, that lives in order for things to be, in order that things—but also myself and the others—show themselves as they are. This means, a life in devotion, a life outside itself, outside oneself [*hors de soi*]" (*MNM*, 122). At a 1975 conference entitled "Spiritual and Intellectual Man," in the context of a private seminar ("The Origin and the End of Europe"), Patočka speaks of the project of such a mode of being of self-sacrifice, devotion, and existence outside one's self, in terms of an "exposition to the negative." Living outside oneself—in the open and in the void, so to speak, these aspects of what Patočka determines as self-sacrifice—is the project of "a *new* life," a spiritual life. Patočka avers: "In contrast to ordinary life which confines itself to never questioned self-evidence and security, never aiming at anything beyond, spiritual man lives expressly from the negative" (*LS*, 247). For the Czech philosopher, spiritual life is not only a life that chooses to be at home in negative experiences and that "lives in uprootedness," thus understood; it is also the project of Europe with which he seeks to confront contemporary European spirit, "which for the last three hundred years set out to conquer the world, wanting to understand and dominate things on the basis of things, and in the absence of world" (*LS*, 248, 210–11).

Even though Patočka never explicitly refers to the Platonic motive of the care of the soul in the context of his revision of Husserl's conception of the life-world, which, as we have seen, is not for the Czech phenomenologist the world in the proper sense, and which he, therefore, replaces with his conception of the natural world as the total, or global, movement of human existence, the analysis of the three movements is precisely the framework within which this motive becomes a determining theme. The third movement of the breakthrough of the possibility of authenticity in a life of devotion and sacrifice of a self that is chained to itself, in opposition to the primal movement of a fusion with roots, the earth, or the sacred, and the second movement of the inauthentic mode of being in everydayness, represents the ontological structure within which the theme of the care of the soul becomes meaningful. Supposing that these reasons are considered insufficient to justify the connection, the following remark by Patočka should put all questions to rest. He writes: "Life in devotion is, in a certain sense, eternal life. . . . Life that devotes itself lives outside itself and is the attestation of the authenticity of this 'outside itself' by way of that which it renounces. Such life is thus the beginning of a community of those who understand themselves in renouncement and devotion." For, indeed, the care of the soul, insofar as it is the embryonic idea of Europe, is the project of a life in a breakaway from the natural temptations that the first and the second movement provide—that is, a life in its own right, independent, however fragile, from nature, a life that is immortal in a certain sense—in short, spiritual life.

According to the essay from *Heretical Essays* entitled "Europe and the European Heritage Until the End of the Nineteenth Century" and "Is Technological Civilization Decadent, and Why?"—as well as *Plato and Europe*—the notion of the care of the soul is nothing less than *the* "bequest of ancient Greek philosophy" (*HE*, 82)—that is, the spiritual foundation that has been determinative for the project of Europe. As is well known, this theme of the care of the soul is a fundamental elementary notion in Plato's earliest dialogues—around which all of Socrates' concerns are gathered. But, according to Patočka this concern with the care of the soul is also the central theme of Platonic philosophy as a whole insofar as it is driven by the aspiration for a good life (*PE*, 195). Yet even though this Socratic motive is central to Patočka's thought, he refers only obliquely to its sources in the Platonic texts, without discussing or expanding on this motive in the context of the dialogues that are devoted to this question. Therefore, a brief digression to the Platonic texts may be warranted here. In the *Apology* Socrates repeatedly accuses his fellow citizens of only giving their "attention to acquiring as much money as possible, and . . . reputation and honor," and he exhorts them to give "attention or thought to truth and understanding and the perfection of [their] soul."[19] *Alciabides I* is, undoubtedly, the dialogue that, in spite of its contested authenticity, provides the most methodical exposition of the theme in question.

The long digression on the care of the soul occurs in *Alcibiades I* after Socrates has made Alcibiades—who though seeking public office has had to acknowledge that he has not the necessary skills to do so and lacks knowledge about the kind of agreement that in ruling over other human beings is to be striven for—aware that he does not know what he is saying and is unconscious of himself. Alcibiades is thus led to acknowledge that he must take care of himself—that is, first, discover himself. Indeed, in order to take care of and to better oneself, self-knowledge—a knowledge of the true nature of the self, that is, of the self itself (*auto tauto*) is necessary. The self, or the soul (*psyche*), is the man himself (*psyche estin anthropos*). As Socrates argues, "there is nothing which may be called more properly ourselves than the soul" (*DP* 1:667, 130d). Furthermore, as that which moves the body, the soul is "the user of the body" (*DP* 1:666, 129e). According to the dialogue, the soul, which "rules the body," is to the body as the user is to the used, the workman to his tool, while everything else is merely something that belongs to him (*DP* 1:666, 130a).

It follows from all of this that to take care of oneself is "to take care of the soul, and look to that" (*DP* 1:669, 132c). But since such care requires knowing the soul, Socrates resorts in the dialogue to an interpretation of the Delphian precept "Know Thyself" in which he compares self-knowing to self-seeing. For the eye to see itself, the eye must look into a reflecting surface such as a mirror. Yet another person's eye is precisely such a mirror. Socrates asks Alcibiades: "Did you ever observe that the face of the person looking into the eye of another is reflected as in a mirror; and in the visual organ which is over against him, and which is called the pupil, there is a sort of image of the person looking?" (*DP* 1:670, 133a). By looking into the eye of an other, one comes face to face with oneself on condition that one look at that in the eye of the other that is the most perfect. Socrates avers, "the eye, looking at another eye, and at that in the eye which is the most perfect, and which is the instrument of vision, will there see itself" (*DP* 1:670, 133a). The self-seeing that the eye achieves—and, mutatis mutandis, self-knowledge of the soul—is not only a function of what is most perfect in the eye itself—in other words, the "virtue of the eye" (*ophthalmou arete*)—such self-perception also sets a standard for bettering seeing and, by extension, bettering oneself (*DP* 1:670, 133b). As Socrates puts it, "if the soul, my dear Alcibiades, is ever to know herself, must she not look at the soul; and especially at that part of the soul where resides her virtue, which is wisdom (*sophia*), and at any other which is like this" (*DP* 1:670, 130b). Now that part of the soul that has to do with wisdom and knowledge is the part that is most divine. It is, says Socrates, "that part of the soul which resembles God; and he who looks at this and at the whole class of things divine, at God and at Wisdom, will be most likely to know himself" (*DP* 1:671, 133c). Just as a mirror, when compared to the reflecting virtue of the eye, is "truer and clearer and bright," so "also God is by his nature a clearer and brighter mirror than the most excellent part of our soul" when compared to the soul of another. Self-knowledge by virtue of a glance into what is most perfect in the soul of another must thus ultimately be foregrounded by a knowledge of the Divine, or the Good. Socrates concludes his digression on self-knowledge and care for one's soul by arguing that "by looking at God we shall use the finest mirror of the human soul and its virtue; and by such means we shall best behold and come to know ourselves" (*DP* 1:671, 133c). The care of the soul—that is, of the self itself, that which we most properly are—thus requires that we come to know the ultimate

Good, and that we measure ourselves up to it, and thus come to resemble in some way the Divine. Furthermore, such care of the soul through looking into what is—that is, through knowledge of the Good—also implies working at a full transparency of oneself. If God is the truest, clearest, and brightest mirror, a soul that reflects itself in such a mirror will have a knowledge of itself comparable to some degree at least to that of the Divine.

As we will see, for Patočka this ideal of clarity and transparency connected to the care of the soul is an intrinsic aspect of this theme that is the embryonic form of Europe. But there is another aspect to this concept that will be equally important for Patočka's account of the European heritage. Plato broaches this aspect in another dialogue, the *Phaedo*, where the care of the soul is linked to a care of death. Preparing to die easily is an essential ingredient of the care of the soul—that is, to achieve purity from everything corporeal, clarity within itself, and, hence, a unity of its own. Particularly in Socrates' second demonstration of the immortality of the soul, it is made clear that for the soul to achieve the necessary purity to become entirely invisible, and thus to be capable of being fully released from the imprisonment of the body, the human being must philosophize, that is, care for death. Philosophy as the care of death "encourages [the soul] to collect and concentrate itself by itself, trusting nothing but its own judgment."[20] Only by making sure that the soul "carries with it no contamination of the body, because it has never willingly associated with it in life, but has shunned it and kept itself separate [*synethroismene hautes eis heauten*, that is, gathered within itself] as its regular practice—in other words, if it has pursued philosophy in the right way and really practiced how to face death easily," the soul will have made itself similar to the other invisible, the divine, and hence become endowed with (a certain) immortality.[21] The care of death consists in making sure that the soul has collected itself within itself, and will, therefore, in death "escape [from the body] independent and uncontaminated," more precisely, separate itself all by itself in purity [*psychen auten kath authen eilikrine apallaxesthai*] from the body.[22] In our discussion of Patočka's understanding of the care of the soul, as the core of what is European, we will see how these two different aspects are intertwined.

As I have already pointed out, the emphasis on the spiritual heritage of Europe is motivated by the diagnosis of Europe's decline, as well as of that of the world. Before returning in greater detail to the theme of the care of the soul, which is precisely this heritage, as well as to the variations that it underwent in the genealogy of Europe, the very nature of the spiritual, and what it is supposed to achieve in the face of the decline, warrants elaboration. Patočka, indeed, raises the question of whether in Europe's heritage there is something that could work for the present situation—namely, in light of the insight that "the world is one of decline" (*PE*, 12). Now, in the introduction to the transcription of the recorded seminar *Plato and Europe*, Patočka proposes that the insight in question is based on "a universal experience." Humankind "has always known, in a certain sense, this general trend—[that] the world is one of decline" (*PE*, 12). As the reference in the context of this statement to the modern sciences suggests, Patočka is referring to the Second Law of Thermodynamics—that is, the law of entropy—which thus only confirms what humankind has from the beginning been aware of in a certain sense. In fact, I believe that it is not a distortion of Patočka's thought to claim that for him "humankind" is intrinsically defined by this universal experience of the decline or decadence of the world. Considering the philosophical assumption that "humankind" is a Greek conception, the fact that, as Patočka notes, the Greek philosophers argued against the belief that the world could age, presupposes precisely "this experience: the world is in decline" (*PE*, 12). Indeed, the philosophical discovery of eternity and immortality goes hand in hand with the universal experience of decline that defines humankind as such. Greek philosophy itself, with its talk about that which never ages, is a response, more precisely, a resistance, to the universal insight in question. "Philosophy says: no, the world is not in decline, because the core of the world is being, and being has no beginning and will not perish, being can neither begin nor end—it is eternal" (*PE*, 12). Undoubtedly, as Patočka admits, the philosophical insistence in Greece on eternity

> from the perspective of modern natural sciences . . . is incomprehensible. But what is encompassed by it? It is after all a resistance, a battle against that fall, against time, against the entire declining tendency of the world and of life. In a certain sense, this battle is understandably futile, but in another sense it is not, because the situation in which man finds himself varies accordingly to how he confronts it. And the freedom of mankind lies—perhaps—exactly in this! The Greeks, the Greek philosophers in whom the Greek spirit is expressed most sharply, expressed human freedom by the term: care of the soul. (*PE*, 13)

From this passage it becomes clear that the origin of philosophy, and its major theme of the care of soul in Greece, is from the start linked to the discovery of eternity and, therefore, of the order of a resistance to the universal experience of the fall of everything that is. Consequently, if the European heritage consists primarily in this concern with the soul, then "Europe" is not so much a project for overcoming all sorts of crises but primarily the figure of the resistance against "the declining tendency of the world and of life." To this general and inevitable trend, the care of the soul ("Europe," in short) opposes a change of attitude, a freedom to resist, even though, ultimately, such resistance may be futile. Rather than the discovery of something universal (humankind as such) on which the commonality of human beings could be grounded, the concept of Europe articulates the project of creating, by way of a change of attitude of the human to him- or herself, a distance to the general, irrevocable, tendency of the universe to a loss of energy and a state of complete homogeneity. As the defining concern in the face of the aging of the world with eternity and immortality demonstrates, the human, by caring for the soul, bracketing as it were the universal experience of decline, achieves a (however futile) freedom from decline, and entropy, and hence a certain ideality or spirituality—in other words, a kind of immortality. Europe, or the care of the soul, then, is, for Patočka, synonymous with a freedom of humankind manifest in the break with, or the distance to, humankind's universal experience of the general fall of the world and all that is. Patočka's question whether the European heritage contains an answer to the present situation arises from his diagnosis that Europe is in the throes of a crisis insofar as it has given up on resisting the universal decline.

But this freedom made possible by the care for the soul is above all the result of a change in attitude with respect to one form of decline. It is an attempt to come to grips with, if not even to overcome, the human being's finitude—that is, mortality.[23] According to Patočka, Plato's philosophy, which, at its core, focuses on the soul as something to be made firm and definite, is also "*melete thanatou*, care for death; care for the soul is inseparable from care for death which becomes true care for life; life (eternal) is born of this direct look at death, of an overcoming of death (perhaps it is nothing but this 'overcoming'). That, however, together with the relation to the Good, identifying with the good . . . means the rule of responsibility, and so of freedom. The soul is absolutely free, that is, it chooses its destiny" (*HE*, 105). Before discussing this passage, and in particular the parenthesis according to which eternal life is, perhaps, nothing but this "overcoming" of death, I point out that before explicitly engaging the theme of the care of the soul in *Plato and Europe*, Patočka makes a detour through Husserlian phenomenology, arguing that this detour will help to "more precisely determine the problem of the soul and the care of the soul as the central European thematic" (*PE*, 15). The theme of the care of the soul, he explains, will be elaborated against the backdrop of Husserl's conception of phenomenological reduction as it has been sketched out in *Ideas I*, chapter 31. Patočka notes that "phenomenological reduction literally means conversion into phenomenon" (*PE*, 15). Let me first attend to this notion of "conversion," which is also the term by means of which the Platonic notion of *anabasis* (the exit from the cave) is commonly translated. As is well known, for Husserl phenomenological reduction consists in a radical change of attitude regarding the natural world—that is, the universal thesis, or positing, underlying all ordinary relations to the world, and according to which the world is real, and there, in advance, independently of me. As Husserl himself underscores on several occasions in chapter 31 of *Ideas I*, such a change of value by which the positing of the existence of the world is "put . . . out of action," excluded, or "parenthesize[d]," "*is a matter in which we are perfectly free [unserer vollkommenen Freiheit].*" He adds: "With regard to *any* positing we can quite freely [*in voller Freiheit*] exercise this particular *epoche, a certain refraining from judgment which is compatible with the unshaken conviction of truth, even with the unshakable conviction of evident truth.*"[24] As a conversion into phenomenon, the phenomenological reduction is thus testimony of an act of perfect, or complete, freedom from the natural world and its underlying theses. Phenomenological reduction shows the subject to be capable of a distance to his or her surrounding world and all that he or she believes with respect to it—a distance that, as Husserl remarks, is compatible with, if not even constitutive of, truth. By grounding the Greek project of life based on the care of the soul, which, according to Patočka, has been determinative for Europe, on what contemporary phenomenology entitles phenomenological reduction, Patočka draws on implications of Husserlian thought that the latter, perhaps, left undeveloped, and he opens up a new way of thinking about Europe. It is from this ability implicit in phenomenological reduction of freeing oneself from the limitations of the natural world, and the subsequent conversion into phenomenon, in light of which the care of the soul is to be understood, that Patočka's specific contribution within the phenomenological tradition to thinking what is European derives.

So what about the phenomenon to which the conversion gives rise? Even though in *Plato and Europe*, Patočka elaborates on the phenomenon in light of the fundamental phenomenological distinction between appearing and what appears, manifesting itself and what is manifest, showing itself and what shows itself, he holds that "this conception—the problem of *manifesting* and *manifestation*—is from the very beginning *the ground of all reflection* of European peoples reflecting upon their situation in a peculiar guise" (*PE*, 42). Even though this fundamental problem breaks through already in Western mythical representations, Greek thought—philosophy in short—is this "entirely new possibility of the human spirit," constituted by a shift from a dimension of the past to that of the actual present, or from what is manifest to manifestation itself—"a possibility that also did not have to be realized and in fact the majority of peoples, even the highly cultured, do not know it at all" (*PE*, 58). From its inception in Greece, the manifest world showing itself in its totality, that is, manifestation itself, is the problem of philosophy, which poses its questions "face to face with the amazing *primeval fact of the manifestation* of the world" (*PE*, 59). Patočka's reminder that philosophy has from the start been concerned with the phenomenon is not simply a reminder of historical interest. It serves to put the Husserlian reflection on the phenomenon, as well as Heidegger's conception of Being, into perspective. Indeed, the reference to Greek thought, and particularly to Platonic philosophy, is indicative of a problem and a task for any reflection on the phenomenon, for if it is true that emerging philosophy has been, from the outset, determined by the problem of the phenomenality of the world, it is also true that rather than thematizing manifesting as such, and answering the question of what manifesting means, philosophy, from early on, has always substituted "some existent that is shown, that manifests itself, that is the object of showing [for] *showing itself*" (*PE*, 40). Patočka, by contrast, seeks to conceive of the phenomenon—manifesting itself—as separate from itself, that is, "in its pure structure *without regard to any kind of reality*" (*PE*, 41)—that is, as a structure that is thus *unreal*—and "as an autonomous lawful ordering" that pertains not to what is manifested but to "the lawfulness of its showing" (*PE*, 144). Although Patočka's reflections on the phenomenon take their starting point in Husserl's phenomenology, he holds that the primacy of the subject—a primacy that, as Patočka realized, is owed to Husserl's concerns with epistemology—prevents Husserlian phenomenology as well from giving the distinction between manifesting and the manifest the sharpness it deserves and from gaining truly universal insights into the phenomenal.[25] To define phenomenology, as Husserl did, as "a teaching about the transcendental subjectivity constituting the world and everything that is encompassed by the world," is, as Patočka remarks, "*insufficiently radical*. In that aspect [i.e., subjectivity], it presents us with a definite existent, that means something *revealed*, although very fluid and refined, instead of *the manifesting* of what is as such" (*PE*, 40; trans. mod.). For phenomenology to truly be a philosophy of manifesting itself, or the phenomenal, rather than a doctrine of phenomena, phenomenology has to recognize that the subject itself is a phenomenon among others. Only an entirely "a-subjective transcendental philosophy"—a title that Patočka explicitly claims for his own undertaking—would be capable of bringing phenomenality as such into view.[26] But, as Patočka's elucidation of the reasons why he has not made use of Heideggerian terminology in defining *showing itself* evidences, showing itself is also "*more primary*," "*more fundamental* and deeper than the problem of being" (*PE*, 133). To the question whether "the problem of being is not just *a part*, a moment of *showing*" (*PE*, 133), Patočka responds that "the problem of showing is deeper, more fundamental, more primary than the problem of being just because I can only get to the problem of being through the problem of showing" (*PE*, 165). After having noted that by conceiving of Being by way of a finite subject—Dasein—Heidegger himself realized "that this manner of thematizing being is still too close to Husserl's subjectivism" (*PE*, 171), Patočka concludes that the entire problematic of Being "has to be thought through again, so that we avoid subjectivistic consequences. That, then, is the grand thing of phenomenology" (*PE*, 176). In sum, the task of phenomenology is to study manifesting itself, or as such, as an autonomous domain in its own right.

Distinct from all phenomena in the common sense—that is, from everything in particular that shows, appears, or manifests itself to us, and with which we are cognitively or practically confronted in daily life—the phenomenon consists in manifesting itself or showing, as such, something in which we have ordinarily no interest. Patočka writes: "*We never know about showing*. Showing, phenomenon, that on the basis of which things are for us what they are, is itself constantly hidden from us" (*PE*,

25). Yet showing itself, the phenomenon, in short, is something on the basis of which alone "we have something like truth and error." Indeed, without manifesting itself, there is nothing—nothing in particular that has manifested itself, and with respect to which alone "truth and falsehood . . . make sense." Now, since "man is most deeply determined by the fact that he is the creature capable of—in contrast to all else in the world—truth and falsehood, good and evil" (*PE*, 25), "the entire essence of man, the whole question of his distinctiveness and his possibilities is connected to the problem of manifesting" (*PE*, 26). As a result, for the human being as a being capable of truth, and who can measure himself up against it, manifesting itself, which is the condition for what is to show itself as it is in truth, is thus "terribly important" (*PE*, 26)—terribly important, precisely, because this is for him, as we will see, an issue of either truth or malediction.

Before discussing how the question of manifesting itself is linked to that of the care of the soul, I need to point out that, according to the Czech phenomenologist, everything that he establishes about such a link is "no longer phenomenology! *Phenomenology* as the teaching about phenomenon is the patient seeking in [a] nonobjective stance, in a stance that does not go after things, that does not use phenomena for the mere unveiling of things" (*PE*, 32). Whereas phenomenology investigates how the things of our immediate exterior surroundings, and the general structures of thought, manifest themselves, as well as the modes in which others appear to us, of how society, or the past, exists for us, and so forth, in an attempt to lay bare the autonomous, and *unreal* domain of the phenomenon itself, Patočka, in *Plato and Europe*, is interested in elucidating the relation between the phenomenon itself and what is, particularly, the human being. More precisely, by seeking, in addition to analyzing phenomena as such, to draw the metaphysical consequences that follow from the factual relation between manifesting itself and what is manifested, Patočka's thought, admittedly, "is already a certain *phenomenological philosophy*" (*PE*, 32). By inquiring into what he calls the "codetermining" (*PE*, 34) of the factual universe by the phenomenon as phenomenon, Patočka seeks to "pronounce certain constructive hypotheses" about the relation between the phenomenon itself and the manifold of actual phenomena (*PE*, 33). As phenomenology in its descriptive form has shown, "the *universum* has this *unreal* side to it, which concerns how the *universum* shows itself" (*PE*, 31). Yet, however independent the structures of appearing are from that which appears, the unreal phenomenal structures are the structures of the world of things that are manifest. Furthermore, if manifesting, or showing itself, is also to be real, that is, if qua manifesting, or showing itself, it is also to manifest or show itself, then, Patočka concludes, "there has to be some kind of actuality . . . to whose composition, to whose structure belongs manifesting as such. There has to be a kind of *real* being that cannot exist otherwise unless something manifests itself to it. . . . The structure of the phenomenon as the phenomenon renders possible the existence of . . . the kind of beings such as man" (*PE*, 31). Manifesting itself, or the phenomenon, thus calls for, and makes possible, the existence of its necessary correlate, a real addressee to whom effective manifesting is addressed—the human being in whom the *unreal* has thus become real. The phenomenon is not without also presupposing a being to whose structure belongs the possibility of being capable of an encounter with the phenomenon—and, as important, also being able to miss this encounter.[27] The theme of the care of the soul originates precisely from this "sudden manifestation of the *unreal* aspect of the universe in man, and its becoming real" (*PE*, 34; trans. mod.).

Before I discuss further this essential relation between the soul and manifesting itself, a brief remark is warranted. Patočka speaks repeatedly of the care of the soul in terms of a glance, an intuition, or look-into-what-is (*nahlédnutí*) (*PE*, 35). Both in Plato and in Husserl, the look-into-what-is is the intellectual apprehension of "the evidence made possible by the thing itself which by itself offers itself and shows itself to the eye" (*LS*, 182).[28] To care for the soul is "to live from true insight into what is here, what is present" (*PE*, 85), rather than from opinion and tradition. Undoubtedly, by choosing to elaborate in *Plato and Europe* on the theme of the care of the soul from the perspective of phenomenology, Patočka implies that "what is" is, ultimately, understood in terms of showing itself, as the world in totality, or manifestation as such. However, in *Heretical Essays* the Platonic motive for the care of the soul is said to be a function of a look into what eternally is—in short, the Good. How are these two conceptions of the care of the soul to be reconciled? What is the relation between manifesting and the Good? As will become clear when, in Chapter 8, we turn to *Heretical Essays*, it is knowledge of the Good that causes the soul to dialogue with itself—that is, to responsibly examine its every thought so as to achieve full clarity about itself and transparency within itself. As the ground of truth and error, manifesting is the clarity within which the soul that responds to this address rids itself of every obscurity and realizes a life in truth—that is, a being of the phenomenon. The Good is light itself, and the phenomenon is good.

As we have seen, manifesting itself is that on the basis of which there can be truth and error since the latter makes sense only with respect to what has come into an appearance. As a being capable of truth and error, good and evil, the human being's destiny rests, therefore, in a fundamental manner on the problem of manifesting itself. As Patočka remarks, beginning with its inception in Greece, philosophy has conceived of the soul as "just *what is capable of truth* within man." The soul, "precisely because it is concerned about truth, poses the question: how, why does existence in its entirety, manifest itself, how, why does it show itself?" (*PE*, 27). With this the further question arises whether manifesting, showing, the phenomenon, in short, is "human destiny," and whether it bestows on the human being a task that he or she can either meet or miss. Patočka asks: "Is not manifesting, light in the world, something that distinguishes man from all else, and is not the consequence of this manifesting, which is after all in a certain sense the human privilege, something that also places duties before man? Care of the soul is fundamentally care that follows from the proximity of man to manifesting, to the phenomenon as such, to the manifesting of the world in its whole, that occurs within man, with man" (*PE*, 27). If, indeed, the care of the soul is intrinsically linked to the fact that the human being is the addressee of everything that manifests itself, and, in particular, of showing as such, it follows that care of the soul is imperative in order to be able to respond in an adequate—that is, responsible—fashion to the duties involved by such a claim. At stake is nothing less than living in truth or putting such a life at risk. But there is still another aspect to the care of the soul that we have left in abeyance—care of the soul is also care of death.

The irruption of manifesting in the human being coincides with the sudden awakening of consciousness in the human being. Consciousness is the tear in one particular being—the human being—between the world, which shows itself in its totality, and this one being, which has the privilege of being the addressee of manifesting itself—that is, the human being. But according to Patočka, "man as the exponent of phenomenon pays dearly for this privileged position in the universe. He pays dearly, for while he is conscious of the whole, that this totality shows and manifests itself to him, he also sees his own eccentricity, that he has fallen out from the center, that he is only also a phenomenon, and a precarious phenomenon, one that of course depends on the rest of the world, and that as an ephemera" (*PE*, 34). No doubt, if the world as a whole discloses itself in the human being, it also makes him or her, who is but one being within this world, painfully aware of his or her ephemeral nature, in short, of his or her finitude and mortality. The truth of which humans are capable because the phenomenon discloses itself as such to them is a truth that "shows [the human being] his own precariousness, his place in the universe, which is overpowering in his regard" (*PE*, 35).[29] The becoming real, of manifesting itself in the human being, not only amounts to a consciousness of the world in its totality but also of the human being's awareness of his or her minuteness in the universe, of his or her being a finite and mortal part of the universe at that. Now, according to Patočka, Greek philosophy has its origin in the question "What is man to do . . . in this *most fundamental distress*, that is not dictated by something external but that coincides with the very character of the universe?" (*PE*, 35). Confronted with this question, Greek philosophy "developed a *project of life*, one that transformed damnation into *human greatness*" (*PE*, 35; trans. mod.). By doing this, Greek philosophy made itself into "the foundation of all European life" (*PE*, 35). For the Platonic philosopher to transform the condition of damnation into human greatness, he or she had to "overcome death fundamentally by not fleeing from it but by facing up to it" (*HE*, 105). The Greeks realized that, as far as death is concerned, indeed, two possibilities, at least, are available on the basis of the human being's original situation—one that reflects the human being's natural attitude and another that is based on a radical change in attitude toward death. In caring for death, and opting for the latter radical attitude, the human being proves him- or herself as precisely a human being. This, then, is the point where we need to take up this other aspect of the care of the soul.

What does it mean for the soul to care for death? The radical change of attitude involved in the care of death presupposes, first of all, the possibility of a separation, a distancing from death. For the soul that has cared for itself, and hence freed itself from all its contaminations with the mortal body, death can be held at bay, and tended to, as something that, though inevitable, will only affect the body, which is "human, mortal, multiform, unintelligible, dissoluable, and never self-consistent." Such distancing from death, furthermore, allows the soul, as Plato remarks in the *Phaedo*, to gather within itself or, as Patočka says, to become unified. Collecting itself by distancing itself from death, the soul shows itself to "resemble the divine, immortal, intelligible, uniform, indissoluble, and ever self-consistent and invariable."[30] Finally, by putting a distance between itself and death, the soul that has thus acquired an independence, a freedom, of its own—selfhood in the first place—becomes alive in its own right, as it were, by achieving (a certain kind of) immortality. Let us recall Patočka's words: "life (eternal) is born of this direct look at death, of an overcoming of death (perhaps it is nothing but this 'overcoming')" (*HE*, 105). Surpassing death in a movement of withdrawal and distancing from it is what endows the soul with life, a life of its own, immortal life, a life, hence, that resembles that of the divine. For all the Greek thinkers, whether they conceptualized the idea of an immortal soul or, as the atomists, regarded the soul to be mortal in the end, "the care of the soul can get man—in spite of his short life, his finitude—into a state similar to that of the gods. Why? Because man, or the human soul—that which knows about the whole of the world and of life, that which is able to present this whole before its eyes, that which lives from this position, that which knows about the whole and in that sense is wholly and in the whole within this explicit relation to something certainly immortal, that which is certainly eternal, that which does not pass away, beyond which there is nothing—in this itself it has its own eternity" (*PE*, 13; trans. mod.). The soul, if cared for, is, as we have seen, capable of beholding the world in its totality. For this reason it is not only made to realize the human being's finitude, but it also becomes capable of a liberating distance from this being's ultimate fate. Because of this "essential relation" of being able to take a step back from death and finitude, the soul achieves an immortality that makes it resemble the gods.[31] Patočka writes: "it is only possible to come to grips with death with the thought that man lives an essential relation, which cannot be forfeited either from man or from the world, and that it is the same whether we realize it for a short time or whether it is realized by the gods for a long time—in this it is the same thing" (*PE*, 13; trans. mod.). However provisional, and short, the soul's immortality may prove to be, it is immortality after all. As Patočka remarks, even though in the end the human being is mortal, he is, according to the Greeks, "not any worse off than the being that would have the whole universe in its power, so long as it systematically pursues the phenomenon as such. Human life differs from the life of the gods only in its quantitative dimension, but not in its essence; that is the solution of Greek philosophy" (*PE*, 44). As long as the human being pursues the phenomenon, and tends to death, keeping it at bay, the curse of finitude and mortality is overcome, and the human soul, for however brief a moment, becomes similar to the gods—that is, immortal. "The soul lives in a divine way even if it lives only for a short time. The difference between short and long is no longer an essential difference" (*PE*, 81).

Thanks to the care of the soul, the Greeks were able to transform the sense of damnation into human greatness. Of course, the awareness of one's finitude can only be transformed into greatness—a certain immortality of the human soul—"under certain circumstances: as long as we make this clarity, the phenomenon as such, the phenomenalization of the world, the placing into clarity—the program of all life. All this from looking-into-what-is. Like in our thinking, so in our deeds, always to act with clarity" (*PE*, 35; trans. mod.) The awareness of being cursed with finitude arises, as we have seen, from the fact that the human being is the addressee of showing itself, beholding in the light of manifestation the world in its entirety. This very clarity in which the whole manifests itself to him or her is also the source for the awareness of one's mortality. The project of life defined by the Greeks, and that, according to Patočka, became determinative for European life, consists, precisely, in using this light in a radical attitude toward corporeal death and decline, by which the human soul distances itself from the natural perception of its bodily fate, gathers within itself, and achieves, by way of this act of freedom, a mode of being in its own right. Opting for this possibility, rather than the natural infatuation with death, the human responds to the duty that comes with the original situation of his or her being the addressee of the phenomenon and the site in which manifesting itself becomes real. By choosing the possibility offered by the care of death, the human being "shows himself as a creature who really does make the phenomenon, that means clarity, *truth the law of his life*, and with the help of this law in every domain in which man is involved. *Given certain circumstances, man could make at least the human world a world of truth and justice*. How this can be achieved is the very subject of the care of the soul" (*PE*, 36). The project of life that emerges in Greece with the motif of the care of the soul is not restricted to the individual soul but is essentially a project of life that concerns the life of the community, the life of humankind itself.[32] The care of the soul as that which in human beings is capable of truth "on the basis of a peculiar, untransferable, only-in-man-realized structure of the phenomenon as such" (*PE*, 36), opens up, for the first time, the possibility of a space, a world for human beings separate from everything else, a clearing, as it were, in whose openness a distinct human world can come forth as such. This human world, made possible by the phenomenon, is at the same time to be a world ruled by the law of the phenomenon, in other words, a world of clarity and transparency. The Greeks understood the human being as capable of such a life of truth, and they took up this challenge. As Patočka puts it, "on the basis that he stand between phenomenon and mere existence, man can either *capitulate and degenerate into mere existence,* or he can only then realize himself as a *being of truth, a being of phenomenon*" (*PE*, 36). The goal of the care of the soul is to secure among the two options available for the human being—to be a natural being among other such beings, or a being that, by bracketing its finitude, brings forth a realm of its own—the one by which the human being can create a distinct world on the basis of manifesting itself, one that is similar to the world of the gods, even though it may not last as long as theirs. This is the project of life—a life of truth and justice, a life of transparency, shaped by the Greeks, a project that is also at the heart of European life.

§ 8 The Genealogy of "Europe-Responsibility"

The Greek idea of the care of the soul based on the look-into-what-is constitutes, according to Patočka, the source of European civilization. It is the fundamental heritage that Greece has bequeathed to Europe. However, the idea of the care of the soul undergoes several transformations in a process in which one spiritual heritage leads to another, until, in the seventeenth century, the current decline of Europe begins, a decline whose results, as Patočka claimed in 1974, lie "before our very own eyes: *Europe has disappeared*, probably forever" (*PE*, 89). Furthermore, as we will see, the Greek idea that sets the history of Europe into motion, has itself a history. Therefore, it is possible to speak of a genealogy of the idea of the care of the soul. Since this idea, which has been bequeathed to Europe, for which and to which Europe is thus responsible, is also, as will become increasingly clear, the idea of responsibility—in Jacques Derrida's words, "of responsibility as Europe, of *Europe-responsibility*, through the decoding of a certain history of mysteries, of their incorporation and their repression"—the genealogy of the motif of the care of the soul is also a genealogy of European responsibility, if not even of the concept of responsibility in general (*GD*, 48). In order to demonstrate that the Greek idea of the care of the soul sets off precisely such a genealogy of responsibility, it will be necessary, first, to return to the theme of the care of the soul. But before I do so, several observations and questions, although highly schematic, are warranted.

The first concerns the privilege that Patočka, like Husserl and Heidegger before him, accords to Greece in the constitution of Europe. Even though the idea of the care of the soul suffers several catastrophes, and undergoes several mutations, the Greek heritage is continuously maintained through these catastrophes. In *Plato and Europe* Patočka stresses that although "it is said that European civilization rests on two pillars: one, the Judeo-Christian tradition, the other, antiquity," Europe rests in his understanding on only one pillar, the Greek pillar (*PE*, 89). This is so, he explains, because the peculiar characteristic of European life is "*a looking-in* [*nahlednutí*], Europe is life founded upon seeing what is" (*PE*, 90). The motif of the care of the soul rests on "the primacy of looking-in" (*PE*, 149). However, if the Jewish element is also seen to have been of significance for Europe, "this applies only conditionally, so long as the Jewish element passed through Greek reflection. The Jewish element is only formed by Greek reflection so that it may become the ferment of the new European world" (*PE*, 128). It had "to be Hellenized, it had to pass through Greek thought" (*PE*, 90). If Europe did not remain simply Greek, but also allowed the Hebrew element to become an essential ingredient of European civilization—and, indeed, since Roman times, that is, historically speaking, since the beginning of European history, the Jews belonged, for good or for ill, to the family of European peoples—it is "perhaps [Patočka muses, because] there are certain *immanent* components in Greek thinking itself that required something like that" (*PE*, 149). Yet for the Jewish element to play a role in Europe, the still primarily simple mythic nature of its dogmas and representations had to be Platonized—that is, justified—and its faith had to be transformed into "a purely moral religion."[1] Patočka writes: "The Jewish religion . . . is not purely moral. In the *Decalogue*, and so on, there are undoubtedly moral precepts, but the Jewish God is the wrathful god who punishes in a manner beyond all human measure. And among human measures is also the measure of human insight into what is. Apart from that, the Jewish God is not a matter of a purely moral religion; he is a god of this world, one who arose from this world" (*PE*, 128; trans. mod.). Even for Christian Europe, which, as we will see, is responsible for the most profound transformation of the Greek heritage, the Jewish element is, according to Patočka, of limited significance. Christianity is above all indebted to the Greek heritage. Even though the Christian conception of interiority is only to be found in embryonic form in Plato's conception of the care of the soul, it is "the embryo of European [say, Christian] inwardness—it all grew out from this" (*PE*, 149). Furthermore, the Christian conception of "that world, the other, world of truth and divinity, which is the divinity of pure good—occurs in *Plato* first, it is not present anywhere else" (*PE*, 90). The difference between the world around us—the world of seeming (*doxa*)—and the world of true being "exists only in Plato. This difference crossed into Christian theology from Plato. It did not cross there from the Jewish religion. Only here, on this basis, was something like the theological conception of divinity of transcendence able to arise" (*PE*, 128). For Europe as a project for life, as Patočka understands it, Hebrew thought, in the end, bears on this project only to the extent that it has been completely Hellenized. Now, as we will see, Christianity, according to Patočka, has not yet achieved what it promised. More precisely, it has not even thought out the radical implications of the new version of the care of the soul that it brought to Europe. Indeed, the *Heretical Essays* hold out the possibility of a Christian Europe that would finally make good on what announced itself with its emergence in the shape of the Holy Roman Empire of the German Nation—that is a genuinely Christian Europe.

The second observation concerns the significance of Rome, Byzantium, and Islam, for the formation of Europe. Compared to Husserl and Heidegger, for whom Europe is exclusively indebted to the Greek heritage, Patočka, for whom the Greek element enjoys a priority as well in its formation, conceives of the Greek legacy as the substrate of all the transformations that the idea of the care of the soul undergoes in the history of Europe. Jerusalem, as we have seen, plays a role in Europe although only insofar as it has been mediated by Athens. Although Patočka does not explicitly broach the confluence of Islamic and European heritages, both Jewish and Greek, especially during the Middle Ages, when the most vibrant intellectual and cultural force in Europe arose from Islam, whose flourishing center in many respects was to be found in Spain, at least his writings carve out the place for such a discussion. Hereafter, while discussing the genealogy of Europe, it will become clear that Rome—the Roman Empire—is not simply one form in which the Greek spirit became realized but a form whose memory was passed on to Christian Europe as a spiritual heritage. However, Europe—that is, basically, Western Europe united under the banner of Christianity during the Holy Roman Empire of the German Nation—renews the Roman attempt to realize the Greek model by advocating a duality between spiritual and secular power, one in which the spiritual power has the ultimate "sovereignty with respect to secular power, something [as Patočka holds] achieved here alone" (*HE*, 80). Rome, therefore, cannot simply be ignored, as is the case in Husserl's appraisal of what is European, or construed as an inevitable deformation of the Greek originary insights and accomplishments, as it is for Heidegger. Yet, as Patočka argues, the perception that Western Europe unified under the banner of Christianity "is but one of the versions of the idea of the holy empire of which there are three versions: beside the West European one also a Byzantine and an Islamic one" (*HE*, 80). Whereas the sacrum imperium Christian style, which unifies Western Europe, "crystallized on the basis of the historical theology contained in the *Epistle to the Hebrews* and in Paul's *Epistle to the Romans*" (*HE*, 81), and promoted the separation of *imperium* and *sacerdotium*, the Islamic version of the holy empire was grounded "in the prophetic ideal and so approximating the Judaic conception" (*HE*, 80). If in the Islamic version of the holy empire, religion and sovereignty were united, the Constantinian model of the holy empire, which rests on the recognition of the Christian church's authority in national education, hence, of its ethical propensity regarding the formation of a state in which secular and spiritual communities coincide, nonetheless, knew a spiritual hierarchy as well as established institutions such as those of the emperor and the patriarch.[2] Yet, if it is true that the spiritual heritage of the Roman Empire underlies all three versions of the sacrum imperium, then Islam and Byzantium are also indebted to Greek philosophy, as well as to the theme of the care of the soul that is the bequest of ancient Greek philosophy. Although the Western European version of the Holy Empire may have given rise to a particular form of conceiving of the care of the soul, the very principle of Europe is, therefore, not its exclusive property right, since it is shared at least with the "other Europe"—that is, Eastern Europe—and with the Islamic world. Western Europe's continued attempts to delimit itself against the Byzantine East, both politically and spiritually, as well as its efforts to stem militarily the Arab expansion from the seventh century on, also make it difficult, especially from a historical point of view, to ignore at least the indirect contributions of Byzantium and Islam to what is European.

The third observation to be made is about the unchanging substrate of European life. Husserl's conception of the Greek idea of a universal rational science, which during the Renaissance underwent a radical transformation giving rise to the objectivist paradigm of the modern sciences, contained in nuce the totality of all the basic features of what is

European—universality, apodicticity, responsibility—and that have only to be rediscovered and reactivated by transcendental phenomenology in the attempt to overcome the crisis of the European sciences (even though this rediscovery may also imply a transformation of the basic features that make up Europe). The thought of Being, which for Heidegger irrupts in Greece, and became that which in being forgotten shaped metaphysics and the destiny of Europe, confronts the thinker with the risky task, one that can go astray, of articulating the very claims of Being on which the destiny of Europe depends. For Patočka, for whom the Platonic motif of the care of the soul represents the embryo from which Europe developed, the Greek heritage undergoes a series of transformations in which heritage builds on heritage and transforms it in unpredictable ways. For example, the idea of humankind as such, which is, for Husserl, in essence, already present in the Greek notion of rationality and universality, is for the historically minded thinker Patočka only a product of Hellenism. Or take the motif of the care of the soul: even though its emphasis on the immortality of the soul can be seen to point to a transformation of myth into religion, nothing within its Greek version seems to predestine it for the specific realization that it achieves within Christianity. Furthermore, since Christianity still falls short of its own promise, the transformation that the Greek idea of the care of the soul might undergo at the hands of a heretical Christianity suggest that such a transformation comes with at least some unpredictable consequences. However new—new not in the usual sense but truly new—a heretically Christian conception of the care of the soul may be, there is nothing in Patočka's thought to suggest that such a realization of the Greek idea would be the last possible one.

The fourth point to be made concerns the relation between myth and philosophy in Patočka. In distinction from Husserl, for whom the idea of Europe as the idea of a universal rational science is that of a clearly cut break with myth, and from Heidegger, for whom the thought of Being that irrupts into thought in early Greece in order to become the destiny of the West, even though this thought is initially not essentially different from myth understood in an originary sense (namely as Saying), stands in a radical difference to what later became known as myth and religion, "Greek primeval philosophy," and in fact "all of Greek philosophy" has for Patočka, "a *mythical framework*" (*PE*, 42). For the Czech thinker, the difference between *episteme* and *doxa* is not one of simple opposition. Indeed, in *Plato and Europe*, Patočka argues that "myth is not something that mankind can shake off entirely and radically" (*PE*, 43). Indeed, as beings living in truth, the human beings who always live "*in the natural world*, in a world that manifests itself" in totality to them, cannot live without myth because myth is the "first, radical still-*unreflected manifestation*" of manifesting (*PE*, 43). Because "*myth is truth*," myth is inextricably intertwined with philosophical thought from the Greek philosophies on to those that follow, "which are not in their fundamentals anything but their reprise, their repeating" (*PE*, 43). But the manner in which Patočka conceives of the development of the embryo of European life—that is, in terms of a history of catastrophes and radical renewals in which the very continuity of the motif has also a paralyzing function since the inherited solutions to, and problems of earlier configurations of the care of the soul prevent the new paradigms from coming fully into their own—is also indicative of a continuity, rather than of a radical caesura between philosophy and *doxa*. Yet, notwithstanding the acknowledgment of a complex of relations between philosophy and *doxa* (including myth and religion), as well as between a new version of the motif of the care of the soul and a previous one that it replaces after its catastrophic failure—relations that further complicate Husserl's conception of the radical difference between *episteme* and *doxa*, as well as Heidegger's thought of what constitutes a beginning—Patočka's heretically Christian version of the care of the soul, which still remains to be thought, not to mention realized, seems radical to the point of breaking not only with all traditionalisms but with the very tradition to which it owes its motif.

Finally, a remark on Patočka's understanding of history is necessary before engaging the genealogy of the motif of the care of the soul, hence, the genealogy of responsibility, and before attempting to pinpoint as precisely as possible what, according to Patočka, specifically is Europe. For, indeed, this question of specificity is no longer simply one of Europe versus (itself and) the world, since, besides Europe, the Greek heritage also shapes the Eastern and Islamic worlds. However, if in spite of the fact that Western Europe, Eastern Europe, and the Islamic world all share the Greek motif of the care of the soul, Patočka can contend, in *Plato and Europe*, that "history is the history of Europe; there does not exist any other" (*PE*, 212), then the specificity of Europe must lie with the manner in which the care of the soul became realized there as opposed to Eastern Europe and the Islamic world. But let us first demarcate European civilization from other civilizations, which "understandably have [of course] their past and their recorded past" (*PE*, 221). Human beings are historical beings, and consequently every civilization in its own manner is historical and evolves in its own way. Yet, as Patočka argues, in a recourse to Husserl, in order to understand these other civilizations one has "to penetrate into [their] distinctive principles" (*PE*, 221)—that is, into the myth or the tradition with which human beings in these civilizations identify—and in which one remains enclosed once one has gotten into them:

> They have this peculiar stamp that you must immerse yourself in them, step into the continuity of their tradition. Not so in Europe. Everyone understands European civilization, because the principle of European civilization is—roughly spoken—two times two is four. From that arises a singular continuity and the possibility of generalization. For that reason, European civilization became universal, while those others, should they be generalized, would signify the swallowing up of all others by a particular tradition, but not by the principle of insight into the nature of things. (*PE*, 221)[3]

Notwithstanding the fact that there are also traditions in Europe—Patočka names, for example, "the Christian tradition or the tradition of classical literature"—the look-into-what-is, as "the most characteristic thing about European civilization" (*PE*, 221), is what renders it capable of universalization. Compared to other civilizations, "European civilization is abstract. For this reason, European history could generalize itself in such a way" (*PE*, 223). This possibility of generalization allowed Europe to penetrate "beyond the original sphere" and to bring with it science, technology, and so forth (*PE*, 221–22).[4] It is this very possibility of generalization that also gives European history its "specific continuum, phrased in the way we have become used to: antiquity, Middles Ages, and so forth" (*PE*, 222). If history is something specifically European—the history of Europe—something that, as Patočka holds, we project only, and force, upon other civilizations, it is because only an abstract principle such as the Platonic Good, the phenomenological phenomenon, or the nature of things, which is the object of the glance into what is, can provide the continuum for a development and expansion that is a history in an emphatic sense.

The foundation of European civilization is the insight into the nature of what is, as opposed to all other civilizations that are founded on tradition. Yet, as we have seen, both Byzantium and the Islamic world share with Western Europe the spiritual foundation of Greece and a development phrased in periods analogous to those that occurred in Europe. Why then can Patočka maintain the claim that history is the history of Europe—of Western Europe alone? The answer to this question, I believe, is to be found in Patočka's understanding of the Christian shape of the theme of the care of the soul and of the heretical possibilities that Christianity harbors for the future.

Before I take up in some detail the transformation in European history of the motif of the care of the soul, a fresh look at this theme is required. The conception of the care of the soul as the essential heritage of Europe encompasses "something like *the ideal of the truthful life*, that is a life that, as much as in praxis as in its activity of thinking, always directs itself by *looking-in*" (*PE*, 107). Caring for one's soul is a task, and as Patočka emphasizes, in the *Heretical Essays*, an infinite, or, rather, lifelong and never ceasing task. Looking-in does not eventually come to rest after the intuition of what is. Rather, its project is without end: "What, though, makes humans just and truthful is their *care for their soul*. Care for the soul is the bequest of ancient Greek philosophy. Care of the soul means that truth is something not given once and for all, nor merely a matter of observing and acknowledging the observed, but rather a lifelong inquiry, a self-controlling, self-unifying intellectual and vital practice" (*HE*, 82). Whether looking at the Platonic Good or the phenomenological idea of showing itself, the soul's care of itself amounts to "a constant conversation of the soul with itself and with others. Conversation with others is always a conversation of the soul with itself at the same time, and care of the soul takes place in this conversation" (*PE*, 137). Such constant conversation, or dialogue, of the soul with itself presupposes a "willingness to let oneself be questioned" (*PE*, 92) and "consists in that we constantly examine our speech," "examining what is good" (*PE*, 120). The care of the soul, which "takes place through *questioning thinking*" (*PE*, 91)—that is, a thinking that questions—thus amounts to "exposing oneself to criticism" (*PE*, 108), "self-overcoming" oneself in the process—that is, regarding everything that has not been "suitably clarified" (*PE*, 91). This stance of relentless inquiring corresponds to a "kind of *epoche* . . . that is exceptionally positive" (*PE*, 92), in that in the face of contradiction it provides not only a firm and certain ground but also one that gives unity to the soul. "Only a completely clear and unified, not contradicting oneself, but rather consistent speech about everything, about anything at all, about which it is possible to think meaningfully, only this kind of absolutely coherent speech then may mean the existence, the creation of the internally unified soul, which, because its thoughts are *binding*, is not split apart, torn into various mutually contradictory opinions" (*PE*, 92). The care of the soul, which, for Patočka, as we have seen, constitutes the very core of philosophy, thus shows that "philosophy has as its ideal complete responsibility, in thought as much as in practical life, meaning to regulate everything according to insight" (*PE*, 138). As Patočka notes, the ideal that emerges for the first time in Plato, under the name of the care of the soul, consists in a demand: "that everything man does and thinks has to be answered for" (*PE*, 95). This ideal of responsibility, which guides philosophy insofar as its core is formed by the care of the soul, is coeval with the ideal, or demand, of "radical clarity": "There exists a certain primacy of clarity and effort for clarity against its opposite from the moment that philosophy is philosophy. Philosophy wants clarity, and as far as possible a radical one, yet radical clarity leads it to see *limits* of this clarity and that man lives in this equivocacy, in this peculiar polarity" (*PE*, 139).

As we noted previously, the care of the soul is the answer of the Greek philosopher to the natural state of decadence and decline, hence, also to the inauthenticity of everydayness. As the essential heritage of European life, this motif undergoes several transformations during the history of Europe. Its first shape is that of Athens, the quintessence of Greek life, but also of the Roman civitas, for in its beginnings Rome was not yet fundamentally different from the Greek *polis*. After the catastrophe of the Greek cities in the wake of the Persian wars, the Greek "inheritance of thinking about a state where philosophers might live, about a state of justice founded not on mere tradition, but rather on *looking-in*" (*PE*, 88), was carried on by the Hellenistic philosophers, in particular, the Stoics, who took for their "chief task the transformation of the classical philosophy of the Socratic-Platonic tradition into the educational leaven of the universal state which Rome ultimately most successfully represented" (*HE*, 80–81). But the Roman Empire realizes the Greek heritage also in a shape that is marked by a reflection on the failure of the Greek polis. As Patočka observes, the Greek idea on which the Roman Empire rests is an idea "matured in reflection into the greatness and the failure of the *polis* and the global significance and misery of the Greeks within their characteristic social framework in which they defied mere quantitative superiority [of the Persians] only to discredit and destroy both themselves and this framework" (*HE*, 81–82). Indeed, "in the Roman Empire the care of the soul assumes the form of striving for a rule of law throughout the global community affected by the empire" (*HE*, 83). Replacing the Platonic Good with the state of right—a state "free of any grounding in ethnic, territorial, or governmental foundation" (*HE*, 81)—the Roman Empire sought to realize the Greek idea of a community in which philosophers could live by educating humankind about what is universal about human beings, and thus in view of the integration of everyone, independently of his or her ethnic origins, into a universal empire. But "this empire succumbed to catastrophe just as the Greek polis before it. In the final analysis, it fell because, just like the Greek polis, it was not capable of convincing its public that it was a state of justice" (*PE*, 89). What brought the Roman Empire down was nothing less than "the catastrophic failure [of its educational] program" (*HE*, 81). It is replaced by the Western Christian Holy Empire in which the inheritance of the Roman Empire, which itself is a transformation of the Greek heritage, is transformed one more time. Not only does the Holy Roman Empire of the German Nation embrace a community that is considerably broader than the Roman-Mediterranean had ever been, but the idea of the care of the soul undergoes a new transformation here as well in that, rather than being founded on the relations between human beings, as was the case in the Roman Empire, by "disciplining inner humanity and giving it greater depth," it is now based on a deepened interiority and a relation to absolute truth—to God as a Person (*HE*, 83). The new community to which the Holy Empire gives rise is not anymore one of "the earthly state of the caesars . . . but rather a city based directly on a truth which is not of this but of the other world and whose norms and primordial model are set not by human but by divine power and by a sacred history entering into human history and drawing it into itself" (*HE*, 81). But in the sixteenth century a turn occurs that leads to the progressive loss of what unified Europe hitherto. The new motif that at this time comes to the fore is no longer the "care *for the soul*, the care to *be*, but rather the care to *have*, care for the external world and its conquest," which from then on became the dominant concern (*HE*, 83). However, the unity and universality of Europe is not simply eroded because of exterior reasons, or the emergence of an opposite principle, but primarily because of the legacy of the Platonic motif itself, or rather, the Platonic solution to the project of the care of the soul, which, as we have seen, has been the heritage that has been kept alive through all the catastrophes and renewals.

In the essay "Is Technological Civilization Decadent, and Why?" Patočka remarks that the reason why Christian Europe failed in its attempt to unify and universalize is due not only to the fact that the Holy Empire inherited the problems of the Roman Empire but also to Platonism itself. Although from early on Christianity appropriated Platonic and Socratic thought for its own purposes, this very heritage of the Greek conception of the care of the soul has also been an impediment to the development of a Christian Europe.[5] The continuity of the motif of the care of the soul has thus also a retarding effect on the new turns that this problematic undergoes and prevents new transformations, particularly its Christian reconception, to fully realize themselves.

Before I can elaborate on Patočka's response to the current state of Europe, it is necessary to further highlight the theme of responsibility, which is inseparable from the problematic of care of the soul and the struggle against decadence and decline. I turn, therefore, to *Heretical Essays*, particularly to the essay "Is Technological Civilization Decadent, and Why?" In line with what we have already established about the universal human experience of decay, decadence, and decline, Patočka shows there that even though the human being "can never not be interested in [its] own being" (*HE*, 98), the human being's ordinary, or natural condition—the condition of everydayness—is the condition of alienation, or estrangement. Avoidance of being oneself is more pleasurable, and comes naturally, Patočka observes. By contrast, "being themselves is something that does not come naturally [to human beings]. It is always an achievement" (*HE*, 98; trans. mod.). Compared to avoidance, escape, and deviation into inauthenticity, being oneself implies assuming responsibility that "bears and 'exposes itself'" (*HE*, 98) and the explicit attempt to resolutely *lead* one's life and accomplish it by resisting the lures of inauthenticity. Now even though the human being qua human being cannot not be interested in his or her being, and is thus caught from the outset in a responsibility for and to him- or herself whether or not he or she wants it, true, authentic being requires taking explicitly upon oneself the "decision [that] has been made about us before," or in advance (*HE*, 98). In distinction from the inauthenticity of everydayness, authenticity, by resisting the natural tendency to deviate from one's responsibility to oneself, is of the order of the extraordinary. Authenticity as determinate responsibility for one's being entails a defiance of everydayness. But, as Patočka points out, everydayness is also to be contrasted with the dimension of the demonic and the passions as they manifest themselves, for example, in the exceptional, that is, in the feast: "The exceptional, the holiday also unburdens, though not by escaping from responsibility but rather by revealing that dimension of life in which the point is not the burden of responsibility and *escape* from it but where, rather, we are *enraptured*, where something more powerful than our free possibility, our responsibility, seems to break into our life and bestow on it a meaning which it would not know otherwise" (*HE*, 98–99). By falling for the demonic and the passions, the human being does not escape from responsibility to him- or herself into the world of the "They" in order to become estranged from him- or herself in the manner of ordinary everydayness; rather the human being is swept away, enraptured, and surprised by a power that transports him or her into a dimension beyond the struggle for ourselves, beyond responsibility and escape, beyond authenticity and inauthenticity, "as if only now true life stood before [him or her], as if this 'new life' had no need to care for the dimension of responsibility" (*HE*, 99). What is experienced in the presence of the demonic, and when the human being is prey to passion, is nothing less than the sacred as a force that is not in our power (unlike in the case of the authentic and the inauthentic), and which can transform our life making us also oblivious to our responsibilities although in a manner different from the one that obtains in everyday life. Of this "distinction between the sacred and the profane [which] is distinct from that of authenticity-responsibility and escape," Patočka says that "it has to be related to responsibility by means other than escape, it simply cannot be overpowered, it has to be grafted on to responsible life" (*HE*, 99). "The sacred, the domain of the holy, represents an other, different counterpart to the everyday" than the quest for authenticity (*HE*, 100). Undoubtedly, demonic ecstasy tears the human being from his or her bondage to life and the objects in the everyday, but rather than setting him or her free, such rapture deepens self-estrangement insofar as demonic ecstasy also alienates one from his or her own possibilities and his or her essential responsibility toward them. Yet if the overwhelming power of the demonic, even though it tears the human being away from all concerns with responsibility for him- or herself, "needs to be brought into a relation with responsibility as originally and primarily it is not" (*HE*, 100–101), if, more precisely, it needs to be incorporated (as the French translation puts it) into responsible life, this is, perhaps, because of an intrinsic want regarding the dimension of authenticity.[6] Even though the human being is a being that cannot escape being interested in him- or herself and that, therefore, is potentially capable of authenticity, the lures of the world of the They are so powerful that responsible life must incorporate the power of the sacred as a necessary supplement, notwithstanding the fact that, at first, the sacred alienates the human being entirely from the dimension of authenticity and inauthenticity. Simply put, the Heideggerian concern with authenticity needs to be complemented by the dimension of the sacred, as if finite human beings were incapable of taking responsibility for themselves all by themselves. But such grafting of the sacred onto the sphere of authenticity also hints at a transformation of the sacred itself. To be precise, a transformation of the sacred into religion is required for such grafting to be possible. Patočka writes: "This bringing into relation to responsibility, that is, to the domain of human authenticity and truth, is probably the kernel of the history of all religions. Religion is not the sacred, nor does it arise directly from the experience of sacral orgies and rites; rather, it is where the sacred qua demonic is being explicitly overcome. Sacral experiences pass over religious as soon as there is an attempt to introduce responsibility into the sacred or to regulate the sacred thereby" (*HE*, 101). Religion overcomes the sacred qua demonic not simply by annihilating it but by subjecting it to the rules that pertain to the domain of responsibility. Although the incorporation of the sacred into the sphere of authenticity is the accomplishment of religion, explicit clarity about this accomplishment is achieved only in "the ontological experience of philosophy" (*HE*, 101). In *Plato and Europe* Patočka credits Plato for having brought about the transformation of myth into religion, but it is safe to assume that, for Patočka, the primarily Greek conception of responsibility (including its Heideggerian interpretation) becomes truly amalgamated with a sacred that has been transformed into religion in Christianity alone.

If history—that is, the history of Europe, the only history that, according to Patočka, merits to be called so—is "foremost a history of the soul" (*HE*, 103), this is so because the dawn of history coincides with the awakening protest of the human being against not only the lures of the demonic and the orgiastic but also with a developing sense of "our inmost, full and irreplaceable being," hence also with a resistance against the decline and decadence of everydayness and the world of the They. History starts with the resistance of the human being against the fervor of a total immersion in, or fusion with, the imminence of natural life that the sacred brings about, and the dawning concern that he or she makes a difference with respect to the undifferentiated continuum of life as such. The awareness of such difference, which coincides with the awakening of a responsibility toward what is properly human, sets the human being also into a relation of opposition to everydayness and decadence. In other words, history begins with the emergence of an "I," or self. For us to form a self "consists in not losing ourselves in the sacred, not simply surrendering our selves within it, but rather in living through the whole opposition of the sacred and the profane with the dimension of the problematic which we uncover in the responsible questioning in a quest for clarity with the sobriety of the everyday, but also with an active daring for the vertigo it brings; *overcoming* everydayness without collapsing in self-forgetting into the region of darkness, however tempting" (*HE*, 102). I wish to emphasize that the clarity, or lucidity, that characterizes the emerging "I" at the dawn of history, and which consists in the awareness that apart from the orgiastic cults and rites there is another possibility for overcoming decadent life—that is, life in the world of the They, life in the world of labor—by caring for one's "inmost, full and irreplaceable being," does not render the "I" blind or deaf to the attraction of losing oneself in the sacred. The clarity of the "I" that has become aware of the dimension of authenticity incorporates, as it were, an acceptance of the lures of the vertigo that darkness can bring about. History as resistance against decadence in all its forms begins with an "I" that, rather than having cut all ties to the sacred, has interiorized, and thus inwardly mastered, it by "confronting internally its essential ground to which human unclarity, that refuge of our life's routines, opens the way when it has been shaken to the very foundations" (*HE*, 102). Interiorizing the sacred becomes possible when human unclarity has been dispelled and when it becomes clear that the human being can only participate in the life of decadence by simultaneously seeking refuge in orgiastic fusion. Interiorization of the sacred thus also means recognizing a certain raison d'être of the sacred (which can be put to use in responsible life).

History begins with "the emergence of humans who master the original dilemma of human possibilities by discovering the authentic, unique I," and for this reason history is the history of this inner process, that is, "foremost a history of the soul" (*HE*, 103).[7] The reflection on history that accompanies history from the start—that is, philosophy—centers, therefore, first and foremost on the soul. This is especially the case in Plato's thought, which "at its core is focused on the soul as that which makes it something firm and definite" (*HE*, 103). For Plato it is a question of rendering "our soul into that firm crystal of being, an untarnished steel crystal in the view of eternity, which represents one of the possibilities of the being which bears within it the source of movement, of deciding its being or nonbeing, that is, dissolution in the uncertainty of instinct and unclarified tradition" (*HE*, 82). This striking image of the soul as a firm crystal highlights the crisp if not metal(lic) clarity and flawless transparency that Greek philosophy seeks to achieve for the soul.[8] Philosophy, which Eugen Fink characterized, in what Patočka terms an "apt description," namely, "as an attempt to think light without shadow," is dedicated to the task of "being the nonecstatic, nonorgiastic counterpart and inmost resolution of the problem posed by everydayness, regardless of the structure of society" (*HE*, 103). Compared to the orgiastic overcoming of everydayness by plunging into the shades of the night, Greek philosophical thought, with its exigency of a crystal clear transparency of the soul, understands itself as a radical answer to the question of the everyday and natural decadence. As an ontology, Greek philosophical thought is also, at the same time, a philosophy of the soul. Throughout all of antiquity, philosophy, according to Patočka, "lives up to its calling to be the realm in which our I arrives at itself as well as at the lived experience [of] its being which it has grasped at last" (*HE*, 104). By looking at what, in distinction from the ever-changing reality of the sublunar world, is eternal—authentic, transcendent being, the order of the cosmos, the Good—and by conversing with itself in inner dialogue, the soul achieves a steadfastness, a unity, a form that "make it capable of resisting the pressure of various questions and problems which would otherwise drive the soul hither and yon" (*HE*, 104). The look-into-what-is, which, according to the Platonic conception of the care of the soul, makes the soul capable of responsibly caring for itself, is a look at something objectively existing, something that the soul can know and subsequently emulate.[9] No longer wavering, and subject to the vertigo caused by indecision, the soul thus finally becomes itself—that is, an autonomous, self-responsible being that reflects, however briefly, the immovable being of true being and is, hence, immortal, as it were.

As I have already noted, philosophy as the care of the soul conceives of itself as a radical alternative to the sacred, the demonic, and the orgiastic in overcoming everydayness and decadence. Immortality, as well, no longer means the same thing as with the mysteries. Patočka points out that immortality, which is "inseparably linked with [the soul's inner] dialogue, is . . . different from the immortality of the mysteries. For the first time in history, it is individual immortality, individual because inner, inseparably bound up with its own achievement. Plato's doctrine of the immortality of the soul is the result of the confrontation of the orgiastic with responsibility. Responsibility triumphs over the orgiastic, incorporates it as a subordinate movement, as *Eros*" (*HE*, 105). The immortality to which responsible life gives rise, which in looking at light steadies its vision and becomes transparent through and through, is individual immortality first and foremost because it is the accomplishment (through resistance) of the self, or the soul, of that which, as we have seen, makes of the human an individual human being (even though, as we will see later, such individuality is still a far cry from the singular human being, that is, the ultimate agent of responsibility in Patočka's genealogy of responsibility). Immortality, consequently, is no longer one of living things in general, which perpetuate life as a whole, and of the species, through procreation, and whose deathless everlastingness is celebrated by the mysteries and the orgiastic cults. However, the orgiastic has not been entirely eliminated from the philosophical alternative to everydayness and decadence. Subordinated in the form Eros, the orgiastic realm "is brought into a relation to the sphere of responsibility" (*HE*, 101). Incorporated in the form of love, the orgiastic has, indeed, become one of the possible means in the search for, and the ascent to, the Good. But what follows from this is that the Platonic resolution of the problem of everydayness and decadence by way of, what I would term, an ontology of light—a resolution with which Patočka will take issue—is not as completely severed from the orgiastic as it would pretend. This is evident from Patočka's claim that the Platonic journey after the Good, which takes the form of internal dialogue, is "the new *mystery* of the soul" (*HE*, 105). The soul's care for authenticity through looking-into-what-is is a mystery for having interiorized, or incorporated, mastered, and subordinated, yet not eliminated, the mysteries. Furthermore, Patočka refers to the Platonic version of the care of the soul as "a new, light mythology." This mythology of light "grows on the basis of the duality of the authentic/responsible and the exceptional/orgiastic: the orgiastic is not removed but is disciplined and made subservient" (*HE*, 106). Since Platonic philosophy is at its core care for the soul, it follows that philosophy, precisely because it is all about light, is not entirely removed from the mysteries, myth, and mythology.¹⁰ Perhaps one could venture to say that because in the mystery of the soul and the new mythology of light the realm of the sacred and of myth has been rendered subservient to the philosophical concerns with authenticity and responsibility, philosophy is, or at least implies, a mythology and a myth that have been reshaped at the hands of these concerns. Platonic philosophy, perhaps, is nothing other than mythology made reasonable and responsible.¹¹

When as a result of the catastrophe of the polis-civitas, the latter is superseded by the Roman principality—that is, when the community of equals in freedom is replaced by the state as a transcendent entity within the framework of the social—the whole complex of motifs that are interwoven in the care of the soul remains the foundation of the new version of the theme in question, although it is acted out in a different way. As Patočka's reference to the Neoplatonic philosopher Julian the Apostate, who briefly held the imperial throne, suggests, the new mythology of light was vital to the Roman Empire. Indeed, although the responsibility of the citizen of the Roman Empire is no longer primarily one to himself, and in relation to his equals, but to the State as "a transcendent Good" (*HE*, 106), the Roman Empire represents a new and significant episode, or turn, "in the relation between the orgiastic and the discipline of responsibility" (*HE*, 106). Responsibility of the individual toward the state as an objective, though transcendent, existent, which, like the Platonic Good, can be known, and in light of which humankind can be educated, is now to culminate in the realization of a global or universal community—the community of humankind—that is entirely transparent in that it reflects the law without fault. The Holy Roman Empire of the German Nation, which comes into being after the collapse of the Roman Empire, inherits the legacy of the Platonic conception of the care of the soul through the shape the latter took at the hands of the Hellenistic and Roman philosophers. However, if Christianity is a significant episode in the genealogy of responsibility, it is because it sought to overcome the Platonic solution Roman style of the relation between the orgiastic and responsibility in what Patočka describes as "an about face" (*HE*, 106). Before discussing the Christian version of the care of the soul, let me say that notwithstanding the fact that Patočka's description of Christianity in the fifth essay of the *Heretical Essays* is profoundly indebted to medieval theology, particularly to Augustinean theology, it is also, and unmistakably so, a highly unorthodox way of thinking about Christianity.[12]

In both the Greek and Roman models of responsible life the orgiastic dimension is not eliminated but rendered submissive to the goal of ascending to the Good, whether it is the Good understood as the highest object (the Platonic *agathon*) or as the transcendent Roman state. If Christianity overcomes this solution, what then, precisely, does this new turn consist in? Patočka writes: "Christianity could overcome this Platonic solution only by an about-face. Responsible life was itself presented as a gift from something which ultimately, though it has the character of the Good, has also the traits of the inaccessible and forever superior to humans—the traits of the *mysterium* that always has the final word" (*HE*, 106). Before going into any details, the about-face can be said to consist in (1) conceiving of responsibility as a gift made to the human being rather than as an accomplishment by which one realizes his or her inmost nature; (2) conceiving of the Good not as an however noble object but as a Goodness that is absolutely inaccessible and unfathomable to the human being; and (3) taking immortality out of the hands of the human being and making it contingent on a suprahuman being's last word. In other words, the way the Greeks and the Romans thought of the relation of responsible life to the orgiastic undergoes a complete reversal. Broadly speaking, it is no longer responsible life that renders the sacred, the demonic, and the orgiastic subservient to itself, incorporating it so as to become a means among others of the ascent to the Good; rather, it is the sacred, which now has been transformed into religion, that makes responsible life possible. The responsible individual is no longer one who has freed him- or herself from the suprahuman forces of the demonic that until then held sway over him or her; rather, the Good in the shape of a suprahuman God now commands the human being. It is a responsible life in which the mysteries are no longer overcome by way of the "mystery of the soul" but in which the *mysterium* of the gift, which has "the traits of the inaccessible and is forever superior to humans," suppresses not only the Platonic (and Roman) solution to the relation between responsibility and the orgiastic—in other words, the Greek *sophia tou kosmou*, which itself has been turned into a form of the demonic—but, at the limit, the entire dimension of the orgiastic and the demonic.[13]

With Christianity, the Good has become Goodness—that is, no longer an objective and comprehensible being but the attribute, or rather the action or emanation, of God as a Person. Patočka writes: "Christianity, after all, understands the Good differently than Plato—as a self-forgetting goodness and a self-denying (not orgiastic) love. It is not the orgiastic—that remains not only subordinated but, in certain respects, suppressed to the limit—yet it is still a *mysterium tremendum. Tremendum*, for responsibility is now vested not in a humanly comprehensible essence of the Good and the One, but, rather, in an inscrutable relation to the absolute highest being in whose hands we are not externally, but internally" (*HE*, 106; trans. mod.). In spite of its difference from the Platonic Eros, which is a means in the ascent to the Good, and especially from orgiastic sexuality, which "illustrates how inevitably the orgiastic realm is brought into a relation to the sphere of responsibility" (*HE*, 101)—the love of the Christian God is self-effacing and self-denying Goodness, infinite Goodness itself. Goodness seems to have cut not only all relation to the Platonic Good insofar as it eludes all human looking-into-what-is, and is forever incomprehensible, but also seemingly with the dimension of the orgiastic fusion with life in general. Patočka not only seems to have borrowed the expression *mysterium tremendum*, from Rudolf Otto, an affiliate of the Göttingen School of neo-Kantianism, who coined the term (as far as I can judge) and to whom he is also indebted for the opposition, distinct from the Heideggerian one between the authentic and inauthentic, of everydayness and the exception (the feast). *Mysterium*, in the expression in question, denotes, in Otto's words, "the inexpressible mystery (*Geheimnis*) . . . above all creatures"; *tremendum*, rather than being merely an analytical explication of *mysterium*, is a "synthetic attribute to it" that names the *tremor*, or "'fear' that is more than fear proper" by which the "'absolute overpoweringness'" of the numinous shakes and radically unsettles the subject.[14] For Otto, who underscores the continuity from "the daemonic level up to the idea of the 'living' God," the religious experience of the *mysterium tremendum* comprises both the daemonic and "the highest level of all, where the worship of God is purest [and in which] the 'shudder' reappears in a form ennobled beyond measure where the soul, held speechless, trembles inwardly to the farthest fibre of its being."[15] Undoubtedly, Patočka seeks to sever the religious experience of the *mysterium tremendum*, itself the seed of what is (to be) European, off from the daemonic. But Goodness contains within itself in subordinated form the Platonic Good, and if Patočka holds that in Christianity the orgiastic has, at the limit, been suppressed, this means also that rather than being eliminated altogether, the orgiastic remains subordinated as well. Indeed, Goodness is, admittedly, a *mysterium*, one moreover that is *tremendum*, that overcomes one and makes one tremble, not unlike what happens to the human in the realm of the sacred and demonic. Goodness is a mysterium because the call to care for one's soul, hence, the call to responsibility, is no longer rooted in a notion of the Good that is transparent to human vision, and that he or she can freely emulate, but comes from a God who not only cannot be seen but who sees the individual and internally holds him or her in his hands. The gift of responsibility by this self-forgetting Goodness overcomes and overpowers one, makes one tremble, and, paradoxically, frightens one into total submission. Indeed, in Christianity, as understood by Patočka, the Greek conception of the autonomous, indivisible, and free individual who achieves freedom from everydayness and decadence through a relation to the Good, is seen as a danger because such an autonomy of the self is judged as a way of turning away and not responding to the gift of absolute self-denying Goodness. From the perspective of Christianity, Patočka notes, "the freedom of the [Greek] wise man who has overcome the orgiastic can still be understood as demonic, as a will to separation and autonomy, a resistance to total devotion and self-forgetting love in which the true image of God consists. The soul now does not simply seek itself in the ascent of an inner dialogue but also senses its danger" (*HE*, 107).

If "the soul is not a relation to an object, however noble (like the Platonic Good) but rather to a Person who sees into the soul without being itself accessible to view" (*HE*, 107), it follows that in the Christian version of the care of the soul we also encounter a new version of the self, one that differs from the autonomous "I" of the Greek sage, as well as from the citizen of the Roman Empire educated to being a representative of universal humanity. According to Patočka, the Greek "responsible human as such is *I*; it is an individual that is not identical with any role it could possibly assume . . . ; it is a responsible I because in the confrontation with death and in coming to terms with nothingness it takes upon itself what we all must carry out in ourselves, where no one can take our place" (*HE*, 107). Greek responsibility, which is described here in terms that are not accidentally reminiscent of the analyses, in *Being and Time*, of Dasein's relation to death as a relation that is irreplaceably its own, is understood as a responsibility to "what we all must carry out in ourselves," namely, taking our eventual death upon us as something that no one else can do for us. Yet, if the Greek autonomous individual comes into its own by assuming a responsibility for what everyone, each one of us, has to face as his or her irreplaceable dying, then the individual's responsibility is predicated on something general, something that is universally shared by all human beings. Consequently, the Greek "I" or self is only "the responsible human as such," in no way as yet a singular human being. What is new about the Christian version of the care of the soul is that it advances a conception of responsibility for the singular, the unique human being. This singularity of the human being hinges on the *mysterium tremendum*—that is, on being the addressee or donee of self-forgetting and self-denying Goodness, of a gift, in short, which is so immense that the human can never ever hope to adequately respond to it. As a singular being to whom the gift is given as *this* singular individual, who, furthermore, is constitutively incapable of a comparable self-abdication, the human being is, therefore, constitutively guilty—guilty in advance of any irresponsible action, of never being able to responsibly respond to such love. Patočka writes that, in contrast to the Greek responsible individual, individuality in Christianity "is vested in a relation to an infinite love and humans are individuals because they are guilty, and *always* guilty, with respect to it. We all, as individuals, are defined by the uniqueness of our individual placement in the universality of sin" (*HE*, 107). The Christian care of the soul and the Christian conception of human responsibility consist in the demand of complete self-abdication, total relinquishing of autonomy, and the surrender without reservation of all selfhood. The individual becomes a singular, unique individual, precisely by giving up his or her self, which carries within it the danger of striving for separation from God.

Contrary to the Greek conception of the care of the soul, the truth for which the Christian soul struggles is not a truth gained through insight into the essence *of* what is—that is, into "the being which agelessly, eternally is" (*HE*, 108), but that, as the being or truth of this world, also remains of the order of the world, a worldly truth. Instead, the truth striven for in Christianity concerns the destiny of the soul—a destiny that is intimately interlinked with the demand that comes with being the addressee of an infinite gift by a selfless God and that it can never hope to adequately fulfill. The care of the soul, in the face of everydayness and decadence, now assumes the form of a "care for the salvation of the soul" (*HE*, 108). Finding its essential content in "the wholly unique and so definitely self-determining bond of divinity and humanity," the notion of the soul undergoes what Patočka calls an "abyssal deepening of the soul" (*HE*, 108). The soul is now the site of a "unique drama" in which it lives "in anxiety and hope inextricably intertwined, [and in] which [it] trembles in knowledge of its sin and with its whole being offers itself in the sacrifice of penance" (*HE*, 108). In this inner drama that derives from "the abyss in the divine and in the human" (*HE*, 108), the soul, guilty for not being able to responsibly respond to the selfless gift of God, seeks "in the face of death and death eternal" to transform itself morally by offering itself in total abandonment to God, abandoning everything worldly, including its own self, in the hope of redemption and the promise of eternal life. It is a drama, however, whose "chief personage" is "the transcendent God of antiquity combined with the Old Testament Lord of History," because it depends on Him alone whether this drama will be one of salvation and grace (*HE*, 108). According to Patočka, this transformation of the Platonic motif of the care of the soul in Christianity brings for the first time the essential content of the soul into view: "The chief difference [with the Platonic conception] appears to be that it is only now that the inmost content of the soul is revealed, that the truth for which the soul struggles is not the truth of intuition but rather the truth of destiny, bound up with eternal responsibility from which there is no escape *ad seculum seculorum*" (*HE*, 107–8). Indeed, what becomes clear with Christianity is something that, according to Patočka, has never philosophically been grasped, namely, "that the soul is by nature wholly incommensurate with all objective being" (*HE*, 108; trans. mod.). According to this new version of the care of the soul, the soul not only is heterogeneous to anything that objectively exists but also is something that cannot take its lead from a truth that is the truth *of* what is—a worldly truth. What becomes obvious with Christianity is that the soul is first and foremost concerned with "its own being in which, unlike all other existents, it is infinitely interested." The soul's own being is precisely what is in question in the care of the soul since its being is not something that is given. This is precisely what the inner drama reveals in which the infinitely guilty human being chooses to selflessly surrender everything worldly, his or her mortal self included, in the hope of eternal life for his or her own soul. With Christianity it becomes evident that responsibility, that is, the possibility of choice, is intrinsically linked to the soul's possibility of existing in the first place or, rather, of continuing to exist beyond worldly existence. Christianity carries with it the idea that responsibility implies the possibility of choice and, "in this choosing, of arriving at its own self—the idea that the soul is nothing present *before, only afterwards*, that it is historical in all its being and only as such escapes decadence" (*HE*, 108). Everydayness and its decadence is overcome only in a responsibility of the soul not for something that it would already be but for what it is to become in the first place, something specifically different from anything that exists within the world, including the eternal essence of what is. Compared to the unhistorical Greek version according to which the soul overcomes natural decline by achieving a however-temporary state of likeness to what is eternal, in the Christian version the soul surpasses everydayness and decline by being historical through and through. If the care of the soul as the core idea of European life is, as we have seen, resistance to everydayness and decadence, then what Christian Europe opposes to the latter is not cosmology but history.

Whereas in the Platonic understanding of the care of the soul, the soul achieves inner form and unity by living in conformity with the cosmological order and is reflected externally in the ahistorical order of the polis of equals, the Christian conception of the care of the soul is about the soul's becoming. The community founded on a concern with the soul's salvation is a historical community throughout—unified through history—that is, European history. According to Patočka, the genealogy of the Platonic motif, and by extension of responsibility in the face of everyday anonymity, has reached its greatest development thus far in Christianity. Christianity has been able to become the most radical realization of the struggle against decadence because of its abyssal deepening of what it understands by *soul*. Patočka writes: "By virtue of this foundation in the abyssal deepening of the soul, Christianity remains thus far the greatest, unsurpassed but also un-thought-through human outreach that enabled humans to struggle against decadence" (*HE*, 108). But as is evident from the preceding statement, Christianity—that is, as we know it—is not yet the end of the process. If the development of the motif of the care of the soul has not yet been completed with Christianity, it is not simply because the Christian conception of the care of the soul, and its particular kind of resistance against decadence and the orgiastic, has never been really realized; above all, it is because Christianity itself has not yet been able to think through the kind of break with decadence and all forms of *doxa* that it proposes.[16]

If the new conception and configuration of the care of the soul that emerges with Christian Europe fails to achieve both externally—that is, socially and culturally—and internally—that is, in inner contemplative life of the person—what it promises, this is because Europe, in the modern sense—Western Christian Europe—also inherits all "the problems of the Roman Empire" that it supersedes (*HE*, 108). Furthermore, the entirely new type of rationality that developed in modern Europe—a non-Platonic rationalism, which wanting "to master things . . . is mastered by them" (*HE*, 110)—is dominated as well by "the unresolved problem which the Christian era took over from antiquity: transcending the everyday and the orgiastic" (*HE*, 110). Indeed, "Christian theology rejected the Platonic solution, though this theology did accept extensive elements of a solution launched along Platonic lines" (*HE*, 110). Galileo, Patočka remarks, "is, notoriously, a Platonist. It is Plato's metaphysics of the immortal soul that makes it possible for the domination of nature by the human soul to find a place in the Christian world with its unresolved problem of metaphysical philosophy and Christian theology" (*HE*, 111). Conceiving of nature in a Platonic fashion, namely "as that over which [humans who strive for freedom and immortality] stand because they grasp it in eidetic insight" (*HE*, 110), "what had originally in Plato been a bulwark against orgiastic irresponsibility has now passed into the service of everydayness," Patočka notes (*HE*, 112). After the collapse of Christian Europe, and its replacement by technological civilization, this domination of nature for the benefit of the everyday has also produced a "new flood of the orgiastic [as] an inevitable appendage to addiction to things, to their everyday procurement, to bondage to life" (*HE*, 113). As Patočka sees it, the wars and the revolutions that mark the twentieth century are clear symptoms of this return of the orgiastic.

But if Christianity has not adequately thought through the kind of break with the everyday and the orgiastic implied by its conception of the care of the soul, it is also, if not primarily, because Christian theology and philosophy inherited the Platonic motif of the care of the soul and with it Platonism's solution to this motif, that is, its problems as well. Patočka notes that there is much truth in Nietzsche's saying that Christianity is Platonism for the people, because "the Christian God took over the transcendence of the onto-theological conception as a matter of course" (*HE*, 107). Yet even though there is "a fundamental, profound difference" (*HR*, 107) between the Platonic and the Christian conception of the soul,

"Platonic rationalism, the Platonic effort to subject even responsibility itself to objectivity of knowledge, continues to affect the nether layers of the Christian conception" (*HE*, 110). Indeed, many of Plato's major concepts and doctrines, such as, for instance, the doctrine of the ideas, only became truly influential when Christian thinkers interpreted the revelations of the Scriptures in terms of his thought. Because of this lingering Platonism in Christian theology and philosophy, the specifically Christian understanding of responsibility has not as yet been able to find its adequate formulation. To think through the radical implications of the Christian solution for a responsible overcoming of everydayness and decadence is still of the order of a task. It is the task of a radical severing off of Platonism—that is, precisely, the heritage to which Europe owes its distinctness. Only such a break, it would seem, can ensure the radical overcoming of everydayness (and all its doxical forms), including the orgiastic way of escape from the latter. Heretical Christianity, as well as a truly Christian Europe, would thus be radical to the point of having cut all ties with the memory of the Greek solution to the motif of the care of the soul that emerged in antiquity. The truly Christian notion of the care of the soul is a novel concept that at the limit does not owe anything anymore to the genealogy of the Platonic theme. With Europe having probably disappeared forever, this radically new conception of responsibility would, therefore, be a thoroughly new beginning of Europe.

I conclude with a question. As we have seen, the Christian God is a synthesis of the transcendent God of antiquity and the Old Testament Lord of History. This is the question: By radically breaking with Platonism, does heretical Christianity not return to the Jewish element that entered Christianity only by way of Hellenization? Or is heretical Christianity, in contrast, not rather to achieve something entirely new? Based on the third volume of Patočka's Collected Works, which have been published in Czech, Ivan Chvatík has concluded that "what Patočka stands for is a kind of non-Christian Christianity" whose "foremost feature is to abandon the conception of God as the giver of all sense." Although Patočka's thought eliminates God, it "remains religious in character."[17] Indeed, by radically severing all ties with Platonism in the Christian conception of God, that is, with God as a transcendent being, Patočka's Christianity is heretical in that it is one without God, an atheistic Christianity, in short. Let us bear in mind that the Christian God, who gives the singular human being the gift of responsibility, is a God that, like the transcendent God of antiquity, is not of this world. Not only is the Christian God not the Jewish God; He is also a God who holds the human being *internally* in His hands. Furthermore, the drama—that is, the historical happening that unfolds in the soul—is an *inner* drama and, in that, also distinct from the (worldly) history of the Jewish people. But this God that makes the human being tremble from within is not the Christian God, who, as the highest being, is still Platonic, nor is the inner drama Christian in any orthodox sense. "The true image of God" is that of "a Person who sees into the soul without being itself accessible to view" (*HE*, 106–7). Patočka's subsequent observation that "what a Person is" has yet to be "adequately thematized in the Christian perspective" (*HE*, 107) gives us, perhaps, a clue to how a responsibility free of all traces of Platonism would have to be thought. Indeed, according to Patočka's heretical understanding of Christianity God as absolute Other is not an ontologically transcendent God. However absolute and other, God as Person holds the self, or person, in his hands from within. God is thus immanent to the self. The call for responsibility which comes from within must come from oneself as a Person to oneself, from a Person, who is no one other than oneself, but who overcomes oneself as no transcendent being, however noble, (such as the Platonic Good), or a transcendent God, could possibly achieve.[18] This conception of a responsibility that originates exclusively in oneself—in a drama between oneself as a Person and a person—a drama of self-affection in which the soul is seen without seeing and that, hence, does not bring the subject into his or her own—this is, in essence, it seems to me, the heretically Christian idea of responsibility, and hence of a Christian Europe, that Patočka advocates. Such a Europe is also the community of all those singular human beings who, in the absence of any transcendent instance, have been shaken from within by the terrible gift, and the ineluctable duty of responsibility, which in an irreducible dissymmetry to themselves, they have received from themselves. This community is one that, in Patočka's words, consists of "the unity of the shaken but undaunted" (*HE*, 43).

PART IV

Jacques Derrida

§ 9   European Memories

Having evoked various reflections and presentations of Europe ranging from Georg Wilhelm Friedrich Hegel to Paul Valéry and from Edmund Husserl to Martin Heidegger, Jacques Derrida remarks in *The Other Heading* that these European discourses on Europe are dated. Although they are modern discourses and even "the most current, [and, indeed,] nothing is more current," they also date back somehow (*OH*, 26). They are always already traditional discourses in the sense that they speak of Europe from the perspective of its end, as an end (in the sense of *telos*) about to be realized or something that is no longer—something that has come to an end. As the heirs of these discourses, Europeans—like all inheritors—are in mourning. But, according to Derrida, Europe must also assume these traditional discourses, particularly those aspects of them that are of acute concern today. The Europeans' capital, their first and most current duty, is to take responsibility for that heritage of discourses on what Europe is. "We bear the responsibility for this heritage," says Derrida, "right along with the capitalizing memory that we have of it. We did not choose this responsibility; it imposes itself upon us" (*OH*, 28). This responsibility is ours insofar as qua Europeans we are heirs of the discourses in question.

In the brief remarks devoted in *Specters of Marx* to the concept of inheritance in general, Derrida points out that *to be* means to inherit. One is an heir, even before one explicitly assumes or rejects a particular inheritance. "That we *are* heirs does not mean that we *have* or that we *receive* this or that, some inheritance that enriches us one day with this or that, but that the *being* of what we are *is* first of all inheritance, whether

265

we like it or know it or not." Indeed, Derrida continues, "inheritance is never a *given*, it is always a task"; it is something still before us, to which we have to bear witness as that which "we *are* insofar as we *inherit*."[1] For Europeans this task consists above all in *being* such that they assume the memory of Europe. To be by taking responsibility for their inheritance in no way reveals nostalgia or traditionalist fervor. On the contrary, understood as a task, the affirmation of this inheritance does not exclude—indeed, it may even call for a radical transformation of what has been handed down. The prime duty of the European is to take responsibility for this heritage, that is, the modern tradition of reflecting on European identity.[2] This is so not only because these discourses concern being European but also because such identity is always established in relation to alterity, to the other, to the non-European. Responsibility toward this heritage is thus also responsibility to the other. It consists in the double injunction of being faithful to "an idea of Europe, [to] a difference of Europe, but [to] a Europe that consists precisely in not closing itself off in its own identity" (*OH*, 29). In other words, the responsibility that Europeans bear for all of the traditional discourses on European identity, of which "old Europe seems to have exhausted all the possibilities," is thus a responsibility toward responsibility, indeed, toward the concept of responsibility itself (*OH*, 26).

At this point, however, I would only like to highlight the fact that for Derrida the prime responsibility of the European is one toward the tradition of the discourses and counterdiscourses concerning his own identification. This point is made even more explicitly, though in more general terms, in *For What Tomorrow . . . A Dialogue*, where Derrida remarks that "the concept of responsibility has no sense at all outside of an experience of inheritance." We should remind ourselves of this as we turn toward Derrida's discussion of a discourse on Europe that he characterizes as heretical "with respect to all the important [or grand] European discourses" (*GD*, 29). All the possibilities of the grand discourses of Europe have apparently been exhausted. Yet Jan Patočka's views on Europe and European responsibility, which have the capacity to produce explosive implications if extended radically, sound a heretical note within the traditional discourses of the modern Western world, not the least because they also seek to break the ties to a certain memory and to a certain tradition.

In the first two chapters of *The Gift of Death* Derrida engages Patočka's genealogy of European responsibility as it is presented in *Heretical Essays*. To my knowledge, this is the only occasion on which Derrida has broached the work of the Czech phenomenologist. Although his discussion is limited to the *Heretical Essays* and, moreover, largely to one of its essays ("Is Technological Civilization Decadent, and Why?"), it provides an exemplary reading of Patočka's conception of Europe and responsibility, of its intricacies and ambiguities, as well as of the major tenets of Derrida's own conception.[3] Needless to say, *The Gift of Death* is not limited to a discussion of Patočka's views on Europe and responsibility. In this work Derrida also engages the thought of Heidegger, Emmanuel Levinas, and, in particular, Søren Kierkegaard. Although I will briefly, and very schematically, sketch out Derrida's main concerns within the essay as a whole, no comprehensive reading can be attempted here. In any event, we will have to examine in some detail Derrida's assessment in *The Gift of Death* of Patočka's fundamental and original thesis of the *Heretical Essays* and *Plato and Europe*, namely, that the Platonic motif of the care of the soul (*epimeleia tes psyches*) is the embryo of European life and the starting point of the genealogy of responsibility in the history of Europe.[4] Without doing so, we would not be able to illuminate Derrida's own understanding of responsibility, hence of what Europe is.

So, before turning to Derrida's reading of Patočka, let us first remind ourselves, however briefly, of what this Platonic motif is. The notion of the care of the soul is a fundamental and elementary notion in Plato's earliest dialogues, around which all of Socrates' concerns are gathered. Although this theme is to be found primarily in the *Apology*, *Phaedo*, and *Alcibiades I*, it is, according to Patočka, the central issue not only of all Plato's thought but of Greek philosophy as a whole. Let us recall that for the Greeks, the soul—that is, the mover and user of the body—is the human being's true self. As Socrates argues in *Alcibiades I*, "there is nothing which may be called more properly ourselves than the soul" (*DP* 1:667, 130d). For the Greek philosopher, the body is only an instrument, or a tool, for a good life. But the prerequisite for a good life is that the soul be in command of the body. The philosopher's first duty, or responsibility, is, therefore, to get to know him- or herself in order to be able to look to that which is most properly him- or herself, rather than tending to what does not expressly belong to him- or herself: money, reputation, honor, as well as anything bodily. The soul achieves not only self-control (*sophron*) but also purity and transparency within itself by shunning everything corporeal. It is guided in this by the knowledge of what is and emulates the eternal, the unchangeable order of the cosmos, the Divine, or the Good. As is made clear in the *Phaedo*, such severing of all ties to the body culminates in the care of death, which, as this dialogue shows, is an intrinsic part of the care of the soul. By caring for death—that is, by learning how to face death easily—the soul, having freed itself from any contamination with the body, becomes able "to collect and concentrate itself by itself, trusting nothing but its judgment."[5] Thus, within his lifetime the philosopher's soul will achieve a state that resembles the one that only the gods should enjoy and will thus also secure its full release from the body on death.

What unmistakably sets Patočka's discourse apart from the traditional discourses on Europe—particularly those of Husserl and Heidegger—is what Derrida calls Patočka's "essential Christianity" (*GD*, 22). Undoubtedly, Derrida makes this point first of all to distinguish Patočka's interpretation of the theme of the care of the soul from Heidegger's analysis of care (*Sorge*) in *Being and Time* as a fundamental existential structure of Dasein. Heidegger constantly sought to separate his thought from Christianity, while at the same time ontologically recovering—and de-Christianizing—Christian themes and texts by inquiring into their originary possibility. Patočka, on the other hand, "makes an inverse yet symmetrical gesture.... He reontologizes the historic themes of Christianity and attributes to revelation or to the *mysterium tremendum* the ontological content that Heidegger attempts to remove from it" (*GD*, 23). But this reference to an essential Christianity also acknowledges that the emergence of responsibility in the face of everydayness and the sacred is, for Patočka, intimately connected to the history of religion. Patočka is intent on overcoming both the inauthenticity of everydayness and the demonic and the orgiastic that are an escape from it. *Plato and Europe* establishes Plato as the Greek philosopher who brought the motif of the care of the soul into being and also as the thinker who transformed myth into religion, the one who "recommends faith." All differences considered, "faith, as the Greek philosophers saw it, is the foundation of what we call faith in the Christian tradition"; nevertheless, only Christianity is religion in an eminent sense (*PE*, 139). Indeed, as Derrida remarks, Patočka's thought is remarkably consistent in taking "into account the event of Christian mystery as an absolute singularity, a religion par excellence and an irreducible condition for a joint history of the subject, responsibility, and Europe. That is so even if, here and there, the expression 'history of religions' appears in the plural, and even if one can only infer from this plural a reference to Judaic, Islamic, and Christian religions alone, those known as religions of the Book" (*GD*, 2). If the genealogy of responsibility developed by Patočka "follows the traces of a genius of Christianity that is the history of Europe" (*GD*, 3), it is precisely because it is only in, or as, Christian Europe that the motif of the care of the soul—the central theme of what is European—is transformed (or, as we will see, *could* be transformed) into a true principle of responsibility. Christianity is the only religion that can secure the possibility of a responsibility that is truly European and at the same time really realize the concept of responsibility. What thus sets Patočka's reflections on Europe apart from those of Husserl and Heidegger is precisely the significance of religion—particularly, of the religion par excellence, which is Christianity.

The Christianity of Patočka's texts on the care of the soul and European responsibility is not just any Christianity. It is not only an essential but also a heretical conception of Christianity. According to Patočka's highly stratified genealogy of responsibility, the history of the responsible self is built on the heritage of the Platonic conception of the care of the soul through a series of ruptures and repressions "that assure the very tradition they punctuate with their interruptions" (*GD*, 7). Although the novel twist to which Christianity subjects the theme of the care of the soul consists, according to Patočka, in an "about-face" by means of which Christianity seeks to extricate itself from its Platonic inheritance, Christianity has proven unable to think through and draw the radical implications of its mutation of the theme in question precisely because its overcoming of Platonism is not complete (*HE*, 106). As Derrida points out, if European Christianity is at its heart still haunted by the persistent presence of a type of Platonism—and of a type of Platonic politics—it is, according to Patočka, because it "has not sufficiently repressed Platonism in the course of its reversal, and it still mouths its words" (*GD*, 23). Now, the specificity of the reversal that the motif of the care of the soul undergoes in Christianity consists in this: the responsibility of the self or the soul does not derive from knowledge of the Divine, the cosmos, or the Good but from the soul's exposure to the gaze of an other, ultimately the gaze of God as a Person, a gaze that constitutes the soul as a person and, for that, as a responsible self. Indeed, the Christian version of the care of the soul is unable to come into its own because it continues to subordinate responsibility (and decision making) to knowledge, the knowledge of the Good, just as is the case with the Platonic model. Patočka inscribes his discourse on Europe, responsibility, and politics "within the perspective of a Christian eschatology"—that is, within a happening in which Christianity and, by extension, the only true conception of responsibility are still hampered by the remnants of the Platonic heritage. He is thus forced to acknowledge that something "remains 'unthought' in Christianity. Whether ethical or political, the Christian consciousness of responsibility is incapable of reflecting on the Platonic thinking that it represses, and at the same time it is incapable of reflecting on the orgiastic mystery that Platonic thinking incorporates" (*GD*, 24). Christianity's inability to determine the notion and status of "the place and subject of all responsibility, namely, the *person*," is indicative of what remains unthought (*GD*, 24), for in the Christian mystery the person is not in a relation to an objectively knowable transcendent object such as the Platonic Good but to God as a Person, to He who transfixes the self by His gaze without being seen Himself.[6] What follows from this inability and neglect of what Patočka judges to be an inadequate thematization is that Christianity remains only "on the threshold of responsibility. It doesn't thematize what a responsible person *is*, that is, what he *must be*, namely this exposing of the soul to the gaze of another person, of a person as transcendent other, as an other who looks at me, but who looks without the subject-who-says-I being able to reach that other, see her, hold her within the reach of my gaze" (*GD*, 25). Furthermore, as Derrida concludes, "an inadequate thematization of what responsibility is or *must be* is also an *irresponsible* thematization; not knowing, having neither a sufficient knowledge or consciousness of what being *responsible* means, is of itself a lack of responsibility" (*GD*, 25). In sum then, the Christian version of the care of the soul is, in spite of all its radicality, "limited by the weight of what remains unthought, in particular its incorrigible Platonism" (*GD*, 28), an unacknowledged debt, which also explains the inadequate thematization of what makes the soul a truly responsible self.

Christianity is also infused with a certain irresponsibility as far as its conception of responsibility is concerned. Patočka's essential Christianity, then, is a heretical conception of Christianity in that "according to the logic of a messianic eschatology" he advocates a more "thorough thematization" of what sets the Christian notion of the care of the soul apart from the Platonic (and Roman) model, which bears not only on its understanding of responsibility but also on its political realization. Derrida writes:

> Something has not yet arrived, neither at Christianity nor by means of Christianity. What has not yet come about is the fulfillment, within history and in political history, and first and foremost in European politics, of the new responsibility announced by the *mysterium tremendum*. There has not yet been an authentically Christian politics because there remains this residue of the Platonic *polis*. Christian politics must break more definitely and more radically with Greco-Roman Platonic politics in order to finally fulfill the *mysterium tremendum*. Only on this condition will Europe have a future. (*GD*, 28–29)

The realization of a European politics based on a Christian version of the care of the soul would hinge on drawing upon the full philosophical, religious, and political consequences of what is promised with the emergence of Christian Europe. This, however, is possible only on the condition of a radical rupture with the Platonic heritage, that is, precisely with a model of the care of the soul that is predicated on knowledge, in particular, the knowledge of the Good. Undoubtedly, *heretical*, in the title of Patočka's *Heretical Essays*, refers, at first, to the vulgar Marxist conceptions of the philosophy of history. But its heresy, which also marks a rupture with Husserl's and Heidegger's views on history, as Paul Ricoeur has noted, derives, as Derrida implies, from Patočka's hyperbolic conception of Christianity.[7] "Taken to its extreme," Patočka's text is heretical with respect to the grand discourses on Europe by Husserl and Heidegger because it "seems to suggest on the one hand that Europe will not be what it must be until it becomes fully Christian, until the *mysterium tremendum* is adequately thematized. On the other hand it also suggests that the Europe to come will no longer be Greek, Greco-Roman, or even Roman. The most radical insistence of the *mysterium tremendum* would be upon a Europe so new (or so old) that it would be freed from the Greek or Roman memory that is so commonly invoked in speaking of it; freed to the extent of breaking all ties with this memory, becoming heterogeneous to it" (*GD*, 29). Patočka's conception of Europe, even though it is a version of the care of the soul, is heretical with respect to all the traditional discourses on Europe because of its attempt to emancipate Europe from the memory of both Athens and Rome—that is to say, from a memory of responsibility that rests on knowledge of the Good or of the universal state. Built exclusively on the *mysterium tremendum*—in other words, on the unseen gaze of an absolutely selfless Goodness, who shakes the soul (the self or person) because it is unable to adequately respond to this gift of love—Europe is to become something entirely new—something, in other words, that is no longer responsible to the memory of Athens and Rome.[8] Yet, before we can provide a hint of what the implications of this radical break of European responsibility with its Platonic and Roman heritage would be, it is necessary to briefly explore the major aspects of the essential Christian conception of responsibility that orthodox Christianity has failed to make good on.

The Platonic responsible self or soul cares for itself and achieves in this manner a resemblance—however temporary—to the gods by measuring itself against the Good. The Christian self's responsibility rests on its relation to an other. It is neither a relation of the self to itself nor one that the self can freely choose to take upon itself nor one that it can ignore. Rather, "the Christian 'reversal' that converts the Platonic conversion *in turn*, involves the entrance upon the scene of a gift" (*GD*, 40). Patočka argues that, in Christianity, "the responsible life is itself presented as a gift from something which ultimately, though it has the character of the Good, has also the traits of the inaccessible and forever superior to humans—the traits of the *mysterium* that always has the final word" (*HE*, 106). Understanding responsibility as a gift makes all the difference. Such an understanding makes responsibility into a function of an event, the singular event of a gift by another, which, furthermore, is addressed to the human as a singular human being. In fact, the gift, insofar as it is always directed specifically at *this* human being, is constitutive of his singularity and irreplaceability. But, according to Christianity, responsibility is also a gift that comes from an absolute Other, that is, a self-effacing Goodness that gives this gift in selfless love and to which the donee is thus constitutively unable to respond in kind. As a consequence, "there is a structural disproportion or dissymmetry between the finite and responsible mortal on the one hand and the goodness of the infinite gift on the other hand. . . . It inevitably transforms the experience of responsibility into one of guilt: I have never been and never will be up to the level of this infinite goodness nor up to the immensity of the gift, the frameless immensity that must in general define (*in*-define) a gift as such" (*GD*, 51). Addressed to finite beings, the selfless gift is constitutive of their singularity; it also condemns such singular beings to guilt inasmuch as they are responsible. Furthermore, the gift of responsibility that occurs in the *mysterium tremendum* is a gift by a self-denying and self-effacing Goodness, which also remains inaccessible because of its very withdrawal. To be responsible is, in Patočka's words, to stand in an inscrutable relation to "a Person who sees into the soul without being itself accessible to view," and "in whose hands we are not externally, but internally" (*HE*, 106–7). That which makes me responsible is something that remains impenetrable to me—in other words, secret. It is also something that shatters me because I cannot adequately respond to such a self-denying gift. Thus, Platonic responsibility is a function of what Patočka terms looking-in, or looking-into-what-is (*nahlédnuti*)—namely, into eternal being—which, like the Platonic Good, can effectively be known. Christian responsibility, however, is not in the power of the subject, who is overpowered, crushed by it precisely because its source—self-renouncing and self-withdrawing Goodness—remains unfathomable (*HE*, 35). Finally, as Derrida puts it, the gift of responsibility is a gift by "a goodness whose inaccessibility acts as a command to the donee. It subjects its receivers, giving themselves to them as goodness itself but also as law" (*GD*, 41)—that is, as a universality to which the donee is subject as a singular and irreplaceable being. As the result of this gift, Christian responsibility takes the uniqueness and irreplaceability of the singular individual into account precisely by subjecting him or her to a universal Law.

Patočka holds that it is only in Christianity that the most powerful plumbing of the depths of responsibility has occurred—in other words, that only here is it conceived in a truly fundamental manner. He can do so because this conception of responsibility articulates, as it were, the only conditions under which responsibility is possible. In Christianity alone, it becomes clear that "responsibility demands irreplaceable singularity" (*GD*, 51). Christian responsibility is also, therefore, tied to a gift of death—of "*another death*" (*GD*, 40), which is not the one to be found in the Platonic version of the care of the soul. As Derrida reminds us, when Patočka argues that "the *mysterium tremendum* announces, in a manner of speaking, *another death* . . . another way of giving death or of granting oneself death, . . . the word 'gift' is uttered" (*GD*, 40). This gift of death is a gift in an eminent sense. It is the gift by the Other, on which the gift of responsibility itself rests or with which responsibility coincides. Only through this gift of death does access to genuine responsibility become possible, because "only death or rather the apprehension of death can give this irreplaceability [without which there can be no true responsibility], for it is only on the basis of it that one can speak of a responsible subject, of the soul as conscience of self, of myself, etc." (*GD*, 51; trans. mod.). This gift is another way of giving oneself death, first and foremost, in the sense of apprehending death. In the originary Platonic version of the care of the soul, the philosopher, by giving himself death as that which will only affect him as a bodily being, frees himself from death; he collects and gathers himself within himself. Derrida writes that the (philosopher's) self "comes into being as such at the moment when the soul is not only gathering itself in the preparation for death but when it is ready to receive death, giving it to itself even, in an acceptation that delivers it from the body, and at the same time delivers it from the demonic and the orgiastic. By means of the passage to death [*passage de la mort*] the soul attains its own freedom" (*GD*, 40). By contrast, in the Christian paradigm death is apprehended neither as something from which the soul can distance itself through care nor as something from which it can sever itself, thus collecting itself within itself. Christian death is experienced as intrinsically linked to my selfhood, as precisely something that is exclusively mine, that no one can take from me, or assume for me, which constitutes my irreplaceability as a singular self. Let us recall that for Patočka the Christian way in which I give myself death rests on "the gift made to me by God as he holds me in his gaze and in his hands while remaining inaccessible to me, the terribly dissymmetrical gift of the *mysterium tremendum*" (*GD*, 33). The human being to whom this gift is made is no match for the gift of death that accompanies the responsibility to which God's selfless gift calls me. It is a gift that makes the finite subject tremble in terror because he or she is unable to adequately respond to it, the gift of an awareness of death as eternal death. Derrida writes: "For what is given in this trembling, in the actual trembling of terror, is nothing other than death itself, a new significance for death, a new apprehension of death, a new way in which to give oneself death or to put oneself to death. The difference between Platonism and Christianity would be above all 'a reversal in the face of death and of eternal death'" (*GD*, 31). Radically guilty in the face of a gift that is addressed to one in his or her very singularity, the human confronts death—that which is irreducibly his or her own and on which his or her uniqueness hinges—as the complete extinction of him- or herself, unless he or she is redeemed by the grace of God. This gift of death is also the gift of a new way of putting oneself to death in the face of the prospect of eternal death, since to merit the grace of God, the trembling creature must offer its "whole being in the sacrifice of repentance" (*HE*, 108). What Christianity brings to light is not only the fact that without the singularity, or the irreplaceability, of the individual, there cannot be any responsible self but also that if singularity is to be the condition of possibility of responsibility, it cannot be a given but must be constantly in danger of extinction.

The Christian version of the care of the soul plumbs into the soul deeper than Platonism because this responsibility—which originates in the gaze of an unfathomable Other—precedes the subject/object relation that informs the classical version of the responsible self. Derrida writes:

> The dissymmetry of the gaze, this disproportion that relates me, and whatever concerns me, to a gaze that I don't see and that remains secret from me although it commands me, is, according to Patočka, what promises itself [*s'annonce*] in Christian mystery as the frightening, terrifying mystery, the *mysterium tremendum*. Such a terror has no place in the transcendent experience that relates Platonic responsibility to the *agathon*. Nor does it have any place in the politics that is so instituted. But the terror of this secret exceeds and precedes the complacent relation of a subject to an object. (*GD*, 27–28; trans. mod.)

Yet such a radical way of conceiving responsibility is only announced or is only promised by Christianity. Christianity as a whole cannot be identified with this understanding of responsibility because its persistent Platonism has prevented it from thinking through this deepened conception. What is thus announced by Christianity is perhaps no longer anything Christian unless it is Christian in a hyperbolic sense.[9] In any case Christianity remains the privileged locus in which the depths of responsibility can best be plumbed.

At this juncture let me return to the Platonic motif of the care of the soul and the first awakening of responsibility that is the core idea of European life but with which the Christian understanding of the responsible self must also, according to Patočka, make a clear break. Let us thus once again recall that knowledge of what is eternal—justice, beauty, the Good—is the basis of Greek responsible life. Responsibility itself is something public because it is based on knowledge—a kind to which everyone has access in principle. It is possible to account for the concept of responsibility and to universally establish what responsibility and being responsible consists of, but such an understanding of responsibility also implies that the responsible self must be able to give reasons for any of his or her actions and beliefs, publicly whenever possible. According to this Platonic conception of responsibility, "not knowing, having neither a sufficient knowledge or consciousness of what being *responsible* means, is of itself a lack of responsibility. In order to be responsible it is necessary to respond to or answer to what being responsible means" (*GD*, 25). To the extent that the Platonic conception of the care of the soul is the first awakening of and to responsibility and hence that this understanding of responsibility is the first moment in the genealogy of responsibility in (or as) Europe, this demand that knowledge be involved in responsible decision making is at the heart of the history of the concept. It dominates the thought on responsibility in Europe from Plato's to Husserl's reflections on an absolutely self-responsible universal science. Derrida refers to this Greek moment and endorses it, thus highlighting a certain continuity between his own thought and that of Husserl on this issue in question when he writes that responsibility consists, "according to the most convincing and most convinced *doxa*, in *responding*, hence in answering to the other, before the other and before the law, and if possible publicly, answering for itself, its intentions, its aims, and for the name of the agent deemed responsible" (*GD*, 26–27). The Greek understanding of responsibility that constitutes the first moment in Patočka's genealogy of responsibility excludes any secrecy. Although the Platonic moment incorporates demonic mystery, there is no place for secrecy and mystery in the philosophy and politics of the Platonic tradition. Everything is in the open, in the light of day, for all to judge. Like Greek political life, Greek civic responsibility "openly declares that secrecy will not be allowed." It "presents itself as a moment without mystery" (*GD*, 33). The Platonic model of responsibility and politics is, consequently, a model of democracy.

Yet, since the Christian model of responsibility rests on a deepened interiority and is the gift of a selfless Other who remains inscrutable, this new model has a definite place for secrecy, for the *mysterium*, for the mystical, unlike the Greco-Roman version, which supersedes so radically as to break entirely with its memory. Christian responsibility has its origin in a gift, in a "*gift that is not a present*," and it is from the outset tied to secrecy for essential reasons. Indeed, as Derrida points out, "a gift that could be recognized as such in the light of day, a gift destined for recognition, would immediately annul itself. The gift is the secret itself. . . . Secrecy is the last word of the gift which is the last word of the secret" (*GD*, 29–30). Originating in the elusive event of such a gift, even the transition from Platonism and neo-Platonism to Christianity remains obscure; it cannot be simply accounted for in positive terms. But since the gift of responsibility is a gift from a self-effacing Goodness (who holds the human being in his hands from within) to the individual in all his or her creatural singularity, it is "the gift of something that remains inaccessible, unpresentable, and as a consequence secret" (*GD*, 29). The donee is exclusively responsible to the donator, and hence, as Derrida's discussion of the Abrahamic story of the sacrifice of Isaac in the second half of *The Gift of Death* demonstrates, he or she is relieved of the necessity to explain his or her deeds to others. Indeed, being the unique addressee of the gift, the responsible individual must, at the limit, relate to others in an irresponsible fashion. How he or she responds to the divine Law remains secret—that is, unaccounted for—and ultimately secret to him- or herself as well, for such responsible decision making must, in principle, be unaccountable.

How does Derrida respond to this conception of responsibility, a conception that is entirely heterogeneous to the Greek one and to the tradition to which it gave rise, one that he has characterized as "the most convincing and convinced *doxa*"? In seeking to answer this question, let us bear in mind that the Platonic idea of responsibility is the beginning of the genealogy of responsibility in Europe, of the European tradition of thinking about responsibility, although it is, according to Patočka, to be entirely replaced by the Christian model. But the Christian version of responsibility is also part of European memory, which thus consists of at least two different memories regarding what constitutes responsibility, despite Patočka's description of Christian responsibility as thoroughly heterogeneous to its Greek antecedent. Further, since the lingering presence of Platonism in Christianity has prevented a full rupture with the Greek model of responsibility that Christianity is to accomplish, the break with this tradition must be completed if the very essence or future of Europe is ever to be realized. Yet, as we saw at the beginning of this chapter, for Derrida the concept of responsibility makes no sense whatsoever without an experience of inheritance. Consequently, responsibility is first and foremost a responsibility for and to the specific traditions of responsibility that have been bequeathed to us. It is such, first and foremost, a responsibility before any particular responsibilities to oneself, the other, God, the animal, the world, and so forth. Such responsibility toward the various conceptions of responsibility that have been handed down to us, or toward the grand discourses on Europe in which they are laid out, does not exclude selection and critique. But would not any attempt to ignore, reject, or break with one of those legacies be tantamount to irresponsibility? Indeed, if responsibility is first of all a responsibility for and to an inheritance, to abandon or to deliberately renounce a part of the tradition in its entirety would be the gravest irresponsibility, all the more so in the case of a part of the tradition that concerns the concept of responsibility itself. Among the several things that Derrida seeks to achieve in *The Gift of Death*, the attempt to do justice to the conflicting models of responsibility within the European tradition—that is, also of thinking about Europe itself—prevails. The most insistent concern of *The Gift of Death* is that of assuming the heritage of responsibility in all its forms—particularly, the most "living" part of it, that which is most current because it continues to put limits on any traditional view on responsibility that would impose itself at the exclusion of all others. All of the other concerns of *The Gift of Death* presuppose this equitable treatment of the contradictory views on responsibility to be found in the traditional discourses of the modern Western world. But, far from amounting to a wholesale underwriting of all the major positions on responsibility, such responsible treatment does not exclude critique, radical transformation, or the opening to other possible models of understanding responsibility. In fact, as we will see, Derrida's attempt in *The Gift of Death* to respond responsibly to the various facets of the European heritage of responsibility represents a novel concept of responsibility—that is, a novel conception of Europe.

Before I elaborate further on Derrida's response to Patočka in *The Gift of Death*, a brief and very sketchy outline of what this text seeks to achieve is warranted. We should keep in mind Derrida's observation in his first chapter, "Secrets of European Responsibility," that what separates Patočka's interpretation of the motif of the care of the soul from Heidegger's influence is its essential Christianity. Whereas Heidegger constantly seeks to separate himself from Christianity, "repeating on an ontological level Christian themes and texts that have been 'de-Christianized,'" "Patočka makes an inverse yet symmetrical gesture" by ontologizing "the historic themes of Christianity and attribut[ing] to revelation or to the *mysterium tremendum* the ontological content that Heidegger attempts to remove from it." Thus, Derrida holds that Patočka's gesture "amounts to the same thing" as Heidegger's because it is symmetrical and merely the inverse. He adds that Patočka's "own heresy [regarding Christianity] intersects with what one might call, a little provocatively, that other heresy, namely, the twisting or diverting by which the Heideggerian repetition, in its own way, affects Christianity" (*GD*, 23). *The Gift of Death* is, of course, not limited to the mapping of the similarities and differences between Patočka and Heidegger; it also includes an analysis of Levinas and, above all, of Kierkegaard's Protestant interpretation of the Abrahamic story of the aborted sacrifice of Isaac. It is in *The Gift of Death* that Derrida seeks to establish the matrix, if I may call it that, that at once makes these four undeniably distinct positions on responsibility possible but also limits their range, distinctiveness, radicality, and even their originality. Indeed, by inquiring into the various modalities of giving (oneself) death and of taking death (upon oneself), Derrida develops an economic model that accounts for the different positions on responsibility, their mutual contamination and passage into one another—in particular, as regards their overdetermination by themes of Christianity, Platonism, and deliberate de-Christianization, as well as of Judaism. This concern with the intersections between distinct positions also frames Derrida's discussion of Patočka's dismissal of the Platonic conception of responsibility on the basis of a decided predisposition toward Christianity's potential to conceive responsibility, which is not yet adequately thematized, hence, outstanding.

As we have seen, to conform to the most convincing and convinced doxa, that is, the Platonic tradition, the responsible party must know what responsibility means. The responsible self must be able to account for what he or she believes and does, and such rendering of accounts should, whenever possible, be public, taking place in a way that is intelligible to everyone. According to what Derrida describes as "the most reliable continuity," the concept of responsibility requires "a decision or responsible action to answer for itself *consciously*, that is, with knowledge of a thematics of what is done, of what action signifies, its causes, ends, etc." (*GD*, 25). Where this element of knowledge and justification is lacking, decision making is irresponsible. As Derrida emphasizes, "we must continually remind ourselves that some part of irresponsibility insinuates itself wherever one demands responsibility without sufficiently conceptualizing and thematizing what 'responsibility' means" (*GD*, 25–26). Yet, although Derrida subscribes to this demand of knowledge and that of giving reasons for all decisions, demands that are constitutive of the conception of responsibility from Plato to Husserl, he also agrees with Patočka that to subordinate responsibility to objective knowledge—namely, to established theorems and time-honored norms—amounts to merely executing a program fixed in advance and thus to annulling responsibility. Therefore, he can also write:

> Saying that a responsible decision must be taken on the basis of knowledge seems to define the condition of possibility of responsibility (one can't make a responsible decision without science or conscience, without knowing what one is doing, for what reasons, in view of what and under what conditions), at the same time as it defines the condition of impossibility of this same responsibility (if decision-making is relegated to a knowledge that it is content to follow or to develop, then it is no more a responsible decision, it is the technical deployment . . . of a theorem). (*GD*, 24)

In addition to acknowledging with Plato and Husserl that the possibility of responsibility is based on knowledge and on rendering accounts, Derrida thus recognizes another equally compelling demand without which responsibility is not possible. The Christian paradigm exemplifies this further condition of possibility of responsibility. According to this new conception, responsibility requires a break with established or sanctified dogmas (including the most convincing and convinced *doxa*). Rather than seeking conformity, one may have to set oneself apart from what is publicly or commonly accepted. In other words, responsibility is tied here to heresy in all the senses of the term—particularly, as is the case with Patočka, to a "departure from a doctrine, difference within and difference from the officially and publicly stated doctrine and the institutional community that is governed by it" (*GD*, 26). Heresy is not only "an essential condition of responsibility"; it "also destines responsibility to the resistance or dissidence of a type of secrecy. It keeps responsibility apart . . . and in secret. And responsibility *depends on* [*tient à*] what is apart and secret" (*GD*, 26; trans. mod.). Indeed, if knowledge remains only on the threshold of a responsible decision, if a decision is a decision on the condition that it exceeds simple consciousness and simple theoretical determination, the responsible self must, in principle, be unable—that is, run the risk of not being able—to fully account for the singular act constitutive of a responsible decision. It follows from this that responsibility is necessarily linked to the secret—not, of course, in the form of withholding knowledge regarding a specific decision but in the form of an essential inability to ultimately make the reasons for one's actions fully transparent. According to this essential Christian conception of responsibility (which is also, for essential reasons, heretical), decision making without secrecy remains ultimately irresponsible. But, while a decision that is based merely on knowledge annuls responsibility, a decision that forgoes knowledge and defies the demand to give reasons is not without problems that threaten responsibility as well.

As we have seen, there is no place for secrecy or mystery in the Platonic paradigm of responsibility. The Platonic model is a democratic model based on responsibility as universally accessible knowledge and on a demand of transparency. Returning to the memory of Europe, Derrida remarks that as long as Europe pays homage to its Platonic heritage and keeps that memory alive, it "either neglects, represses, or excludes from itself every essential possibility of secrecy and every link between responsibility and the keeping of a secret; everything that allows responsibility to be dedicated to secrecy" (*GD*, 34). But apart from seeking to secure the democratic demand of full transparency and generalized accountability, the fact that this heritage seeks to achieve this demand by neglecting, repressing, or excluding the possibility of secrecy clearly suggests some kind of irresponsibility that is inseparable from the demand in question. As Patočka's analyses of the decadence of modern Europe resulting from technological civilization seek to show, it takes very little for such a democratic model of responsibility and of rendering reason to become totalitarian. Indeed, the legitimate demand intrinsic to the concept of responsibility to publicly account for oneself and one's deeds can easily turn into a means of oppression—as has amply been demonstrated under Stalinism and Zhdanovism in the former Soviet Union, but examples of which can also be found in the United States, with its obsession with public confession—and thus this conception of responsibility based on the demand for knowledge must also, to quote Derrida, "call for respecting whatever refuses a certain responsibility, for example, the responsibility to respond before any and every instituted tribunal" (*OH*, 79).[10] This right not to respond and to keep a secret is the necessary antidote to a conception of responsibility that, based on knowledge, can always become a tool for the benefit of the worst. But the Christian paradigm of responsibility, which rests on the *mysterium tremendum*, by which the unique and singular self is called to responsibility by God's gift alone, harbors a similar, or rather inverse, risk. Christian responsibility requires of the self a complete departure from everything established by *doxa* and tradition, from all rules and doctrines—in particular, from the necessity of having to give accounts to others—so that one's actions will have been exclusively one's own. As such, it is also fraught with the danger of the worst possible irresponsibility. That Christian responsibility could become tied to the worst repression is a possibility as well. Furthermore, to demand of Europe that it abandon all memory of Platonism and become exclusively Christian—by making secrecy and mystery into the sole condition of European politics and responsibility—is tantamount to calling for a reign of arbitrariness, irrationality, and terror.

Against Patočka's attempt to free Christianity from its Platonic foundation and to conceive of a Europe emancipated from both Athens and Rome, Derrida stresses the need to remain faithful to both aspects of European memory. As the inheritors of both conceptions of responsibility, Europeans are what they are thanks to both of these conceptions and the demands that they articulate; hence, they are responsible for and to them. But this double heritage of the meaning of responsibility is not a simple given and does not entail traditionalist submission. Responsibility for and to both traditions demands first of all acknowledging that any one of these conceptions of responsibility is necessarily fraught with risks and dangers. But such responsibility calls not only for the affirmation of what has been inherited but also for the radical transformation of the heritage. In other words, responsibility for and toward the tradition is inevitably heretical.

In response to Patočka's claim that Christianity has failed to adequately thematize what a Person is—that is, the Person that penetrates the soul with its glance without in turn being seen and that constitutes the soul as a responsible self—Derrida writes that such a reference to "inadequate thematization . . . seems to appeal to some ultimate adequacy of thematization that could be accomplished" (*GD*, 27). Let us remind ourselves of the fact that, in the tradition of responsibility, its Greek moment may come the closest to the ideal of full thematization because it demands knowledge of the reasons, the aim, the meaning of what is done and of the circumstances of one's decisions or actions. Derrida emphasizes that we must be continually aware of the fact that whenever we do not sufficiently thematize what *responsibility* means, some irresponsibility insinuates itself into our actions; he also remarks, however, that this is always and everywhere the case. No action, if it is to be a responsible action, is ever consciously or cognitively sufficiently determined. Derrida adds: "One can say *everywhere* a priori and nonempirically" (*GD*, 25–26). If this is so, it is because an action must transcend knowledge to be responsible as well as to include knowledge of what responsibility means. Unless it is the execution of a preestablished theorem or norm, an action merits the title *responsible* only if it is also effectuated without full theoretical determination. It follows from this that the thematization of responsibility is, for structural reasons, always lacking—even in the case of the Platonic notion of responsibility rejected by Patočka on the basis that it makes responsibility a function of the knowledge of the good. This is even more the case for the heretically Christian conception of responsibility. Derrida observes that thematization "is, if not denied, at least strictly limited in its pertinence by that other more radical form of responsibility that exposes me dissymmetrically to the gaze of the other. . . . The concept of responsibility is one of those strange concepts that give food for thought without giving themselves over to thematization. It presents itself neither as a theme nor as a thesis, it gives without being seen [*sans se donner à voir*], without presenting itself in person by means of a 'fact of being seen' that can be phenomenologically intuited" (*GD*, 27). In a move that proves Derrida even more heretical than Patočka, he shows that the concept of responsibility resists all final thematization. It is a "paradoxical concept" in that, in addition to seeking to cognitively unify what responsibility means in one intuition, it also defies such an effort insofar as "it has the structure of a type of secret—what is called, in the code of certain religious practices, mystery. The exercise of responsibility seems to leave no choice but this one, however uncomfortable it may be, of paradox, heresy, and secrecy. More serious still, it must always run the risk of conversion and apostasy: there is no responsibility without a dissident and inventive rupture with respect to tradition, authority, orthodoxy, rule, or doctrine" (*GD*, 27). With this we have already begun to broach Derrida's own—radically heretical—take on responsibility.

Derrida upholds both injunctions of the tradition in question rather than solely privileging the structurally necessary element of secrecy, which Patočka associates with heretical Christianity, to the detriment of the cognitive element in responsibility advanced by Platonism. Yet his innovative interpretation of the heritage of responsibility consists neither in attempting to mediate between both demands nor in establishing their golden mean. Instead, what distinguishes Derrida's interpretation of the Platonic and the Christian heritages is, first of all, the recognition that "the relation between the Platonic and Christian paradigms throughout the history of morality and politics" is defined by the "*aporia of responsibility*" (*GD*, 24). Responsibility toward this inheritance is itself aporetic; it excludes the choice of one of the inherited conceptions of responsibility at the expense of the other; that is, it requires that both traditions be simultaneously honored without any mitigation of the radicality of their demands. The injunctions—on the one hand, of full knowledge of one's actions, on the other, of secrecy—are mutually exclusive; moreover, we are unable to account for either of them. Thus, no program exists that could prescribe a way out of this dilemma.

Responsibility for and to this double heritage requires, then, the invention, each time anew, of a rule according to which both contradictory demands could be met simultaneously or of an action from which such a rule could, after the fact, be construed. Such a rule, which at the same time does justice to the conflicting imperatives, cannot be a rule of their dialectical sublation and reconciliation. It must necessarily be a rule that maintains the aporicity of the demands in the action that responds simultaneously to both imperatives. In this sense the singular and innovative response to the challenge posed by the aporia of responsibility can at the same time also be a principle for any response worth the name. In short, responsibility toward the two paradigms of the tradition requires a response to its conflicting injunctions that must contain within itself the unique rule (principle, or *arche*) from which it is derived; more precisely, it must be a response coeval with this rule in that in its very singularity it can, at the same time, serve also as a universal, or absolute, law for any response in a singularly determined context to the aporetic demands in question. In Patočka's parlance, such responsibility toward the memory of Europe is inevitably heretical. Indeed, the relation to this memory is a responsible one only if the contradictory injunctions are met in a way that amounts to a transformation of the tradition that is new each time, one that is singular. Needless to say, what we have seen in regard to the relation to the memory of Europe is valid for all other responsible decision making as well insofar as it takes place against the backdrop of an experience of tradition. Any responsible decision making must face the demand to give reasons without at the same time being reduced to knowledge that would merely be put into effect.

What, then, is for Derrida European responsibility or responsibility as something specifically European? The conflicting exigencies formulated in the foregoing discussion of the concept of responsibility require the invention of a new way to revive or replay the figure, concept, or idea of Europe. European responsibility is, first of all, this openness to *both* traditions of responsibility that characterize its history—namely, Platonism and Christianity. It consists in exposure to the radically conflicting demands that these two traditions make on their heirs as responsible selves. European responsibility is above all the uncompromising willingness to assume the challenge posed by the aporetic nature of inheritance itself—that is, by the constitutive lack of handed-down rules or norms to negotiate contradiction. Consequently, Europe is the name for a responsibility that goes hand in hand with the necessity of having to invent, each time anew, new ways of meeting mutually exclusive demands. As a simultaneous responsibility to, at first, two opposite traditions, European responsibility consists in not letting one of the traditions overturn, outplay, or outdo the other. By doing justice to its double heritage, and not shunning the necessity of negotiating conflicting demands in the absence of pregiven norms or rules, such responsibility not only entails a radical refusal of traditionalism, for structural reasons, but also is distinguished by openness to other traditions and demands. Indeed, from the moment that Europe is understood as a responsibility to more than one tradition or set of injunctions, its responsiveness and responsibility extend to all other traditions. Apart from being hospitable to other historically and culturally decisive intra-European differences (such as Judaism and Islam, not in the abstract, however, but with all their shades and forms), as well as to the many minor, or marginal, differences within Europe, this principal openness that the name Europe designates consists as well in the demand of unconditional receptiveness of the tradition of the non-European other. But the demand of such unconditional openness to other traditions and injunctions does not exclude the opposite demand, which is heterogeneous to the former, of conditional or determinate responsibility to oneself. One responsibility comes with the other; none is possible without negotiation with its opposite. Responsibility as Europe—that is, Europe as responsibility—outlines a model of decision making that is respectful of mutually exclusive demands within the concept of responsibility itself and that endures the test of exigencies that, since they are equally valid, cannot be mediated except at the unacceptable price of rendering one exigency subservient to the other. If something like Europe exists and can be thought at all, it must be a conception that for structural reasons or for reasons of principle is open to responding to still more injunctions, including injunctions from other, or non-European, traditions. Responsibility as Europe coincides with a mode of being for which identity, or selfhood, is possible only in honoring conflicting, strictly speaking, aporetic injunctions. It means that Europe is the idea of an identity predicated on aporetic demands, hence of a mode of being that structurally is infinitely open—rather than being closed off—to what is other than oneself. Europe thus understood is a name for a project that Europe has still to live up to. But Europe, neither a figure nor concept, neither an idea nor even an Idea in the Kantian sense—all of which presuppose a formal unity of what they represent, or name—is something that can be realized only by way of approximation, something whose very conception remains open, still—perhaps, forever—unfinished, hence, something to come.

§ 10 "This Little Thing
       That Is Europe"

The question of Europe is not merely one question among others. It is, rather, as Jacques Derrida remarks at the beginning of *The Other Heading: Reflections on Today's Europe*, "a question that will always be of current interest." If this is so, it is because this question is not only of current interest to Europeans but because it is a question that by essence projects itself beyond boundaries, particularly, those of a geographical, political, and cultural entity called "Europe." If this topical question is raised today in Europe in the face of, or under the pressure of, "some *imminence*," that is, of something that is occurring now at this very moment, then it is because it is a question that poses itself now and is therefore of some urgency. But as Derrida's reference to "some *imminence*" suggests, that which thus announces itself in Europe, and to which the question of Europe responds, is something that is approaching, that is about to happen or to arrive. Yet it is also that which refuses "itself to anticipation as much as to analogy" and thus "seems to be without precedent." Without yet having a face, resembling nothing, it is also something unique, and, consequently, something of the order of an event whose promise is tinged with a certain degree of monstrosity. The impending event that triggers the question of Europe today is also perhaps a threat. Whether what is imminent presents itself as a chance or as a danger, or even as "at once a chance and a danger," the question that it raises is bound to be more demanding than a mere academic exercise or performance. The question of Europe draws its urgency and actuality from the threat or the chance—or from both—that "is afoot in Europe, in what is still called Europe even if we no longer know very well *what* or *who* goes by this name" (*OH*, 5–6).¹ If the question of Europe is always of topical interest, and if, moreover, the response to this question bears on present-day Europe and what it is to become; if this question is posed at a moment of threat to Europe or a moment of the promise of something new—"a moment for which the word *crisis*, the crisis of Europe or the crisis of the spirit, is perhaps no longer appropriate"—then it follows that the question of Europe is for Europe always the question of the day, the most pressing, if not the ultimate, concern (*OH*, 31). The word *crisis*, which Edmund Husserl, like so many others between World War I and II, used to justify his reflections on Europe, may no longer be appropriate to describe the impending imminence that besets Europe, since *crisis* suggests that, at one point, Europe, or the European spirit, was intact or whole and is only now suffering a critical upheaval. Today, the threat or chance that calls Europe into question and forces the question of Europe upon Europe is something unique, a matter of present interest, while at the same time remaining something that Europe qua "Europe" has always been exposed to: the fact that what it represents is both a promise and a danger. *Europe*, if I may advance something like a definition, is the conception of a world or a life project, which, at every moment—that is, every day—faces the imminence of being "at once a chance and a danger"; of a world, in short, that at every moment confronts the future as both a menace and a chance. If "today" is unique, it is, precisely, because today the pressure of what is approaching as a threat or a chance concerns this very conception of a world. What is imminent today in Europe is not only that Europe may be about to realize the promise of its "concept" (or, on the contrary, to forgo it altogether), but what is imminent is also the very existence of Europe as a conception that is "at once a chance and a danger." Considering the nature of this question on Europe, it should therefore come as no surprise that "this little thing that is Europe" has been a topic of constant interest to Derrida, from *The Problem of Genesis in Husserl's Philosophy* (1953–54) to "A Europe of Hope," the address given on the occasion of *Le monde diplomatique*'s fiftieth anniversary celebration in May 2004, that is, shortly before his death.²

Derrida, in the concluding chapters of the 1953–54 dissertation that he wrote to fulfill the requirements for a diploma of higher education, had already taken up Husserl's definition of Europe as an idea. As an investigation into the difficulties caused by the introduction of the theme of genesis—that is, of time, becoming, and history—in Husserlian phenomenology (which, originally, had only been concerned with the static constitution of the ego), Derrida inquires both into the birth of the idea—the eidetic unity of Europe, in Europe itself—and, vice versa, into how Europe itself is born from this idea, that is, from the idea of philosophy. Based on a minute and careful analysis of some key passages from Husserl's Vienna lecture, as well as from the sections, then available, of *The Crisis of European Sciences and Transcendental Phenomenology*, Derrida highlights a series of unresolved problems, contradictions, and aporias between, on the one hand, Husserl's insistence that as a transcendental idea, the idea of Europe is unrelated to Europe's empirical history, and, on the other hand, his contention that this transcendental idea is born in Europe itself, more precisely, in seventh-century Greece, the one point in real history when the pure idea of philosophy came to be confused with the destiny and the existence of a particular people. As a pure idea, however, the idea of philosophy as an infinite task can, in principle, have no geographical or historical roots, and "in this respect, Europe should be able [as Derrida notes] to be replaced by Asia or by Africa." And yet, in spite of the refusal—particular to phenomenological idealism—to grant the European *eidos* the status of an empirically datable and localized event, Europe, in Husserl's works, is said to be "philosophy's spiritual place of birth, its mysterious and immaterial residence," the place where philosophy inhabits, in his words, "'the heart of certain men.'" Europe, consequently, is endowed with an *eidos* that is also specifically European.[3] A host of further questions and contradictions derive from this basic tension, demonstrating that even the later Husserl had not yet completely clarified the problem of genesis. We do not need to thread out these additional questions and contradictions here, as they primarily concern the difficulties that the project of phenomenology undergoes once it opens itself to the question of history. The resolution of this question will lead Derrida to envision a "radical conversion" that, at the time, he conceived of in terms of a new ontology, which, on the basis of a deepened phenomenology of temporality, was to demonstrate that "at the level of the originary temporal existence, fact and essence, the empirical and the transcendental, are inseparable and dialectically of a piece."[4]

This early work by Derrida is also significant insofar as it had already problematized Husserl's reference to the notion of "crisis," an issue to which Derrida, in his later work, will repeatedly return.[5] Although Husserl explains the crisis that the teleological idea of Europe undergoes in modernity as a result of the sciences' naive desire for formal objectivism (and, hence, of the prephilosophical naturalism they embrace), Derrida remarks, in *The Problem of Genesis in Husserl's Philosophy*, that "the origin of this crisis is not gone into more deeply, precisely because, on the one hand, there is no teleological reason for the crisis and, on the other, because the crisis itself cannot by definition reveal us anything originary" (*PGHP*, 160). The sole explanation that Husserl provides for the internal crisis or decomposition of the idea of Europe is the "forgetting" or "covering up" of its source in transcendental subjectivity, as a result of which the constituted idea in question becomes isolated and is made into something autonomous and absolute. "It is always because at a certain moment a simple constituted product has been taken for absolute, originary and constituting, that the movement of the idea has been interrupted or corrupted in a crisis" (*PGHP*, 171–72). Yet if the idea of philosophy—that is, of Europe—is a transcendental motif, and is as such fully "present to itself from its birth . . . , it is impossible that it should make itself a stranger to itself at a given moment of empirical becoming" (*PGHP*, 170). If, however, this is the case, then this idea can never be the idea *of* philosophy and *of* Europe (alone), that is, its animating *telos*. Understood as fully constituted from the beginning, the essential reasons (that is, the reasons why the idea necessarily undergoes an internal alienation and crisis) cannot be addressed. By the same token it is also impossible to see how the idea of philosophy could be an infinite task, as well as that which necessarily guarantees the teleological progress of this idea in Europe. Indeed, if this idea undergoes a crisis, then it cannot be pure and originary, but instead "from its birth, it negotiates with what is not it" (*PGHP*, 170).[6]

Although the question of the idea of Europe as the idea of philosophy as an infinite task is raised only in the context of Derrida's exploration of the unresolved problems that derive from the introduction of the theme of genesis in phenomenology, the intimate link that Derrida conceives between Europe and (phenomenological) philosophy sets the stage for his ongoing interest in the question, leading him to present himself, over time, as a philosopher *of* Europe. As a thinker of Europe, Derrida has broached the question of Europe on numerous occasions, but this does not mean that he is simply a European thinker. Let us recall what he says at the end of *The Other Heading*: "I am European. . . . But I am not, nor do I feel, European *in every part*, that is, European through and through. . . . I feel European *among other things*" (*OH*, 82–83). What follows from such a position on Europe, which, "beyond all Eurocentrism," is therefore neither Eurocentrist nor anti-Eurocentrist (the latter being just another form of Eurocentrism), is a critical interrogation of European identity understood in terms of what in the grand discourses on Europe is referred to as the "European spirit"—that is, the spiritual unity of Europe.[7] Undoubtedly, similar to his predecessors in the history of phenomenological thought who have pondered over Europe, Europe, for Derrida, is not (or is not simply) a geographical or territorial entity. What Derrida clearly takes issue with, however, is the phenomenologists' understanding of the eidetic unity of Europe in terms of a spiritual unity. Indeed, if the determination of Europe's eidetic unity as a spiritual unity becomes problematic, it is primarily because the concept of spirit suggests a purity of essence that has originated in Europe alone, one that is immanent to Europe, exclusively its own and *of* its own. As Husserl's exclusion of Eskimos, Indians, and gypsies from European humanity demonstrates, the danger of understanding European identity from a purported spiritual unity is that such a conception of European identity risks foreclosing any openness to the other, to everything non-European.[8] This long-standing determination of Europe's identity as spiritual has its roots in the equally venerable assumption that Europe originates in one source alone, whether this source is held to be Greek philosophy or medieval Christianity. Let us recall again Husserl's contention that Europe as the very idea of philosophy—of philosophy as an infinite task, or *telos*— from which Europe itself is born, comes into existence in Greece, and the birth certificate of Europe, and of its unity, is therefore essentially Greek. This has been for Husserl, Heidegger, and even Patočka an unchallenged assumption. Yet in Derrida's reflections on Europe, the continuity between Greece and Europe is not simply overcome. If Derrida's thought can be aligned with that of the three previous thinkers, it is first of all because by acknowledging philosophy's origins in Greek thought, he, one more time, created an international echo to philosophy as a classical discipline. But Derrida's distinguished accomplishment is that while he continued to orient his whole thought toward the heritage of the classical tradition, he complicated at the same time, as we will see, the continuity between Greece and Europe, and this to the point of rendering all talk of a spiritual unity of Europe obsolete. In particular, his questioning of the Greek heritage of Europe results in a reconception of the very eidetic nature of what can and must be called "Europe," a reconception that, considering what the term *idea* has always meant, can thus no longer be referred to as the "idea" of Europe.

As Derrida reminds us, "what we can rigorously call 'philosophy' exists nowhere other than in Greece. While there are certainly very powerful bodies of thought elsewhere, which are other than philosophy, philosophy as a specific project of the thinking of being was born in Greece."[9] Given that "the founding concepts of philosophy are primarily Greek, and [that] it would not be possible to philosophize, or to speak philosophically, outside this medium," any hope for "something . . . still to transpire [*advenir*—that is, to happen] within the tradition by which all philosophers know themselves to be overtaken" requires, as Husserl and Heidegger have argued, each in his own way—a summoning forth of the origin of the tradition in Greece. As Derrida remarks, this appeal to the tradition—that is, Husserl's and Heidegger's conception of "the entirety of philosophy . . . on the basis of its Greek source"—amounts neither "to an occidentalism, nor to a historicism." Such an appeal to the tradition does not entail any relativism, either, since "the truth of philosophy does not depend on its relation to the actuality of the Greek or European event."[10] Indeed, if for both Husserl and Heidegger the advent of philosophy is of the order of an irruption (*Aufbruch or Einbruch*), or the result of a call or claim of Being that occurs in Greece, then the Greek or European *eidos* cannot be reduced to the factuality of this occurrence. Derrida, for his part, does not contest this phenomenological recourse to the origins of the philosophical tradition in the Greek event. Obviously, he does not intend to replace the Greek origins of Europe by another origin. His aim certainly does not consist in advocating a cultural monogenealogy of Europe in Christianity, since a monolithic conception of the identity of Europe, based on exclusion, has been (and still is) opposed in the name of Christianity to the Europe of the other, ignoring the different kinds of faith that, historically speaking, have been (and are more than ever) present in Europe.[11] Even though, as we will see, Derrida multiplies the sources of what is European to such a degree that the originality of Greece as the unique foundation of Europe becomes questionable, I would argue that, for Derrida, the primacy of the Greek moment for understanding Europe (in particular, a future Europe) remains valid, at least to a certain extent. But I would also immediately add that, notwithstanding Derrida's preservation of the Greek origin of the European *eidos*, this affirmation of the Greek moment in the constitution of Europe also entails a novel interpretation of Greece. "Greece," or whatever deserves the name "Greek," is, as we will see from here on, that which actually makes it possible to envision another Europe, a Europe to come, a Europe that in the words of the address "A Europe of Hope"—which speaks clearly to issues of topical concerns, that is, to pressing political concerns of the day—"remains irreplaceable for the world to come" insofar as it is to take on an "irreplaceable . . . responsibility in the anti-globalist [*altermondialiste*] movement between American hegemony, the rise in power of China, and the Arab and Muslim theocracies."[12]

Before I broach Derrida's novel interpretation of the source of the philosophical, and hence of Europe, let me pause here long enough to emphasize that, as opposed to Husserl and Heidegger, and more emphatically than Patočka, Derrida highlights the multiplicity of the sources and identities that intersect in the European heritage. He writes, for example, that "if the heritage of thought (of truth and Being) in which we are inscribed is not solely, neither fundamentally nor originarily Greek, it is no doubt because of other intercrossing and heterogeneous affiliations, of other languages, and other identities which are not simply additions [to this heritage], or secondary accidents (Jewish, Arabic, Christian, Roman, Germanic, and so forth). This is certainly so because European history has not only unfolded a Greek deal [*une donne grecque*]."[13]

In his reflections on European identity Derrida has consistently demanded that these other moments be taken into account. In *Rogues*, for instance, he contends that it is indispensable to examine "what gets passed on, transferred, translated from Europe *by* pre- and post-Koranic Arabic, as well as by Rome."[14] But since the idea of Europe is generally understood to be the idea of philosophy and is, therefore, Greek in origin (although moments such as the Jewish, Arabic, Christian, Roman, and Germanic ones have all played a decisive role in European identity, it is not in the least, or rather precisely, because of their effective assimilation and mediation of what is Greek), it is highly significant that Derrida also raises the question of Chinese or African thought and whether this thought bears on the claim that philosophy is by nature Greek. Here is what Derrida has to say: "Still today, but this is not new, we feel strongly the seriousness of the question of whether philosophy was born in Greece or not, whether it is European or not, whether one can speak of Chinese philosophy, whether one can speak of African philosophy, or whether the destination of philosophy is marked by a singular source, thus by a singular language or a network of singular languages."[15] By evoking the question of whether something like a Chinese or African philosophy is conceivable, and whether philosophy is a function of one language—that is, the Greek idiom—the question becomes, indeed, that of the uniqueness and identity of the Greek source as the source of philosophy, the question, by extension, of Europe itself.[16]

At this juncture a note of caution may be warranted. What is at stake in this interrogation of the uniqueness and originality of the Greek source of philosophy (and Europe) is not a desire to replace the Greek by the non-Greek. As Derrida has forcefully shown in "Violence and Metaphysics," any interpellation of the Greek by the non-Greek is possible only in the language of the Greeks. Only in this language is it possible to state that the question of the non-Greek is a question that is silenced and forgotten in the language of the Greeks.[17] Likewise, to evoke the inner limits of the Greek paradigm by pointing to the Greek idiom or, more generally, to the Indo-European linguistic milieu in which its concept of Being—hence, the ontological question—has its roots, one must confront the fact that the meaning of such limits is intelligible only on the basis of the question concerning the meaning of Being.[18] After having unmasked as empiricism "the true name of the inclination of thought to the Other" that one finds in the thinking of Emmanuel Levinas (together with the renunciation of the concept on the basis of the violence it does to the Other), that is, nonphilosophy, which "contests the resolution and coherence of the logos (philosophy) at its root, instead of letting itself be questioned by the logos," Derrida writes that "nothing can so profoundly *solicit* the Greek logos—philosophy—as this irruption of the totally-other; and nothing can to such an extent reawaken the logos to its origin as to its mortality, its other. But if one calls this experience of the infinitely other Judaism . . . , one must reflect upon the necessity in which this experience finds itself, the injunction by which it is ordered to occur as logos, and to reawaken the Greek in its autistic syntax of his own dream." Any attempt to contest the Greek logos confronts "the necessity to borrow the ways of the unique philosophical logos, which can only invert the 'curvature of space' for the benefit of the same."[19] But, Derrida asks, if it is "necessary to lodge oneself within traditional conceptuality in order to destroy it," is it not also because this necessity "hide(s) . . . some indestructible and unforeseeable resource of the Greek logos? Some unlimited power of envelopment, by which he who attempts to repel it would always already be *overtaken*?"[20] The question that had already animated Derrida's early work on Husserl's conception of the idea of philosophy as the *telos* of Europe—namely, whether its transcendental nature (and its content) does not, from the start, make it an idea that could have arisen elsewhere, and whether, as far as its concern with universality is concerned, it is not an idea that, from the start, is necessarily open to the non-Greek—points to this "indestructible and unforeseeable resource of the Greek logos" that prevents it from being unseated by calling on the non-Greek, whatever the latter's shape. Indeed, what makes philosophy in its Greek form unique is that it inscribes within itself the place of the other, including that of the totally-other. According to Derrida: "In having proffered the *epekeina tes ousias*, in having recognized from its second word (for example, in the *Sophist*) that alterity had to circulate at the origin of meaning, in welcoming alterity in general into the heart of the logos, the Greek thought of Being forever has protected itself against every absolutely *surprising* convocation."[21]

From here on I intend to argue not only that Greece is the origin of Europe because of this "indestructible and unforeseeable resource of the Greek logos" but also that the priority that Greece enjoys in determining Europe's *arche* and *telos* derives precisely from its intrinsic nonidentity. (Needless to say, such priority can no longer be ontological.) First, however, I wish to return to Derrida's statement about the seriousness of the question of whether philosophy as the source of Europe is solely Greek and whether its destination is marked by one language alone or, at best, exclusively, by the Indo-European languages as a whole. He writes:

> This question always has serious consequences. And in a certain way, it is philosophy itself. Which means that, at the same time, one feels led to reaffirm that *philosophia* has a Greek or Greco-European source with all the consequences that that entails, and without that necessarily limiting thereby its universality; or, inversely, since philosophy is the question about its own source, and bears the question of its own limit within itself, then at that moment there is not only no reason why precisely the non-European would not accede to philosophy, but no reason either for the non-European not to be the place of the philosophical question about philosophy.[22]

If the question of the origin of philosophy (which, in a certain way, is philosophy itself) allows for this double possibility—namely, for being thoroughly Greek (yet universal) while being at the same time marked by extrapositionality and hence being non-European (though universal as well)—is it not precisely because the Greek logos *is* this relation to alterity, and is thus constituted by this very possibility of suspending its Greek origin in order to turn itself (or to let itself be turned) not simply into [its] other—that is, another self-identity—but into the passage into (the) other itself?

A moment ago I alluded to a novel interpretation of the source of what is European in Derrida. To reinforce this point I turn now to a little-known text (from which I have already been citing), "'Nous autres Grecs.'"[23] In what amounts to a sweeping transformation of Heidegger's conception of "beginning" (including "the other beginning" as a radically innovative repetition of the first beginning), according to which "Greece" and the Greek idiom is the one and only beginning of philosophy unifying the history of the West (even where the latter has become entirely oblivious to the question of Being that constitutes this beginning), Derrida, in this text, begins by pointing out that "rather than defining some essence or self-identity of what is 'Greek,'" all his (i.e., Derrida's) work on the Greeks has questioned "the identity of a properly so-called referent: 'Greek,' 'the Greeks,' or 'Greece'" (253, 252). All of his own writings on the Greeks, he claims, "intersect in one place, one should say a non-space, in a process of *dislocation*, namely 'there' where the *horizon* of the Greek thing is no longer assured, and where what gives rise [*lieu*] to it, and opens it, delimits it by the same token—that is, neither as a space or system of language, nor as a politico-geographical space; neither as a spiritual figure ('Husserl'), nor as a figure of historicity ('Heidegger')" (252). In other words, in his work on the Greeks Derrida has been interested in what from the very beginning has disowned the Greeks—that is, in "the disownment that from the start happened to them, before and independently of their originality of which some, such as Nietzsche and Heidegger, have dreamt" (262). What Derrida hints at is not only the "Egyptian other" in Greece, to which he has repeatedly drawn attention, "but more generally the irruption of the other, of the wholly other [into what is Greek], which forces open the limits of identification and of the self-relation of language, of the corpus, and the system" (253). The *pharmakon, khōra*, or *hymen* are examples of the traces of such an irruption of otherness in Greek thought, and Derrida remarks that in his texts on Greek topics, "he has sought above all to read 'Greek' words" that could not close upon themselves "and which consequently had already been marked by the irruption of the other (the non-discursive real, the non-Greek, and so forth)" (269). In short, then, rather than concerning himself with the "self-immanence of what is Greek," Derrida has been concerned with a double infraction of what is Greek by the other, the non-European. He notes: "It is not only the non-Greek which drew me towards [*chez*] the Greek (in sum, it is a question of finding out what *chez* means), not merely the other of the Greek (the Egyptian, the barbarian, or whoever is determined by the Greek as *his* other, thus excluded-included, and positioned as in opposition), but the wholly other of the Greek, of his language and the *logos*—that is, the figure of the wholly other which the latter cannot figure out, of which he cannot convey a figure (*infigurable*)" (260). If this other in all its forms irrupts into the Greek from the beginning (thus foreclosing any possibility of a Greek self-identity or self-immanence), the Greek, as the source of Europe, is precisely the figure of a nonclosure upon itself, allowing it to welcome alterity into the logos. As we have seen, if the tradition of thought characteristic of Europe is not fundamentally or originarily Greek, or Greek alone, this is, according to Derrida, undoubtedly because other moments have left their mark on Europe: the Jew, the Christian, the African, the non-Greek in general ("without, however, supposing some other assured identity"); it is, he adds, "above all because what is Greek has never gathered itself or identified itself with itself" (276, 267). Derrida infers from this that "certainly, we [Europeans] are still Greeks, but perhaps other Greeks, since we are not only born from the sole *coup d'envoi grec* [that is, solely from the Greek *Schickung*, or sending on its way, as Heidegger would have said]; that certainly we are still *other* Greeks, having the memory of events that are irreducible to the Greek genealogy, but sufficiently other so as not only to have also altered what is Greek in us, but also so as to carry within us something wholly other *than* what is Greek" (263). He can reach this conclusion, above all, because "we others, we have also inherited that which rendered the Greeks other [different] than themselves" from the start (262).

"The other conception of Europe," or the "*new* figure of Europe," that is invoked in *Fichus* and in *Philosophy in a Time of Terror*, respectively, concerns a Europe that can understand itself as having its origin outside itself.²⁴ Europe's origin is nonidentical to itself; it would thus be a mistake to conceive of it as primarily Greek, with additional Jewish, Christian, and Islamic elements. Rather, Europe's origin is open to multiple origins from the beginning. However, this conception of Europe is made possible, specifically, by the West's philosophical heritage—its Greek heritage—in that from the beginning that which was Greek allowed alterity to circulate within the logos; Europe was able to make good on this heritage only by growing, as Friedrich Nietzsche once put it, "more Greek by the day."²⁵ This conception of Europe is, first of all, the conception or the figure of a self-identity that is at home (*chez*) with itself, precisely to the extent that it is outside itself—decentered, as it were—and hence constituted by an openness and a hospitality that is extended not only to the non-European but also to unpredictable, unforeseeable otherness. Europe names the possibility or the project of such an identity—or rather nonidentity—that is at home with itself precisely by letting itself be disowned by the other; the non-European, and the wholly other. What distinguishes this other conception of Europe, the one that Derrida is thinking about, is that it is the figure of an identity that has the capacity not only for opposition but above all for relating to, and letting itself be claimed by, an other that is not the other of myself. As Karl Jaspers once argued, one of the two fundamental aspects that distinguish Europe is its freedom (which, together with history and science, constitutes Europe's peculiarity), a freedom that keeps it restless and in motion (the other aspect being "life in the face of extremity") and that represents a conception of "life in polarities." He writes: "Europe has itself developed counter-positions to every position. It is perhaps only properly what it is insofar as it is capable of the possibility of being everything [*der Möglichkeit nach alles ist*]." Europe is thus this freedom, or openness, that *from within* has developed all possible oppositions to everything that it posits, including itself. Because of this freedom vis-à-vis all dichotomous counterpositions, Europe is "open not only to conceive of that which comes from outside as being merely in opposition to it, but also of taking it into itself as an element of its own essence." The "dialectical way of being of Europe," Jaspers continues, consists in its being itself by also being, at least potentially, its other, which it is capable of appropriating and folding into itself.²⁶ This ability is so pronounced that the other of Europe even lets itself be conceived as the commencement of Europe, as is the case with Hölderlin, for example, for whom Greece is the Orient of the West.

However, by conceiving of Europe as a figure that, apart from relating to its non-European others, is also open to an other that does not let itself be categorized in terms of self and other—an other to come—the dialectical conception of Europe is not overcome but is inscribed in what it cannot ever hope to appropriate or master. This new figure of Europe is the figure of a certain conversion, passage, or translation, not merely into an other who, or which, bears immediately on my identity by being the commencement of my self (and whose foreignness is thus predetermined by the dialectical relation of self and other) but one who, or which, is foreign in unpredictable and incalculable ways—an other, in short, who, or which, is significant in more ways than just being the commencement of my own self.

As a figure of such a conversion to, or passage into, the other, this new figure of Europe—distinct from Europe as a territory or even a nation-state—is unmistakably a conception whose thrust is universal. But whence the insistence, then, on continuing to call such a conception of unconditional openness and hospitality to the other by the name of *Europe*? If Derrida retains this name for such a conception and task, it is because of the memory of Europe. Europe's own memory—that is, the memory of the idea of responsibility and universality—remains "an indispensable resource" for any attempt to conceive and realize a way of being and action: in short, a political space, beyond the authority of the particular in all its forms. This task, in Greece, has from the beginning been associated with the idea of the lights of *logos* and reason, as well as the Enlightenment, which is another name for "Europe." In an interview with Giovanna Borradori in *Philosophy in a Time of Terror*, Derrida remarks:

> I persist in using this name "Europe," even if in quotation marks, because, in the long and patient deconstruction required for the transformation to-come, the experience Europe inaugurated at the time of the Enlightenment (*Lumières, Aufklärung, Illuminismo*) in the relationship between the political and the theological or, rather, the religious, though still uneven, unfulfilled, relative, and complex, will have left in European political space absolutely original marks with regard to religious doctrine (notice I'm not saying with regard to religion or faith but with regard to the authority of religious doctrine over the political). Such marks can be found neither in the Arab world nor in the Muslim world, nor in the Far East, nor even, and here's the most

sensitive point, in American democracy, in what *in fact* governs not the principles but the predominant reality of American political culture.²⁷

The name *Europe* imposes itself as a conception and as a task of universality, and that for Derrida means also the task of a public space (i.e., the political), which, by inscribing the relation to the other and especially to the other to-come into the heart of the self, draws on the resources of what promised itself with the irruption in Greece of the thought of a logos that allows alterity to circulate within it. Since there is no thinking without memory, without inherited concepts, the name *Europe*, used to designate a new figure of universality (and the political), not only draws on the resources provided by its European heritage but also remains faithful to Europe's own memory, rather than forsaking it.

Now, since I have spoken of this other conception of Europe as a figure of conversion and passage into other(s), a cautionary remark is warranted. Such a figure does not entail reversibility of self and other, what is one's own and the foreign, the familiar and the alien. If it is true, as Hannah Arendt has noted in *The Human Condition*, "that the Platonic tradition of philosophical as well as political thought [which] started with a reversal [of the Homeric world order, by locating ordinary life, the life of the senses, in the underworld of the cave], and that this original reversal determined to a large extent the thought pattern into which Western philosophy almost automatically fell wherever it was not animated by a great and original philosophical impetus," with the result that "academic philosophy, as a matter of fact, has ever been dominated by . . . never-ending reversals," then the new figure of Europe is not Greek in this latter sense. The reversibility of thought formations and systems of thought—the fact "that they can be turned 'upside down' or 'downside up' at any moment" that characterizes the Western tradition starting with the philosophical schools in late antiquity—a reversibility made possible "once Plato had succeeded in making the . . . structural elements and concepts [of thought] reversible," does not occur as a result of an exposure of thought to otherness. It needs no more, Arendt remarks, "than purely intellectual experience, an experience within the framework of conceptual thinking itself." Furthermore, "the concepts themselves [that are inverted] remain the same no matter where they are placed in the various systematic orders."²⁸ In other words, in reversibility the sphere or realm of the same remains fully intact; no opening to otherness in all its unpredictability occurs there. The horizon is not even enlarged; it certainly is not pierced (as it must be if the openness is to be unconditional) by inverting self and other. Reversibility is a function of, and a way of, securing sameness: a celebration of sameness, as it were. By contrast, Europe as the figure of a logos within which alterity circulates from its inception (of a passage, or a certain conversion into the non-European and into an other that escapes the categorical distinction between European and non-European), rather than turning the self into the other, and hence the other into the self, implies a radical reinscription or reconception of what is European given that, from the start, Europe has been dislocated from itself to such a degree that it is open and hospitable to what it does not, and cannot, determine. This very opening to an other to-come—that is, to an other that is not only unpredictable but also has no assured identity—prevents the passage into the other from becoming a passage into one's own other or, more generally, into any other that is determined or determinable in advance. This opening to an unforeseeable other prevents the passage from being a passage into an identifiable and enduring sameness, in short, into another form of self-identity, one that would be the reverse, for example, of one's original identity. Indeed, through the exposure not only to identifiable others but also to unforeseeable others—that is, wholly-others—Europe as the figure of passing, transition, or translation undoes both the specularity and the symmetrical imbrication of self and other. As a consequence, "Europe" as the figure of such a passage presupposes neither a prior identity to be overcome nor a new one to be achieved. Rather, by opening itself to the undetermined and undeterminable other, it is nothing but an unconditional openness to otherness, nothing but the figure of a passage into an other itself. Europe as a figure of passage, transition, transformation into otherness suggests a conception of identity that is always already the occurrence of an exposure to what is non-European, not only regarding what is other than Europe but also other than the non-European. As such an exposure, vulnerable to otherness and at the same time hospitable, Europe is also another term for—another figure of—deconstruction.

Reversibility is without risk, since the other, or the foreign to and into which the self reverts, is only the opposite of oneself (thus the self can always reassert itself in the other, or reappropriate it). At all moments reversibility announces only the same. By contrast, that which makes the new figure of Europe the figure of a passage or conversion into the other, that is, a promise, is precisely the fact that such transition and transformation is also charged with danger. However, without the threat posed by its promise Europe would not be a promise to begin with. Without its inherent danger it would also lack all universal appeal.

§ 11   De-closing the Horizon

Since Husserl—who, while attempting, in *Ideas*, to account for what really takes place in experience—introduced for the first time the concept of horizon as the foremost instrument of his analytic of intentionality (in order to conceptualize and analyze the specific mode of apprehension of the contextuality in which all experience of things takes place, that is, the pre-predicative assumption in natural life of the existence of the world, or the co-meant existence of the world in all judgments about particular things), any reference to this concept in phenomenological or postphenomenological thought is also a reference to "world." Indeed, Husserl was the first to provide a thoughtfully developed concept of the world as a horizon that guides all understanding of whatever is encountered in the world. As a lawfully ordered interconnectedness of sense references, the "world," whether a particular world or the One world that we all have in common, names the circumference, or frame, within which things can appear as things experienced and which guides their intelligibility at all levels of understanding. However different, both the particular worlds and the One world are horizons. In natural experience "the vital horizon [*lebendiger Horizont*]" of the active apperception of transcendent things is made up of the open infinity of all potential perceptions (based on all that which is given in nonthematic fashion, together with the thing in focus), as well as by a thing's proximity to the other things by which it always finds itself surrounded (C, 149).[1] By contrast, the universal horizon of the One world is the open space for the manifold particular worlds, with their mobile and hence expandable and modifiable horizons, and that thus also transcends them as the universal dimension that makes all horizonal appearing and experience possible.

As we have seen in our discussion of the life-world in Chapter 3, in *The Crisis of European Sciences and Transcendental Phenomenology* Husserl makes a sharp distinction between the way particular things are apprehended within their own particular worlds and the world horizon itself. Whereas in "normal, unbroken, coherent life . . . world is the universal field into which all our acts, whether of experiencing, of knowing, or of outward action, are directed" without any explicit or thematic awareness of the horizonality of experience, the world as universal horizon is the result of a reflective attitude directed at the different ways in which the conscious having of the world occurs in natural life (*C*, 144). Only in this new universal direction of interest does horizonality become thematic. As Elisabeth Ströker notes: "'Horizonality' is not a title for a descriptively discovered complex within the natural attitude, but rather a title for what is phenomenologically exhibited in pure consciousness. As the basic structure of the objectively appearing world, it requires a search for the corresponding processes on the side of experience. For according to the universal *a priori* correlation between world and consciousness, the world must present itself in consciousness, and consciousness must maintain the structural conditions for the constitution of the world."[2] The One world, which transcends all other particular worlds—the *koinon*, or universal world—is something distinct from a partial horizon. But in no way does the One world horizon amount to a universalizing expansion of one such particular horizon or of the sum total of all particular horizons. The horizon of horizons, which can never be adequately apprehended in intuitive self-givenness, must be built, as we saw in Chapter 3, from an analysis of the intersubjective meaning-giving acts of a transcendental Ego sedimented in the particular horizons of the life-world. The ultimate horizon of the One world is, indeed, an idea, more precisely, an Idea in the Kantian sense.

The concept of horizon and, in particular, the world-horizon—understood either as the product of intersubjective meaning constitution (Husserl); or as that which guides all understanding of Being, namely, time (Heidegger); or as the extrasubjective objectivity that underpins all functions of the understanding of beings in the sphere of phenomenality (Patočka)—plays a considerable role in Derrida's thought as well.[3] From early on he has repeatedly broached this theme, which, in *Sur parole*, he even termed "a grand philosophical question."[4] Considering the capital importance in phenomenological thought of this concept, it is somewhat surprising, at first, to remark that on almost all occasions at which Derrida raises the question of the horizon, he is strongly critical of it. Although Derrida's treatment of this concept would warrant an extensive discussion, we must confine ourselves to some very succinct observations. First, however, a brief reminder of the Greek origin of the word may be appropriate. *Horizon* derives from the verb *horizein*, to divide or separate from, as a border or boundary. *Horismos* means limit, and *horizon* is a separating circle. Not only does the verb *horizein* thus refer to a marking out, or tracing, of borders by which a setting into limits occurs, but according to Liddell and Scott, it also signifies "to ordain," "to determine," and "to lay down." Now, for Derrida, a horizon is "an inevitably totalizing horizon," and on occasion he even speaks of it as being "dark, threatening and threatened."[5] One of Derrida's earliest discussions of Husserl's concept of horizon occurs in his 1962 commentary on Husserl's "Origin of Geometry," where Husserl defines the world (i.e., "the universe of Objects insofar as it is linguistically expressible in its being and its being-such") as the infinite horizon of every possible experience. Derrida writes:

> Thus, the signification of the world as horizon is clearly explicated, i.e., as the infinitely open common place for everything we can encounter in front of and for ourselves. In front of and for ourselves implies, then, given as an object. The world, therefore, is essentially determined by the dative and horizontal dimension of being perceived [*l'être-perçu*] in a gaze whose object must always be able to be a *theorem*. Geometrical exemplariness undoubtedly results from the fact that, as an "abstract" material science, this exemplariness treats the spatiality of bodies (which is only one of the body's eidetic components), i.e., treats what confers sense on the notion of horizon and object. Despite all the antagonistic motifs which animate phenomenology, space's privilege therein is in certain respects remarkable. It testifies to that "objectivist" tendency which Husserl simultaneously opposes so vigorously, and yet which is only a period, an essential, and therefore irreducible, movement of thought.[6]

In Husserlian phenomenology horizonality, or the world as a horizon, is thus a concept that is fundamentally linked to the bodily and spatial structures of the universe, the very same ones on which, as we saw in

Chapter 2, the theoretical gaze that found expression in the exact sciences bases its claim of universality. The horizon is the infinite spatial openness for the manifestation of everything that lets itself be encountered as a bodily object, and it draws its very meaning from this eidetic component of bodily things. But, as we have also seen, the world of objects and, mutatis mutandis, the horizon (if indeed the latter pertains, first and foremost, to corporeal things in space) is not, for Husserl, the entire world. Husserl's transcendentalist approach to the life-world, his search for a more encompassing universality than the one offered by the sciences, stands therefore in an antagonistic relation to this very notion of horizonality. But in spite of the fact that Husserl, in *The Crisis of European Sciences and Transcendental Phenomenology*, sought to open the horizon up to include the universal structure of the accomplishments of world-constitution by the intersubjective acts of the transcendental ego, the objectivist conception of the horizon, as Derrida would seem to suggest, continues to cast a shadow on Husserl's broader conception of horizonality. If in his later works Derrida then speaks of the necessity to exceed, pierce, perforate, puncture, or even burst open the horizon, something, indeed, that from a phenomenological perspective can only be, if not simply a provocation then at least complete nonsense, it is first of all in order to break the hold of geometry on the horizon or, more accurately, on our way of thinking world and universality.

This outrageous demand to pierce the horizon rests first and foremost on Derrida's inquiry into the coming about, or, what he also calls, the "invention of the entirely other"—invention, since in distinction from the programmable other who arrives in the order of the same, one has to prepare for the entirely other—that is, a coming about "that allows the coming of a still unanticipatable alterity and for which no horizon of waiting as yet seems ready, in place, available."[7] More generally, the demand in question devolves from Derrida's probing of the nature of an event and from his examination of the necessary conditions of eventness. In "The University Without Condition" Derrida contends that "if there is any, if there is such a thing [as an event], the pure singular eventness of *what* arrives or of *who* arrives and arrives *to me* (which is what I call the *arrivant*), it would suppose an *irruption* that punctures the horizon, *interrupting* any performative organization, any convention, or any context that can be dominated by a conventionality."[8] Even though Derrida takes issue here with the rules and conventions that, according to speech act theory, make a performative event possible, one can extend his critique of conventions and conventionality to the whole sphere of doxical beliefs, customs, and habits. Without interruption, not only of the horizonality of a theorizable world of objects but also of the horizon of expectations, anticipations, and precomprehensions characteristic of the life-world, no event, strictly speaking, will ever be able to occur. To take this one step further: without piercing the horizon, whether in the sense of *episteme* or in the sense of *doxa*, without bursting open the objectivist horizon of the exact sciences, or the subjectivist one of everyday beliefs, conventions, and expectations, no world worth its name—that is, no universal world—can come into being.

Let us keep the broader implications of Derrida's demand to burst open the horizon in mind as we now return to a discussion of some of his critical observations about the phenomenological concept of horizon. Especially when horizon is understood as "a horizon of anticipation or precomprehension," a formulation that recalls Husserl's talk, in *Experience and Judgment*, of the "structure of anticipation and fulfillment" characteristic of a horizon, a horizon is seen as "a *horizon*, period," and is subject to suspicion.[9] In "Force of Law," for example, Derrida writes: "One of the reasons I'm keeping such a distance from all these horizons—from the Kantian regulative idea or from the messianic advent, for example, or at least from their conventional interpretation—is that they are, precisely *horizons*. As its Greek name suggests, a horizon is both the opening and the limit of that opening that defines an infinite progress or a period of waiting."[10] Derrida's criticism of the notion of horizon—which, as I remarked earlier, occurs in particular in his discussion of what constitutes an event—aims at dislocating the space in which something takes place, in which it is opened up but, by the same stroke, is also encased within certain limits. In his commentary on Husserl's "Origin of Geometry" Derrida had already pointed out that the notion of horizon in Husserl's phenomenology concerns the concrete—because experienced—conditions of possibility of history, that is, "a primordial knowledge" presupposed by "the totality of possible historical experiences." He notes: "Horizon is the always-already-there of a future which keeps the indetermination of its infinite openness even though this future was *announced* to consciousness. As the structural determination of every material indeterminacy, a horizon is always virtually present in every experience; for it is at once the unity and the incompletion for that experience—the anticipated unity in every incompletion."[11] Besides being intimately linked to world, horizonality is also determinative of history insofar as the latter concerns the expansion of the world to the One universal world that is shared by all. The paradox of the horizon, however, is that it both opens up the indeterminacy of the future and closes it in the same breath by anticipating what that future brings. Yet, while in this early Derridean text the horizon only seems to anticipate structurally and determine the future in advance, it does not seem to interfere with the material indeterminacy of the latter. By contrast, all references to the horizon in Derrida's later work would seem to suggest that, as a structure of anticipation and precomprehension, the horizon also encroaches on the material indeterminacy of future events, and this to such a degree that any history (and, by the same token, any world worth its name) becomes impossible. Indeed, structured by anticipation and precomprehension, the horizon describes a space (and a time) in which whatever happens remains controllable and programmable—always already possible—in short, anticipatable and even calculable. What occurs within a horizon "is of the order of the masterable possible, it is the unfolding of what is already possible. It is of the order of power, of the 'I can,' 'I may,' or 'I am empowered to. . . . ' No surprise, thus no event in the strong sense." Where there is a horizon, "an event worthy of the name cannot arrive. If what arrives belongs to the horizon of the possible, or even of a possible performative, it does not arrive, it does not happen, in the full sense of the word."[12] Now since, within the horizon, an event can only take place on the condition that the horizon master it as something possible in advance (thereby precluding any surprise), Derrida proclaims the need to exceed, pierce, perforate, puncture, or even burst open the horizon (all these being expressions that mark his discussion of horizonality). Already in "Signature, Event, Context," where horizonality is discussed in terms of the communication of consciousnesses or presences within which the linguistic and semantic transport of meaning (*vouloir-dire*) occurs (as well as in terms of the semantic and hermeneutic horizon, that is, the horizon of sense, which commands the notion of communication within which all meaning takes place), the nuclear traits characteristic of writing (in the sense of archewriting) were said to exceed and puncture (*excédé ou crevé*) these horizons.[13] In a debate over the hermeneutic conception of the horizon in *Spurs*, Derrida adds that "reading [as well], which is to relate to writing, is to perforate such an horizon or the hermeneutic veil."[14] As I have pointed out, in speaking of eventness Derrida observes that if there is such a thing as an "event in the strong sense . . . it would suppose an *irruption* that punctures [*crève*] the horizon."[15] Furthermore, in regard to "revolution," understood as an interruption of, and a radical caesura in, the ordinary course of history, that is, as an event that does not let itself be preprogrammed, Derrida notes that "in a certain way, as the only event worthy of the name, [a revolution] exceeds every possible horizon, every *horizon of the possible*—and therefore of potency and power."[16] However, if the thought of the event—or for that matter of revolution, responsibility, decision, the coming of the other, and so forth—requires exceeding, puncturing, piercing, or perforating the horizon, this in no way implies abandoning or simply doing away with the horizon altogether. However provocative the talk in question may be, puncturing the horizon does not entail the all-out rejection of phenomenological horizonality. Undoubtedly, Derrida has occasionally linked the occurrence of an event to the absence altogether of a horizon. In *Sur parole* he remarks: "It is the absence of the horizon which is the condition of the event. . . . The absence of the horizon causes fear, but it is perhaps the condition for something unheard of to happen."[17] However, as Derrida's reference, in *For What Tomorrow . . . A Dialogue*, to the necessity of "maintain[ing a] horizon without horizon," if something such as unconditional hospitality is to be thought, demonstrates, the notion of horizon is not to be relinquished once and for all.[18] It is certainly true, as Helmut Kuhn remarks, that "by its very nature every horizon is 'open.' As we move from the center toward the circumference fresh horizons open up. We are constantly invited to transcend the boundary of our field of vision."[19] But it is also true that all these horizons are at the same time framed by what, in Husserl's words, is "the horizon of all horizons"—that is, the ultimate foundation of all actual and potential experience in an idea, which although merely regulative, and hence only the object of an infinite approximation or fulfillment, nonetheless suggests a preclosed whole. In his call for the puncturing of the horizon, Derrida would then seem to extend to the horizon of all horizons, that is, the universal horizon of the world, the constitutive transcendence of all particular horizons. If, however, the horizon of all horizons is an idea in the Kantian sense, this horizon, rather as something always already given, is, as we saw in Chapter 3, also a horizon in the making, if it is not even an idea itself in the making. In light of Derrida's emphasis, in "Violence and

Metaphysics," that, contrary to what Levinas contends, Husserl never held that the perception of a transcendent thing could be completed in full adequation (and hence, could be fully determined once and for all), and that the infinite horizons within which a thing is experienced cannot be reduced to disposable present objects, the call for puncturing the horizon could in a certain way be tantamount to thinking faithfully Husserl's conception of horizon (as an idea in the Kantian sense) to its radical conclusion. Indeed, in the essay in question, Derrida points out that

> the *Idea in the Kantian sense* designates the infinite overflowing of a horizon which, by reason of an absolute and essential necessity which itself is absolutely principled and irreducible, *never* can become an object itself, or be completed, *equaled*, by the intuition of an object.... In phenomenology there is never a constitution of horizons, but horizons of constitution. That the infinity of the Husserlian horizon has the form of an indefinite opening, and that it offers itself without any possible end to the negativity of constitution (of the work of objectivation)—does this not certainly keep it from all totalization, from the illusion of the immediate presence of a plenitudinous infinity in which the other suddenly becomes unfindable?[20]

As an idea in the Kantian sense, the ultimate horizon, which frames all other horizons, can thus not be a constituted totality. Yet, even though nothing that takes place in it is ever fully determinable, this horizon, notwithstanding the impossibility of its ever providing a definite sense for that which occurs within it, remains something with respect to which everything that occurs becomes intelligible. If alterity is to have a chance to manifest itself, then even a horizon that can only be approximated in an infinite process must be pierced.

While only a burst horizon could allow something singular—that is, something other, hence, incalculable—to occur, an unforeseeable event is one that is also "necessarily without horizon."[21] However, in the same way as a "horizon without horizon" implies the freeing of the horizon of its enclosing circumference within, and with respect to which, alone, things can and must appear without therefore relinquishing all relation to it, just so does an event without horizon merely refer to a given horizon's inability semantically to saturate in advance the sense of such an event, and thus to strip it of its singularity. To be recognized as an unforeseeable and radically singular event (as something universal, to the extent that it does not yield to inexorably particular expectations and precomprehensions), the event—a singular universal, as it were—must at the same time burst open the horizon, be without a horizon, and negotiate its lack of intelligibility with some sort of horizon in order to be experienced and recognized as a singular event. Phenomenologically speaking, the demand to do away with the horizon as such is an absurdity, but as the formula of a "horizon without horizon" (or of an event without horizon) indicates, any call to puncture the horizon seeks first and foremost not only the cutting open of particular horizons (even if they may not have those "firm walls" or, more precisely, the "walls hard as steel [*stahlharte Wand*]" that, according to Max Scheler, enclose the "milieu" of human beings, that is, their worlds, or in Husserlian terms, their home worlds) but above all the cutting open of the ultimate meaning-giving horizon, the universal horizon of the world, in order for an experience of alterity to be possible and to open the space for the unforeseeable to come.[22] Only by bursting open the horizon qua "horizon of the wait," in relation to which one waits only for what one already expects in advance; only by "awaiting without a horizon of the wait" is a "*just* opening" toward "the event that cannot be awaited *as such*, or recognized in advance therefore [possible], to the event as the foreigner itself, to her or him for whom one must leave an empty place, always, in memory of the hope."[23]

If, however, an event is "*what comes to pass* only once, a single time, a first and last time, in an always singular, unique, exceptional, irreplaceable, unforeseeable, and incalculable fashion," in short, "*what* happens or *who* happens precisely there where . . . one no longer *sees it coming*, no longer horizontally: *without prospect or horizon*," then for an event to happen not only is the end (*la fin*) of the horizon required but also—implicated by the latter—the end of "teleology, the calculable program, foresight, and providence."[24] Indeed, wherever there is a horizon, whatever happens is seen to be coming from, or to happen in light of, this horizon. A horizon as a horizon of precomprehension is always already also a horizon of anticipation and teleological determination. Whatever happens within it has therefore already been present in some way: "It has already arrived or happened and is thus neutralized in its irruption. Everywhere there is a horizon and where we can see something coming from out of some teleology or ideal horizon, some horizon of an idea, that is, from out of the seeing [*voir*] or the knowing [*savoir*] of an *eidos*, everywhere that ideality is possible . . . this horizontal ideality, the horizon of this ideality, will have neutralized in advance the event, along with everything that, in any historicity worthy of this name, requires the eventfulness of the event."²⁵ Derrida's reservation regarding all horizons includes the one provided by the Idea in a Kantian sense, that is, not only by an idea of adequate determinability to which everything converges as toward a limit on which, however, it never fully closes in, but also as that from which everything that occurs is already ideally prefigured, progressively accomplishing it, even if there is no ultimate fulfillment to this process.²⁶ A horizon as a Kantian Idea, as a regulative idea for every event, is consequently also something that neutralizes the event in its very unpredictability—and hence, the singularity—that alone makes it an event worthy of the name. A horizon that thus serves as a *telos* of both precomprehension and anticipation is by the same token that which also inhibits all historicity. Derrida writes: "Whenever a *telos* or teleology comes to orient, order, and make possible a historicity, it annuls that historicity by the same token and neutralizes the unforeseeable and incalculable irruption, the singular and exceptional alterity of *what* [*ce qui*] comes, or indeed of *who* [*qui*] comes, that without which, or the one without whom, nothing happens or arrives. It is not only the question of the *telos* that is posed here but that of the horizon and of any horizontal *seeing-come* in general."²⁷ What follows from all of this is that if the horizon is the horizon of the world, and in particular of the world that is common to all, that is, the universal world, this world is not *the* world since in it every event is instantly neutralized: It would be a world in which nothing happens and thus not a world at all. Strictly speaking, the world opened up by the horizon is enclosed within limits that prevent anything nonanticipated and nonprecomprehended from happening within its overture. It is, therefore, not an openness to begin with, if openness implies exposure toward otherness, singularity, the incalculable, the to come. No world worthy of its name comes into being within a horizon. A first condition for a world to open up would thus entail bursting open the horizon as anticipatory and teleological—and that always means archeo-teleological—determination.

Undoubtedly, the reflections on world that I have considered so far in this book—by Husserl, Heidegger, Patočka—largely abide by this archeo-teleological schema. Yet, as I have also intimated, for Husserl the world as the one, universal world is not only nothing given but is always in the making, and this not only in the sense of never achieving in its progressive approximation of the idea of such a world any definitive fulfillment or adequation but perhaps also in the sense that even this idea is not fully given in advance but also announces an infinite process of idealization. Similarly, in the case of Heidegger, the originary world, in which a particular people could accomplish its destiny is not a given either: for it to occur this people would not only have to take that by which it is addressed from the beginning—the strange injunction of Being—upon itself, but it would also have to expose itself to other beginnings—entirely other beginnings—with the result that the originary world to be founded may no longer be fully determinable in advance. Situated, as it were, between Husserl's life-world and Heidegger's originary world, Patočka's conception of world as the asubjective phenomenal foundation of all appearing is also not of the order of an essence given once and for all. Constituted by movements whose structures can lay claim to universality, Patočka's revised conception of world not only has an intrinsic dynamic and temporal dimension but is essentially open, structurally inhibited from closing upon itself, given that movement—especially the third movement of truth—is also one of being ahead of oneself and formative of a life outside of oneself. But only in Derrida does bursting open the horizon with its archeo-teleological structure of anticipation and pre-comprehension become a condition (one among others, as we will see) for a world to come into existence at all. Occasionally, while speaking of the world, Derrida adds "if something like it exists [*s'il y en a*]."[28] The world in question here is *the* world, the world as shared, or to be shared, by everyone. However, such a universal world could exist solely on the condition that it take the form of an openness hospitable to the other in its absolute, that is, unanticipatable and possibly even unintelligible otherness. "World," according to Derrida, is not only not a given, but there is, strictly speaking, no such thing yet as the world, that is, if world is indeed a world shared by all, one not only constituted by exposure to the other of oneself but also by the other, which is not determinable in respect to oneself, that is, the other to come. In spite of all the current talk about globalization or, rather, *mondialisation*, we are today more worldless than ever, according to Derrida.[29] In *Rogues*, for example, he remarks that the context inherited from the end of the cold war consists of "a so-called globalization or *mondialisation* that is more inegalitarian and violent than ever, a globalization that is, therefore, only simply alleged and actually less global or worldwide than ever, where *the* world, therefore, is not even there, and where we, we who are worldless, *weltlos*, *form* a world only against the backdrop of a nonworld where there is neither world nor even that poorness-in-world that Heidegger attributes to animals (which would be, according to him, *weltarm*)."[30] In the absence of *the* world (a universal world shared by all), and in the presence of one particular world that is formed against the backdrop of the rest of the world to which world is denied (and that therefore is no world either), in light of this "abyss of the without-world," a reflection on the conditions of world becomes imperative. Before taking up this concern with the conditions of possibility for *the* world, let us also remind ourselves that, just as with the three other thinkers I have dealt with in this work, the thought of *the* world is also, in Derrida, intrinsically connected to what has been called "Europe."

Reflecting in "The University Without Condition" on the concept of world, Derrida points out that "this notion of world is charged with a great deal of semantic history, notably a Christian history: the world . . . is neither the universe, nor the earth, nor the terrestrial globe, nor the *cosmos*." Yet if this concept is obscure, it is precisely because "in its European, Greek, Jewish, Christian, Islamic history, between science, philosophy, and faith, . . . the world is wrongly identified with the earth, with the humans on earth here below, or with the heavenly world above, the cosmos, the universe and so forth." Heidegger is mentioned in this context, who, "beginning with *Sein und Zeit*, will have sought to remove the concept of world and of being-in-the-world from these Greek or Christian presuppositions."[31] A similar attempt to reconceive of the notion of world occurs in "The University Without Condition," where an investigation into the proposition that, given the expiatory signification of work or labor in the Christian conception of world, the world would only begin where work or labor comes to an end. More precisely, this attempt to retrieve a different concept of world inquires into the "as if" of the statement "*as if* the world began where work ends, as if the mondialisation du monde . . . had as both its horizon and its origin in the disappearance of what we call *le travail,*" so as to be able both to interrupt the archeo-teleological determination of the world by the horizon of work as expiation, and to examine the possibility, or virtuality, of world happening like an event as a result of work coming to its end.[32] If Derrida's effort to conceive of world in distinction from work or, rather, labor is reminiscent of Hannah Arendt's elaborations on the concept of world in *The Human Condition*, so is his linkage of the origin of the world to nativity:

> With the birth of a child—the first figure of the absolute arrivant— ... there will be someone who speaks, someone irreplaceable, an absolute initiative, another origin of the world. Even if this initiative dissolves in analysis or returns to ashes, it remains as a clinker of absoluteness [*une escarbille d'absolu*]. ... What is absolutely new is not this, rather than that; it is the fact that it arrives only once. It is what is marked by a date (a unique moment and place), and it is always a birth or a death that a date dates. ... What resists analysis is birth and death: always the origin and the end of a world.³³

Even though the child who is born is only "the first figure" of the arrivant with whom a world begins—any event that bursts open the horizon is, as I have indicated, an opening of world—we will hereafter pursue Derrida's elaborations on birth as the event in which *the* world originates and death as the end of the world. Indeed, as we will see, the birth of the child is not simply a unique opening *to* the world, but it is above all a unique opening *of* the world itself; consequently, the death of another is not merely the disappearance of one singular world but also of the world itself.³⁴ We need to consider two short pieces in this context, both of which appeared more or less at the same time: "Uninterrupted Dialogue: Between Two Infinities, the Poem" and the "Avant-propos" to the French edition of *The Work of Mourning*, entitled *Chaque fois unique, la fin du monde*.³⁵ But first we need to recall Derrida's statement in *Rogues* about our worldlessness, which also concerns the *Da* (*là*) that, according to Heidegger, is the open site, or world, of our Dasein as human beings. Derrida writes:

> there [*là*] where *the* world ... is not even there, and where [*là*] we, we who are worldless, *weltlos*, there [*là*] where we *form* a world against the backdrop of a nonworld, there [*là*] where there is neither world nor even that poorness-in-world that Heidegger attributes to animals ... within this abyss of the without-world, this abyss without support, indeed on the condition of this absence of support, of bottom, ground, or foundation, it is as if one *bore*, or carried, the other, as if I felt, without support and hypothesis, *borne* by the other and *borne* toward the other, there [*là*] where, as Celan says, *Die Welt ist fort, ich muss dich tragen*: the world goes away; the world disappears; I must bear you, there [*là*] where the world would no longer or would not yet be,

where [*là*] the world would distance itself, get lost in the distance, or be still to come.³⁶

Needless to say, in order to tease out, in particular, the cluster of the manifold intertwined ways in which the "there" of Da-sein composes with this absence of world, this dense and difficult passage would require a lengthy commentary. For the moment, however, it must suffice that I point out that where and when worldlessness reigns, where and when there is no longer any form of horizon structuring the relations between the one and the other, this "there," where there is no world, may "possibly" be the sole possible site in which *the* world could break into this worldlessness and for *the* world to come. Within the abyss of worldlessness we are, in Leonard Lawlor's words, "without alibi in relation to the others."³⁷ Indeed, without the support of any ground or limits of a horizon, it is as if we were carried by the other or others (within me or beside me) who, by their singularity, are the opening up or event of worlding. Rather than the accomplishment of a transcendental ego, *the* world—that is, the world in its most elementary and most universal traits—happens only with the other as an absolutely singular arrivant who, in the event of arriving, opens up the world within which I am borne toward him or her, carry him or her, and are myself carried. *The* world, qua the universal world, the one that on condition of no support emerges with the irruption of the absolutely singular other, is this minimal web of imbricated relations between self and other, in which the other carries me, and in carrying me bestows on me the responsibility to carry him or her (or it). *The* world, rather than being the intersubjective accomplishment of a transcendental ego, is a function not only of the other's nativity, and my indebtedness to him or her, but also of the responsibility that I have in relation to the other and the world itself that he or she opens up when this world comes to an end with his or her death.³⁸

To better grasp such an emergence of *the* world, let us turn to Derrida's memorial conference on Hans-Georg Gadamer, *Béliers*, published in English under the title "Uninterrupted Dialogue: Between Two Infinities, the Poem." In the context of an analysis of the conception of dialogue, Derrida explains that in every dialogue one of the partners will from the beginning have been doomed "to carry alone, in himself, both the dialogue that he must pursue beyond the interruption [by the death of the other] and the memory of the first interruption [as the condition of comprehension and understanding]. And carry the world of the other . . . the world after the end of the world." With the above-quoted line by Paul Celan in mind—*Die Welt ist fort, ich muss dich tragen*—Derrida continues:

> For every time, and every time singularly, every time irreplaceably, every time infinitely, death is nothing less than the end *of the* world. Not *only one* end among others, the end of someone or of something *in the world*, the end of a life or of a living being. Death neither puts an end to someone in the world nor to *a* world among others. Death marks every time, every time in defiance of arithmetic, the absolute end of the one and only world, of that which everyone opens as one and only one world, the end of the unique world, the end of the totality of that which is or can be presented as the origin of the world for any unique living being, be it human or not.³⁹

With the death of the other it is not only one particular world that comes to an end. The death of the other is not simply the disappearance of another's world within the existing world. It is not only the end of the unique world of one individual to whom it ceases to appear. Rather, and above all, the death of the other affects the world in its totality as world. The death of the other is nothing less than the disappearance of *the* world itself, the world as a whole, the only world there is—that is, the world we all share in common. In the "Avant-propos" to *Chaque fois unique, la fin du monde* Derrida writes: "Every time death declares *the end of the world in totality*, the end of any possible world, and *every time the end of the world as a unique, hence irreplaceable, hence infinite, totality*." In other words, in addition to being the end of the one and only world there is, and hence of the very possibility of world as such, the death of an other not only means that with it one singular world comes to an end in a unique fashion but also that this one and only world is itself the unique and irreplaceable totality of *the* world. Every time a death occurs, it is as if it were a repetition of the disappearance of the unique and irreplaceable one world, the only one there is—and this every time, moreover, in a singular and irreversible way. Derrida remarks: "As if the *repetition* of the end of an infinite whole were still possible: the end of the world *itself*, the only world there is, every time. Singularly, irreversibly. For the other and in a strange way also for the provisional survivor who endures its impossible experience." The obvious part of this statement refers to the fact that for anyone who dies, the disappearance of his or her unique world is, paradoxically, a repetition of the end of what is unique to such a degree that it suffers no repetition. But according to Derrida, he or she who survives the other undergoes the "impossible experience" of such singular repetition as well. It is to this possibility for the provisional survivor to repeat in a singular fashion this coming to an end of the unique one and only world itself that we now must turn. Obviously, the easy part of this claim refers to the fact that the survivor will in turn die and that his or her death will be the impossible repetition of the unique one and only world coming to an end in a unique way. Yet to repeat the unique disappearance of the one and only world itself after the death of an other also means that in every singular case in which a death occurs, and one world (which is also the world itself) disappears, there is no more return of the world itself. The death of a singular other confronts the survivor with "the always open possibility—that is to say, the necessity of the possibility of a non-return—of the end of the world as the end of all resurrection." Death means that there is no world to succeed the disappearance of the one and only world by the death of the other. Furthermore, what one calls "world" is determined by what is called "death." It is not the end of just one world, as if "one world could always survive another one" or as if "there were more than one world." Indeed, as Derrida remarks: "death, death itself, if there is something like it, leaves no place, not the slightest chance, for the replacement and the survival of the sole and unique world, of the "sole and unique" that makes of each living thing (animal, human or divine), a sole and unique living being."[40]

Let us now return to "Uninterrupted Dialogue," where wordlessness was established as a condition for the possibility of the irruption of the world to come. World, in the sense of the one and only world shared by all is, as seen, linked to the event of the arrival of the arrivant in all his, her, or its singularity but also comes to an absolute end with the death of the other as this singular and irreplaceable being. Upon the death of the other, "the survivor, then, remains alone. Beyond the world of the other, he is also in some fashion beyond or before the world itself. In the world outside the world and deprived of the world. In the least, he feels solely responsible, assigned to carry both the other and *his* world, the other and *the* world that have disappeared, responsible without world (*weltlos*), without the soil of any world, thenceforth, in a world without world, as if without earth beyond the end of the world."[41] The impossible experience of the survivor, that of repeating the end of the world, which occurs with the death of the other, consists, then, in "carrying"—that is, in taking the responsibility upon oneself—not only for the other's world that disappeared with his death but, above all, for the unique one and only world that disappeared with him. Although worldless, this responsibility for the world that has come to an end is the sole hope for there to be the world, for it to come. To carry the worldlessness that results from the disappearance of the other is precisely to carry the responsibility to and for the only world there can be. World, then, in the sense of the universal world, is a function of carrying that which, thanks to the arrival of the singular other, opened up as *the* world of all in all its uniqueness but that inevitably disappeared forever with him or her. It is only thanks to the arrival of the other that I, by definition a survivor, own a world. When that world disappears with the death of the other (who, for Derrida, is not restricted to the human other but can be the animal or divine other as well) and I become worldless, it is only by carrying the other and his world (which in all its uniqueness is the very world itself) that there can possibly be another one and unique world. Far from being given, the only possible way for *the* world to be is that the "I," as a survivor, responsibly carries, in a unique way, the departed's unique world that emerged with his or her arrival. There is thus hope for a world, a world of hope—that is, for *the* world, the absolute or universal world—solely on the condition of repeating the end of the world; this is an aporetic condition, no doubt, but in this also an unconditional condition for there to be *the* world.

Although Derrida speaks of birth and death as the origin and end of *a* world, that is, the singular world of a singular human being—a world in an existential-empirical sense within the world of the many singular and concrete worlds of singular human beings—this world is, ontologically speaking, different from the world itself, the one and absolute world that comes into being with the arrival of the newcomer and to an end with his or her final departure. This latter world is not the essence of the many worlds, a world ontologically more real than all the singular worlds. The one and only world, the unique world for all, that opens with the arrival of an other, however unique it is insofar as it is the world in common that comes into being with this precisely singular individual, is no longer either simply *his* or *her* world. Nor is this universal world grounded in the sole and unique act of the creation of an "I." The one and unique world that opens with the birth, that is, in this absolute and irreducibly new moment, of an other, opens only as a promise. *The* world is only ever promised, and hence contingent on the response by the one to whom the promise is made, when he or she survives the other. This, then, is also the reason why, when *the* world comes to an end with the departure of the other, the survivor, left without the world, is by definition a survivor in that he or she carries the responsibility to and for that world that has come to an end. If the one and absolute world is only ever promised, the survivor is the addressee of this promise and is thus requested to carry the other and the world that disappeared with him or her—to responsibly respond to this request, or to turn it down, thus abrogating the absolute initiative that the other's arrival represented and to remain without a, or rather *the*, world.

By conceiving of the other as the one who, in his, her, or its arrival opens up *the* world for me (and for all others), one that disappears again with the departure of the other, bestowing on the thus worldless "I" (and all others) a responsibility for and to the world itself, the argument is from the start "transcendental" rather than empirical, historical, or cultural. Nor is it an argument for an immutable essence of the world. But in his reflection on "world," Derrida does not therefore argue for plural worlds, for world in the plural, if such plurality is understood in an empirical way. If European rationality has been linked to the thought of the universal, the point is not to confront it with a plurality of other worlds, for what such diversity achieves or proves is not enough. Undoubtedly, the other has his or her own particular world, one of the countless worlds particular to individuals (as well as to different cultures), and this world disappears as well again with the departure of the other. But to think of "world," it is not sufficient to advocate a plurality of worlds; on the contrary, such plurality of particular worlds not only presupposes the one world itself, the world for all, opened up by the singular event of the other's arrival; the very concept of particular worlds also relies on an unthought, and more often than not, essentialist conception of "world." However, this unthought, and essentialist, notion of world that commonly subtends all understanding of particular worlds is not *the* world— the world promised to me by the arrival of the other and to which I am thus bound to responsibly respond, in particular, at the moment of the other's death. The very world itself that needs to be thought as one to which and for which I have a responsibility, in that it comes into being as a promise with the coming of the other, and will come to an end with his or her death, is not a substantialist, or essentialist, world. Paradoxically, the distinction between the singular and the universal traverses the problematic of *the* world itself. The universal world is always a unique world and therefore prone to disappearance; irreducibly unique, it is nevertheless *the* absolute world. Its very singularity "constitutes" its universality. The universal world is plural in a structural sense in that it is opened up by everyone and everything that happens to arrive. This irreducible uniqueness of the world, its singularity, and at the same time, its oneness, founds my responsibility to and for it.

What I have elaborated so far about the world shows that there is *the* world only on condition that it is an openness for the other in his or her absolute singularity, opened up by the arrival of this unique other, and at the same coming to an end with his, her, or its death. Thus only by being worldless, with no ground supporting him or her, can the survivor, by carrying the other who has disappeared, and with him or her *the* world that opened up with his or her arrival, carry on the world. From this point on I intend to discuss a few other such conditions under which alone the world promises itself. But first, what has all of this to do with "Europe"? Significantly, the conditions of possibility for *the* world are also the conditions of European responsibility; hence "world" is intimately linked with the notion of Europe that, whatever it is, can no longer be an idea since, as a horizon structured by precomprehension and anticipation, Europe would precisely lack the openness for the event, the singular, the other to arrive—in other words, to be a promise of *the* world. Only a pierced horizon opens up the possibility for an event to occur, an event that, if it is indeed worthy of the name, will in turn burst open every horizon, that is, every teleological world-horizon of precomprehension and anticipation.

These conditions for there to be a promise of *the* world—for a world that would thus be open and hospitable to the foreigner and to what is foreign—rather than just a plurality of worlds by definition confined by horizons and built on exclusion—are not conditions for the best world. As the universal world, *the* world, or, to refer to the title of part 2 of *Rogues*, the world of "the Enlightenment to come," is not per se free of all danger, violence, or evil.[42] In spite of all the evils that have been committed in the name of universality, the conditions under which the world would truly be universal are at the same time only conditions for a world that would be of lesser evil. These conditions have a priori status, for as I have already pointed out, if there is to be such a thing as *the* world, it *must* be open to the alien, the singular, and the event. If these conditions are a priori, this does not imply that they are universally accepted but only that they are based on a universal injunction or ought: if there is such a thing as *the* world, then it *must* be structured in such a way as unconditionally to allow singularity within it. Otherwise, it remains a particular world. What Max Scheler said about the peculiar essence of ethical values is also valid for the a priori structures of *the* world: whether or not everyone possesses factual evidence of these conditions is unimportant. By contrast, what is important is that everyone can in principle comprehend these conditions, in the same way as everyone is capable of grasping geometrical and mathematical evidence.[43] Finally, if these ideal conditions (without which there is no such thing as *the* world itself, that is, a world without a delimiting horizon) are gathered under the name *Europe*, it follows that this name names the unique and singular way in which a universal world is conceived. Even though the name *Europe* singularizes the thought of the a priori conditions for a universal world, this thought remains nonetheless "a universal beyond all relativism, culturalism, ethnocentrism, and especially nationalism."[44] In other words, this is a universality that, despite its name, is beyond all Eurocentrism.

Whereas for Husserl, the universality of the idealities—and in particular of the structures of the life-world—is transindividual and, although detached from particular peoples, tied to humanity as a whole, the originary world conceived by Heidegger is first of all linked to the Greeks. It is a world projected for a particular people, one that creates the conditions for them to have a history and a world. However, as we have also seen, the indispensable conditions for a people to have a world are such that this people has to raise itself to universality by freeing itself of everything of the order of the native, such as ethnicity, race, nationalism, and so forth. Even though Heidegger shuns the term, it is this very process of pulling up the roots, of becoming unmoored, which allows other peoples—the Germans, first and foremost, but metonymically all of Europe as well—to measure themselves up against such an originary world in order to find their own world in a "dialectics" of sorts between self and other, rather than simply applying this "universality" deeply sunk into singularity to itself. As is manifest from *The Other Heading*, for Derrida the value of universality, to the extent that "it must be linked to the value of exemplarity," is inscribed "in the proper body of a singularity, of an idiom or a culture, whether this singularity be individual, social, national, state, federal, confederal, or not." But "the self-affirmation of an identity," "whether it takes a national form or not, a refined, hospitable or aggressively xenophobic form or not . . . always claims to be responding to the call or assignation of the universal. There are no exceptions to this law. No cultural identity presents itself as the opaque body of an untranslatable idiom, but always, on the contrary, as the irreplaceable *inscription* of the universal in the singular, the *unique testimony* to the human essence and to what is proper to man" (*OH*, 72–73). Whereas for Husserl the universality of the life-world, even though it is constantly in the making, bears on humanity as a whole, and whereas for Heidegger the intimate articulation between an originary world and a particular people invites an *Auseinandersetzung* with this world in the process of which another people can find its own originary world without having to surrender its singularity, for Derrida the relation between universality and singularity is antinomic. At all moments two distinct laws—one law according to which all universality is necessarily inscribed in a singular identity, and another law according to which no singularity can pretend to being a unique identity without at the same time claiming to represent in exemplary fashion the value of humanity itself—imperatively demand to be observed at the same time without a given rule that would determine in advance the solution of their aporetic injunctions. The conflict between a universality that must always be singular, and a singularity that cannot but lay claim to universality, has always to be negotiated in every singular instance in a singular way, that is, by inventing a rule that is itself irreducibly singular.

So far we have discussed several necessary conditions for something like a common world to have a possibility of coming into being: it must be free of any archeo-teleological circularity and open to the arrival of the unforeseeable, the noncalculable, or the foreign, in short, to the other. Other conditions include unconditional friendship, unconditional forgiveness, and last, but not least, a relation to animals based on the least violence. To conclude I will evoke two further conditions for there to be a world that, moreover, evidences the intrinsic link between the demand for one and unique world and the singularity of "Europe." To discuss the first of these conditions (which concerns the condition of possibility of identity), I turn to a close reading of several pages from *The Other Heading*.

In his lecture "Hölderlin's Earth and Heaven" Heidegger adds to the two questions posed by Valéry in "La crise de l'esprit" about the future fate of Europe (that is, whether Europe will turn into a mere promontory of the Asian continent or remain the brain of the terrestrial globe) a third one regarding the origin of Europe in Greece. Derrida poses, in *The Other Heading*, the question of what is called "Europe" precisely because one no longer knows anymore exactly what Europe is (if one ever did). In other words, the question raised in this text concerns the identity of Europe. After having expressed as "an axiom of finitude" the sentiment that *we* old and anachronistic Europeans, although "younger than ever . . . since a certain Europe does not yet exist . . . are like these young people who get up, at dawn, already old and tired," because all options for bringing about a new Europe seem already to have been exhausted, Derrida advances a second, this time, discursive, axiom. First, however, let us bear in mind what an axiom is: since Aristotle, at least, the term *axioma* refers to a statement that serves as the premise of an argument and for which no proof can be, or needs to be, provided because it is either apodictically self-evident or because it is held to include an implicit definition of the terms it contains. It follows from this that an axiom necessarily implies or requires faith, trust, or credence in the worthiness of what the axiom advances. As Derrida remarks in *Religion*, "an *axiom* always affirms, as its name indicates, a value, a price; it confirms or promises an evaluation that should remain intact and entail, like every value, an act of faith."[45] If by proceeding to speak in the first-person plural—"we"—about the "feeling of an old, anachronistic European, youthful and tired of his very age," Derrida surreptitiously moves "from the feeling to the axiom," it is clear that this feeling is not a private one but one that, in principle, is intelligible to all Europeans at least. The second axiom, which one may call an axiom of infinity, no longer concerns the aporetic *we* of "we Europeans," but "a very dry necessity" regarding the identity of Europe itself, as well as of identity in general (*OH*, 9), it calls on the understanding of everyone.[46] "In a somewhat dogmatic way" the second axiom articulates a preliminary condition, if not a universal law, whose consequences affect the very possibility of establishing what is proper to a culture, European or not. This second axiom is thus one that in principle is apodictically self-evident and can be understood or reconstructed by anyone. Since culture, as is generally admitted, represents what is proper—the innermost own—to a particular world, the law in question concerns the latter's identity. But for what follows, let us also not lose sight of the fact that, while articulating an axiom that is preliminary to giving meaning to assertions about European identity, a law is formulated that also concerns self-identification in general. As is to be seen, this linkage is not fortuitous. Now, as regards this second axiom, Derrida writes:

> *what is proper to a culture is to not be identical to itself.* Not to not have an identity, but not to be able to identify itself, to be able to say "me" or "we"; to be able to take the form of a subject only in the non-identity to itself or, if you prefer, only in the difference *with itself* [*avec soi*]. There is no culture or cultural identity without this difference *with itself.* A strange and slightly violent syntax: "with itself" [*avec soi*] also means "at home (with itself)" [*chez soi*] (with, *avec,* is *"chez," apud hoc*). In this case, self-difference, difference to itself [*différence à soi*], that which differs and diverges from itself, of itself, would also be the *difference (from) with itself* [*différence (d')avec soi*], a difference at once internal and irreducible to the "at home (with itself)" [*chez soi*]. It would gather and divide just as irreducibly the center or hearth [*foyer*] of the "at home (with itself)." In truth, it would gather this center, relating it to itself, only to the extent that it would open it up to this divergence. (*OH*, 9–10)

Whereas for Heidegger one does not possess what is properly one's own, but has to acquire it in a confrontation with what is alien to oneself, for Derrida that which is proper to a culture, and provides it with an identity, requires a complex structural difference within itself in order to be able to be this identifiable and identifying innermost own to begin with. First, a difference with itself as a minimal divergence (*écart*) dividing any "itself" is necessary in order for this self to relate to itself at all and thus to be able to identify itself as properly this or that. But, although "strange and slightly violent," "with itself" (*avec soi*) can also be held to mean at (one's) home or a home that is one's own (*chez soi*). The home, however, is the place where one receives or puts up an other. In other words, whereas the difference with itself as a minimal divide within the self is that which allows any relation to oneself, this difference, as one that also affects one's being at home in and with oneself, concerns the very openness of the itself as the home that is one's own to the other. Indeed, since identity makes sense only in relation to, and in distinction from, other identities, it must from the start welcome the arrival and let itself be inhabited by the other. From the beginning, being at home or, what *Monolingualism of the Other* refers to as "the very order of one's home (*chez-soi*), of the house (*casa*), of the home [*chez*]," is marked by the internal difference caused by the structural opening or hospitality to the other.[47] Elsewhere Derrida writes that the "home [*chez-soi*] in general . . . welcomes the absolute *arrivant*," that is, the yet nameless event of the coming of the other.[48] Understood as at one's home, the "with itself" is thus also divided by a "difference (from) with itself [*différence (d') avec soi*]," which, while deferring the relation of the self to itself, exposes the "itself" to the other and is, therefore, the condition of possibility for any itself to relate to others. More precisely, a fundamental unhomeliness inhabits all athomeness insofar as the athome has first to be the place in which one receives the other for it to be an abode as well in which I am with myself. As Jan Patočka observes in a seemingly paradoxical statement: "the others are [even] the originary at-home [*le chez-soi originel*]" (*MNM*, 37).[49] In any event, the "difference to itself (*à soi*)" required for there to be an identifiable property of a culture is twofold. Its two distinct and strangely interconnected differences—the difference with and from itself (which are, therefore, also akin to what I have elsewhere called "infrastructures")[50]—provide the necessary divides for any itself to gather itself into its own. At the same time, the itself is only identical to itself at the price of opening and housing these differences that also irreducibly divide it.[51] To sum up, then, identity, cultural or not, presupposes not only an internal difference (the difference with itself) within which that which is to be identical with itself turns upon itself to affect itself, but since all identity necessarily becomes established in relation to and in distinction from another identity, it also presupposes a difference from itself, so as to be open to others, that is, other identities—but, as is to be seen, also to others that are not (yet) identifiable.[52]

Although the axiom regarding identity is stated in the context of a reflection on today's Europe, it is an axiom that bears on identification in general. With this, however, the question of the exact relation of Europe to this universal law arises. Derrida asks: "Will the Europe of yesterday, of tomorrow, and of today have been merely an example of this law? One example among others? Or will it have been the exemplary possibility of this law?" (*OH*, 11).[53] Since this law stipulates that the formation of identity presupposes a double nonidentity, it is tempting, of course, to ignore the difference with and from oneself and to cultivate exclusively the specific identity that this difference has made possible. Europe will have merely been an example of the law in question if it has only been engaged in cultivating, through repetition, the identity that both differences made possible. However, for a "Europe beyond all the exhausted programs of Eurocentrism and anti-Eurocentrism" to be possible, Europe must "be torn away from self-identification as repetition of itself" (*OH*, 12–13). It must change direction, and head for that which, in the formation of identity, prevents all identifying self-closure. Let us remind ourselves with Derrida that "it is always in the figure of the Western heading and of the final headland or point that Europe determines and cultivates itself: it is in this figure that Europe identifies itself, identifies with itself, and thus identifies its own cultural identity, in the being-for-itself of what is most proper to it" (*OH*, 25). Indeed, Europe has not only always understood itself as "a geographical headland or heading," that is, in Valéry's words, as the advanced point of a "cape" of the Asian continent—that is, "the Western heading"—but also as "a spiritual heading, at once as project, task, or infinite—that is to say universal—idea" or "the *final* headland." As such, it has also interfused its self-image with that of "a heading of world civilization or human culture in general. The idea of an advanced point of *exemplarity* is the *idea of the* European *idea*, its *eidos*, at once as *arché*—the idea of beginning but also of commanding ... and as *telos*, the idea of the end, of a limit that accomplishes, or that puts an end to the whole point of achievement, right there at the point of completion" (*OH*, 24–25). Europe has thus repeatedly conceived of itself as a head or cape—the brain of the globe, or the promontory of the Asian continent—that is, as "the *eschaton* in general" and as "the pole, the end, the *telos* of an oriented, calculated, deliberate, voluntary, ordered movement: ordered most often by the *man* in charge" rather than by a woman (*OH*, 14). However, Europe could also be "the exemplary possibility" of the universal law of identity and identification, if, by freeing itself from the horizon of the *eschaton* that teleologically orients it, it becomes the singular and unique openness of *the* world.[54] For this to occur, today's Europe, Europe on this singular day, has to head in another direction than that identified by its traditional efforts at understanding itself as "our heading," by recalling "that there is another heading, the heading being not only ours [*le nôtre*] but of the other [*l'autre*], not only that which we identify, calculate, and decide upon, but the *heading of the other*, before which we must respond, and which we must *remember, of which* we must *remind ourselves*, the heading of the other being perhaps the first condition of an identity or identification that is not an egocentrism destructive of oneself and the other" (*OH*, 15). For Europe to change directions implies, first of all, reminding itself of the universal conditions under which it (as any other culture as well) can (and must) gather itself into an identity, namely, that any identity in which one can be at home must already be in wait for the other, and must thus be "inhabited" by him, her, or it, and to whom or which all self-identification must, therefore, responsibly answer. This other or others have their own headings—their own goals, horizons, and *tele*—so that for us to remember, call upon, and recall ourselves to the other heading—a heading within European culture itself that differs from the prevalent heading, but above all the headings of the non-European other—is also to acknowledge that our own heading is indebted to headings, that is, directions and destinations, different from ours.[55] Calling on this heading of the other that reaches into one's own identity, reminding oneself of it, and responding to it as something that is not of our own making, prevents identification from self-destructive closure.

One of Derrida's undeniable accomplishments is to have consistently taken into account the logical and conceptual fact that a strict concept of the other implies an irreducible strangeness. An other is *stricto sensu* an other only if absolutely singular and foreign. Derrida has, therefore, at all moments in dealing with an other who or which is other to and from myself, inscribed the place—be it an empty place or seat like the one reserved for Elijah at the dinner table during the seder—of an otherness beyond the other who as *my* other is always already determined from my perspective, hence, made predictable and identifiable. To hold open this space for an other to come—an other singular enough to be an other and hence noncategorizable in terms of the other of myself—is an exigency of thought, a necessity demanded by the thought of the other itself. What follows from this necessity to reserve a place for an otherness that is not anticipatable or precomprehensible is that if to recall our own heading to the "*other heading*, and especially the *heading of the other*" is "perhaps" the "first condition" of a nonegocentric identity, its second condition is "perhaps" the openness to an otherness that is so other that it cannot be categorized in terms of the self/other divide.[56] Consistent with Valéry's terminology, the many meanings of which are itemized and enlarged upon in *The Other Heading*, Derrida terms this other "the *other of the heading*." The second condition of a nonegocentric identity is thus the necessity to recall oneself "to a relation of identity with the other that no longer obeys the form, the sign, or the logic of the heading, nor even of the *anti-heading*—of beheading, or decapitation" (*OH*, 15). For identity to forgo self-destructive closure on itself, it is not sufficient to relate to other headings, and in particular to the heading, the direction, the goal, the *telos*, of the other—"the other heading"—as an other who is one's opposite. Such an identity must as well expose itself to "the other *of* the heading"—to an other, in short, which does not let itself be identified by way of a goal with respect to which he, she, or it could be made intelligible. "The other *of* the heading," to which the "cultural identity of Europe" would have to respond in order to be "perhaps" an identity that responsibly responds to and for itself, as well as to and for the other, refers to an other that no end makes foreseeable and comprehensible in advance. For identity not to self-destruct by closing itself off and withdrawing within itself, it would have to "orient" itself toward an other that defies all horizonality.

Let us remind ourselves again of the fact that these elaborations on the conditions under which an identity would perhaps no longer be self-destructive not only bear on identity in general but also on Europe's cultural identity as perhaps "the exemplary possibility of this law" (*OH*, 11). Even though the question of Europe as a heading is an old European question, one that, as Derrida remarks, "should remain, even beyond all answers" because it is Europe's constant question, the question that constitutes it, this question about its status as a head, a goal, a direction (as opposed to other headings) not only seems to have become unavoidable today, but it also poses itself in a novel fashion since "the experience of the *other heading* or of the other of *the* heading presents itself in an absolutely new way" (*OH*, 17). Imminent in Europe is nothing less than the possibility of the singular event of thinking in a new way about European identity, and about identity in general. Furthermore, if this event is today imminent in Europe, the conclusion is also that this is the unique time of its occurrence, since as an event today, it arrives only once. What happens in such a unique fashion comes of course with an inevitable responsibility. After having suggested that a double exposure to the other may perhaps be necessary for identity to be nonegocentric, Derrida avers: "And what if Europe were this: the opening onto a history for which the changing of the heading, the relation to the other heading or to the other of the heading, is experienced as always possible? An opening and a non-exclusion for which Europe would in some way be responsible?

For which Europe *would be*, in a constitutive way, this very responsibility? As if the very concept of responsibility were responsible, right up to its emancipation, for a European birth certificate?" (*OH*, 17). The law regarding identification and identity is a universal and apodictic law. Yet the two conditions under which identity may be responsible to itself and the other are modalized by a "perhaps" that suspends certainty, or rather, expresses the only certainty that is possible in this context. The "what if" followed by the imperfect "were" with which the conditional proposition about the "essence" of Europe opens, indicates a lack of certitude as well, but it also suggests—and above all expresses—a desire or wish for what Europe is or ought to be.[57] In addition, insofar as it is preceded by the conjunction "and," the suggestion or wish in question is also subject to the possibility that Europe might *not* be what is advanced about it. Yet what is thus advanced about Europe is not merely a hypothesis or a call (*appel*). Derrida notes:

> No, I believe, rather, that *this is taking place now*. (But it is also necessary, for this, to begin to think that this "now" would be neither present, nor current, nor the present of some current event.) Not that it arrives, that it happens or has already happened, not that it is already *presently* given. I believe, rather, that this event takes place as that which comes, as that which seeks or promises itself *today*, in Europe, the today of a Europe whose borders are not given—no more than its name, Europe being here only a paleonymic appellation. I believe that if there is any event today, it is taking place here, in this act of memory that consists in betraying a certain order of capital in order to be faithful to the other heading and the other of the heading. (*OH*, 30–31)

Nothing in particular substantiates the belief that, indeed, an opening onto a history that would no longer be self-enclosed within its arche-teleological limits at the exclusion of the other is actually taking place. But if there is a today in Europe, and thus also some imminence, it becomes inevitable to wager that what seeks or promises itself in Europe is the opening onto a history that responds to the *telos* of the other, to the model offered by the other, and what is irreducible to a *telos* as well as a model. Such a wager—or what Hume refers to as "custom" and "belief"—is not only an inevitable "anticipation" in the form of the "as if." If it is "*also* necessary to anticipate and to keep the heading" (*OH*, 18), it is in order to prevent that which is imminent, and thus coming, from being a threat rather than a promise. What is imminent in Europe, when

Europe is thought of in terms of the singular instant of *today*—that is, of a here and now that is entirely new—is therefore unique, and because unanticipatable and forfeiting precomprehension, it is potentially both a chance and a danger. Only the belief that what is coming is the coming of an other Europe, one that cultivates the culture of the other, can forestall, as it were, the worst from happening.

As we have seen, horizons and *tele* neutralize in advance that which comes today in all its uniqueness and singularity. Therefore, for a world to be a world, one that is open to the event, the other, the horizon, must be pierced, and the *telos* must open itself to the ends of the other and to that which escapes the determination of ends altogether. As the need to believe that what happens today in Europe is the opening to a world and history in which the change of headings and of the other of the heading is acknowledged—rather than the nightmare of the worst—demonstrates, it is not a question of arguing for a horizonless and nonoriented world. Such a world would not only be no world; it would be a hellish non- or unworld. Absolute openness to the other, for sure, could mean the end of any world. If a world is only one on condition of letting the other come, this world is also necessarily one that imposes conditions on the other to prevent, though without any assurance whatsoever, the possibility of the worst violence. There is no such thing as a world without a horizon, without an *arche* and a *telos*; there is no such thing as a world that does not in advance neutralize to some extent the absolutely new and the absolute *arrivant*. Such neutralization also deprives the other of his or her otherness, no doubt, but it necessarily also seeks in this manner to prevent that which yet has no face from becoming the face of the monstrous. As a result, that which announces itself *as* the unanticipatable and nonidentifiable in today's Europe, and for which one does not yet have a memory, must not only be welcomed; it must also be met with suspicion. As the European memory tells us, it is also necessary "to anticipate and keep the heading [*garder le cap*], for under the banner—which can also be a slogan—of the unanticipatable or the absolutely new, we can fear seeing return the phantom of the worst, the one we have already identified" (*OH*, 18).

Heretofore Europe has been determined in terms of so many Eurocentric and anti-Eurocentric programs, which by now are exhausted. The new experience of the *telos* of the other, or of the other of the *telos* that Europe currently undergoes according to *The Other Heading*, as well as the new questioning of its relation to its others and to what may come, does not provoke a new definition of the essence of Europe. Rather, what arises from this new experience is a question about Europe, one that ventures a hypothesis about Europe and simultaneously expresses a desire of what and how it ought to be—an "essence" of Europe that, rather than having always already been its true essence, is an absolutely new essence, an essence in a new sense, one that announces itself as a promise to forestall the danger of the worst and that, as the modality of the question suggests, may never come once and for all, but remain in coming.

Without abandoning the questioning mode, Derrida asks whether this new "essence" of Europe were not its openness to a history that, rather than being archeo-teleologically closed upon itself, would be one that acknowledges that the *telos* that orients it, including the relation to the ends or aims of others that can no longer be identified as other, can always be subject to change. Undoubtedly, there is no history without an identifiable cape or *telos* in which an identity, ahead of itself in anticipation, dreams of gathering itself. But at the same time, "history also presupposes that the heading not be *given*, that it is not to be identifiable in advance and once and for all," for otherwise nothing would happen. "The irruption of the new, the unicity of the other *today* should be awaited *as such*. . . . It should be anticipated *as* the unforeseeable, the *unanticipatable*, the non-masterable, non-identifiable, in short, as that of which one does not yet have a memory" (*OH*, 18). An openness to a history, which, although not *telos*-free, but in which one's own heading is in a constant negotiation with the heading of the other and the other of the heading, would not only represent an overture to such a history, but it would also be the first day of a history based on nonexclusion, that is, a history that would respond to the other, the other's ends, and the absolute singularity and eventness of what is not categorizable. In other words, such a history of which Europe might be and ought to be the beginning is a responsible history. The Europe that, perhaps, announces itself in this way today is one that would be responsible for such a non-archeo-teleological history. Or more precisely, such a Europe "*would be*, in a constitutive way, this very responsibility." In a clear, but also critical, reference to Husserl's contention that the idea of responsibility has teleologically oriented European history from its inception in Greece onward, Derrida suggests that Europe would only be this openness to a nonexclusive history if it were to identify itself with this responsibility just *as if* the concept of responsibility would be European in origin, and even coincide with the birth of Europe—that is, the birth of a Europe still to come.[58]

A Europe of this kind would also be a Europe whose identity heeds the universal law advanced by the second axiom. In fact, as should by now be clear, if this universal law is stated in the context of the question of European cultural identity, it is because Europe is not merely one example among others of this universal law. On the contrary, what perhaps promises itself today in Europe is a Europe that would be "the exemplary possibility of this law," a Europe that would, indeed, identify itself with the cultivation of "the difference-to-oneself (*with oneself*) that constitutes identity [rather than] confining [itself] to an identity wherein this difference remains *gathered*" (*OH*, 11). If Europe is not merely an example of this universal law, it is because it is intimately linked to Europe as the singular time (today) and space of its emergence. Europe may be "the exemplary possibility of this law" because this law is what perhaps announces itself as a unique event in today's Europe. This law, from all we have seen, is not only a universal law for identity-formation. It is at the same time a law that stipulates the conditions for a history that would no longer exclude the other, the singular, the event, and so forth; in other words, this law articulates the indispensable conditions for something that merits the name of world—the one world—to be possible. The law in question is thus that of *the* world in the face of an impending threat that what arrives could be a threat of a monstrous nonworld. If in Europe today a Europe emerges that is the exemplary possibility of the universal law for the one world we all could have in common, *the* world is then, undoubtedly, intimately, and in exemplary fashion, tied to Europe. But that of which Europe is the promise—*the* world—is at the same time that which also dissolves it in its exemplary singularity, turning it into a mere example, as it were, of this universal world.

If there is to be such a thing as *the* world, it will be possible only under certain conditions. Only when they are met can the world be a world worth its name, namely, one in which the other, the event, and the singular, however absolute, are welcomed. Where this does not happen, *the* world will not exist. But this welcome must, of course, also be constantly negotiated with European memory, which also reminds us that the absolutely new can also be that of past horrors. It is in this sense that one can understand Derrida's statement that "one could show that, in a certain way, Europe today, here and now, originates in Auschwitz as much as it does in Greece, Christianity, the Empires, and the Revolutions of '89 and '17."⁵⁹ For Derrida all these conditions are inextricably tied to Europe, not merely because of all the great discourses and programs on Europe that, although exhausted, are also "unforgettable. . . . (We cannot and must not forget them since they do not forget us)" (*OH*, 13). Indeed, Europe is also intrinsically imbricated in the promise of a universal world because today the possibility of an entirely new way of thinking about this one world may be in the offing in a Europe in which the world is linked to the responsibility to and for the arrivant but in which the old memory could also provide the means for preventing the arrival of the new from being the arrival of the worst. What promises itself in Europe is neither the utopia of a world of innocence nor the nightmare of a world of terror by the absolute other but a world of the least possible evil. Only such a world would be *the* world. But such a world, as we have seen, is also "only" a promise. So far we have discussed several of the conditions that, as should also have become evident, are intrinsically imbricated in one another and that must be met for such a world to happen. In conclusion we will briefly broach one additional condition for *the* world to have a chance to occur.

After conjuring, in *Of Hospitality*, the current conflicts in Europe, in particular the restructuring of state-national borders in the former Yugoslavia and USSR, Derrida opens a parenthesis: "Whatever the enigma of this name and the 'thing' to which it refers, 'Europe' perhaps designates the time and space propitious to this unique event: it was in Europe that the *law* of universal hospitality received its most radical and probably most formalized definition—for instance in Kant's text, *Perpetual Peace*, a constant point of reference for us and throughout the whole tradition that has carried it on."⁶⁰ Derrida's planned address to the International Parliament of Writers in 1996 in favor of the formation of a network throughout Europe of "cities of refuge" permits gauging the importance of universal hospitality—and per extension, of Europe, where its law received its most radical definition. Indeed, in *On Cosmopolitanism and Forgiveness*, while evoking the need "to cultivate an ethics of hospitality," he writes that "hospitality is culture itself and not simply one ethics amongst others." Let us bear in mind what we have seen regarding the twofold culture *of* the other that all relation to oneself and all self-identification necessarily presupposes. Indeed, hospitality concerns ipseity, being with self itself—that is, all with-oneself, *chez-soi*, and *bei sich*—hence, all athomeness, in other words, the *ethos* and the ethical: "Insofar as it has to do with the *ethos*, that is, the residence, one's home, the familiar place of dwelling, inasmuch as it is a manner of being there, the manner in which we relate to ourselves and to others, to others as our own or as foreigners, *ethics is hospitality*; ethics is so thoroughly coextensive with the experience of hospitality."[61] If ethos and ethics are understood from the habitat or sojourn, then being at home is inextricably intertwined with the welcoming of the other, the foreigner, in the place where one oneself dwells. *Stricto sensu*, the foreigner is not only to be understood "on the basis of the circumscribed field of *ethos* or ethics, of habitat or time spent as *ethos*," but, as Derrida points out in *Of Hospitality*, as the master of the house, although at home, "comes to enter his home through the guest—who comes from outside. The master thus enters from the inside *as if* he came from the outside. He enters his home thanks to the visitor, by the grace of the visitor."[62] In other words, it is *as if* only the stranger could "liberate the power of his host" to be at home in his or her own home by welcoming him or her. It is only ever *as if* the host were the master of his or her home, since without the foreigner he or she would not enjoy the difference with him- or herself required to establish him- or herself as sovereign in his or her own house. Derrida writes: "It's *as if* the master, *qua* master, were prisoner of his place and his power, of his ipseity, of his subjectivity," and as if, only by inviting the stranger to stay in his or her home could the host become the master of the home to begin with.[63] But if, on the one hand, hospitality is culture itself insofar as it is the culture *of* the other—cultivating the other and the other's culture—thereby allowing for something like self-identity to form; and if, on the other hand, universal hospitality is not one ethics among others but, as the unconditional Law of hospitality, the Law for all particular ethics, then all sorts of tensions, modifications, and even perversions can come to characterize the relations of self and other, host and guest. Precisely because hospitality and ethics are coextensive, "for this very reason, and because being at home with oneself (*l'être-soi chez soi—l'ipséité même*—the other within oneself) supposes a reception or inclusion of the other which one seeks to appropriate, control, and master according to different modalities of violence, there is a history of hospitality, an always possible perversion of *the* law of hospitality (which can appear unconditional), and of the laws which come to limit and condition it in its inscription as a law."[64] As indicated, according to Derrida, "Europe" designates the time and place where the law of universal hospitality found its most radical expression. Undoubtedly, the reference here is to what in *Cosmopolitanism and Forgiveness* is called "*the* Great Law of Hospitality—an unconditional Law, both singular and universal, which order[s] that the borders be open to each and every one, to every other, to all who might come, without question or without their even having to identify who they are or whence they came."[65] Without *the* law of universal hospitality, that is, without the unconditional exposure to what arrives, the "horizon without horizon," without which *the* world cannot exist, cannot be maintained. The injunction of absolute hospitality must be distinguished from the *laws* of universality that regulate the "*hospitality of invitation.* [By contrast] pure or *unconditional* hospitality assumes that the one arriving has not been invited to the place where I remain master of my domain and where I control my house, my territory, my language, where (according, on the contrary, to the rules of *conditional* hospitality) he should in some way conform to the accepted rules of the place that welcomes him. Pure hospitality consists in leaving one's house open to the unforeseeable arrival, which can be an intrusion, even a dangerous intrusion, liable eventually to cause harm."[66] Without such unconditional openness to the arrivant there is no prospect for *the* world but only imprisonment in a space that is not even one's own. Yet even though it is one of the requisite conditions to raise any hope for *the* world to occur, "unconditional hospitality can also have perverse effects."[67] Unconditional hospitality is absolutely corrupt from the start; lacking all decision and responsibility on the part of the host, it can turn out to be an invitation to unforeseeable violence and evil. For *the* world to possibly be a world of lesser evil, hospitality must therefore combine with the conditional laws of hospitality, which is not to say that these laws could not in turn become corrupted as well. In any event, two laws must enter into a collusion for there to be such a thing as *the* world—two antinomic, aporetic laws:

> *The* law of unlimited hospitality (to give the new arrival all of one's home and oneself, to give him or her one's own, our own, without asking a name, or compensation, or the fulfilment of even the smallest condition), and on the other hand, the *laws* (in the plural), those rights and duties that are always conditioned and conditional, as they are defined by the Greco-Roman tradition and even the Judeo-Christian one, by all of law and all of philosophy of law up to Kant and Hegel in particular, across the family, civil society, and the State.[68]

Hospitality becomes constitutive of *the* world at the moment when *the* law of absolute hospitality in all its "universal singularity" enters into an irreconcilable conflict with the many laws that regulate hospitality and according to which hospitality is offered as a right or a duty to a foreigner provided with a family name, for instance, or provided with the social status of being a foreigner.[69] Apart from the fact that this collision is antinomic because two irreducibly different laws—the one universal Law of hospitality and the multiplicity of laws—confront each other, it is, moreover, a conflict of asymmetric laws. Without the Law of unconditional hospitality there cannot even be a concept of hospitality, a concept *stricto sensu* of what amounts to hospitality, nor can there be the laws that condition hospitality by submitting it to rules. But these two laws are not only contradictory; they are also inseparable, both excluding and implying one another:

> But even while keeping itself above the laws of hospitality, *the* unconditional law of hospitality needs the laws, it *requires* them. This demand is constitutive. It wouldn't be the effectively unconditional law, the law, if it didn't *have to become* effective, concrete, determined, if that were not its being as having-to-be. It would risk being abstract, utopian, illusory, and so turning over into its opposite. In order to be what it is, *the* law thus needs the laws, which, however, deny it, or at any rate threaten it, sometimes corrupt or pervert it. And must always be able to do this . . . And vice versa, conditional laws would cease to be laws of hospitality if they were not guided, given inspiration, given aspiration, required, even, by the law of unconditional hospitality.[70]

To conclude then: "Europe" is not only associated with the universal Law of hospitality, and the demand that comes with this law to become effective at all moments by way of determined laws—such as, for instance, those that govern "cities of refuge." Although there are, undoubtedly, multifarious laws of hospitality, "Europe" also stands for the demand that in all of these laws the injunction of absolute or unconditional hospitality be the guiding force. Indeed, the very demand of piercing the horizon in order for the event to be able to happen, or the singular arrivant to arrive, is not yet sufficient for there to be one world. Hospitality to any other, and particularly the other who or which cannot be identified in advance, must take on concrete forms, such as laws, by which this unconditional openness becomes effective. For this to be possible, however, the unconditional openness to the absolute other, which itself could spell definite disaster, needs to be *limited* by what Derrida calls the unconditional and unlimited *Law* of hospitality, which, although leaving one's house open to the unforeseeable and thus liable to cause harm, is at the same time the Law of *hospitality*. As precisely the Law of *hospitality*, this Law, therefore, allows also for particular laws of hospitality that impose specific conditions on the other. Only on this condition is it possible to maintain the horizon without a horizon required for a world to be *the* world to begin with, while also preventing this world from becoming a world of violence and evil. "Europe" designates the universal conditions, more precisely, the antinomic or aporetic injunctions for the world to be an *ethos* in which all—past, present, and even the not anticipatable beings (human and nonhuman)—can dwell. A world, in short, of the least violence and the least evil. "Europe," rather than guaranteeing such a possibility, is only the promise of such a world. However, as a promise of a world of lesser evil, such a promise turned into a program in the name of *Europe*, one that qua program thus forecloses the possibility of the coming of the unexpected, could also turn out to be the promise of the worst. Without this inevitable risk, however, there is also no chance that the impossible promised by "Europe" may become effective as a possibility.

Epilogue

Although this examination has repeatedly broached the question of why the name *Europe* should continue to designate a kind of universality and a conception of world that, decidedly, are no longer Eurocentric (nor therefore anti-Eurocentric), and that in all their aspects and ramifications barely resemble the conception of universality (or universality point) with which Europe has commonly been associated, I wish to return to this question one more time. For many, universality is a European invention. It is a philosophical and, for some, an ideological construct that intends to justify and embellish its historical pretensions with respect to the non-European world. Universality is generally considered to amount to Europe's historical and cultural imposition on the rest of the world and to imply an overriding and denying of all singularities.[1] Undoubtedly, the title of "universality" has served Europe, beginning with the conception of "the unity of the world in the mode of submission"—that is, with the imperial unification of the Roman Empire—to justify its hegemony until its world-political and economic decline in the twentieth century. Stoicism's contribution to this philosophical idea of a unity totalized by way of one sole sovereign power may well have consisted in formalizing this model of universality.[2] Marcus Aurelius, himself a Stoic after all, became an emperor. For those who seek to understand universality as a simple translation of the merely factual power of Europe and European arrogance, the connection that I have made in this book—between the thought of universality and Europe—will only serve as further confirmation of what, in essence, is a misunderstanding of universality—namely, that universality is dismissive of particularity and singularity. Universality, however, or, for that matter, reason, is not a threat to particularity per se. On the contrary, particularity only makes sense with respect to universality. Though certain forms that this concept has assumed in order to legitimate and mask domination are indeed intended to root out singularity and difference, universality, understood as the domination of the particular by the universal, has very little resemblance to the concept of universality that, from its inception in Greece, has dominated most of the Western philosophical tradition.[3] As a consequence, the rapidly dwindling influence of Europe within a globalized world, and the so-called postcolonial "provincialization of Europe," in no way affects the validity and pertinence of this classical philosophical concept. And its potentialities are invoked by Husserl when the project of universality is shown to imply not only the demand for thought to be all-embracing, and seek to account for everything that is, but also that it rationally justify any claims that are made—that is, to publicly, and in a verifiable manner, render account. Universality as an exigency of thought has, from its start in Greece and Europe, implied critical self-justification, and hence a responsibility to all others. This is the very reason why in this book the concept of universality has been shown to be predicated on singularity as distinct from particularity. Undoubtedly, the demand to transcend all customary beliefs and the exigency of radical self-criticism that goes along with the concept of universality is experienced as a foreign imposition on all particular opinions and entrenched positions that (whatever the particular reasons may be) consider themselves beyond the necessity to explain themselves to others. The demands inscribed in the idea of universality are exacting demands, but they are not demands that would only be limited to non-Europeans. As I have also shown, this very exogeneity of the universal is, independently of its intrinsic link to singularity, something that offers the possibility for becoming binding to everyone in the first place. Nonetheless, it is also true that the development that the concept of universality undergoes in the hands of Heidegger, Patočka, and especially Derrida, drawing as it does on the untapped resources of the classical, and in particular, Husserlian conception of universality, has led to a conception of universality and world in which the role of the other and the foreign is so determinant that, admittedly, it is hard to see what such a conception still might have to do with Europe.

Because the conception of universality that has emerged from our discussion is one that is not discriminatory of singularities but is, rather, itself predicated on singularity—hence a true openness to others—resistance to associating this conception with "Europe" is to be expected since that name, today, smacks of parochialism. In light of Europe's accelerating disappearance as a world power, such designation will be held in suspicion for many reasons, reasons that are too obvious to require spelling out here. Let me therefore only say that if the connection between such a universality and Europe is contested, it may first of all be because of what one understands, or rather misunderstands, by "Europe." If "Europe" is taken to refer to a geographical entity, or to the however-ill-determined economic, cultural, and political identity of present-day Europe, one would be hard-pressed to discover any traces in it of the radical openness to the other advocated by the new conception of universality and world. But if universality and Europe are intrinsically linked, then this can only be the case if "Europe" is not understood as a geographical entity but, in Husserl's words, as a spiritual figure, in short, as a philosophical concept or conception itself. Furthermore, if it seems problematic to relate a newly enlightened conception of universality to something called "Europe," it may also be because of a lack of clarity regarding the relation of the philosophical concept of Europe to Europe as a particular part of the world—something that is more generally reflected in the relation between universality and singularity.

Husserl's, Heidegger's, Patočka's, and Derrida's reflections are all attempts to reawaken the demand for universality and for a world (that would be one world shared by all) in the name of Europe. Undoubtedly, some other great world-cultures have raised themselves to the thought of universality. It is therefore not a question here of arguing that thought—which is thought only on condition of seeking universal validity—only emerged with the Greeks. Yet only in Greece did thought develop in a way that had no likeness anywhere else. Though this is certainly not sufficient to argue for the supremacy of Greek thought, more important is the fact that it is only in Greece that thought became defined as such. By developing a logic, for example, it provided the criteria to be able to identify thought itself. On this basis alone, thought became capable of demanding (of itself and of everything that pretends to be thought) that it account for itself in a way that is in essence intelligible to everyone. Only in Europe does the concept of universality entail the demand for a responsible self-justification and hence a constitutive openness to every other. There is no question that this conception of universality is a philosophical invention that occurred solely in Europe. In Husserl's words, it is not, however, therefore "a fiction, not a dispensable invention without significance" (*C*, 336). For indeed, if one faces what the demands are that are tied to the idea of universality, they are minimal exigencies for there to be *the* world to begin with. Hence, whether they are sufficient or not, they are the only option, in the last instance, to avert barbarism. The name *Europe* is synonymous with this, and only this specific understanding of universal thought. "Europe" signifies nothing more—but also nothing less—than the project of a world subject to the demand of universal intelligibility, public justification of all claims and deeds, and, hence, of an openness to, and responsibility toward, all others. If, therefore, all the authors I have discussed continue to link the notions of universality, responsibility, and world to "Europe," it is in recognition of the fact that these concepts, in the specific way in which they are interlinked, are of European descent or have a European birth certificate. Manifestly, by probing the untapped possibilities of the concept of universality and world, their own elaborations take place in a debate astutely aware of the interconnectedness of the thought of universality and Europe in philosophical, and especially phenomenological, thought. If the kind of universality and world that emerges from these discussions is still associated with "Europe," then it is not only in recognition of this historical linkage of the two topics in philosophical thought but also because the resources for expanding on it are drawn precisely from this context. To not recognize the intrinsic link between universality and Europe would not only mean being oblivious to something that is, after all, a matter of fact; it would also be to think ahistorically. The need to keep "Europe" as a name for a conception of universality where hospitality to the foreigner is essential is based on the recognition of an indebtedness to the emergence of the concept of universality in Greece and the tradition to which this thought has given rise. And it is, furthermore, the resources of this tradition that are instrumental to the further development of this concept.

But the question of why one should still refer to such a universality returns because, as has been seen, this is a conception that also transcends its site of emergence, tearing itself away from the singular conditions that have given rise to it. Nothing in this concept prevents it from emerging somewhere other than in Europe. Thought as a form of life—whether one that yields at all moments to the precepts of reason or one that cultivates the culture of the other, and thus also promises a new way of thinking about political freedom and equality—this conception of universality can perhaps "be realized more effectively in other cultures and parts of the world than in Europe itself."[4] To cling to the name *Europe*—is this not then a nostalgia for a past Europe, for its original hegemony? In short, is it not one more manifestation of Eurocentrism, albeit a particularly refined and sophisticated version? Needless to say, such nostalgia for a lost Europe is, of course, always a temptation and a danger. It is the temptation to claim that only European rationality has the privilege of uprooting itself and of having alone the disposal of alterity, of other cultures and traditions—cultures and traditions that are themselves deemed to be stuck in particularity, incapable of self-transcendence. Yet even though the "Europe" of universal openness and responsibility to the other no longer belongs to Europe as a geographical, political, economic, and cultural entity, "the name of Europe remains—and Europe is not to be confounded with the world."[5] To continue designating this impossible identity of a self-dispossessing universality according to the name of *Europe* is, first of all, to acknowledge this difference; it is not to claim a patent for universality as a European invention so as to further nurture the illusory hope of dominating all other cultures and traditions. Continuing to designate this model of universality by the name *Europe* is a way to account for this conception. It is a way to let others name and judge it from outside rather than to impose it on him or her. By labeling this conception "Europe," one acknowledges the intimate connection of all thought (including the thought of what is universal and what a world for all means) to a singular "agent"—singular tradition, locality, and history—thereby guarding the concept from becoming abstract and forcing the particular into subservience and submission. Furthermore, as I pointed out in my introduction, the very eccentricity of the name *Europe* all by itself justifies its being used to name universality and exposure to otherness.

Throughout this book I have insisted on the intrinsic link between the universal and the singular. From Husserl's discussion of a universal rational science having its roots in the life-world, to Heidegger's linkage of an originary world to the history of a people, to Patočka's conception of a community of responsibility predicated on the absolute singularity of its members, to Derrida's claim that the concept or idea of universality as an infinite task itself emerges in a finite space and time, we have seen that a singularity can only identify itself by simultaneously appealing to universality. This link has not simply been acknowledged; it has also been consistently argued that the finitude of the universal implies no relativism whatsoever. Still, if the thought of universality—universality being not of the order of a fixed and abstract essence, but being constituted by aporetic injunctions, a task that is, moreover, an infinite task—arises in a tight relation to singularity, the addressee of the demands of universality is, first of all, this very singularity itself. The finite singularity that first invented the concept of universality is also the first subject *of* this thought. Europe is the first addressee of this thought of uprooting oneself in order to become open to the other, a demand that goes as far as to include Europe's own de-Europeanization. Originating in Europe, the idea of "Europe" as the idea of *the* world is, first of all, a challenge to the European. For this very reason this conception of universality (one that not only challenges all others but above all its own inventor) is one that, in principle, could also have arisen elsewhere. And yet the culture *of* the other presupposed by this conception interdicts imposing it on others. Hence, the need to continue to call it by the name of *Europe*.

Although the thought of universality emerged in a necessary conjunction with Europe, as a universal thought it cannot suffer remaining enclosed in a singular name. Precisely because *Europe* is the name for universality, that is, for an openness and exposure to the other, the very injunctions that constitute universality also require that this name, as a proper and singular name, and as a name of a singularity, be abandoned. If Europe, rather than being a figure, an idea, or a *telos*, is not only an answer to the foreign but an answer as well that, rather than being given from a place that would properly be one's own, is given from a place that does not properly belong to oneself, then this place of Europe is one of "an anonymous Europe, one which has received—just as any one of us have—its name from somewhere else."[6] As the name for the universal, *Europe* is not simply a self-effacing name; the place where the injunction to respond responsibly to the other arises (whether the other is within or without) is a place that cannot name itself. It can only be named by the other. If Europe is to be the thought and practice of an openness to the other that is not offset by an anticipation of what or who the other is, but that meets the challenge of the other's singularity and unpredictableness, then Europe's name can never be *its* name, one that it would have given to itself and by means of which it could identify itself. Yet precisely because it is named "Europe" by an other, Europe, as the thought of universality and *the* world, cannot simply shed its name. At the same time, being in essence a response to the call and challenge of the other, Europe is, by nature, undefinable, unidentifiable, and thus without a name. Although such anonymity demands being named by the other within and outside Europe, any name—the name of *Europe* included—can also be parted with. For the thought of universality and the world, *Europe* is thus also just one name among other possible names.

The majority of the thinkers discussed in this book have consistently tied the thought of universality to Europe, even if it is a Europe that is still to come. This is the case in attempts to elaborate a conception of universality and world that is not only distinct from the current understanding of universality, as an abstract construct intended on overriding singularity, but also from the classical, and even Husserlian, conception of it—conceptions that, on occasion, go as far as relinquishing the term *universality* itself, as is the case with Heidegger. This is also the case with Derrida who, on several occasions, has insisted on the need "to take the old name of Europe at once very seriously and cautiously, that is, to take it lightly, only in quotation marks, as the best paleonym, in a certain situation, for what we recall (to ourselves) or what we promise (ourselves)" (*OH*, 82). As Derrida explains, a paleonym is an "*old name*" that, in an operation "that in the last analysis refuses to be governed by a teleo-eschatological horizon," is maintained for "strategic reasons in order to launch a new concept."[7] As we have seen, in his writings on Europe Derrida has consistently and forcefully made a case for continuing to refer to the new conception of universality, world, and responsibility that he elaborated by the old name of *Europe*. But on one occasion at least, he has also advocated the need "to become a bit iconoclastic with regard to the European discourses on today's Europe. Iconoclastic with respect to the names of Europe, in the name of Europe" (*PEF*, 35). Such a breaking with the venerable images or names of Europe is not motivated by an anti-European or anti-Eurocentrist sentiment. On the contrary, it is an operation to be undertaken in the name of what, in Europe, promised itself as the thought of universality and the thought of a world that would be truly hospitable to the foreign. In his contribution to the 1992 conference in Strasbourg, France, "Penser l'Europe à ses frontières," after having admitted that, in a certain way, "Europe today, here and now, comes as much from Auschwitz as it does from Greece, Christianity, the Empires, and the Revolutions of '89 and '17," Derrida broaches the question of the proper name. Certainly, the name *Auschwitz* refers to the effacement of the name, not only insofar as this name has come to substitute itself for other names of disasters, European and non-European alike, thus "re-centering everything, the whole of Europe and of Europe alone, around one crime and one foundational trauma on the basis of which it would identify, reassemble and relate to itself." But, as Derrida points out as well, "Auschwitz is also the effacement of the name, of the proper name in a different sense. Auschwitz has come to signify the project of an annihilation that reduces the possibility of memory, the name, and witnessing to cinders. Today, we pose the question of Europe, of what is called and what one names Europe, from these experiences of the effacement of names—from their happening and their possibility" (*PEF*, 30). As this event of the radical effacement of names, Auschwitz has made manifest "the essential and originary crisis that is opened up by the apprehension of the name," above all, of "Europe" (*PEF*, 33). Indeed, as we have seen at the beginning of this book, "Europe," although a proper name whose referent is a singular and irreplaceable existent, is also in a strange way a common noun, and as such this name carries also an ideal and universal concept which extends well beyond its body (*PEF*, 27). Now, let us remind ourselves that the world is *the* world only if it is the space and time of history, the event of the arrival of the arrivant, and responsibility. For *the* world to be responsive, and hospitable to the alien, the foreigner, the other, this world must not, as we have seen, yield to an enclosing horizon, an archeo-teleological circular history, nor to a name that, in advance, has already decided what this coming world will always already have been. "Europe" is such a "semantico-archeo-teleological" name with which one must break (without forgetting it) "if one wishes (hypothesis) that something happens, and comes . . . that is, if one wishes that something *other* comes, that, consequently, something comes to the other and from the other" (*PEF*, 33–34). An "other experience of the name" rooted in the apprehension of the difference within the name—the difference between the proper name and the common name that meaningfully saturates the singular existent that the proper name refers to—one that thus breaks with its semantico-archeo-teleological saturation of the event and advent of the other, but that does not forget the event, is required for something to happen if there is to be such a thing as an event at all (*PEF*, 34).

Consequently, the name of *Europe* must be maintained to designate the thought of universality, hospitality, and responsibility that arose in

Europe and, drawing on the resources of this tradition, has found its most radical development in the thinkers I have discussed. However, in order for there to be the other and the event, for responsibility, hospitality, and history to take place, the name *Europe* must also be abandoned. Jean-Luc Nancy has proposed "to rename Europe 'Euruopa,' the one that sees far into the distance, to no longer name her" (*PEF*, 15). As the one who looks far ahead, Europe can leave its name and all of its presumed identity behind. Yet, to simply drop Europe's name would also mean to cease being faithful to its memory. In fact, it is not simply a question of either being faithful to the memories of Europe or of preferring the openness of the open to its opposite. Rather, the question is how to meet both contradictory exigencies of preserving and abandoning Europe's name at the same time. Only by simultaneously facing these inexorably aporetic injunctions can there "possibly" be such a thing as *the* world.

Notes

Introduction

1. Such is, for example, the judgment of Gérard Granel in the preface to his French translation of Husserl's work. See Granel, preface to *La Crise des sciences européennes et la phénoménologie transcendantale*; as well as my discussion of Granel's claim in Gasché, "In Light of Light."
2. Lübbe, "Geteilte Souveränität."
3. Undoubtedly, the topos of the critical self-referentiality of European discursive history is a distinguished feature of all the grand discourses about Europe. But rather than pointing to learned references, let me only quote part of a statement by "an elderly Englishman and local resident" in some African country, as reported by Ryszard Kapuściński in his fascinating book *The Shadow of the Sun*:

> His view: That the strength of Europe and of its culture, in contrast to other cultures, lies in its bent for criticism, above all, for self-criticism—in its art of analysis and inquiry, in its endless seeking, in its restlessness. The European mind recognizes that it has limitations, accepts its imperfections, is skeptical, doubtful, questioning. Other cultures do not have this critical spirit. More—they are inclined to pride, to thinking that all that belongs to them is perfect; they are, in short, uncritical in relation to themselves. They consider all criticism to be a malevolent attack, a sign of discrimination, of racism, etc. Representatives of these cultures treat criticism as a personal insult, as a deliberate attempt to humiliate them, as a form of sadism even. If you tell them that the city is dirty, they treat this as if you said that they were dirty themselves, had dirty ears, or dirty nails. (227–28)

Kapuściński, who follows up this evaluation of African culture with the critical question regarding its generalization to all African cultures, has on more than one occasion forcefully put this so-called Western culture of self-criticism radically into question. Indeed, whenever such a culture is made into something that the West has effectively accomplished, it only serves to ideologically buttress superiority and domination. The recent reaction in the United States to the reluctance of "Old Europe" to support the U.S.-led invasion of Iraq is clear proof that lack of self-criticism is just as prevalent in the West as it is in the so-called Third World.

4. For the concept of "Euroanalysis" see Valdinoci, *La traversée de l'immanence.*

5. In his investigation of European anti-Americanism, after having linked the process of critical self-reflection and self-cognition to a comprehensive secularization of life-worlds, Dan Diner singles out the United States, rather than Europe, as the paradigm of universalism and the culture of self-referentiality: America is "properly speaking more a country of humanity than the rest of the world which is primarily formed in particular ways" (Diner, *Feindbild Amerika,* 198–99).

6. Gollwitzer, "Europa."

7. Valéry, *History and Politics,* 323.

8. See the proceedings of a conference on Europe entitled *Penser l'Europe à ses frontières,* 90; hereafter cited parenthetically in the text as *PEF.*

9. Guénoun, *Hypothèses sur l'Europe,* 358. In what sense is *schema* to be understood here? Considering Guénoun's thesis that Europe is synonymous with "world"—world understood exclusively in terms of imperial domination—that is, the world that emerges with Rome, Europe as a schema may have to be understood in light of St. Paul's reference to the *skema* of the world as the figure of that which passes in Corinthians. See in this respect also Brague, *La sagesse du monde,* 84.

10. Derrida, *Demeure,* 19.

11. Aristotle, "Politics," 2107.1327b19–30.

12. See Koslowski and Brague, *Vaterland Europa,* 14.

13. Schulze, "Europa als historische Idee," 3.

14. Di Cesare, "Die Heimat der Verschiedenheit, 109–10.

15. Herodotus, *The Histories,* 285. For a sample of the many representations of this popular myth from antiquity to the Renaissance, see Plessen, *Idee Europa,* 44–53.

16. Guénoun, *Hypothèses sur l'Europe,* 42.

17. The myth of Europa is thus above all a myth of separation and hence coeval with the birth of philosophy as a generalized criticism. See Wismann, "Une introduction," 24.

18. Cited in Rougemont, *The Idea of Europe,* 28.

19. Nancy, "Euryopa" (this essay has also been published in *Terra Lingonna* [Langres: Lycée Diderot, Jan. 1995]). For an extensive discussion of this essay see Gasché, "Alongside the Horizon."

20. Jaspers, "Vom europäischen Geist," 238.

21. Openness to the other, as I will show, is the first characteristic of Europe insofar as its idea includes universality. However, given the current inflationary references to the other—which more often than not are merely moralizing gestures that fetishize the other (or Other) and, at the same time, prevent all exposure by the self by preserving the notion of the subject—it may be well to point out right from the beginning that such openness is understood here in an ontological, and more precisely, structural sense. Openness to the other, thus understood, is constitutive of all ipseity, and for this very reason such openness is also occluded. Since a relation to the other in the sense of a differentiation from the other is a necessary requisite for all identity formation, the self is always already open to the other, although most of the time it is in the mode of a denial of the other. In other words, openness to the other is not of the order of a moralistic demand addressed to a self first enclosed within itself since such self-enclosure and defense against the other already presupposes a primary irruption of the other into the self. Furthermore, as a structural relation to the other, such a relation in no way predicates in advance the nature of the other, who can, indeed, be good or evil.

22. In this respect compare also Derrida's remarks in his contribution to the 1992 conference on Europe in Strasbourg, on the implications of the peculiarity of preceding the proper name *Europe* with a definite article (*l'Europe*, rather than simply *Europe*) in French (*Penser l'Europe à ses frontières*, 24–28).

23. Leibniz, *New Essays Concerning Human Understanding*, 307.

24. Ibid., 308.

25. "Europe is a figure," says Denis Guénoun in *Hypothèses sur l'Europe* (191), which, to my knowledge, is the most elaborated exposition on the concept of figure in relation to Europe. As such, his work would need an extensive discussion, which I cannot undertake here. Guénoun equates "figure" (by which Europe constitutes and sets itself apart from Islam) with the universal (whose idea emerges in Europe) returning to, or folding itself upon itself. He writes: "'Europe' is one of the names of the return of the universal upon itself, that is of the universal as figure" (23).

26. See my "Zur Figur des Archipels."

27. *Penser l'Europe à ses frontières*, 78.

28. "Europe has always been the land of the limit. From the limit one can—to speak with Kant—understand its cosmopolitical viewpoint. Europe has always been in a border situation. It has recognized itself as 'limit,' and, as a result, as the starting point for discoveries and inventions. It recognizes itself as horizon—'horizon' means in Greek 'limit.' From a geographical experience, the experience of the horizon, respectively of the limit, became a philosophical and political experience, and finally an experience of thought" (Di Cesare, "Die Heimat der Verschiedenheit," 121).

29. Weidner, "Vorwort," 17.
30. Simon, "Europa als philosophische Idee," 15.
31. Nancy, "La naissance continuée de l'Europe," 254.

Chapter 1

1. Husserl, *Die Krisis . . . Ergänzungsband*, 108. In this supplementary volume of texts regarding *Die Krisis*, Husserl also points out that "the crisis has its origin in a crisis of the human being's self-understanding" (138). Throughout my notes I will use *Die Krisis . . . Ergänzungsband* to reference Husserl's *Die Krisis der europäischen Wissenschaften und die transzendentale Phänomenologie. Ergänzungsband: Texte aus dem Nachlass, 1934–1937*. I will use *Die Krisis* to reference *Die Krisis der europäischen Wissenschaften und die transzendentale Phänomenologie*.
2. Jacques Derrida has qualified Husserl's inclusion of the English Dominions and the United States within the spiritual shape of Europe, and his exclusion of the Eskimos and gypsies from that shape, as both comic and sinister. Sinister, no doubt, if one considers the date and place at which Husserl delivered the Vienna lecture, comic because, in his case, this reference to Eskimos and gypsies is certainly not a form of racism! (see Derrida, *Of Spirit*, 120–21). It must also be noted, however, that if the English Dominions and the United States constitute elements in the spiritual shape of Europe, "whereas the Eskimos or Indians presented as curiosities at fairs, or the Gypsies, who constantly wander about Europe, do not" (273), it is precisely because Husserl thinks of "Europe" as a life-project around certain tasks and supported by certain institutions. Although his disparaging remarks about the Eskimos, Indians, and gypsies reflect widespread prejudices of the time, they are in no way to be construed as racist. Husserl's rejection of a human zoology in the Vienna lecture categorically eliminates such a possibility. One must thus inquire into what the reasons are for which Husserl may have thought (however unseemly) that Eskimos, Indians, and gypsies are not part of the European life-project. Without taking into account that Europe is a goal to be accomplished, that is, an immanently practical undertaking, these reasons are difficult to understand. Only active and willed participation makes one participate in a practical goal. First, it needs to be remarked that the Eskimos and Indians he excludes are only those who serve as curiosities at fairs. They are not active and creative contributors to the realization of the founding idea of Europe. The gypsies, by contrast, are excluded because by not settling in the cultural and educational institutions through which Europe seeks to realize its idea, they themselves exclude themselves from the task that Europe represents. Still another issue is Husserl's contention in a study from 1934, advanced in the context of a discussion of the question of national and transnational historicity, namely that "a Papua has no biography, and a Papua tribe no life history, no

history of its people, in any serious (strict) sense" (Husserl, *Die Krisis . . . Ergänzungsband*, 56–57). Even though tribes are, in the same way as nations, and supranations, personal unities of a higher order, and thus have history, it is difficult to see why precisely a Papua, and a Papua tribe, should be excluded from this possibility.

3. Although Husserl refers on one occasion to "the two sources of meaning [*Sinnesquellen*] from which European humanity sprang forth in antiquity: Greek philosophy and Jewish-Christian monotheism," *The Crisis*, as well as all the texts written in connection within, highlight only the Greek component. If the Roman-Christian aspect of Europe is mentioned at all—as in the following passage: "The originary inauguration of theory, that is, science in the Greek nation, extends from the whole transnational unity of the Mediterranean world and the expanding Roman state into the Roman-Christian peoples that emerge from it"—it is, it would seem, only to make the religious aspects of Europe subservient to the Greek inaugural event (Husserl, *Die Krisis . . . Ergänzungsband*, 109, 12).

4. The crisis in question is thus not one of the sciences' scientificity and exactitude. Even though they have abandoned all relations to the vital interests of humankind, their exactitude remains without doubt. Nor is Husserl's critique motivated by historical and cultural concerns. It is not a form of cultural criticism. Since what is at stake for Husserl is the self-understanding of humanity, his critique of the sciences is motivated, as Ernst Wolfgang Orth remarks, by the question of the intentionality of life and takes place in view of the intentional self-clarification of subjectivity (see Orth, *Edmund Husserls "Krisis der europäischen Wissenschaften und die transzendentale Phänomenologie,"* 56). For a general discussion of the meaning of *crisis* in this Husserlian work, see also Lübbe, "Husserl und die europäische Krise," 66–67.

5. Husserl writes in the Vienna lecture: "There is something unique here that is recognized in us by all other human groups, too, something that, quite apart from all considerations of utility, becomes a motive for them to Europeanize themselves even in their unbroken will to spiritual self-preservation; whereas we, if we understand ourselves properly, would never Indianize ourselves, for example" (*C*, 275). Easily construed as an example of European arrogance, this passage, when read in context, only says that the "universal" attraction that Europe exercises is due to its spiritual shape, which unsettles the dialectic between the foreign and the familiar. Europeanization is not the same as colonization. If "Europe" signifies transgressing one's customs and traditions toward what is universally human, then there can only be self-Europeanization.

6. Fink, *Studien zur Phänomenologie, 1930–39*, 183.

7. Husserl, *Die Krisis*, 427.

8. Ibid., 393, 485.

9. Even though the Phoenician origins of Thales may only be part of the legend that surrounds the first Greek philosopher, his cosmology drew on a Semitic cosmogony and his astronomical predictions on methods imported from Babylon. Xenophanes and Pythagoras left Greece as a result of the Iranian invasions and the political revolutions to become stateless emigrants or founders of the colonies of Sicily and Italy. As Clémence Ramnoux remarks: "From the great Mileseans on until the third generation of the Pythagoreans and the Eleatics, the Presocratic schools flourished at the extremities of the Greek lands: in close proximity to the Asian civilizations, or very near the Western barbarians. From there, they swept back in groups of friends or individual travelers, to the centers of continental Greece, and especially to Athens" (Ramnoux, "Les Présocratiques," 409).

10. Cohen, *Kommentar zur Kritik der reinen Vernunft*, 161. See also 153, where Cohen speaks of "transcendental tasks." Although the notion of "infinite tasks" cannot explicitly be found in Kant himself, by linking the notion in question, for example, to the categorical imperative, Kant undoubtedly anticipated this terminological formation. (However, the expression "infinite tasks," in conjunction with hermeneutics, is already present in Friedrich Schleiermacher. See Grondin, "Hermeneutik," 1365.) As I have noted, the source of Husserl's concept of infinite tasks is most likely the neo-Kantian interpretation, particularly, by Hermann Cohen, of the "thing-in-itself," who, by not distinguishing between this concept of transcendental aesthetics and the noumenon as a concept of the understanding, interprets the "thing-in-itself" as a task. After having commented in his "*Kommentar zur Kritik der reinen Vernunft*," Kant's statement that "the concept of the noumenon . . . is a task [*Aufgabe*] unavoidably bound up with the limitation of our sensibility" regarding objects that are entirely disconnected from sensible intuition (Kant, *Critique of Pure Reason*, 293; trans. mod.), Cohen characterizes the "thing-in-itself" in exactly the same terms in *Kants Theorie der Erfahrung* (660–61). But the most extensive connection between task and thing-in-itself interpreted as idea, and hence as infinite, occurs in Cohen, *Kants Begründung der Aesthetik*: "The idea is never an appearance, but always a thing-in-itself. Since, furthermore, every idea governs a particular purposiveness, every kind of purposiveness is therefore a particular kind of thing-in-itself. However, the thing-in-itself signifies always a task by which reason limits understanding which without reason would have to recognize its own limits as regards its own tasks. Aesthetic purposiveness represents as well such [a] task in the form of the aesthetic idea, as a 'suprasensible ground,' as a thing-in-itself of consciousness" (208). I thank Juan Manuel Garrido for these references.

11. Indeed, as will become clear, philosophy for Husserl is inextricably linked to the concept of humanity as such. In *The Crisis* he describes "philosophy as a function of the humanization of the human being; as the humanization of 'the

human being in its entirety,' that is, of mankind; as the human being in its final form which, at the same time, is the beginning form for the very first form of development of mankind toward a reason proper to mankind" (Husserl, *Die Krisis*, 429).

12. Undoubtedly, in spite of Husserl's criticism of anthropologism, the very determination of the human being in view of an end, that is, as a being addressed by transcendental telos, qualifies Husserl's thought, as Derrida has pointed out in "The Ends of Man," as a humanism, more specifically, as a transcendental humanism (see Derrida, *Margins of Philosophy*, 122–23). However, given the fact that this telos consists, as we will see, in the infinite task of "universal critique," this transcendental humanism also complexifies from within the metaphysical way of thinking. This reconceptualization of the telos does not, of course, put metaphysics as such into question. It is an intrametaphysical move, one in the name of a general metaphysics.

13. As Françoise Dastur remarks, "the human being is no longer the name for a mundane or natural reality, but the correlate of a teleological project, of an infinite task. In fact, it is a question of philosophical man since the idea of philosophy, that is the project of a universal science, is for Husserl the *telos* of history" (Dastur, *Husserl*, 107).

14. Speaking of the birth of philosophy, Jacques Derrida remarks that one can be in agreement with Husserl and Heidegger that it is born in ancient Greece "as the universal project of a will to deracination. If philosophy has a root (Greece), its project consists at the same time in pulling up the roots and in making it sure that what is thought in Greece—and later in Germany, according to Heidegger—is delivered in 'more than one language.' Philosophy, then, is delivered; it tends at least toward liberating itself, from the start, from its linguistic, territorial, ethnic, and cultural limitations" (Derrida and Roudinesco, *For What Tomorrow . . . A Dialogue*, 18).

15. Husserl, *Die Krisis . . . Ergänzungsband*, 15–16. In response to an easily foreseeable misunderstanding regarding the way he conceives of this expansion of Europe, Husserl writes: "Europe arose from the expansion of the rational internationality of the Roman empire. It was possible to call this expansion a Romanization, which itself included Hellenization by way [of] Hellenistic philosophy. Yet, what thus came into being as a relatively accomplished figure was nonetheless something new, that is, the incorporation [*Aufnahme*] of the thus transformed spirituality of the included nation. In the same way, the expanded Europe will no longer be Europe. And yet, it will be a continuation of what until now has been the fundamental nature of Europe, but also an extraordinary deepening of it" (16).

16. In the same way as "critique," "correction," as a means to achieve adjustments and rectifications, of say, apperceptions, is a distinctively Husser-

lian philosophical and historical concept (see, e.g., Husserl, *Die Krisis*, 501). Regarding Husserl's thesis that the theoretical attitude of the philosopher is the foundation for a new type of community, see also Max Scheler's elaboration on how new "moral value-qualities [can] be comprehended for the first time in history ... in the feeling insight [*fühlende Blicke*] of *a single individual*" and subsequently become binding for everyone, hence universal, without however being therefore universal in the sense of '*Allgemeingültigkeit*'" (Scheler, *Formalism in Ethics and Non-Formal Ethics of Values*, 272–73).

17. The "reorientation" realized by Greece, and as a result of which Greek philosophy turns to "the worldliness of the world, and this in accordance with the latter's double universality—the universality of being and the generality of proprieties that belong to it in totality, and that hence concern all its particularities," is unique, Husserl contends. "The religious contemplation of the world, and even the priesterly speculation about the world that we find in the case of the Oriental peoples, is not that of the *epoche*, and the reorientation of the ways of looking at things that has just been described. This religious contemplation and speculation about the world is 'interested.' Historically speaking it was only a preliminary stage for the breakthrough of Greek 'theoria'" (Husserl, *Die Krisis . . . Ergänzungsband*, 218). For the way in which the breakthrough of philosophy is prepared in myth and religion see also Husserl, "Fünf Ausätze über Erneuerung, 60-72."

18. Even though the idea of universality demands of Europe (as a geographical entity) that it rise above its natural determinations, this idea still merits being called "Europe" since, born in Europe, it concerns the European first of all.

19. For a fine discussion of Husserl's interpretation of the Greek inaugural event see Held, "Husserl und die Griechen."

20. Husserl, "Philosophy as Rigorous Science," 137.

21. Schlegel, *Philosophical Fragments*, 14.

22. Husserl refers already to the philosopher as a functionary of humankind in the *Kaizo* articles (1923). See Gniazdowski, "Phänomenologie und Politik," 76–77.

23. Husserl, *Die Krisis . . . Ergänzungsband*, 237.

24. See *C*, 144. What sets the philosopher apart from the sage of both Greek and non-European extraction is the "vocational," more precisely professional (*Beruf*), nature of philosophical life. In Husserl's repeated reflection on profession, the latter is intimately linked to the temporary suspension in the lifeworld of all concerns other than those demanded by the profession and hence, in the case of the philosophical profession, to the *epoche*.

25. Ogawa, "Eurozentrismus, Eurozentrik und Ent-Europäisierung," 129.

26. Aristotle, "Nicomachean Ethics," 1729.1094a24.

27. Nancy, "Dies Irae," 41–42. In this context see also Heidegger's contention

that *telos* is not a goal or a purpose but must be thought from *peras*, that is, from that within which a movement or an action achieves completion (*Fertigkeit*). See, e.g., Heidegger, *Grundbegriffe der aristotelischen Philosophie*, 38–39, 85.

28. Held, "Heimwelt, Fremdwelt, die eine Welt," 329. Derrida observes that the universal at which philosophy aims "is not a given, the way an essence would be; rather, it announces an infinite process of *universalization*" (Derrida and Roudinesco, *For What Tomorrow*, 18).

29. Husserl, *Die Krisis*, 465. See also the discussion of *doxa* in Landgrebe, *The Phenomenology of Edmund Husserl*, 184–85.

30. Even though Husserl undertakes a reevaluation of *doxa*, in a way reminiscent of Aristotle's defense of *empeiria*, this reevaluation is ambiguous, Bernhard Waldenfels has argued, because it is valorized only in the face of scientific reason. Philosophical reason remains privileged reason. For Husserl it is never a question of granting *doxa* a right of its own, not to speak of a privileged position. See Waldenfels, "Die verachtete Doxa."

31. Biemel, "Zur Bedeutung von Doxa und Episteme im Umkreis der Krisis-Thematik," 18.

32. Schumann, "Lebenswelt als Unterlage der Phänomenologie," 86.

33. Ricoeur, *A l'école de la phénoménologie*, 174.

34. With the thinkers following Husserl (Heidegger, Derrida), the intimate relation between the universal and the particular has become a more central question.

35. See Cacciari, *Der Archipel Europa*, 123–24.

36. Husserl adds: "Through the criticism of theoretical reason, everything becomes relativized. Truth and being receive a new meaning, that of the irrelative 'in-itself.' Traditional norms of all kind are confronted with the objective norm, the norm of objective transnational, all-human truth." For, indeed, "the capacity of reason, or evidence of universal human validity, is the capacity to repeat, account for, and ground [such] validity at will" (Husserl, *Die Krisis . . . Ergänzungsband*, 7, 12, 15).

37. Husserl, *Die Krisis . . . Ergänzungsband*, 228.

38. On this score see Husserl's critique of the Enlightenment understanding of rationalism as based on an objectivistic and naturalistic conception of reason (*C*, 290–94), and from which it follows that genuine rationalism, for him, is based on the practice of self-knowledge (*C*, 297–98). Since rationality requires that any claim must be able to be justified just as much before oneself as before all others, rationality amounts to "nothing other than the extreme radicalism of philosophical self-responsibility" (Husserl, *Die Krisis*, 426). Indeed, in Husserl the question of rationality coincides with one of the apodictic foundations of knowledge.

39. From this fundamental incompletion of the sciences owed to their infinite

desire to cognitively grasp all that is, Jaspers concludes that Europe, insofar as it coincides with the idea of science, "is therefore not complete, and as a result that of which it is fundamentally capable, has always still to show itself" (Jaspers, "Vom europäischen Geist," 246).

40. This double sense of "all-embracing" recoups the double meaning of "universality," when Husserl writes: "Philosophy must be [the] universal science of the world, universal in a double sense—concerned with the universals of the world, and with everything in the worlds—insofar as this makes sense" (Husserl, *Die Krisis*, 497).

41. Ibid., 429–30.
42. Husserl, *Ideas*, 60, 382–83.
43. Husserl, *Die Krisis*, 397.
44. Ibid., 426, 430.
45. Ibid., 426.
46. Ibid., 428.
47. Ibid., 423.
48. Ibid., 427.
49. Ricoeur, *Husserl*, 160.
50. Held, "Husserls These von der Europäisierung der Menschheit," 17–18.
51. Held, "Heimwelt, Fremdwelt, die eine Welt," 305–6.

Chapter 2

1. The naivete of Greek philosophy is that of its objectivism, but, as Husserl points out, this objectivism differs from that of the modern sciences. See Husserl, *Die Krisis . . . Ergänzungsband*, 161–62.

2. Husserl, *Die Krisis*, 483; see also 455.

3. For further distinction between imaginary ideality of the morphological type in the pregeometrical life-world and the ideality of pure geometry, see Derrida, *Edmund Husserl's Origin of Geometry*, 122–26, 133.

4. Husserl makes the distinction when he writes: "What arises first is the idea of continuation which is repeatable with unconditional generality, with its own self-evidence, as a freely thinkable and self-evident possible infinity, rather than the open endlessness [of 'imperfect but perfectible subjective representations' of, for example, an individual thing]: rather than finite iteration, this is iteration within the sphere of the unconditional 'again-and-again,' of what can be renewed with ideal freedom" (*C*, 346).

5. For the connection between idealization, objectification, and method see, e.g., *C*, 348.

6. In the appendix "The Origin of Geometry," it is made clear that the very formal-logical self-evidence of all the geometrical propositions that Galileo in-

herited relieved him from the need to reactivate the actual, that is, the truth-meaning, of geometry (see *C,* 366–67).

7. For a discussion of the notion of the abstract in Husserl see Kuhn, "The Phenomenological Concept of 'Horizon,'" 117.

8. Derrida, *Edmund Husserl's Origin of Geometry,* 127. Indeed, in the Vienna lecture Husserl asserts that in the mathematics of antiquity "was accomplished the first discovery of both infinite ideals and infinite tasks. This becomes for all later times the guiding star of the sciences" (*C,* 293). For a discussion of this apparent contradiction see Derrida, *Edmund Husserl's Origin of Geometry,* 127–41. He writes: "despite the closedness of the system, we are *within* mathematical infinity because we have definitively idealized and gone beyond the factual and sensible finitudes. The infinite infinity of the modern revolution can then be announced in the finite infinity of Antiquity's creation" (*C,* 130).

9. Throughout *The Crisis* Husserl portrays Galileo as the founder of the modern sciences. If Johannes Kepler's, René Descartes', Christiaan Huygens's, Robert Boyle's, and Isaac Newton's (to name a few) contributions are not mentioned, it is because Husserl subsumes their philosophical theories, mathematical innovations, and new observations under the one name "Galileo." For this reason scholars of the history of the sciences have more often than not questioned the accuracy of Husserl's account of the genesis of modern science. Indeed, the historians of the sciences have objected to the privilege accorded to Galileo. It has been argued that Galileo's real accomplishment does not consist in the mathematization of nature, as Husserl contends, but in the discovery of the relativity of movement and rest. Furthermore, as François De Gandt has pointed out, Husserl draws his knowledge about Galileo "from a Galilean vulgate of sorts that was prevalent at his time, and which was strongly marked by Neo-Kantianism, by way of Hermann Cohen, Paul Natorp, and Ernst Cassirer" (De Gandt, *Husserl et Galilée,* 97–98). Hence, the "objectivist" depiction of Galileo's conception of nature with which Husserl takes issue throughout the book, at the expense of Galileo's novel openness to the sensible world, and its enrichment through observation and verification. In light of all of this it is therefore necessary to strongly stress that Husserl's account, in *The Crisis,* of the birth of the new sciences, in which the discussion of Galileo dominates at the expense of equally important and perhaps, from a historical perspective, more important figures is not at all intended as a history of the sciences or a mundane history of ideas. Indeed, the history developed in part 2 of *The Crisis* is a history executed in a transcendental-phenomenological attitude, as Elisabeth Ströker notes—that is, "a limine a history within the frame of the already presupposed phenomenological epoche" (Ströker, "Geschichte und Lebenswelt als Sinnesfundament der Wissenschaften in Edmund Husserls Spätwerk," 113). Husserl's inquiry into the ways Galilean science, which he construes as the completion of the efforts

of various thinkers, such as Vieta, who preceded him (whom Husserl singles out because, according to De Gandt, in contrast to others, the latter achieved a higher level of abstraction and formalism), and in which the name "Galileo" does not primarily refer to the historical figure but serves as a designation for an epochal state of mind, is one into "the way of thinking which motivates the idea of the new physics" (*C*, 33), its presupposed self-evidences, and "undetermined general anticipations a priori" (*C*, 36), in short, into the subjective processes of this creation. Husserl writes: "Our concern is to achieve complete clarity on the idea and task of a physics which in its Galilean form originally determined modern philosophy, [to understand it] as it appeared in Galileo's own motivation, and to understand what flowed into this motivation from what was traditionally taken for granted and thus remained an unclarified presupposition of meaning, as well as what was later added as seemingly obvious, but which changed its actual meaning." Thus Husserl can conclude that "in this connection it is not necessary to go more concretely into the first beginnings of the enactment of Galileo's physics and of the development of its method" (*C*, 42–43). Inquiring into the intentional structures and the original evidences that constituted the new scientific spirit, the mathematization of nature appears as the very precondition on the basis of which experimentation and the discovery of the relativity of movement and rest acquire their scientific significance in the first place. To claim that Husserl misrepresents Galileo's achievement misses out on the thrust of Husserl's analysis, the philosophically innovative aspects of his account of the fundamental evidences constitutive of the modern sciences.

10. Holding that the sciences and their history are grounded in the life-world does not amount to relativizing them "in the sense of a social or just epistemological constructivism." As Hans-Jörg Rheinberger has argued, Husserl's aim in grounding the sciences in the life-world is the establishment of a "historical epistemology" (as opposed to pure history of science), an aim that shows Husserl in the proximity of the work of Ludwik Fleck (Rheinberger, "Zur Historizität wissenschaftlichen Wissens," 34–36).

11. Husserl, *Die Krisis . . . Ergänzungsband*, 122.

12. Derrida, *Edmund Husserl's Origin of Geometry*, 71–72.

13. Husserl writes that "the perfection-limit of the secondary qualities is not measurable; it is only 'intuitable.' But it is intersubjectively determined and determinable through relation to the mathematical limits of the primary characteristics" (*C*, 310).

14. Paul Ricoeur also remarks that in spite of its geniality Galileo's "working hypothesis, for lack of self-criticism, is not recognized [by Galileo] as the audacity of spirit at work. Soon this 'indirect mathematization of nature' could verify itself only by the success of its extension, without which the circle of hypo-

thetical anticipation and unending verification could never be broken, for every enigma of induction is inscribed within this circle" (Ricoeur, *Husserl*, 163).

15. Let me also point out that if the natural sciences achieve compelling apodicticity regarding the idealized spatiotemporal shapes by grounding them logically, it is to be assumed that in the case of idealities that are no longer of the order of bodily shapes, their universal reconstructability may have to have recourse to other than logical means.

16. Husserl, *Die Krisis . . . Ergänzungsband*, 178.

17. Undoubtedly, as a whole, Husserl's *Crisis* cannot be correctly understood without taking the part titled "The Way into Phenomenological Transcendental Philosophy from Psychology" into account. In spite of a number of difficulties, if not even aporias and paradoxes, that characterize Husserl's last way into transcendental philosophy, its argument parallels that of the first way but culminates in an original conclusion not found in the first part, namely that "the transcendental ego is not just 'another' ego besides or above, as it were, the empirical ego. Rather it is me as transcendental ego, that, after all, is 'the same ego that in the worldly sphere is a human ego.' . . . For that both are 'the same' means, if we follow Husserl's ways of thought more closely, nothing but that I as transcendental ego am only a specific kind of living my factual ego myself" (Ströker, "Psychologie," 84). I add to this that it is precisely this "identification" of transcendental and empiricopsychological ego that forcefully brings to bear the tendentially universal structures associated with the transcendental ego—and hence also the ethical demands that come with these structures—on the empirical ego.

Chapter 3

1. Husserl distinguishes between free and bound idealities in *Experience and Judgment*, 267. See also Dastur, *Husserl*, 111.

2. Husserl, "Philosophy as Rigorous Science," 147.

3. See Kern, "Die Lebenswelt als Grundlagenproblem der objektiven Wissenschaften und als universales Wahrheits- und Seinsproblem," 69. Let me also point out that the term *life-world* can be found as early as 1921 in Heidegger. In his lectures from 1921 and 1922, the "life-world," which is said to be experienced in the shape of either Dasein's *Umwelt*, *Mitwelt*, or *Selbstwelt*, is a term that comprises also all of these different worlds. See Heidegger, *Phänomenologische Interpretationen zu Aristoteles*, 94.

4. Husserl, *Formal and Transcendental Logic*, 292.

5. Ricoeur, *A l'école de la phénoménologie*, 292. Not unlike the analytic of Dasein, which Heidegger develops in *Being and Time* only as far as is required by the leading question of the inquiry—the question of Being—Husserl does not

aim at unfolding a full-fledged exposition of the life-world. As is quite clear from chapter 51 of *The Crisis*, no "ontology of the life-world" is intended.

6. Husserl writes that all scientific judgments "are judgments based on the ground of the life-world, that is to say, on the ground of a universal validity concerning what is. This universal validity is produced through a life of validity of subjects (which is constantly in motion), together with the certitude that comes with it, and which validates through all experiences and validation of experience" (Husserl, *Die Krisis*, 465).

7. Let me also point out that the life-world remains "constantly in the validity of being." It is "the permanent foundation of knowledge [*Gewissheitsgrund*]" and is known as such. It is, therefore, "as far as its being is concerned, not the object of an *epoche*" (Husserl, *Die Krisis*, 398–400).

8. Let me also add here that Husserl does not valorize the life-world as a richer world that would have been lost as a result of the developing sciences and that would need to be retrieved again. Hans Blumenberg writes: "Wenn Husserl den Sinn der europäischen Geistesgeschichte darin sieht, 'die universale Selbstverständlichkeit des Seins der Welt . . . in eine Verständlichkeit zu verwandeln' (VI, 184) und seine Phänomenologie von ihm als Erfüllung dieses Geschichtssinnes ausgegeben wird, und zwar gerade als 'Auflösung der Selbstverständlichkeiten . . . in ihre transzendentalen Fraglichkeiten' (VI, 187), dann kann eben für ihn die Lebenswelt als das Universum, sich behauptender Selbstverständlichkeiten keinen Heilssinn haben." And: "Die Lebenswelt hat also keineswegs die Fülle und Üppigkeit eines mythischen Paradieses und nicht die dazu gehörige Unschuld" (Blumenberg, *Wirklichkeiten in denen wir leben*, 23–25).

9. Ströker, "Geschichte und Lebenswelt als Sinnesfundament der Wissenschaften in Edmund Husserls Spätwerk," 117.

10. In the appendices to *The Crisis* devoted to Descartes, Husserl clearly demarcates his conception of *epoche* from Descartes' universal doubt and remarks that the *epoche* "is not universal doubt, which no one is capable or powerful enough to enact in any serious way." "A truly universal doubt concerning the world is out of [the] question," Husserl remarks. Compared to Descartes' method of doubt, the method of the *epoche* is "a purified Cartesian method" (Husserl, *Die Krisis*, 407–9). Rather than deciding on being or nonbeing, "the uncomparable significance" of the *epoche* consists in a disregard (*Absehen*), or abstention (*Enthaltung*), "from the total validity of the world with all the values that this includes, whether experiential or cognitive; from all interests, and all acts that relate to something in the world, or are to be related to the world, and that therefore belong themselves as such to the world." In other words, taking no account of, or holding off, the naive and straightforward positioning of the world, the *epoche* permits shifting one's attention to the acts of consciousness

by which the world is constituted, and to discover something that is not of the order of the world itself, namely, "the pure ego" (ibid., 410, 469, 410).

11. Yet, as Husserl also remarks, the theories that the sciences produce through a "continued building-up of activities" acquire "the character of validities for the life-world, adding themselves as such to its own composition and belonging to it even before that as a horizon of possible accomplishments for developing science" (*C*, 131). On how science becomes incorporated into the life-world, see Ströker, "Geschichte und Lebenswelt als Sinnesfundament der Wissenschaften in Edmund Husserls Spätwerk," 121. As this interacting between the concrete life-world, as "the grounding soil" (*C*, 131) of the sciences, and the sciences themselves suggests, the concept "life-world" is multifaceted.

12. The subjective a priori structures that Husserl unearths are anything but subjective and relative. They are the "objective" par excellence, in a sense, however, that necessarily differs from what *objective* means in the sciences.

13. Husserl, *Die Krisis . . . Ergänzungsband*, 183.

14. The reflective attitude is made possible by waking life in the life-world, but it also implies a complete reorientation of interest—a reorientation that makes the world-horizon thematic as such.

15. Husserl, *Die Krisis . . . Ergänzungsband*, 93.

16. Let me also mention that critique is involved in the formation of the ego's identity. Pointing to the essential role that temporalization occupies for the ego's identity, Husserl writes that as "now actually present," the ego is temporalized in that it "has contact with its past ego, even though the latter is precisely no longer present: it can have a dialogue with it and critique it, as it can others" (*C*, 172).

17. Husserl, *Die Krisis*, 415.

18. See ibid., 416–17.

19. Husserl's claim that the primal "I" of the *epoche* constitutes intersubjectivity, adding itself to it merely as a privileged member, "namely as the I *of* the transcendental Others [*als Ich der transzendentalen Andern*]," that is, as the "I" that constitutes the transcendental Others, implies that each "I" itself must, freely one could say, constitute "in itself an other as other" (*C*, 185). This constitution of the other, which, as various analyses in *The Crisis* suggest, takes place in analogy to the ways in which an actual "I" constitutes "itself in self-temporalization as enduring through 'its' pasts" (*C*, 185), rather than encroaching on the other, throws the recognition of the other onto the self and turns it into a task, an infinite task, at that, if the other is to be recognized in its otherness.

20. As Derrida has pointed out, Husserl's renewed concept of universal form remains caught within metaphysics because this new concept is attained through an analysis of the ego. See Derrida, "Form and Meaning," 158, 169, 172.

21. Supposing that one continues to think in periods, or epochs, would Derrida's thought not have to be construed as opening up a third epoch of infinity,

one following the mathematical infinite, including that of Husserl's infinite rational tasks? But Derrida's structural or infrastructural conception of the infinite may make it impossible to speak of it as inaugurating a new epoch.

Chapter 4

1. For a detailed history of both terms see Köhler, "Abendland."
2. Heidegger, *Zu Hölderlin*, 160.
3. Apart from standing in no relation of contrast to the Orient, because the Occident must be understood in the perspective of the history of Being, the Orient, or rather what has become of it, no longer differs in an essential manner from the Occident. Kah Kyung Cho writes: "The Occident does not stand in opposition to the Orient insofar as the latter has also been overcome by the planetary phenomenon of 'world-darkening,' or the desertion of Being. One could even speak of an Orient that has become 'occidental' insofar as its venerable tradition has been replaced by the uniform power of technology and the usual phenomena of the rule of subjectivity" (Cho, "Der Abstieg über den Humanismus," 159).
4. Heidegger, *Zu Hölderlin*, 157. See also 146, where Heidegger writes: "Destiny [*Geschick*] is the sending [*Schickung*] from the Orient into the Occident."
5. It is in this sense that one may have to understand Heidegger's remark to Elisabeth Blochmann that "the 'Occident' [had] come probably already to an end [*untergegangen*] at a time when no one yet spoke of it. For a long time other 'powers' are *real*." These powers are the powers of technology. Heidegger continues: "Yet the question remains whether this reality is a beginning or only the end of a process which has determined the age of modernity for three centuries" (Heidegger and Blochmann, *Briefwechsel, 1918–1969*, 92).
6. Heidegger, *Denkerfahrungen, 1910–1976*, 21.
7. In a lecture from 1936 Heidegger singles out two things on which the possibility of saving Europe rests: apart from overcoming their own rootlessness and fragmentation, "the European peoples have to be protected from the Asiatic." If German philosophy is in a privileged position as far as the task of saving Europe is concerned, it is because, notwithstanding its elaboration of modern mathematical thought in the shape of the systems of Idealism, the most intrinsic trait of German philosophy consists in its attempt to establish an originary point of departure for philosophy's first question about Being (Heidegger, "Europa und die deutsche Philosophie," 31, 40). But if this thrust of German philosophical thought leads it consistently back to the inception of philosophy in Greece, it is not only because the question of Being emerges with the early Greek thinkers but also because of the separation from the Asiatic that comes with this question upon which the Occident is grounded. Following a long tradition that has

determined the West's specificity by demarcating it from the Asiatic, Heidegger remarks that "'Heraclitus' is the name of an originary power of the occidental-Germanic historical Dasein, that is, as regards its first confrontation [*Auseinandersetzung*] with the 'Asiatic.'" It comes therefore as no surprise if the notion of destiny (*Schicksal*) to be found in Hölderlin's thought is also said to be "a creative overcoming of the Asiatic representation of destiny" (*HHGR*, 134, 173).

8. Heidegger, *Zu Hölderlin*, 141.
9. According to Heidegger, Spengler not only "calculated [*errechnet*]" the decline of the Western world, but his very conception of decline is one of calculating thought (*EGT*, 17; the translator renders the German *errechnet* with "predicted").
10. Heidegger, *Heraklit*, 65.
11. Heidegger, *Zu Hölderlin*, 140, 157.
12. Heidegger, *On the Way to Language*, 194.
13. Heidegger, *What Is Called Thinking?* 70.
14. Cited from *EGT*, 17.
15. Heidegger, *What Is Called Thinking?* 178.
16. Heidegger, *On the Way to Language*, 16 (see also 15).
17. Dastur, "Europa und der 'andere Anfang,'" 195.
18. In this context also see "*Spiegel* Interview with Martin Heidegger." Even though in what follows I will show that, notwithstanding the presence in Heidegger's thought of certain themes consonant with Nazi ideology and discourse (for example, *Volk*, historicality, community, Earth), or his sharp criticism of certain assumptions or positions (for instance, the demand of universality or the idea of cosmopolitism), these themes and criticisms are considerably more complex than his hurried critics hold (critics, who eager to dismiss his thought as fascist, or fascistic, disregard the philosophical nature of Heidegger's thought). This is in no way an attempt to exonerate or to minimize any of his political aberrations. Nor is such complexification in any way indicative of a lessened critical vigilance, of a desire to depict Heidegger as simply an opponent of the movement. Indeed, as Domenico Losurdo has recalled, National Socialism was never a monolithic movement or ideology. He argues compellingly for the necessity "to break with the stereotype of an ideological monolithism of the Nazi regime and to bring out its internal contradictions because it is only on this basis that one can understand the relation that Heidegger entertains with the political reality of his time" (Losurdo, *Heidegger et l'idéologie de la guerre*, 146). Consequently, if after 1935 Heidegger takes on positions that seem to contradict Nazi ideology, this does not yet imply per se that he is critical of the movement as a whole but possibly only of important cultural trends within Nazism itself, which, in his view, may have held the movement hostage.
19. Riedel, "Heideggers europäische Wendung," 48.

20. Although Heidegger's disagreement with the movement bore from the beginning on the question of racism, it broadened after the turn, as is evidenced from the *Introduction to Metaphysics*, but also from the debate with Nietzsche in his lectures of the late 1930s and early 1940s, a debate that includes almost all other aspects of National Socialism. Yet as Philippe Lacoue-Labarthe rightly remarks: "But the unacceptable did not prevent compromises, and he compromised with a 'movement' for which anti-Semitism was a fundamental principle, not the product of some ideological excrescence with which one might choose to agree or disagree" (Lacoue-Labarthe, *Heidegger, Art and Politics*, 33).

21. See Lefort, "L'imaginaire de la crise," 535.

22. Derrida, *Of Spirit*, 60–61.

23. Derrida, *Rogues*, 124–25.

24. For an excellent discussion of Heidegger's account of the notion of crisis from *Being and Time* to "The End of Philosophy and the Task of Thinking," in which he explicitly takes issue with the Husserlian conception of crisis, see Baas, "De Husserl à Heidegger: l'épuisement critique de la raison," unpublished manuscript.

25. Heidegger, "The Time of the World Picture," 133.

26. If it is true that after World War II Heidegger no longer refers to Germany (and only rarely to Europe), but more generally to the Occident, the finitist logic—which, as we will see, links the question of Being to an always singular articulation by a specific historical Dasein—remains the same.

27. Since both Greek and German are not just any languages among others—indeed, in the *Introduction to Metaphysics* these two languages are said to be the most spiritual—Heidegger's foregrounding of the thought of Being in language and the history of a peoples is not in any way relativistic. However, it is not therefore necessarily Eurocentric. On this account see Derrida, *Of Spirit*, 69–72.

28. For the history of this other concept of universality, to which Heidegger thought Being must be related, see Courtine, "Un peuple métaphysique."

29. For Heidegger the other great beginnings are thus not incommensurate with the Greek beginning. By contrast, Derrida, as we will see, acknowledges the possibility of heterogeneous beginnings, as well as of (unpredictable) beginnings still to come, and ties the openness of such beginnings to the very responsibilities of "Europe."

30. As early as the Freiburger lectures, questionableness is linked to Dasein's self-illumination. See, for example, the lectures from 1921 to 1922, where Heidegger writes: "The proper foundation of philosophy is the radical existential seizing and temporalization of questionableness; to put oneself as well as life, including the decisive effectuations into questionableness is the fundamental seiz-

ing of all radical illumination" (Heidegger, *Phänomenologische Interpretationen zu Aristoteles*, 35).

31. In fact, as Heidegger remarks in the *Introduction to Metaphysics*, the question of what humanity is and what historically it has to be can only be asked within the context of the question of Being itself (*IM*, 152–53).

32. See, for example, *Hölderlins Hymnen "Germanien" und "Der Rhein,"* where Heidegger, speaking of the question of Being, refers to Being as "the strangeness of the questionworthy" (*HHGR*, 270). If this question requires a radical break with everything customary, and particularly with the homely, it does not necessarily give rise to an uprootedness (*Bodenlosigkeit*). In anticipation of what I will demonstrate, being at home in unhomeliness is, paradoxically, the only authentic way to have roots.

33. The category of history, and by implication the category of particularity (as opposed to universalism), has been, as Losurdo has shown in *Heidegger et l'idéologie de la guerre*, part and parcel of the ideology of war that arose in Germany (though not in Germany alone) during World War I and later became, in a radicalized form, an essential ingredient of Nazism. According to Losurdo, Heidegger's insistent concern with history and historicality remains indebted to this ideology. But the history and historicality of which Heidegger speaks, which binds the thrust of the universal, is in no way that of a particularity—*völkisch*, for example—of an empirically concrete tradition with its particular customs and habits, be it that of the Greeks or Germans.

34. In an addendum to the Parmenides lectures (1942–43), after having said that "modern man is by essence the 'subject,'" Heidegger writes: "Only because he is the 'subject' can his I or his Ego become essential. And the fact that a Thou is set in opposition to the I, thereby relegating the I to its limits and raising the I-Thou relation to prominence, and the fact that the place of the individual is then taken by the community, the nation, the people, the continent, and the planet, these in no way, metaphysically speaking, cancel out the subjectivity of modern man, but in fact for the first time lead it into its unconditioned state" (*P*, 165). See also, in "Letter of Humanism," the remark that "every nationalism is metaphysically an anthropologism, and as such subjectivism" (*BW*, 221). It is also rather ironic that while Heidegger is frequently criticized for not having paid much attention in his analysis of Dasein to the individual's status as a member of a community, he is also criticized for his concern with the "people." Undoubtedly, at the time this was a highly charged concept, and Heidegger's attempt to reinterpret it according to the analysis of Dasein was politically naive. Few critics, however, have been sensitive to how the analytic of Dasein informs and inflects Heidegger's conception of this notion. By contrast, for a superb analysis of the history of the notion of a people in Heidegger's work, and of how

from the beginning it is thought in terms of Dasein, see Phillips, *Heidegger's Volk*.

35. Heidegger writes: "Only a historical people is truly a people. However, it is historical only when it takes place [*geschieht*] from out of the ground of the center of Being, when the between is there, when demigods, the creators, bring about the happening as history [*das Geschehen als Geschichte*]" (*HHGR*, 284).

36. Heidegger still uses this same image of Europe's lying between the pincers of America and Russia in a letter from 1952 to Hannah Arendt: "The world is increasingly becoming darker. Here quarrelsomeness is tantamount. Given the disastrous situation within the great pincers one would expect something different. 'Europe' is merely a name to which one can barely give any content anymore" (Arendt and Heidegger, *Briefe, 1925–1975*, 137–38).

37. In "Letter on Humanism" (1946) Heidegger writes that "whoever takes 'communism' only as a 'party' or a 'Weltanschauung' is thinking too shallowly, just as those who by the term 'Americanism' mean, and mean derogatorily, nothing more than a particular lifestyle." Rather both *Americanism* and *communism* have to be understood world-historically, that is, in relation to "world" as the opening in which the human being is in the nearness of Being. However, in contrast to the lectures from 1935, in which both America and Russia are accused of involving a loss of world, the "Letter on Humanism" makes a distinction in that in communism, insofar as it seeks to overcome the human being's alienation or estrangement, "an elemental experience of what is world-historical speaks out," in that in it, undoubtedly, a glimpse of what *world* means for Being-human occurs. The danger that Europe faces also differs slightly here from the assessment of 1935: "The danger into which Europe as it has hitherto existed is ever more clearly forced consists presumably in the fact above all that its thinking—once its glory—is falling behind in the essential course of dawning world destiny which nevertheless in the basic traits of its essential provenance remains European by definition." The danger into which Europe is forced concerns primarily its impotence to address in a thinking manner the dawning world destiny of a loss of world in general, and this, above all, is because its forms of thinking are metaphysical. Even though the world destiny in question remains European, metaphysics as the Western mode of thought, for essential reasons, is incapable of achieving this task of coming to grips with this destiny that is in the making, because it is an inability that arises from its own European essence. "No metaphysics, whether idealistic, materialistic, or Christian, can in accord with its essence [*ihrem Wesen nach*], and surely not in its own attempts to explicate itself, 'get a hold on' this destiny yet, and that means thoughtfully to reach and gather together what in the fullest sense of Being now is." Unlike the 1935 claim that salvation can come exclusively from the center of Europe, Heidegger now anticipates help from outside of Europe (*BW*, 220–21).

38. Except for the ominous passage toward the end of the 1935 lectures (in which Heidegger, in the context of a discussion critical of the *Wertphilosophien* of the time, as well as of "what is peddled about nowadays as the philosophies of National Socialism," invokes "the inner truth and greatness of [the] movement [namely, the encounter between global technology and modern humanity]" [*IM*, 213]), Heidegger is, in *Introduction to Metaphysics*, critical, at least in an implicit fashion, of Nazism. Indeed, if Germany is characterized as being caught in the pincers of America and Russia, of technologization and mass organization respectively, everything that is established about both powers, in particular, the loss of distance, the vanishing of history from all Dasein of the people, the triumph of mass meetings, and the acceptance of a boxer (the reference is most likely to the legendary heavyweight champion Max Schmeling, a cult figure during the Weimar Republic, who was also embraced by Hitler—who, in *Mein Kampf,* glorified boxing) as a great man of the people, applies to Nazi Germany (see *IM*, 40). What happens in Nazi Germany is nothing less than the simultaneous Americanization and Bolshevikization of Europe. In the context of a discussion of the different ways in which spirit has become disempowered, Heidegger's critical account of the misinterpretation of spirit as intelligence, that is, as a tool in the service of something else, "whose handling can be taught and learned," is of particular interest here. He writes: "Whether this service of intelligence now relates to the regulation and mastery of the material relations of production (as in Marxism) or in general to the clever ordering and clarification of everything that lies before us and is already posited (as in positivism) [hence, as in America], or whether it fulfils itself in organizing and directing the vital resources and race of a people [*Lebensmasse und Rasse eines Volkes*]—be this as it may, the spirit as intelligence becomes the powerless superstructure to something else, which, because it is spirit-less or even hostile to spirit, counts as authentic reality" (49). In other words, Marxism, positivism, and Nazi ideology (since the reference to "the vital resources and race of a people" is a clear reference to Nazism) are, metaphysically speaking, the same and share the same misinterpretation of spirit. What is at work in all three is what Heidegger will characterize as the demonic, the unleashed power of the average, the mediocre, and the indifferent that has become autonomous. Consequently, the so-called inner truth and greatness of National Socialism is restricted to its beginning only. Undoubtedly, this notorious statement—in the same way as the reference in the lectures of *Hölderlin's Hymn "The Ister"* (1942) to "the historical uniqueness" (*HHI*, 80) and "historical singularity" (*HHI*, 86) of National Socialism—must be interpreted in the context of Heidegger's understanding of what constitutes a beginning. However, the question to be asked here concerns Heidegger's conviction that, in principle, a beginning was made with National Socialism that was subsequently betrayed by the movement itself. Indeed, what possibly could have motivated Heidegger

to believe that National Socialism at one point had the status of a "beginning" that was necessarily great? It is this belief by Heidegger in a truth of fascism that motivated Philippe Lacoue-Labarthe to speak of Heidegger's "archi-fascism," which Heidegger then opposes to real fascism (Lacoue-Labarthe, *Heidegger and the Politics of Poetry*, 66).

39. This assessment changes as the later Heidegger recognizes several great beginnings, in "Hölderlin's Earth and Heaven," but as well in the *Spiegel* interview, where he acknowledges that change may even come from Russia or China.

40. See Riedel, "Heideggers europäische Wendung," 53. Originally, however, this reference to a people of the middle concerns the people of ancient Greece (distinct from Europe). According to Aristotle, within the habitable world the states of Greece lie in the middle, between those who live in Europe ("full of spirit, but wanting in intelligence and skill; and therefore . . . retain comparative freedom, but have no political organization, and are incapable of ruling over others") and the natives of Asia (who are "intelligent and inventive, but . . . are wanting in spirit, and therefore . . . always in a state of subjection and slavery"). Aristotle, "Politics," 7.7.20–24.

41. See Lacoue-Labarthe, *Heidegger, Art and Politics*, 78–95.

42. Volpi, "Heidegger et la romanité philosophique," 11.

43. See also Derrida's analysis of this definition of *spirit* in the Rectorship Address, particularly his comments on Heidegger's "politics" of the quotation marks with respect to the notion of spirit, in Derrida, *Of Spirit*, 37–46, 66–67.

Chapter 5

1. See also Heidegger, *Über den Anfang*.

2. This un-Greek manner of thinking Greece is, first and foremost, Roman. See, e.g., *HHI*, 54.

3. See, in particular, Lacoue-Labarthe, *Poétique de l'histoire*, 22–24.

4. Ricoeur, "Note introductive," 17.

5. Franco Volpi, by contrast, argues that the question of "philosophical Romanity" is not "a *de facto* question to which one could respond by referring to the historical reality and importance of the philosophical Roman and Latin tradition, but, rather, a *de jure* question, or a question *de possibilitate*. It is a question of knowing which kind of legitimacy and possibility there is within the specific horizon of the Latin and the Romanist languages for a thinking that claims to be *philosophical*, and which, as such appropriates an originary Greek tradition, transforming it by way of another language and integrating it into another civilization" (Volpi, "Heidegger et la romanité philosophique, 5–6). However, if the Latin world already presupposes the birth of philosophy in Greece, does it not follow from this that any new philosophical beginning in the Roman

or Latin tradition is either a fall away from the former or, if it is a *philosophical* beginning, the same Greek beginning all over again? If it is as originary as the Greek beginning, it cannot, strictly speaking, be a philosophical beginning. It can only be another beginning.

6. A different question concerns the extent to which the Jewish-Christian tradition had first to be assimilated by the Greek tradition, before it could become an intrinsic part of Europe—as is, in particular, the case in Jan Patočka's *Plato and Europe*. See Dastur, "Europa und der 'andere Anfang,'" 189. See also Held, "Europa und die interkulturelle Verständigung," 98, on the two beginnings of Europe, the Greek and the Roman-Latin; as well as Chiereghin, "Der griechische Anfang Europas und die Frage der Romanitas," 205–7.

7. However, it remains the case that the priority Heidegger assigns to the Greek moment in the history of Europe, and that is seen as preferable to the Roman moment that follows it, is established postfactum. As a consequence, the Greek moment cannot but be haunted by what impoverishes it, and even betrays it.

8. It is possible to object, as Lacoue-Labarthe has, to Heidegger's understanding of what constitutes a beginning on the basis that such a beginning corresponds to the way he conceived of the National Socialist revolution. But is not such a conception of what constitutes a beginning a necessary ingredient of any "revolution" in the modern sense, that is, in conformity with the American and French revolutions? As Hannah Arendt has argued, revolution in the modern sense implies as an essential trait the experience of beginning something radically new, i.e., a pathos of novelty. She writes: "Only where this pathos of novelty is present and where novelty is connected with the idea of freedom are we entitled to speak of revolution" (Arendt, *On Revolution*, 34). Indeed, is not such a concept of a beginning a necessity of thought? If a beginning is indeed to be a beginning, it must be a radical break with everything that precedes it. From the level of principle, such a conception of the beginning can only be opened to questioning through an inquiry into the structural traits that limit its range from within such a beginning and require its opening up to something other than itself.

9. In the same way as in Husserl, in whose work it cannot be a question of a servile reproduction of the Greek beginning, given that this beginning is precisely the advent of universal critique, the German people are not simply to imitate what emerged in Greece because what emerged there was the possibility of a transgression of all pregiven models. If, indeed, Heidegger can be seen to follow in the footsteps of the Reformation, which rejected the neoclassical or the Latin imitation of Antiquity, as Philippe Lacoue-Labarthe has shown, it is also the case that the way the Germans are to be Greeks must, according to the Greek model, be free of both this Greek model and of all other cultural para-

digms (Lacoue-Labarthe, *Heidegger, Art and Politics*, 78–79). How such a radical rejection of all influences, admixtures, etc. could condition a radical openness to otherness remains to be seen.

10. Zarader, *The Unthought Debt*, 86, 124–25.

11. Heidegger, *Nietzsche*, 4:100. As Marramao points out, Heidegger's understanding of the new world of the modern age in terms of nihilism shows that, rather than inquiring into the religious roots of modern humanism and historicism, as Karl Löwith had proposed in *Meaning and History*, he is exclusively concerned with its metaphysical origin (Marramao, *Die Säkularisierung der westlichen Welt*, 97). Let me also point out that Hannah Arendt voices a critique similar to Heidegger's when she writes: "Whatever the word 'secular' is meant to signify in current usage, historically it cannot possibly be equated with worldliness; modern man at any rate did not gain this world when he lost the other world" (Arendt, *The Human Condition*, 320).

12. Heidegger, *1. Nietzsches Metaphysik. 2. Einleitung in die Philosophie*, 108.

13. See also Volpi, "Heidegger et la romanité philosophique," 16.

14. For a discussion of how successful Heidegger is in dechristianizing fundamental ontology and what he calls thinking, see Derrida, *Of Spirit*; and Derrida, *The Gift of Death*. See also Didier Franck's discussion not only of Heidegger's frequent recourse to Christian thought (and Latin language) to gain access to Greek thought properly speaking, in particular, to the ontological difference. In this context Franck's analysis of Heidegger's dechristianizing translation and interpretation in *Grundbegriffe der Metaphysik* (396) of Saint Paul's statement that "the creature [and the creation as a whole] waiteth for the manifestation of the sons of God" (Romans 8:19) as an ontological determination of the poverty of world characteristic of the animal and life in general is of particular significance (Franck, *Heidegger et le christianisme*, 99–110).

15. Dennis J. Schmidt's wonderful discussion in his *On Germans and Other Greeks*, of Heidegger's interpretation of Sophocles' *Antigone* in *Introduction to Metaphysics*, has been for me the starting point of my attempt in this, and, particularly, in the next chapter, to tie Heidegger's conception of Europe and the West to this strange figure that, as Schmidt argues, is not of the order of the Western canon but rather "the quality which the West and its traditions of metaphysics and Christianity cannot grasp" (260), but which in all its foreignness is precisely, as I will hold, the figure of what began in Greece, that is, the project of an originary world, which Europe and the West must, according to Heidegger, encounter again in order to find and win a world of their own. The pages that follow are dedicated to Dennis Schmidt. See also my review article on Schmidt's work, "Felicities and Infelicities of a Model," esp. 295–98.

16. If Greek thinking poetry accomplished a determination of what or who is human in a way specifically its own, that is, distinct from what happens in

the poetizing thinking of Heraclitus and Parmenides, it is by way of its poetic nature, but it is poetic not in the sense of meeting the requirements of a genre of poetry such as tragedy.

17. For a more detailed discussion of this evocation of primal history, its relation to mythology, and especially to poetry (*Dichtung*), see "Prologue: Heidegger's Onto-Mythology," in Lacoue-Labarthe, *Heidegger and the Politics of Poetry*, 3–16.

18. Heidegger, *What Is Called Thinking?* 10. For a discussion of *-logy*, as in "mythology," see Heidegger, *Identity and Difference*, 58–59.

19. Heidegger, *What Is Called Thinking?* 10.

20. Lacoue-Labarthe, *Heidegger and the Politics of Poetry*, 14. See also Franck, *Heidegger et le christianisme*, 104; and Zarader, *The Unthought Debt*.

21. I leave aside the question about the origin of the words *mythos* and *tragedy* in Greek language. Even if Heidegger contends in *What Is Philosophy?* that the Greek language is a language unlike any other language in that it is universal from the start, a reference (in the form of a trace) to what the Greek language overcomes within the Greek idiom to become universal remains inscribed within it. This is all the more the case because what Heidegger calls "Greek" is the result of, to use a Heideggerian term, a belated "phenomenological construction" (see Heidegger, *Being and Time*, 428; trans. mod.).

22. Reinhardt, *Sophokles*, 73–74. After having distanced himself from "the famous Hegelian interpretation of the tragic conflict as one between two equally valid principles, state and family," Reinhardt writes in the introduction to his 1961 translation of *Antigone* that

in *Antigone* the political becomes the counteraction to the divine. The political is represented by the new "general" Creon. He faces the divine in the figure of Antigone. . . . The conflict arises because the political in all its extremity as it is represented by Creon encroaches on the sphere of the eternal, that is, of "the unwritten laws," and because the obedience to the gods by the incensed and ardent young woman turns into a provocation as it collides with political power. Not two equally valid principles clash with one another. Political might, which does not know its limits, becomes, where it should open to insight, increasingly blind. Inseparably connected to its error is its self-assertion, its attitude. One of the Greek words for this is *authadia* [stubbornness, willfulness, arrogance]. Significant for the projection of power is the fact that the latter uses this word again and again to accuse Antigone. (Sophocles, *Antigone*, 9–10)

In *Hölderlin's Hymn "The Ister"* Heidegger echoes Reinhardt when he writes: "The two main figures, Creon and Antigone, do not stand opposed to one another like darkness and light, black and white, guilty and innocent. What is essential to each *is* as it is from out of the unity of essence and nonessence, yet in a different way in each case" (*HHI*, 52).

23. Reinhardt, *Sophokles*, 85.

24. Ibid., 263.

25. Taminiaux, *Le théâtre des philosophes*, 193.

26. It also follows from this that poetizing thinking, which "conceptually" unfolds this poetizing knowing, cannot be theoretical either (see *HHI*, 106, 111).

27. Let me also emphasize that by taking into her innermost own that against which nothing can avail, and which therefore is also "something altogether of no avail [*das, wogegen nichts auszurichten ist und was daher selbst das schlechthin Unausrichtbare bleibt*]" (*HHI*, 100)—in sum, by taking her point of departure in Being that because it is overwhelming—Antigone's actions are impossible actions, that is, actions that are actions in the first place, actions based in decision in the face of that which is the impossible.

28. Other names that come to mind for that which determines Antigone's action is the Heraclitean "cosmos," or "ever-living Fire," which "was not created by any one of the gods or of mankind" (Freeman, *Ancilla to the Pre-Socratic Philosophers*, 26); "what the Greeks experienced in the name Moira as the dispensing of portions. Gods and men are subordinated to Moira" (Heidegger, *Early Greek Thinking*, 55); or even "nature" as when, in "As When on a Holiday . . . " Hölderlin writes of nature that it "is older than the ages and above the gods of Occident and Orient" (*EHP*, 69). According to Heidegger, all of these are other names for Being.

29. Aristotle, "Rhetoric," 2189–90.1375a–75b. Aristotle also qualifies the one who, instead of following the written laws, obeys and remains faithful to the unwritten law as the better person.

30. Heidegger, *Zu Hölderlin*, 29–30.

Chapter 6

1. This lack of concern with the noetic dimension of the phenomena in question also explains why Husserl could have perceived Heidegger's discussion of everydayness and being-in-the-world to be merely anthropological descriptions.

2. Although hereafter tragic, rather than epic, poetry will be singled out by Heidegger as world-founding, the reference to Homer as the poet who gave the Greeks their gods already presupposes that Homer's *Iliad* is a tragic work. Indeed, Heidegger's understanding of Homer's *Iliad* is inscribed in the tradition that starts with Plato's reading of Achilles in books 2 and 3 of *Republic* (as well as Aristotle's elaborations on the differences and similarities between epic and tragedy in *Poetics*) and that sees in Homer, at least as far as the thematic level is concerned, a precursor of the tragic poets.

3. Heidegger, *Being and Time*, 62.

4. See also in this context *HHGR*, 251, where Heidegger notes that the essence

of something—the human being, for example—must always be "thought from the extreme limit. The standards for the determination of the essence can only be found there where the creators overstretch their capacities [*die Schaffenden über ihr Vermögen sich übernehmen*]."

5. Heidegger, *Vorträge und Aufsätze*, 137.
6. Heidegger, *On the Way to Language*, 90.
7. Pöggeler, *Schicksal und Geschichte*, 139, 134. Even though Heidegger once referred to *Antigone* in a lecture from 1919 (see Heidegger, *Zur Bestimmung der Philosophie*, 74), Pöggeler remarks that "a turn in Heidegger's thought was needed to permit an appreciation of this Greek tragedy" (115–16). After "a first distancing from political engagement Heidegger [not only] announced a lecture on Hölderlin's hymns for the winter 1934–35," but he also turns to Sophocles' *Antigone*, for which, according to Pöggeler, there was no place within National Socialism, obviously, because of the motif of resistance associated with the tragedy. "Yet Heidegger oriented himself [or, rather, reoriented himself at that moment] after the Antigone of Sophocles in the translation and interpretation by Hölderlin" (11).
8. Reinhardt, "Hölderlin und Sophokles," 382.
9. Ibid., 385.
10. At the end of his 1959 lecture "Hölderlin's Heaven and Earth," Heidegger draws attention to the fact that Hölderlin signed the poem discussed in the lecture—"Greece"—"Scardanelli," and remarks: "a foreign name, just as the poet had to reconcile himself and his ownmost self, that is, had to submit and resign, to something foreign [*gleich als müsste auch der Dichter sich und sein Eigenstes in ein Fremdes schicken, d.h. bringen und fügen*]" (*EHP*, 205).
11. Husserl, *Die Krisis*, 427.
12. Even though Heidegger seeks help and instruction from a Greek tragedy in the lectures on metaphysics from 1935 in order to clarify the difficult and strange determination of Being and Being-human in the pre-Socratic philosophers, he barely reflects on tragedy itself. However, in the Parmenides lectures several years later, he admits that the realm of "Greek tragedy is still entirely sealed off to us" (*P*, 73). Indeed, if the realm of Greek tragedy is still obscure to us, it is because the nature of truth—i.e., the "conflictual essence [*streithaften Wesens*] of *aletheia*"—remains obscure to us. Yet it is from the Greek understanding of truth that "the rise and the fall of man"—that is, "the possibility, and the necessity, of 'tragedy' itself" arises (*P*, 90). Furthermore, the "pre-eminence of the tragic word in their tragedies," in short, "the tragic word's essential ambiguity," whose saying also conceals what it says, and which explains our difficulty of relating to the realm of Greek tragedy, rests as well on the Greeks' understanding of Being and truth (*P*, 79).
13. Heidegger, *Zu Hölderlin*, 8, 18–19.

14. Ibid., 27.

15. Ibid., 28–30.

16. As Pöggeler has shown, Heidegger's interpretations of the tragedy are also marked "by a plurality of translations of the first choral ode of *Antigone*." In what follows I do not intend to take these differences into account, not the least because, as Pöggeler notes, this plurality "is outplayed by the tendency to retrieve the one origin of our history for a new beginning," and this is my exclusive concern here (Pöggeler, *Schicksal und Geschichte*, 158). For similar reasons I will not discuss Heidegger's translation of Sophocles itself. Repudiating ordinary opinion, but especially the science of philology, which, just like all other sciences, objectifies everything that it approaches, Heidegger holds that there is no "Sophocles as such [*an sich*]" (*HHGR*, 145). However, several very general observations may be warranted: (1) any discussion of the translation and interpretation of the choral ode in *Introduction to Metaphysics* must heed what Heidegger establishes about the inevitable violence that comes with any translation and interpretation; (2) the violence (*Gewalt*) in question cannot be taken in any ordinary sense but must evidently be understood in terms of *walten* (holding sway) that determines *Gewalt* and *Gewalt-tätigkeit*, which Heidegger highlights in his discussion of Being and Being-human in these lectures; (3) the translation and interpretation of this choral ode names what the Greeks left unsaid but what must be named if what is Greek is again to become something to be thought today (see, in particular, "Das abendländische Gespräch," in Heidegger, *Zu Hölderlin*, 104). Heidegger's translation and interpretation rests on his contention that in conformity with their understanding of *aletheia*, the Greek thinkers and poets observe silence precisely insofar as they are sayers (see, e.g., *P*, 73); (4) what Heidegger makes the Greek words say, and by extension the choral ode as a whole, is not of the order of a historically, scientifically identifiable referent. Rather it is something that, according to Heidegger, announced or promised itself in Greece in order to be covered up by what followed; (5) as regards the often contested translation of *deinon* as uncanny, or rather as unhomely (*unheimlich*), let me point out that this translation permits Heidegger to tease out and name the way according to which the Greeks must have understood the violence and violence-doing that pervades the choral ode.

17. Nietzsche, *Early Greek Philosophy and Other Essays*, 52.

18. For this very reason uncanniness is also not of the order of an intuitable essence of the human being—that is, an essence present at hand or a fixed characteristic and condition that could be sought out.

19. To understand in what sense Being as *dike* is violently overwhelming, let us also recall Heidegger's claim, in *Hölderlins Hymnen "Germanien" und "Der Rhein,"* that Being *is* in the mode of enmity (*Feindseligkeit*). Such enmity, however, is also the highest bliss (*Seligkeit*) in that it intimately, that is, chiasmati-

cally, interconnects what stands against one another (*HHGR*, 256–257; see also 245).

20. Heidegger's reflections on the reasons why the Greeks considered the artwork and authentic art as *techne* in an emphatic sense clearly demonstrate that art only exemplifies what is valid of all other *techne* and machinations that the human being directs against the overwhelming sway of Being (see *IM*, 170). There is no aestheticist valorization of the artwork here. All the human being's machinations are forms of *techne*. They are all, without exception, attempts to master the overwhelming sway of being by putting Being into work in a particular being, which as a being that *is*, forces Being to be the open in which everything else can become manifest as itself and as such.

21. Otto, *The Idea of the Holy*, 40. For a fine discussion of the history of the notion of the uncanny see Masschelein, "Unheimlich/das Unheimliche."

22. Heidegger, *Being and Time*, 233.

23. In the lectures in *Hölderlin's Hymn "The Ister"* Heidegger writes that to translate *to deinon* as uncanny is to think it "in the direction of the non-ordinary. . . . We mean the uncanny in the sense of that which is not at home—not homely in that which is homely. It is for this reason that the un-homely [*das Un-heimische*] can, as a consequence, also be 'uncanny' [*unheimlich*] in the sense of something that has an alienating or 'frightening' effect that gives anxiety" (*HHI*, 71). Let me also mention here that in the context of a discussion of the affect of fear in his interpretation of Aristotle's *Rhetoric* in the 1924 lectures at Marburg, Heidegger links speech to anxiety and the feeling of uncanniness that accompanies it: "When we feel uncanny, we begin to speak. This is a hint at the *genesis of speaking in terms of Dasein*, that is, at how speaking is connected to the fundamental determination of Dasein which is characterized by *uncanniness*" (Heidegger, *Grundbegriffe der aristotelischen Philosophie*, 261).

24. Such moving out of the limits of the homely is also intimately linked to the Greek understanding of freedom as essentially the freedom of movement. Hannah Arendt writes that "being able to depart [*Aufbrechen-können*] for where we will is the prototypical gesture of being free" (Arendt, *Men in Dark Times*, 9).

25. For having drawn the two (contradictory) concepts of *pantaporos* and *aporos*, respectively, of *hupsipolis* and *apolis* together in oxymora, rather than linking the first to the end of the previous line and the last to the first word of the following verse, Heidegger has, of course, brought on the wrath of the philologists. See Pöggeler, *Schicksal und Geschichte*, 23, 137.

26. Heidegger, *Grundbegriffe der aristotelischen Philosophie*, 46–49, 56.

27. In "On the Essence of the Ground" Heidegger points out that Dasein, insofar as it "transcends," is essentially "*world-forming*, 'forming' [*bildend*] in the multiple sense that it lets world occur, and through the world gives itself an

original view (form [Bild]) that is not explicitly grasped, yet functions precisely as a paradigmatic form (*Vor-bild*) for all manifest beings, among which each respective Dasein itself belongs" (Heidegger, *Pathmarks*, 123). The image of this world projected by Greek Dasein is the *polis* in the sense defined above; or differently put, world and *polis* are the same for Greek Dasein, which is thus, in an essential sense, a historical and "political" Dasein.

28. Would such a nonpoetic or thoughtful way of articulating the essence of the human being—his or her unhomely athomeness—not also have to put the poetic words of thoughtful poetizing—the words *uncanny* and *hearth* (and perhaps, even the word *tragic*)—into brackets by translating them differently into thoughtful words?

29. Heidegger finds further proof of this understanding of the hearth as Being in the *Phaedrus*, where Plato says of Hestia, the goddess of the hearth, that she is the most steadfast and the middle of the Olymp (*HHI*, 113–15).

30. In the lectures on "The Ister" it is said that, for Hölderlin, that in which the Germans have to become at home "is whatever belongs to the fatherland of the Germans. Whatever is of the fatherland is itself at home with mother earth" (*HHI*, 49). As is evident, at least from "Hölderlin's Earth and Heaven," where Heidegger comments on the poet's use of the adjective form of the term *fatherland*, fatherland "means the relatedness of the land as to the supreme God" (*EHP*, 206), in other words, to the principle of the divine itself, not Zeus, but what Hölderlin, in "Remarks on 'Antigone,'" refers to as "the more real [*eigentlicheren*] Zeus" (Hölderlin, *Essays and Letters on Theory*, 113). Incarnated in mother earth (Gaia?), the native land becomes the fatherland.

31. In the debate on the much discussed "patriotic reversal [*vaterländische Umkehr*]," according to which the later Hölderlin would have left his earlier infatuation for Greece behind in order to turn to the fatherland of the Germans, Heidegger takes a definite stand by highlighting in "Hölderlin's Earth and Heaven" the late poem "Greece" (see, in particular, *EHP*, 206). The following elaborations on the fundamental law of homecoming are subtended by the contention that if the principle of a *vaterländische Umkehr* concerns the finding of what is one's own, it occurs necessarily within both Greece and Germany. Beda Allemann writes that the reversal in question is to be understood as a movement that takes place "*within* the domain of a fatherland, be it that of the Greeks or the Hesperians. On the basis alone of the tension between gods and men, Empedoclean-Titanic union and royally pure distinction, something like a relation between Greece and Hesperia becomes possible to begin with" (Allemann, *Hölderlin und Heidegger*, 43).

32. Speaking of Hölderlin's encounter with Sophocles and Pindar in his search for what is German, Heidegger writes: "What is one's own, which the poetic meditation and telling is concerned with finding and appropriating, itself

contains the relations to that foreign through which coming to be at home takes its path. In this way, the foreign of one's own, but also the poets of these foreign parts, are determined in their singularity" (*HHI*, 49).

33. See Françoise Dastur's discussion of the Böhlendorff letter in Dastur, *Hölderlin*, esp. 32.

34. Heidegger, *Denkerfahrungen, 1910–1976*, 16–17.

35. Well before Derrida, who, in *The Other Heading*, took up Valéry's famous essay, Heidegger thus had already had recourse to this text in his elaborations on Europe. Let me also point out that according to Gonzague de Reynold and Denis de Rougemont, the image of Europe as a cape "has been a commonplace among geographers for centuries" (Rougemont, *The Idea of Europe*, 30). But the more direct source of Valéry's reference to Europe as a small cape of the Asiatic continent, or the brain of the entire planet, could also have been Theodor Lessing, a theoretician of decline, who, based on reasons of demography, writes in 1916 that "using a not all too bold image one could say that our part of the world relates to Asia like the brain to the rest of the body. In the same way as the brain, because of its light, free, and autocratic position up there in the head, is called to guide the whole heavy and unconscious mass of the body, so does this protruding and severed little island of Europe, which is attached to the dreaming trunk of old mother Earth, seem, like a minuscule head on a massive stem, to be authorized to begin the domination of the whole world of men" (Lessing, *Untergang der Erde am Geist*, 21).

Chapter 7

1. In this essay Patočka argues that European civilization, because it is based on continuous rationalization, is a civilization that, distinct from all previous forms of high civilization, has achieved effective universality by evacuating the religious (also the emotional and irrational) kernel around which civilizations have been commonly organized to the margins. Patočka characterizes this highly secularized civilization as "rational over-civilization" (*LS*, 109). He writes: "Over-civilization means universalism. Universalism is rationalist, but its essence implies non-totality" (*LS*, 114) because it is limited to just one function of life, that is, one that concerns solely the objective and impersonal aspects of life. Indeed, "initially over-civilization does not present itself as a principle for a renewal of life in its entirety" (*LS*, 120). But if, according to Patočka's diagnosis, which, in many ways, echoes Husserl's *Krisis*, the rational civilization of Europe is currently in crisis, it is because it has become critically divided into opposing conceptions of rationality, one of which even threatens Europe with extinction. Whereas moderate over-civilization acknowledges the limitation of the universal

thrust of European rationality to one function of life—one that is objective and impersonal—and thus remains open to tradition and the ideas of previous civilization, radical over-civilization does not want to acknowledge these internal limits of universality and seeks to dominate life in its entirety by eliminating all the functions of life that do not conform to objective and impersonal rationality—that is, ultimately, religion in its entirety. Yet the European crisis is not limited to this division of European rationality into two opposite forms of rationality and conceptions of universality; moderate over-civilization, which is the only answer to the threat posed by the radical version of over-civilization, is in crisis as well. Needless to say, the particular traditions tolerated by moderate over-civilization exert a conservative thrust and threaten moderate over-civilization with a conservative and dogmatic regression toward previous stages of mere civilization. According to Patočka, the moderate form of over-civilization, which takes its inspiration "from the model of the ancient individualist civilizations of Greece and, although to a lesser extent, from Israel," rests on two values: "the value of scientific truth and the value of human freedom, i.e., the recognition of the human being by the human being as being an equal" (*LS*, 212–22). Furthermore, originating in "the struggles from the sixteenth to the eighteenth century about autonomy in the context of the central question regarding the determination of life's ultimate meaning: the religious self-determination of the individual before God" (*LS*, 119), the value of human freedom—more broadly, of religious liberalism—becomes an intrinsic and even indispensable ingredient of over-civilization in its moderate form. Indeed, insofar as over-civilization implies a universal principle, and thus expects that "the ideas impose themselves by way of the model of rational argumentation, in a purely internal process of exposition, deduction, critique, doubt, counter-criticism, and so forth," freedom of thought is necessary as a protection of finite reason (*LS*, 120). In other words, moderation in over-civilization implies "the inclusion of something that does not belong to the purely rational system of instrumentality" (*LS*, 142), and that negates it. Yet this principle of negation is also in a process of being weakened, if not even of disappearing altogether. Without the complementarity between finite rationality and its negation, whose "concrete expression [according to Patočka] is the maintenance of the Christian tradition" (*LS*, 154), moderate over-civilization is, indeed, in jeopardy. Yet today the balance between these two plateaus no longer exists, and, therefore, moderate over-civilization is in a crisis. Patočka writes: "The crisis of liberalism, and, more generally, of over-civilization is perhaps linked to the fact that *ratio* as an element of life and of the diffusion of this form of civilization is not the element of ultimate decision, and of resolution, as regards the relation of the human being to its ultimate limits. Ratio cannot live alone: its essence is such that it is not enough for life as a whole to live upon. It demands to be completed or replaced by something else" (*LS*, 155).

2. For a fine discussion of Patočka's notion of over-civilization, and on how the dangers that threaten rationality according to him in 1950 differ from Husserl's assessment in the 1930s of the crisis that Europe faces, see Crépon, "Penser l'Europe avec Patočka," 36–44.

3. Ibid., 32.

4. Ibid., 33.

5. Ibid., 34.

6. Ibid., 35.

7. In *Plato and Europe* Patočka explains at great length that the idea of the care of the soul exists even in Democrates, although the expression is not found there, and that Aristotle, although he does not talk about it, builds on this motive.

8. Patočka, *Le monde naturel comme problème philosophique*.

9. Patočka, *Le monde naturel et le mouvement de l'existence humaine*; Patočka, "Réflexion sur l'Europe."

10. Ricoeur, "Preface to the French Edition," x.

11. For an evaluation of how Heidegger's philosophy bears on Patočka's revision of Husserl's conception of the life-world, see, in particular, Patočka's "Afterword" in the second edition of *Le monde naturel comme problème philosophique* (168–81). For Patočka's proximity and indebtedness to Heidegger, whose philosophy of finitude he considered as the completion of the phenomenological project, see also Dastur, *La phénoménologie en questions*, 214, 222–24.

12. The implication of understanding human life as movement is that existence is essentially corporeal. This important aspect of Patočka's work would require a study of its own.

13. For an excellent account of both how the life-world, according to Patočka, is anchored in practical life rather than primarily in its philosophical determination, and the three movements by which it is constituted, see Srubar, "Vom begründeten Leben."

14. See also Patočka, "La conception aristotélicienne du mouvement."

15. In *Heretical Essays* Patočka calls these three movements "the movement of acceptance, the movement of defense, and the movement of truth" (*HE*, 29). Whereas in the movement of acceptance the human being preserves and secures his or her introduction into, and acceptance by, the world, in the movement of defense he or she surrenders his or her self, "disposing of the self," and in the movement of truth the human being achieves "a proper relation to manifestation as such—that is, to that which makes manifestation possible" (*HE*, 30, 33).

16. However, pointing to the names that Patočka gives to the three movements of life—that is, the three ways of being-in-the-world—which constitute the natural world, namely, the movements of taking root, of escape, and of breakthrough, Paul Ricoeur has argued that rather than corresponding to "Heidegger's triad of becoming, having-been, and presence, Patočka substitutes

an essentially corporeal triad" to the latter's essentially temporal triad (Ricoeur, "Jan Patočka et le nihilisme," 87).

17. See also *HE*, where Patočka writes that in this second sense of *natural* the natural world as the prehistoric world is natural because it refers to "the community of all it contains as something given, something that simply manifests itself. It is a community of gods and mortals, the shared lifespace of those dependent on the nourishing earth and the heavenly lights and of those who are not so dependent and who thus constitute the most wondrous mystery of this world" (25).

18. See *MNPH*, 181.

19. Plato, *The Collected Dialogues*, 16 (29d–e; see also 30a).

20. Ibid., 66 (83a).

21. Ibid., 63–64 (80c–e).

22. Ibid., 64 (81c).

23. In his study of the motif of the care of the soul as a key term of the heritage and the future of Europe, according to Patočka, Marc Crépon argues that as a response to the general decline of all beings, this motif concerns primarily a different relation between life and death, and a different way of comportment in the face of death, and thus advocates another kind of attachment to life than the one of ordinary life and its turning away in anxiety from death. More precisely, the topos of the care of the soul is the only way of confronting nihilism and the lack of a meaning of life. He writes: "What Socrates in his very death has bequeathed to Europe is that life is worth living only if it is 'life in truth,' and that this dignity can only be experienced at the risk of life itself, at the risk of a life which at that moment becomes detached from the anxiety of death. In the same way as it becomes a question of loving life *differently*, it is a question confronting death *differently*" (Crépon, *Altérités de l'Europe*, 175).

24. Husserl, *Ideas Pertaining to a Pure Phenomenology and to a Phenomenological Philosophy*, 59–60.

25. See Bégout, "La phénoménologie décapitée?" 379, 382.

26. Patočka, *Papiers phénoménologiques*, 261. For an excellent discussion of the conception of an asubjective phenomenology see Garrido, "'Appearing as Such' in Patočka's A-Subjective Phenomenology."

27. The human being, as Patočka conceives of him or her, is in no way a subject constitutive of the phenomena; rather, as the one for whom things appear, he or she is "an 'outcome' in the same way as everything else" (Patočka, *Papiers phénoménologiques*, 127). See also Deniau, "Phénoménologie asubjective et herméneutique," 355–56.

28. If, as we will see, Patočka puts the Platonic conception of the care of the soul into question, a whole range of Platonic, but also Husserlian, themes becomes problematic by implication, not only the Platonic conception of the

look into what is but also the Platonic and especially Husserlian conception of donation and evidence, and, ultimately, the notion of subjectivity.

29. Before becoming the explicit concern of reflection in the shape of philosophy, the experience and consciousness that by being the site in which the world as world discloses itself to him or her, the human being is condemned to the awareness of his or her finitude, hence that he or she is "at the same time a creature of *truth and [that] this truth is damnation for him*," is already the theme of mythic consciousness "at a certain stage." "This consciousness—that man as the caretaker of phenomenon is at the same time the only creature who knows that its phenomenal domain has an end—is at the beginning of this entire reflection [on the care of the soul]. An awareness that man is a creature of truth—which means of the phenomenon—and that this is his *damnation*—is already present in the mythical world" (*PE*, 35). Patočka refers to the biblical myth of the tree of knowledge, the Sumeric myth of the cultural hero Gilgamesh and Enkidu, the Greek myths of Heracles and, in particular, Oedipus, to make his point (*PE*, 35).

30. Plato, *The Collected Dialogues*, 63 (80b).

31. For a short history of the concept of immortality in Greece see Arendt, *The Life of the Mind*, 1:129–38. The Platonic conception of immortality is not the same as the Christian conception of eternal life as the *summum bonum*. Patočka does not always seem to clearly distinguish between the two.

32. In *Plato and Europe* Patočka distinguishes three aspects from which the care of the soul is thematized in Plato's philosophy: "in one way as the complete plan of existence, in another as the plan of a political life, and in yet another as the clarification of what the soul is in itself" (*PE*, 86).

Chapter 8

1. Yet as Marlène Zarader has pointed out, for a non-Greek culture such as Hebraic culture, to intervene in the field of Greek and European thought and culture (even if this occurs on this culture's own terms) means that this non-Greek culture has "a property enabling it to be thus inscribed and to bring something to the field in its own fashion. But, if that is possible, then it is because a thinking was in action there, a thinking that did not correspond to the Greek comprehension of the term, and which consequently demanded another definition of its essence" (Zarader, *The Unthought Debt*, 81).

2. A brief reference to the Constantinian model is to be found in *HE* (68). See also Dempf, *Sacrum imperium*, 106–8. Patočka's discussion in *Heretical Essays* of the Holy Empire of the German Nation is to a large extent based on Dempf's work.

3. As a reader of Hannah Arendt's *The Human Condition*, Patočka might have

had a passage from this work in mind in which Arendt argues that with the introspection characteristic of modern thought as it originated in Cartesian reason, the structure of the human mind—its faculty of reasoning—becomes the universal ground that everybody cannot but share. She writes: "The fact that, given the problem of two plus two we all will come out with the same answer, four, is henceforth the very model of common-sense reasoning." It must be added, however, that for Arendt this model for what is universal is the outcome of the world-loss of modern philosophy:

> The mind of this man [who with Descartes and Hobbes is determined by his faculty of deducing and concluding]—to remain in the sphere of mathematics—no longer looks upon "two-and-two-are-four" as an equation in which two sides balance in self-evident harmony, but understands the equation as the expression of a process in which two and two *become* four in order to generate further processes of addition which eventually will lead into the infinite. This faculty the modern age calls common-sense reasoning; it is the playing of the mind with itself, which comes to pass when the mind is shut off from all reality and "senses" only itself. (Arendt, *The Human Condition*, 283–84; see also Arendt, *On Revolution*, 193)

4. As Patočka remarks, whether this is a superiority is an open question, since the abstract civilization of Europe puts the human being continuously into question. "Man is constantly problematic" (*PE*, 223).

5. If it is true that even early Christianity's self-articulation was framed by Greek conceptuality, it is also true that the Platonism that, according to Patočka, haunts Christianity from the beginning is a thoroughly Christianized understanding of Plato's thought.

6. Since the relation between the demonic or the orgiastic onto the sphere of responsibility—a sphere that is essentially the discovery of the Greek genius—is not an originary given, the grafting in question is of the order of an accomplishment.

7. The polis, as the proper place of history, is only the exterior form of the soul.

8. The comparison of the soul to a steel crystal would seem to contradict its transparency. Although the image clearly serves Patočka only to highlight the soul's steadfastness, rather than any opacity, it is, perhaps, also already a hint that ultimately Plato's ontology of light is not possible without a dark kernel.

9. Considering that the Platonic Good is not an *eidos* but only an *idea*, it has no fixed contours and cannot, therefore, as Patočka suggests, be fully and clearly known. See Gadamer, "Europa und die Oikumene," 77.

10. For Patočka's understanding of the relation between philosophy and myth see *PE*, 51–52.

11. Light is, perhaps, nothing else than the breakaway from the everyday and darkness, purified and elevated as such to the level of a philosopheme.

12. Augustine could as well be the theologian whom Patočka has in mind when he accuses Christianity of having failed in overcoming Platonism (the laws of nature are a reflection of the divine in Augustine!).

13. Although Christian noncosmic mystery stands in a bipolar opposition to the Greek mystical orgiastic cults, remainders of Orphic "emotional identification" (*Einsfühlung*) remain present in Christianity. But as Max Scheler has argued, these authentic forms of identification (*Einsgefühl*) are now grounded in the love of the person of Christ. He writes:

> No reasonable person will be led to the almost ludicrously profane notion, that Paul's *enduesthai Christon*, his "putting on of Christ," his being "rooted and built up in," "suffering in," "crucified with," "dead and risen again in" Him represent nothing more than fellow-feeling or pity for Christ, or that they are identical with the mere belief that all this once happened in the world, and happened "for me" and for my salvation. On the contrary, it is as clear as day that in their orphic obscurity and morbid ecstasy of passion, these utterances of St. Paul refer to something totally different from mere fellow-feeling or understanding. . . . He is expressing a true identification in form and essence . . . of Christ's Person with his own. (Scheler, *The Nature of Sympathy*, 85–86).

14. Otto, *The Idea of the Holy*, 13, 19, 25.

15. Ibid., 23, 17.

16. Already while discussing the Christian conception of God as a person, Patočka noted that "what a Person is, that really is not adequately thematized in the Christian perspective" (*HE*, 107).

17. Chvatík, "The Heretical Conception of the European Legacy in the Late Essays of Jan Patočka," 23.

18. This is also the point where one can see to what extent Patočka's understanding of Christianity is heretical: a Christianity radically freed from Platonism is a Christianity in which God is reduced to a nonsymmetric radical difference within the self itself. From a phenomenological point of view one may also wonder in what sense this relation of (God as) Person to the person is still linked up with the question of manifesting itself, which is central, according to Patočka, to the motif of the care of the soul. Could this internal difference within the self not be conceived as, precisely, the asubjective opening within which all manifestation takes place? Analyzing, in *The Gift of Death*, how giving oneself death and taking one's death upon oneself are intertwined in the formation of the singularity of the self, Derrida remarks that "the question becomes concentrated in this 'oneself,' in the identity [*le même*] or oneself [*le soi-même*] of the mortal or dying self. 'Who' or 'what' gives itself death or takes it upon themselves or itself?" (*GD*, 45). As Derrida argues, in what I would characterize as a deduction in a transcendental, or quasi-transcendental, style, this structure of oneself, in which, moreover, I relate to myself and have a secret relationship with myself insofar as I witness myself within me without seeing myself seeing,

is above all the very site of the constitution of God understood as a transcendent being (*GD*, 108–9).

Chapter 9

1. Derrida, *Specters of Marx*, 54. In "Deconstruction of Actuality" Derrida writes:

> If to inherit is to reaffirm an injunction, not only a possession but also an assignation to be decoded, then we are only what we inherit. Our being is an inheritance, the language we speak is an inheritance. Hölderlin more or less says that language has been given us so that we may testify to what we inherit. Not the inheritance we have or receive, but the one that we are, through and through. What we are, we inherit. And we inherit the language that serves to testify to the fact that we are what we inherit. A paradoxical circle within which one must struggle and decide, by means of decisions that both inherit and invent—necessarily without any set norm or program—one's own norms. (Derrida, *Negotiations*, 111)

2. Derrida's reference to heritage, and the responsibility to it, does not necessarily imply that he would dismiss the notion of "tradition." Let me only emphasize that, in contrast to Gadamer, Derrida does not hold tradition to be homogeneous. Indeed, within the tradition one finds "dominant structures, discourses which silence others, by covering or destroying the archive" (Derrida, *Politics of Friendship*, 233). Even though repeatedly he notes that "it is no longer possible to *use* seriously the words of tradition" (Derrida, "Some Statements and Truisms About Neologisms, Newisms, Postisms, Parasitisms, and Other Small Seismisms," 74), and that in the end all concepts of the tradition have to be put aside, he also "reaffirm[s] the necessity of returning to them, at least under erasure" (Derrida, *Psyche*, 2:2). Responsibility to the tradition and its deconstruction go hand in hand.

3. Derrida does not seem to have been familiar with the basic tenets of Patočka's later phenomenology, in particular, his reinterpretation of the Husserlian conception of the life-world (see Chap. 7 above). Nonetheless, Derrida's reading of the essay in question is a very fine account of Patočka's thought.

4. This genealogy also raises the question whether it is not also modeled in accordance with the tripartite movement that, according to Patočka, makes up the natural world of the human being (see Chap. 7 above).

5. Plato, *The Collected Dialogues*, 66 (83a).

6. In spite of the decidedly emphatic and crucial role of the conception of person for his thought, Patočka provides little to no information about how this concept, which undoubtedly belongs to the fund of resources of Christian theology, is to be understood. However, from the contexts in which Patočka

speaks of the person, it is clear that this notion serves to name the individual human being's absolute singularity. To my knowledge, Patočka never explains the philosophical sources for this concept. Undoubtedly, Saint Augustine and Duns Scotus, according to whom the human being is a singular being created in His image by a Creator-God who Himself is a Person, could have acted as models for Patočka's understanding of person. But it seems to me that the more likely, and more immediate, source is Max Scheler's phenomenological, sociological, and metaphysical idea of person, as well as his person-based ethics. Distinct from the human being qua human being, the Ego (*Ich*), the subject, and in particular, the subject of reason (the moral person, according to Kant), Scheler understands *person* as the radically individualized and concrete center of all acts (and, hence, as a spiritual unity, or totality)—that is, as the *absolute* individual. (God, in this sense, is then, of course, "the person of all persons.") As the individualized center of all the performed acts, the person exists and lives only in the performance of intentional acts, experiencing him- or herself in the reflection upon these acts as being responsible for them, and, hence, as a "value-essence [*Wertwesen*]" that is both personal and individual in nature, "essence" having here nothing to do with universality, since it is "given only in one particular individual." All lived experiences of personal obligations are grounded in the prior experience of one's individual value-essence. Scheler writes: "It is this value-essence of a personal *and* individual nature that I also designate 'personal salvation.'" The link of Scheler's idea of person to that of Patočka becomes tangible, especially, when Scheler ties such personal salvation to an evidential insight into a good in which I experience a

> reference [*Hinweis*] to me which is contained (descriptively put) in the special non-formal content of this good-in-itself, something that comes from this *content* and points to "me," something that whispers, "For you." . . . This, therefore, is to catch sight of the value-essence of my person—in religious terms, of the value-picture, so to speak, which God's love draws and bears before me insofar as this love is directed to *me*. This peculiar individual *value-content* is the basis on which a consciousness of an individual ought is built, that is, the evidential knowledge of a "good-in-itself" but precisely in the sense of a "good-in-itself-for-*me*." (Scheler, *Formalism in Ethics and Non-Formal Ethics of Values*, 489–90)

In more general terms the question to be posed would have to concern the extent to which Patočka's heretically Christian conception of ethics is indebted to what Scheler, in *The Nature of Sympathy*, calls, a *noncosmic* ethos—that is, an ethos based on love for the person, which originates in historical-occidental Christendom with the gospel of Jesus—that is, this combination of "Jewish and Roman notions of mastery over Nature (which are alien and even hostile to identification [*Einsfühlung*]), with the romantic, Graeco-Hellenistic view of the world, and both of these with the Gospel of Jesus." Breaking both with the cult of Orphism and *Einsfühlung* with the cosmos, whose ultimate root is Eros, the acosmic ethos "creates an entirely new plane of purely *spiritual* relationships of men to things, to one another, and to God"—that is, as far as man and God are concerned, relations of genuine sympathy and spontaneous love, as well as a "'belief in' [*Glauben an*]," "experienced as a gift, a grace, a favour granted, not as a personal achievement of one's own," in the person as a Master's figure by whom the disciple is "grip[ped], and seized, and overwhelm[ed]" (Scheler, *The Nature of Sympathy*, 83–84, 86–87).

7. Ricoeur, "Preface to the French Edition," ix.

8. Indeed, as Hannah Arendt has pointed out, "Goodness in an absolute sense, as distinguished from the 'good-for' or the 'excellent' in Greek Roman antiquity, became known in our civilization only with the rise of Christianity." The analysis of Goodness provided in *The Human Condition*, and in which Arendt highlights the constitutive secrecy of good works, which must remain hidden even to the one who performs them—a good deed being good only on condition that it is forgotten at the moment it is done—as well as Goodness's intrinsic hostility toward the public realm, converges in many respects with what Patočka—a reader of Arendt—says about this notion, as well as with all the implications that Derrida draws in systematic fashion from this conception in *The Gift of Death*. See Arendt, *The Human Condition*, 73–77.

9. Derrida asks: "Is the reference to this abyssal dissymmetry that occurs when one is exposed to the gaze of the other a motif that derives firstly and uniquely from Christianity, even if it be from an inadequately thematized Christianity? Let us leave aside the question of whether one finds something that at least represents its equivalent 'before' or 'after' the Gospels, in Judaism or in Islam" (*GD*, 28).

10. See also Derrida, *Passions*.

Chapter 10

1. Derrida, *The Other Heading*, 5–6. It is certainly appropriate here to recall the historical context that frames Derrida's text, an abbreviated version of which was delivered during a colloquium on "European Cultural Identity" in Turin in 1990. On several occasions Derrida refers in the text to the tremor that at the time (that is, before the first Gulf War) shook Central and Eastern Europe in particular, but the following passage perhaps sums up the situation in the most succinct way: "With the destruction of the Berlin Wall and the unification of Germany in sight, with a *perestroika* that is still uncertain, with all the diverse movements of 'democratizations,' and with all the legitimate but sometimes ambiguous aspirations for national sovereignty, there is in *today*'s day and age the

reopening and denaturalization of [the] monstrous partitions" that resulted from World War II (62–63).

2. Derrida, *Demeure*, 19.

3. Derrida, *The Problem of Genesis in Husserl's Philosophy*, 155–56.

4. Ibid., 159. Although in this early work the contradictions in Husserl's reflection on Europe are believed to be resolvable through a new dialectical ontology, the notion of aporia present in this work already hints at Derrida's later work, in which the failure to reconcile the aporetic tension is precisely the condition for a relation to what is to come. One could perhaps say that the new figure of Europe that Derrida envisions consists in its endurance of all the conflicting positions (and the demands that they imply) found in Husserl's elaborations on Europe.

5. See *OH*, 31–34; as well as Derrida, *Of Spirit*, 120–22.

6. By suffering alienation as the result of confusing the constituted with that which constitutes, the crisis reveals itself to be of historical necessity rooted in the indefinitely synthetic character of the idea. It is in this synthetic nature of the idea that Derrida locates the possibility and necessity of the crisis (see *PGHP*, 172).

7. Derrida, *Rogues*, 158.

8. Derrida, *Of Spirit*, 120.

9. Derrida and Roudinesco, *For What Tomorrow . . . A Dialogue*, 18. Derrida continues:

> But it was born—and we can follow Husserl and Heidegger in this—as the universal project of a will to deracination. If philosophy has a root (Greece), its project consists at the same time in pulling up the roots and in making it such that what is thought in Greece—and later in Germany, according to Heidegger—is delivered into "more than one language." Philosophy, then, is delivered; it tends at least toward liberating itself, from the start, from its linguistic, territorial, ethnic, and cultural limitations. The universal projected in this way is not a given, the way an essence would be; rather, it announces an infinite process of universalization. (18)

10. Derrida, *Writing and Difference*, 81, 311.

11. If the Christian conception of Europe also means that Europe's mission consists in defending Christian values, then this would be one more reason why Derrida does not seek to replace the Greek origin with a Christian one. Only the Greek origin provides the necessary structures that can secure an identity of Europe that does not consist in the defense of the particular values of particular traditions. It is thus necessary to distinguish Derrida's approach to Europe from that of a historical scholar such as Jacques Le Goff, for example, who in *The Birth of Europe* has forcefully argued that Europe begins with the Christian Middle Ages, as does also Rémi Brague in his cultural study *Europe, la voie romaine*. However, if Brague's work, which rather than focusing on the content of

European culture considers its *form* alone—more precisely, the form of Europe's relation to what is proper to it—would require a more detailed discussion, it is because Brague's Christian Europe resembles, on the surface at least, Derrida's account of Europe, which relies on untapped resources of Greek philosophical thought. Compared, however, to Derrida's philosophical analysis of the relations of Europe to itself and its others, Brague's cultural history of Europe thinks of Romanity as the form of Europe's relation to its sources in terms of "a model of cultural praxis," first and foremost (Brague, *Europe, la voie romaine*, 175). If Europe, according to Brague, is essentially Roman—"Roman" referring to the world of the Latin tongue that lasted until the Middle Ages and beyond in those who thought and wrote in Latin—it is because the paradigm of Romanity is the reason why Europe is, and also can be, Greek and Jewish. Romanity, or the "Roman" structure, consists of being torn away from an origin of one's own and being ahead of oneself by having one's source in the experience, transmission, and appropriation of cultures experienced as foreign, such as Greek and Jewish culture. Hence Brague's contention that "we are 'Greek' and 'Jewish,' and can be so only because we are first 'Roman'" (31). Romanity is the paradigm for transmitting what is not of one's own making. However, since the Roman attitude itself is not truly the Romans' propriety because the Greeks were already Roman in this sense, although without the specifically Roman experience of a feeling of inferiority (42–43), Romanity is additionally to be characterized by its experience of its own secondariness and, in particular, by a complex of inferiority regarding the accomplishments of the foreign sources that it transmitted and diffused without ever hoping to surpass them. Europe, according to Brague, distinguishes itself from other cultural worlds such as Islam and Judaism on the basis of "its particular mode of relating to what is one's own (*propre*): the appropriation of what is experienced as foreign" (103). This "cultural secondariness seems to govern the relation to the other in the cultural history of Europe" (116) but also in its relation to its own past, which is "a past that has never been its own," something other than itself from which it is also irreparably estranged (125). Consequently, to say that Europe is Christian is to say that it is secondary in relation to Judaism, hence 'Roman'" (145). Brague concludes that Europe has deliberately sought this secondariness (123) and that Europeans have "the consciousness of being latecomers, having to reach back to a source that 'we' are not and which has never been 'us.' From this consciousness derives a displacement of the cultural identity of Europe such that it has no other identity than an eccentric identity" (125).

12. Derrida, "A Europe of Hope," 410. Derrida eschews the English "globalization" and the German "Globalisierung," keeping instead the French word *mondialisation*—which has no equivalent in English (although, on one occasion, he suggests "worldization" as a possible translation)—to refer to the phenom-

enon in question, "so as to maintain a reference to the world—*monde, Welt, mundus*—which is neither the globe nor the cosmos" (Derrida, "The University Without Condition," 203, 223). "Altermondialiste," which is not the equivalent of "antiglobalization," refers, therefore, to the demand for another world. For a fine discussion of the difference, according to Derrida, between the Anglo-American *globalization* and the Latinate French *mondialisation*, see Li, "Elliptical Interruptions, or, Why Derrida Prefers *Mondialisation* to Globalization."

13. Derrida, "'Nous autres Grecs,'" 267.

14. Derrida, *Rogues*, 31. In this context he raises the troubling question of the absence of Aristotle's "Politics" in the Islamic translation, reception, and mediation of Greek philosophy (31–32).

15. Derrida, *Points . . . Interviews, 1974–1994*, 377.

16. In his intervention to the conference "Penser l'Europe à ses frontières," at Strasbourg (France) in November 1992, Derrida also remarked that "one could demonstrate that, in a certain way, Europe today, here, and now, comes as much from Auschwitz as from Greece, Christianity, the Empires, and the revolutions of '89 or '17" (*PEF*, 29–30).

17. Derrida, *Writing and Difference*, 133.

18. Derrida, *Margins of Philosophy*, 125.

19. Derrida, *Writing and Difference*, 152 (trans. mod.).

20. Ibid., 111–12.

21. Ibid., 153.

22. Derrida, *Points . . . Interviews*, 377.

23. This piece is a response to papers by Eric Alliez and Francis Wolff presented at a symposium organized by Barbara Cassin in 1990 at the Sorbonne on the contemporary appropriation of antiquity. Derrida's response was written for the publication of the proceedings. All page references in the text refer to the piece in question.

24. Derrida, *Fichus*, 51; Borradori, *Philosophy in a Time of Terror*, 116.

25. Nietzsche, *The Will to Power*, 225n419–26n419.

26. Jaspers, "Vom europäischen Geist," 240. In this essay from 1946, which defines the specificity of Europe—in particular, the development of science and technology—as a result of the constitutive influence of antiquity and Christianity, such a life in polarities is traced back above all to the Scriptures, which, "as the foundation of European life, contain in a unique fashion the polarities in itself" (240; see also 261).

27. Borradori, *Philosophy in a Time of Terror*, 116–17. In "A Europe of Hope" Derrida adds: "I believe that, without Eurocentric illusions and pretensions, without the slightest pro-European nationalism, without even much trust in Europe as it is or in the direction it is taking, we must fight for what this name represents today, with the memory of the Enlightenment, of course, but also

with a guilty conscience for a responsible awareness of the totalitarian, genocidal, and colonialist crimes of the past" (410).

28. Arendt, *The Human Condition*, 292–93.

Chapter 11

1. For the distinction between inner and outer horizon by which the horizon of the perception of a thing is made see Kuhn, "The Phenomenological Concept of Horizon," 112.
2. Ströker, *Husserl's Transcendental Phenomenology*, 90.
3. Derrida, *Sur parole*, 49.
4. For a succinct discussion of Patočka's conception of the horizon see Srubar, "Vom begründeten Leben," 14.
5. See Liddell and Scott, *A Greek-English Lexicon*; Derrida, *Specters of Marx*, 28, 52.
6. Derrida, *Edmund Husserl's Origin of Geometry*, 82–83 (trans. mod.).
7. Derrida, "Psyche," 55.
8. Derrida, "The University Without Condition," 234.
9. Husserl, *Experience and Judgment*, 89; Derrida, "The University Without Condition," 234.
10. Derrida, "Force of Law," 967 (trans. mod.).
11. Derrida, *Edmund Husserl's Origin of Geometry*, 117.
12. Derrida, "The University Without Condition," 234.
13. Derrida, *Margins of Philosophy*, 316, 329.
14. Derrida, *Spurs*, 127 (trans. mod.).
15. Derrida, "The University Without Condition," 234.
16. Derrida and Roudinesco, *For What Tomorrow . . . A Dialogue*, 83.
17. Derrida, *Sur parole*, 50.
18. Derrida and Roudinesco, *For What Tomorrow . . . A Dialogue*, 60.
19. Kuhn, "The Phenomenological Concept of Horizon," 108.
20. Derrida, *Writing and Difference*, 120–21.
21. Derrida, *Rogues*, xiv.
22. Scheler, *Formalism in Ethics and Non-Formal Ethics of Values*, 144–45.
23. Derrida, *Specters of Marx*, 65.
24. Derrida, *Rogues*, 135.
25. Ibid., 143.
26. From his early work to his contribution to Giovanna Borradori's *Philosophy in a Time of Terror*, Derrida consistently expressed reservations regarding the

Idea in a Kantian sense, that is, the regulative idea. However, it is significant that the succinct critique of the Idea in a Kantian sense found in Derrida's interview with Borradori is preceded by the following observation: "my reservations are not straightforward objections. They are precisely reservations. For lack of anything better, if we can say this about a regulative idea, the regulative idea remains perhaps an ultimate reservation. Though such a last recourse risks becoming an alibi, it retains a certain dignity; I cannot swear that I will not one day give in to it" (Borradori, *Philosophy in a Time of Terror*, 133–34).

27. Derrida, *Rogues*, 128.
28. Derrida, *Chaque fois unique, la fin du monde*, 11.
29. In "The University Without Condition" Derrida explains that if he keeps the French term "*mondialisation du monde* . . . the worldwide-ization of the world," to translate "what the Anglo-Saxon countries call 'globalization,' in German *Globalisierung*," it is "to maintain a reference to the world—monde, Welt, mundus—which is neither the globe nor the cosmos" (Derrida, "The University Without Condition," 203, 223).
30. Derrida, *Rogues*, 155. For an excellent discussion of the implications of Derrida's claim that, contrary to what Heidegger asserts, the human is poor in world, see Lawlor, *This Is Not Sufficient*, 70.
31. Derrida, "The University Without Condition," 224.
32. Ibid., 223–24.
33. Derrida, *Negotiations*, 104 (trans. mod.).
34. In an essay devoted to the connection of "Europe" and the concept of "world," Klaus Held invokes the German expression "that a child at birth 'beholds the light of the world' [*das Licht der Welt erblickt*]," and, in an explicit reference to Arendt's concept of nativity, he remarks that "the German expression does not mean to say that the world is so full of light that it thereby gives occasion for great optimism. It means to say much more that the world's being there is luminous because it raises itself from the darkness of the Nothing, which event is awe-inspiring within the attunement of wonder. With every birth of a human being this darkness is newly broken and the world is brought forth as the light for the appearing of things. In this sense, every birth possesses a world-creating character" (Held, "The Origin of Europe with the Greek Discovery of the World," 96–97).
35. Derrida, "Uninterrupted Dialogue"; Derrida, *Chaque fois unique, la fin du monde*, 9–11.
36. Derrida, *Rogues*, 155 (trans. mod.).
37. Lawlor, *This Is Not Sufficient*, 96.

38. Derrida's conception of the world is the result not only of a critical debate with Heidegger's conception of death, which primarily concerns the individual's own death rather than that of the other, but also, and perhaps more fundamentally, with Husserl's analyses of intersubjectivity in the constitution of the world.

39. Derrida, "Uninterrupted Dialogue," 8. For an additional commentary on this passage see my *Views and Interviews*, 6–7.

40. Derrida, *Chaque fois unique, la fin du monde*, 9–11. We should remember, too, Derrida's contention that for death to be only the end of one world, but not of the world itself, one must postulate the existence of some God.

41. Derrida, "Uninterrupted Dialogue," 8.

42. Derrida, *Rogues*, 115.

43. Scheler, *Formalism in Ethics and Non-Formal Ethics of Values*, 271–73.

44. Derrida, *Rogues*, 149.

45. Reinhardt, *Religion*, 58.

46. In "Feeling the Debt" I have tried to show that these two axioms—one of which is of the order of a nonprivate sentiment, the other of the order of the conceptual, or discursive—relate to one another as empirical and transcendental experiences, that, despite their tension, are inseparably bound together. For a fine discussion of Derrida's *The Other Heading* and how Derrida's great texts of the 1960s loom behind his developments on Europe, see Redfield, "Derrida, Europe, Today," esp. 380–81. Much less in sync with Derrida's thought is Han, "Zu Derridas Gedanken über Europa in *Das andere Kap*." Han is greatly bewildered, if not taken aback, by the fact that Derrida links the demand for openness to the other to the question of the woman, which supposedly is one of the reasons why, according to Han, Derrida's demand for a Europe open to the other would remain deeply abstract (186–87).

47. Derrida, *Monolingualism of the Other*, 88.

48. Derrida, *Aporias*, 34.

49. Patočka, *Le monde naturel et le mouvement de l'existence humaine*, 37.

50. See Gasché, *The Tain of the Mirror*, 142–224.

51. All identity and all identification presupposes the law of this twofold difference. But whereas all cultural identity and identification is based on this law, it is also the case that identity and identification in general require culture: "there is no self-relation, no relation to oneself, without culture, but a culture of oneself as a culture of the other, a culture of the double genitive and of the difference to oneself. The grammar of the double genitive also signals that a culture never has a single origin" (*OH*, 10). What this means is not only that the way in which the universal law of identity forms self-relation and self-identity is always idiomatic and singular but also that because of the difference to oneself as a difference from oneself, one's own culture will always be based on a cultivating of the other, as well as of the other's culture. Differently worded, one's own culture will not only be indebted in depth to the culture of the other, at the same time it will

have to be dispossessed by the other's culture. All culture of one's own originates, therefore, not in oneself alone but, above all, in this cultivation of the culture of the other, as well, and this other's culture.

52. Rémi Brague has argued that what distinguishes European culture is that, for it, "the source is exterior." Whereas the cultural history of the Byzantine world is determined by the belief of a continuity with Hellenism, which the Byzantine Greek considers to be his own direct past and legacy, as a result of which the past to be reappropriated is always only one's own past; and whereas the turn to the sources in the cultural history of Islam, despite all its efforts to open itself to knowledge that comes from outside, is marked by a desire to appropriate its own sources in all their purity (in particular, the period of Medina, when the prophet established his community), Greece, as his or her origin, is for the European of the order of a past that has never been his or her own. Hence, "culture, for the European, cannot be something that he possesses and that would constitute his identity. On the contrary culture is for him something fundamentally foreign and requires an effort of appropriation. Only through the effort of a detour through an anteriority and the foreign does the European find access to what is his own." European identity, for this reason, is necessarily an "eccentric identity" (Brague, *Europe, la voie romaine*, 125–33). In contradistinction to Brague's historical and cultural approach to the question of Europe, Derrida's second axiom regarding cultural identity pertains just as much to other cultures as it does to Europe. If Europe enjoys a privilege at all, it is not because Europe would already enjoy this "eccentric identity" that Brague refers to, which he labels as a chance (133), but because Europe harbors perhaps the promise of such an eccentric identity.

53. If a double difference to oneself is required for a culture to gather itself into itself, the question, furthermore, becomes whether one is "more faithful to the heritage of a culture by cultivating the difference-to-oneself (*with oneself*) that constitutes identity or by confining oneself to an identity wherein this difference remains gathered" (*OH*, 11).

54. Michael B. Naas has explored Derrida's critique in *The Other Heading* of the logic of the example that pervades all the discourses on Europe, arguing that Derrida's ultimate concern is with that which qua "irreducible singularity . . . can have no example" (Naas, "Introduction," lv). But since no singularity can present itself without laying claim to universality, must it not, however unrepeatable, also demand for itself the status of exemplary example?

55. For an excellent account of how other, already constituted, cultural identities invoked by the second axiom interact with the identity of Europe, see Crépon, *Altérités de l'Europe*, 57–58.

56. Although the law stated by the second axiom is universal and apodictic, its implication for nonegocentric identity comes with a lesser degree of certainty because whether such an identity is truly open to the other is only in the other's court.

57. A similar use of "what if" opens another proposition on the "essence" of Europe in Derrida's contribution to the conference "Penser l'Europe à ses frontières," held in Strasbourg, France, in 1992. Following a characterization of Europe in terms of different ways of portage (*porter, se rapporter, transporter, exporter, deporter,* and so forth), Derrida submits: "And what if Europe were the history of an unending, and by definition open series of deportations, violent as well, of persons or peoples, from their supposedly proper site, such that the very idea of a European site would be mortally exposed to a history of these deportations that have always begun and are never finished?" (*PEF,* 21).

58. For a more detailed discussion of Derrida's understanding of the concept of responsibility see Gasché, "L'étrange concept de responsabilité."

59. *Penser l'Europe à ses frontières,* 29–30.

60. Derrida and Dufourmantelle, *Of Hospitality,* 141.

61. Derrida, *On Cosmopolitanism and Forgiveness,* 16–17.

62. Derrida and Dufourmantelle, *Of Hospitality,* 125.

63. Ibid., 123–25. For a fine discussion of the significance of the "as if" (which opens here all these conditional comparative propositions regarding the relations of self and other, host and guest), see Johnson, "*As If* the Time Were Now."

64. Derrida, *On Cosmopolitanism and Forgiveness,* 16–17.

65. Ibid., 18.

66. Derrida and Roudinesco, *For What Tomorrow . . . A Dialogue,* 59.

67. Ibid.

68. Derrida and Dufourmantelle, *Of Hospitality,* 77.

69. Ibid., 79.

70. Ibid.

Epilogue

1. In Joachim Ritter's words, for all peoples, Europe and Europeanization is "the universal that asserts itself in the particular" (Ritter, "Europäisierung als europäisches Problem," 321).

2. Guénoun, *Hypothèses sur l'Europe,* 250.

3. See, for example, Socrates' discussion in the *Philebus* of the only way worthy of the dialectician to consider how the one relates to the many, namely, by way of definite numbers that represent the intermediate link between both (Plato, *The Collected Dialogues,* 1094 [18a–c]).

4. Baruzzi, *Europas Autonomie,* 148.

5. Crépon, *Altérités de l'Europe,* 189.

6. Waldenfels, "Europa angesichts des Fremden," 143–44.

7. Derrida, *Positions,* 71.

Bibliography

Allemann, Beda. *Hölderlin und Heidegger.* Freiburg: Atlantis Verlag, 1954.
Arendt, Hannah. *The Human Condition.* Chicago: University of Chicago Press, 1958.
———. *The Life of the Mind.* Vol. 1, *Thinking.* New York: Harcourt Brace Jovanovich, 1978.
———. *Men in Dark Times.* New York: Harcourt, Brace and World, 1968.
———. *On Revolution.* New York: Viking Penguin, 1987.
Arendt, Hannah, and Martin Heidegger. *Briefe, 1925–1975.* Frankfurt/Main: Klostermann, 1999.
Aristotle. "Nicomachean Ethics." In Barnes, *The Complete Works of Aristotle,* 2:1729–1867.
———. "Politics." In Barnes, *The Complete Works of Aristotle,* 2:1986–2129.
———. "Rhetoric." In Barnes, *The Complete Works of Aristotle,* 2:2152–2269.
Baas, Bernard. "De Husserl à Heidegger: L'épuisement critique de la raison." Unpublished manuscript.
Barnes, Jonathan, ed. *The Complete Works of Aristotle.* 2 vols. Princeton, NJ: Princeton University Press, 1985.
Baruzzi, Arno. *Europas Autonomie.* Würzburg: Ergon Verlag, 1999.
Bégout, Bruce. "La phénoménologie décapitée? Perspectives et difficultés de la phénoménologie asubjective de Jan Patočka." *Chiasmi International* 4 (2002): 377–409.
Biemel, Walter. "Zur Bedeutung von Doxa und Episteme im Umkreis der Krisis-Thematik." In Ströker, *Lebenswelt und Wissenschaft in der Philosophie Edmund Husserls,* 10–22.
Blochmann, Elisabeth, and Martin Heidegger. *Briefwechsel, 1918–1969.* Marbach am Neckar: Deutsches Literaturarchiv, 1990.
Blumenberg, Hans. *Wirklichkeiten in denen wir leben.* Stuttgart: Reclam, 1981.

Borradori, Giovanna, ed. *Philosophy in a Time of Terror: Dialogues with Jürgen Habermas and Jacques Derrida.* Chicago: University of Chicago Press, 2003.
Brague, Rémi. *Europe, la voie romaine.* Paris: Criterion, 1993.
———. *La sagesse du monde: Histoire de l'expérience humaine de l'univers.* Paris: Fayard, 1999.
Cacciari, Massimo. *Der Archipel Europa.* Köln: DuMont, 1998.
Chiereghin, Franco. "Der griechische Anfang Europas und die Frage der Romanitas." In Gander, *Europa und die Philosophie,* 197–223.
Cho, Kah Kyung. "Der Abstieg über den Humanismus: West-Östliche Wege im Denken Heideggers." In Gander, *Europa und die Philosophie,* 143–74.
Chvatík, Ivan. "The Heretical Conception of the European Legacy in the Late Essays of Jan Patočka." www.cts.cuni.cz/new/data/Rep8aafe27d.doc.
Cohen, Hermann. *Kants Begründung der Aesthetik.* Berlin: Ferdinand Dümmlers Verlagsbuchhandlung, 1889.
———. *Kants Theorie der Erfahrung.* Berlin: Bruno Cassirer, 1918.
———. *Kommentar zur Kritik der reinen Vernunft.* Leipzig: Felix Meiner, 1917.
Courtine, Jean-François. "Un peuple métaphysique." *Revue de Métaphysique et de Morale* 3 (2001): 39–61.
Crépon, Marc. *Altérités de l'Europe.* Paris: Galilée, 2006.
———. "Penser l'Europe avec Patočka: Réflexions sur l'altérité." *Esprit* 12 (2004): 28–44.
Dastur, Françoise. "Europa und der 'andere Anfang.'" In Gander, *Europa und die Philosophie,* 185–96.
———. *Hölderlin: Le retournement natal/tragédie et poésie.* La Versanne: Encre Marine, 1997.
———. *Husserl: Des mathématiques à l'histoire.* Paris: Presses Universitaires de France, 1995.
———. *La phénoménologie en questions: Langage, altérité, temporalité, finitude.* Paris: Vrin, 2004.
De Gandt, François. *Husserl et Galilée: Sur la crise des sciences européennes.* Paris: Vrin, 2004.
Dempf, Alois. *Sacrum imperium: Geschichts- und Staatsphilosophie des Mittelalters und der politischen Renaissance.* Darmstadt: Wissenschaftliche Buchgesellschaft, 1954.
Deniau, Guy. "Phénoménologie asubjective et herméneutique: Patočka et Gadamer." *Chiasmi International* 4 (2002): 351–73.
Derrida, Jacques. *Aporias.* Trans. T. Dutoit. Stanford, CA: Stanford University Press, 1993.
———. *Chaque fois unique, la fin du monde.* Ed. P.-A. Brault and M. Naas. Paris: Galilée, 2001.

———. *Demeure: Fiction and Testimony.* Trans. E. Rottenberg. Stanford, CA: Stanford University Press, 2000.
———. *Edmund Husserl's Origin of Geometry: An Introduction.* Trans. J. P. Leavey. Stony Brook, NY: Nicolas Hays, 1979.
———. "A Europe of Hope." Trans. P. DeArmitt, J. Malle, and K. Saghafi. *Epoché* 10, no. 2 (spring 2006): 407–12.
———. *Fichus: Discours de Francfort.* Paris: Galilée, 2002.
———. "Force of Law: The Mystical Foundations of Authority." Trans. M. Quaintance. *Cardozo Law Review* 11, nos. 5–6 (1990): 919–1045.
———. "Form and Meaning: A Note on the Phenomenology of Language." In Derrida, *Margins of Philosophy*, 155–74.
———. *The Gift of Death.* Trans. D. Wills. Chicago: University of Chicago Press, 1992.
———. *Margins of Philosophy.* Trans. A. Bass. Chicago: University of Chicago Press, 1982.
———. *Monolingualism of the Other; or, The Prosthesis of Origin.* Trans. P. Mensah. Stanford, CA: Stanford University Press, 1988.
———. *Negotiations: Interventions and Interviews, 1971–2001.* Trans. E. Rottenberg. Stanford, CA: Stanford University Press, 2002.
———. "Nous autres Grecs." In *Nos Grecs et leurs modernes: Les stratégies contemporaines d'appropriation de l'antiquité*, ed. B. Cassin, 251–76. Paris: Seuil, 1992.
———. *Of Spirit: Heidegger and the Question.* Trans. G. Bennington and R. Bowlby. Chicago: University of Chicago Press, 1989.
———. *On Cosmopolitanism and Forgiveness.* Trans. M. Dooley and M. Hughes. New York: Routledge, 2001.
———. *The Other Heading: Reflections on Today's Europe.* Trans. P.-A. Brault and M. B. Naas. Bloomington: Indiana University Press, 1992.
———. *Passions.* Paris: Galilée, 1993.
———. *Points . . . Interviews, 1974–1994.* Trans. E. Weber. Stanford, CA: Stanford University Press, 1995.
———. *Politics of Friendship.* Trans. G. Collins. London: Verso, 1997.
———. *Positions.* Trans. A. Bass. Chicago: University of Chicago Press, 1981.
———. *The Problem of Genesis in Husserl's Philosophy.* Trans. M. Hobson. Chicago: University of Chicago Press, 2003.
———. *Psyche: Inventions of the Other.* Ed. P. Kamuf and E. Rottenberg. 2 vols. Stanford, CA: Stanford University Press, 2008.
———. "Psyche: Inventions of the Other." Trans. C. Porter. In *Reading de Man Reading*, ed. L. Waters and W. Godzich, 25–65. Minneapolis: University of Minnesota Press, 1989.

---. *Rogues: Two Essays on Reason.* Trans. P.-A. Brault and M. Naas. Stanford, CA: Stanford University Press, 2005.

---. "Some Statements and Truisms About Neologisms, Newisms, Postisms, Parisitisms, and Other Small Seismisms." Trans. A. Tomiche. In *The States of "Theory": History, Art, and Critical Discourse*, ed. D. Carroll, 63–94. New York: Columbia University Press, 1990.

---. *Specters of Marx: The State of the Debt, the Work of Mourning and the New International.* Trans. P. Kamuf. New York: Routledge, 1994.

---. *Spurs: Nietzsche's Styles.* Trans. B. Harlow. Chicago: University of Chicago Press, 1979.

---. *Sur parole: Instantanés philosophiques.* La Tour d'Aigues: Editions de l'aube, 2005.

---. "Uninterrupted Dialogue: Between Two Infinities, the Poem." Trans. T. Dutoit and P. Romanski. *Research in Phenomenology* 34 (2004): 3–19.

---. "The University Without Condition." In Derrida, *Without Alibi*, 202–37.

---. *Without Alibi.* Trans. P. Kamuf. Stanford, CA: Stanford University Press, 2000.

---. *Writing and Difference.* Trans. A. Bass. Chicago: University of Chicago Press, 1979.

Derrida, Jacques, and Anne Dufourmantelle. *Of Hospitality.* Trans. R. Bowlby. Stanford, CA: Stanford University Press, 2000.

Derrida, Jacques, and Elisabeth Roudinesco. *For What Tomorrow . . . A Dialogue.* Trans. J. Fort. Stanford, CA: Stanford University Press, 2004.

Derrida, Jacques, and G. Vattimo, eds. *Religion.* Stanford, CA: Stanford University Press, 1998.

Di Cesare, Donatella. "Die Heimat der Verschiedenheit: Über die plurale Identität Europas." In Stegmaier, *Europa Philosophie*, 109–22.

Diner, Dan. *Feindbild Amerika: Über die Beständigkeit eines Ressentiments.* Munich: Propyläen, 2003.

Fink, Eugen. *Studien zur Phänomenologie, 1930–1939.* The Hague: Nijhoff, 1966.

Franck, Didier. *Heidegger et le christianisme: L'explication silencieuse.* Paris: Presses Universitaires de France, 2004.

Freeman, Kathleen. *Ancilla to the Pre-Socratic Philosophers.* Cambridge, MA: Harvard University Press, 1983.

Gadamer, Hans-Georg. "Europa und die Oikumene." In Gander, *Europa und die Philosophie*, 67–86.

Gander, Hans-Helmuth, ed. *Europa und die Philosophie.* Frankfurt/Main: Klostermann, 1993.

Garrido, Juan Manuel. "'Appearing as Such' in Patočka's A-Subjective Phenomenology." *Philosophy Today* 51, no. 3 (2007): 124–39.

Gasché, Rodolphe. "Alongside the Horizon." In *On Jean-Luc Nancy: The Sense of Philosophy*, ed. D. Sheppard, S. Sparks, and C. Thomas, 140–56. London: Routledge, 1997.

———. "Feeling the Debt: On Europe." In *Future Crossings: Literature Between Philosophy and Cultural Studies*, ed. K. Ziarek and S. Deane, 123–46. Evanston, IL: Northwestern University Press, 2000.

———. "Felicities and Infelicities of a Model: Tragedy and the Present." *Research in Phenomenology* 33 (2003): 287–98.

———. "In Light of Light: On Jan Patočka's Notion of Europe." In *The Politics of Deconstruction*, ed. M. McQuillan, 116–36. London: Pluto, 2007.

———. "L'étrange concept de responsabilité." In *La démocratie à venir: Autour de Jacques Derrida*, ed. M. L. Mallet, 361–74. Paris: Galileé, 2004.

———. *The Tain of the Mirror: Derrida and the Philosophy of Reflection*. Cambridge, MA: Harvard University Press, 1986.

———. *Views and Interviews: On "Deconstruction" in America*. Aurora, CO: Davis Group, 2007.

———. "Zur Figur des Archipels." Trans. K. Thiele. In Weidner, *Figuren des europäischen*, 235–45.

Gniazdowski, Andrzey. "Phänomenologie und Politik: Husserls These von der Erneuerung der Menschheit." *Der Begriff des Subjekts in der modernen und postmodernen Philosophie*, ed. D. Dybel and H. J. Sandkühler, 82–96. Frankfurt/Main: Peter Lang, 2004.

Gollwitzer, Heinz. "Europa." In *Historisches Wörterbuch der Philosophie*, ed. J. Ritter, 2:824–28. Darmstadt: Wissenschaftliche Buchgesellschaft, 1972.

Granel, Gérard. Preface to *La Crise des sciences européennes et la phénoménologie transcendantale*, by Edmund Husserl. Trans. G. Granel, v–vii. Paris: Gallimard, 1976.

Grondin, Jean. "Hermeneutik." In *Historisches Wörterbuch der Rhetorik*, ed. G. Ueding, 3:1350–74. Tübingen: Max Niemeyer, 1966.

Guénoun, Denis. *Hypothèses sur l'Europe: Un essai de philosophie*. Belfort: Circé, 2000.

Han, Byung-Chul. "Zu Derridas Gedanken über Europa in *Das andere Kap*." In Stegmaier, *Europa Philosophie*, 177–88.

Heidegger, Martin. "The Age of the World Picture." In *The Question Concerning Technology and Other Essays*, trans. W. Lowitt, 115–54. New York: Harper & Row, 1977.

———. *Basic Writings*, ed. D. F. Krell. New York: Harper & Row, 1977.

———. *Being and Time*. Trans. J. Macquarrie and E. Robinson. New York: Harper & Row, 1962.

———. *Denkerfahrungen, 1910–1976*. Frankfurt/Main: Klostermann, 1983.

———. *Early Greek Thinking*. Trans. D. F. Krell and D. A. Capuzzi. New York: Harper & Row, 1975.
———. *Elucidations of Hölderlin's Poetry*. Trans. K. Hoeller. Amherst, NY: Prometheus Books, 2000.
———. "Europa und die deutsche Philosophie." In Gander, *Europa und die Philosophie*, 31–41.
———. *Grundbegriffe der aristotelischen Philosophie. Gesamtausgabe*, Vol. 18. Frankfurt/Main: Klostermann, 2002.
———. *Grundbegriffe der Metaphysik. Gesamtausgabe*, Vol. 29/30. Frankfurt/Main: Klostermann, 1983.
———. *Heraklit. 1. Der Anfang des abendländischen Denkens. 2. Logik. Heraklits Lehre vom Logos. Gesamtausgabe*, Vol. 55. Frankfurt/Main: Klostermann, 1979.
———. *Hölderlins Hymne "Andenken." Gesamtausgabe*, Vol. 52. Frankfurt/Main: Klostermann, 1982.
———. *Hölderlins Hymnen "Germanien" und "Der Rhein." Gesamtausgabe*, Vol. 39. Frankfurt/Main: Klostermann, 1980.
———. *Hölderlin's Hymn "The Ister."* Trans. W. McNeill and J. Davis. Bloomington: Indiana University Press, 1996.
———. *Identity and Difference*. Trans. J. Stambaugh. New York: Harper & Row, 1969.
———. *Introduction to Metaphysics*. Trans. G. Fried and R. Polt. New Haven, CT: Yale University Press, 2000.
———. *Nietzsche*. Vol. 4. Trans. F. A. Capuzzi. San Francisco: Harper & Row, 1982.
———. *1. Nietzsches Metaphysik. 2. Einleitung in die Philosophie. Denken und Dichten. Gesamtausgabe*, Vol. 50. Frankfurt/Main: Klostermann, 1990.
———. *On the Way to Language*. Trans. P. D. Hertz. New York: Harper & Row, 1982.
———. *Parmenides*. Trans. A. Schuwer and R. Rojcewics. Bloomington: Indiana University Press, 1992.
———. *Pathmarks*. Trans. W. McNeill. Cambridge, UK: Cambridge University Press, 1998.
———. *Phänomenologische Interpretationen zu Aristoteles: Einführung in die phänomenologische Forschung. Gesamtausgabe*, Vol. 61. Frankfurt/Main: Klostermann, 1985.
———. *Über den Anfang. Gesamtausgabe*, Vol. 70. Frankfurt/Main: Klostermann, 2005.
———. *Vorträge und Aufsätze*. Pfullingen: Neske, 1954.
———. *What Is Called Thinking?* Trans. J. G. Gray. New York: Harper & Row, 1968.

———. *What Is Philosophy?* Trans. W. Kluback and J. T. Wilde. Estover: Vision Press, 1989.

———. *Zu Hölderlin: Griechenlandreisen. Gesamtausgabe*, Vol. 75. Frankfurt/Main: Klostermann, 2000.

———. *Zur Bestimmung der Philosophie. Gesamtausgabe*, Vol. 56–57. Frankfurt/Main: Klostermann, 1987.

Held, Klaus. "Europa und die interkulturelle Verständigung." In Gander, *Europa und die Philosophie*, 87–103.

———. "Heimwelt, Fremdwelt, die eine Welt." In *Phänomenologische Forschungen* 24/25, ed. E. W. Orth, 304–37. Freiburg/Munich: Karl Alber, 1991.

———. "Husserl und die Griechen." *Phänomenologische Forschungen* 22, ed. E. W. Orth, 137–76. Freiburg/Munich: Karl Alber, 1989.

———. "Husserls These von der Europäisierung der Menschheit." In *Phänomenologie im Widerstreit. Zum 50. Todestag Edmund Husserls*, ed. C. Jamme and O. Pöggeler, 13–39. Frankfurt/Main: Suhrkamp, 1989.

———. "The Origin of Europe with the Greek Discovery of the World." *Epoché* 7, no. 1 (fall 2002): 81–195.

Herodotus. *The Histories*. Trans. A. de Sélincourt. Harmondsworth: Penguin, 1972.

Hölderlin, Friedrich. *Essays and Letters on Theory*. Ed. T. Pfau. Albany: State University of New York Press, 1988.

Husserl, Edmund. *Aufsätze und Vorträge (1922–1937)*. Ed. T. Nenon and H. R. Sepp. *Husserliana*, Vol. 27. Dordrecht: Kluwer, 1989.

———. *The Crisis of European Sciences and Transcendental Phenomenology*. Trans. D. Carr. Evanston, IL: Northwestern University Press, 1970.

———. *Die Krisis der europäischen Wissenschaften und die transzendentale Phänomenologie*. Ed. W. Biemel. *Husserliana*, Vol. 6. The Hague: Nijhoff, 1962.

———. *Die Krisis der europäischen Wissenschaften und die transzendentale Phänomenologie. Ergänzungsband: Texte aus dem Nachlass, 1934–1937*. Ed. R. N. Smid. *Husserliana*, Vol. 29. Dordrecht: Kluwer, 1993.

———. *Experience and Judgment: Investigations in a Genealogy of Logic*. Trans. J. S. Churchill and K. Ameriks. London: Routledge & Kegan Paul, 1973.

———. *Formal and Transcendental Logic*. Trans. D. Cairns. The Hague: Nijhoff, 1978.

———. "Fünf Ausätze über Erneuerung." In Husserl, *Aufsätze und Vorträge (1922–1937)*, 3–122.

———. *Ideas: General Introduction to Pure Phenomenology*. Trans. W. R. Boyce Gibson. New York: Humanities Press, 1967.

———. *Ideas Pertaining to a Pure Phenomenology and to a Phenomenological Philosophy: First Book: General Introduction to a Pure Phenomenology*. Trans. F. Kersten. The Hague: Nijhoff, 1982.

———. "Philosophy as Rigorous Science." In *Phenomenology and the Crisis of Philosophy*, trans. Q. Lauer, 71–147. New York: Harper & Row, 1965.

Jaspers, Karl. "Vom europäischen Geist." In *Rechenschaft und Ausblick: Reden und Aufsätze*, 233–64. Munich: Piper Verlag, 1951.

Johnson, David E. "*As If* the Time Were Now: Deconstructing Agamben." *South Atlantic Quarterly* 106, no. 2 (spring 2007): 265–90.

Kant, Immanuel. *Critique of Pure Reason*. Trans. N. K. Smith. New York: St. Martin's, 1965.

Kapuściński, Ryszard. *The Shadow of the Sun: My African Life*. Trans. K. Glowczewska. Allen Lane: Penguin, 2001.

Kern, Iso. "Die Lebenswelt als Grundlagenproblem der objektiven Wissenschaften und als universales Wahrheits- und Seinsproblem." In Ströker, *Lebenswelt und Wissenschaft in der Philosophie Edmund Husserls*, 68–78.

Köhler, Oskar. "Abendland." *Theologische Realenzyklopädie*. 1:17–42. Berlin: de Gruyter, 1977.

Koslowski, Peter, and Rémi Brague. *Vaterland Europa: Europäische und nationale Identität im Konflikt*. Vienna: Passagen Verlag, 1997.

Kuhn, Helmut. "The Phenomenological Concept of 'Horizon.'" In *Philosophical Essays in Memory of Edmund Husserl*, ed. M. Farber, 106–23. New York: Greenwood Press, 1968.

Lacoue-Labarthe, Philippe. *Heidegger and the Politics of Poetry*. Trans. J. Fort. Urbana: University of Illinois Press, 2007.

———. *Heidegger, Art and Politics: The Fiction of the Political*. Trans. C. Turner. Oxford: Basil Blackwell, 1990.

———. *Poétique de l'histoire*. Paris: Galilée, 2002.

Landgrebe, Ludwig. *The Phenomenology of Edmund Husserl: Six Essays*. Ed. D. Welton. Ithaca, NY: Cornell University Press, 1981.

Lawlor, Leonard. *This Is Not Sufficient: An Essay on Animality and Human Nature in Derrida*. New York: Columbia University Press, 2007.

Lefort, Claude. "L'imaginaire de la crise." *Commentaire* 20, no. 79 (autumn 1997): 525–36.

Le désir d'Europe. Strasbourg: Carrefour des Littératures de Strasbourg, 1992.

Le Goff, Jacques. *The Birth of Europe*. Oxford: Blackwell, 2005.

Leibniz, Gottfried Wilhelm. *New Essays Concerning Human Understanding*. Trans. A. G. Langley. La Salle, IL: Open Court, 1949.

Lessing, Theodor. *Untergang der Erde am Geist: Europa und Asien*. Hannover: Wolf Albrecht Adam Verlag, 1925.

Li, Victor. "Elliptical Interruptions, or, Why Derrida Prefers *Mondialisation* to Globalization." *New Centennial Review* 7, no. 2 (fall 2007): 141–54.

Liddell, Henry George, and Robert Scott. *A Greek-English Lexicon*. Oxford: Clarendon Press, 1968.

Losurdo, Domenico. *Heidegger et l'idéologie de la guerre.* Trans. J. M. Buée. Paris: Presses Universitaires de France, 1998.
Löwith, Karl. *Meaning and History.* Chicago: University of Chicago Press, 1949.
Lübbe, Hermann. "Geteilte Souveränität: Die Transformation des Staates in der europäischen Einigung." *Information Philosophie* 3 (1994): 5–13.
———. "Husserl und die europäische Krise." In *Bewusstsein in Geschichten: Studien zur Phänomenologie der Subjektivität,* by Hermann Lübbe, 63–80. Freiburg: Rombach, 1972.
Marramao, Giacomo. *Die Säkularisierung der westlichen Welt.* Trans. G. Memmert. Frankfurt/Main: Inserl Verlag, 1966.
Masschelein, Anneleen. "Unheimlich/das Unheimliche." *Aesthetische Grundbegriffe.* Vol. 5, ed. Karlheinz Barck, Martin Fontius, Dieter Schlenstedt, Burkhart Steinwachs, and Friedrich Wolfzettel, 241–60. Stuttgart/Weimar: J. B. Metzler, 2005.
Naas, Michael B. "Introduction: For Example." In Derrida, *The Other Heading,* vii–lix.
Nancy, Jean-Luc. "Dies Irae." In *La faculté de juger,"* ed. J. Derrida, V. Descombes, G. Kortian, P. Lacoue-Labarthe, J.-F. Lyotard, J.-L. Nancy, 9–54. Paris: Minuit, 1985.
———. "Euryopa: Le regard au loin." In *Contributions,* a prepublication of the proceedings of a conference at the University of Leipzig, May 11–14, 1994, 5–15. Leipzig: University of Leipzig Press, 1994.
———. "La naissance continuée de l'Europe." In *Le désir d'Europe,* 253–55. Strasbourg: Carrefour des Littératures de Strasbourg, 1992.
Nietzsche, Friedrich. *Early Greek Philosophy and Other Essays.* Vol. 2 of *The Complete Works.* New York: Russell and Russell, 1964.
———. *The Will to Power.* Ed. W. Kaufmann. New York: Vintage Books, 1968.
Ogawa, Tadashi. "Eurozentrismus, Eurozentrik und Ent-Europäisierung." In *Grund und Grenze des Bewusstseins: Interkulturelle Phänomenologie aus japanischer Sicht,* 121–31. Würzburg: Königshausen & Neumann, 2001.
Orth, Ernst Wolfgang. *Edmund Husserls "Krisis der europäischen Wissenschaften und die transzendentale Phänomenologie."* Darmstadt: Wissenschaftliche Buchgesellschaft, 1999.
———. "Einleitung. Jan Patočka und die Phänomenologie." In Orth, *Studien zur Philosophie von Jan* Patočka, 7–9.
———, ed. *Studien zur Philosophie von Jan Patočka.* Munich: Karl Alber Verlag, 1985.

Otto, Rudolf. *The Idea of the Holy: An Inquiry into the Non-rational Factor in the Idea of the Divine and Its Relation to the Rational.* Trans. J. W. Harvey. London: Oxford University Press, 1957.

Patočka, Jan. "Afterword." In *Le monde naturel comme problème philosophique.* Trans. J. Danek and H. Declève. The Hague: Nijhoff, 1976.

———. *Heretical Essays in the Philosophy of History.* Trans. E. Kohak. Chicago: Open Court, 1966.

———. "La conception aristotelicienne du mouvement: Signification philosophique et recherches historiques." In Patočka, *Le monde naturel comme problème philosophique,* 127–38.

———. *Le monde naturel comme problème philosophique.* Trans. J. Danek and H. Declève. The Hague: Nijhoff, 1976.

———. *Le monde naturel et le mouvement de l'existence humaine.* Trans. E. Abrams. Dordrecht: Kluwer, 1988.

———. *Liberté et sacrifice: Ecrits politiques.* Trans. E. Abrams. Genoble: Jérôme Millon, 1990.

———. *Papiers phénoménologiques.* Trans. E. Abrams. Grenoble: Jérôme Millon, 1995.

———. *Plato and Europe.* Trans. P. Lom. Stanford, CA: Stanford University Press, 2002.

———. "Réflexion sur l'Europe." In Patočka, *Liberté et sacrifice,* 181–213.

Penser l'Europe à ses frontières, 7–10 novembre 1992. Ed. D. Guénoun. Strasbourg: Editions de l'aube, 1993.

Phillips, James. *Heidegger's Volk: Between National Socialism and Poetry.* Stanford, CA: Stanford University Press, 2005.

Plato. *The Collected Dialogues.* Ed. E. Hamilton and H. Cairns. Princeton, NJ: Princeton University Press, 1980.

———. *The Dialogues of Plato.* Trans. B. Jowett. Vol. 1. Oxford: Clarendon Press, 1875.

Plessen, Marie-Louise von, ed. *Idee Europa: Entwürfe zum "Ewigen Frieden." Ordnungen und Utopien für die Gestaltung Europas von der pax romana zur Europäischen Union.* Berlin: Deutsches Historisches Museum, 2003.

Pöggeler, Otto. *Schicksal und Geschichte: Antigone im Spiegel der Deutungen und Gestaltungen seit Hegel und Hölderlin.* Munich: Wilhelm Fink Verlag, 2004.

Ramnoux, Clémence. "Les Présocratiques." In *Histoire de la philosophie,* ed. B. Parain, 1:405–48. Paris: Gallimard, 1969.

Redfield, Marc. "Derrida, Europe, Today." *South Atlantic Quarterly* 106, no. 2 (spring 2007): 373–92.

Reinhardt, Karl. "Hölderlin und Sophokles." In *Tradition und Geist: Gesammelte Essays zur Dichtung,* ed. Carl Becker, 381–97. Göttingen: Vandenhoeck & Ruprecht, 1960.

———. *Sophokles*. Frankfurt/Main: Klostermann, 2006.
Rheinberger, Hans-Jörg. "Zur Historizität wissenschaftlichen Wissens: Ludwik Fleck, Edmund Husserl." In *Epistemologie des Konkreten: Studien zur Geschichte der modernen Biologie*, 21–36. Frankfurt/Main: Suhrkamp, 2006.
Ricoeur, Paul. *A l'école de la phénoménologie*. Paris: Vrin, 1993.
———. *Husserl: An Analysis of His Phenomenology*. Trans. E. G. Ballard and L. E. Embree. Evanston, IL: Northwestern University Press, 1967.
———. "Jan Patočka et le nihilisme." In *Lectures 1: Autour du politique*, 69–73. Paris: Seuil, 1991.
———. "Note introductive." In *Heidegger et la question de dieu*, ed. R. Kearney and J. S. O'Leary, 17. Paris: Grasset, 1980.
———. "Preface to the French Edition [of Jan Patočka's *Heretical Essays*]." In Patočka, *Heretical Essays in the Philosophy of Europe*, vii–xvi.
Riedel, Manfred. "Heideggers europäische Wendung." In Gander, *Europa und die Philosophie*, 43–66.
Ritter, Joachim. "Europäisierung als europäisches Problem." In *Metaphysik und Politik: Studien zu Aristoteles und Hegel*, 321–40. Frankfurt/Main: Suhrkamp, 1977.
Rougemont, Denis de. *The Idea of Europe*. Trans. N. Guterman. New York: Macmillan, 1966.
Scheler, Max. *Formalism in Ethics and Non-Formal Ethics of Values: A New Attempt Toward the Foundation of an Ethical Formalism*. Trans. M. S. Frings and R. L. Funk. Evanston, IL: Northwestern University Press, 1973.
———. *The Nature of Sympathy*. Trans. P. Heath. London: Routledge & Kegan Paul, 1954.
Schlegel, Friedrich. *Philosophical Fragments*. Trans. P. Firchow. Minneapolis: University of Minnesota Press, 1991.
Schmidt, Dennis J. *On Germans and Other Greeks: Tragedy and Ethical Life*. Bloomington: Indiana University Press, 2001.
Schulze, Hagen. "Europa als historische Idee." In Stegmaier, *Europa Philosophie*, 1–13.
Schumann, Karl. "Lebenswelt als Unterlage der Phänomenologie." In Ströker, *Lebenswelt und Wissenschaft in der Philosophie Edmund Husserls*, 79–91.
Simon, Josef. "Europa als philosophische Idee." In Stegmaier, *Europa Philosophie*, 15–35.
Sophocles. *Antigone*. Trans. K. Reinhardt. Göttingen: Vandenhoeck & Ruprecht, 1961.
"*Spiegel* Interview with Martin Heidegger." In *Martin Heidegger and National Socialism: Questions and Answers*, ed. G. Neske and E. Kettering, 41-46. New York: Paragon, 1990.

Srubar, Ilja. "Vom begründeten Leben: Zu Jan Patočkas praktischer Philosophie." In Orth, *Studien zur Philosophie von Jan* Patočka, 10–31.
Stegmaier, Werner, ed. *Europa Philosophie*. Berlin: de Gruyter, 2003.
Ströker, Elisabeth. "Geschichte und Lebenswelt als Sinnesfundament der Wissenschaften in Edmund Husserls Spätwerk." In Ströker, *Lebenswelt und Wissenschaft in der Philosophie Edmund Husserls*, 107–23.
———. *Husserl's Transcendental Phenomenology*. Trans. L. Hardy. Stanford, CA: Stanford University Press, 1993.
———. "Krise der europäischen Wissenschaften als Krise der Kultur: Husserls Europa Gedanke in seinem Spätwerk." In Stegmaier, *Europa Philosophie*, 123–39.
———, ed. *Lebenswelt und Wissenschaft in der Philosophie Edmund Husserls*. Frankfurt/Main: Klostermann, 1979.
———. "Psychologie: A New Way into Transcendental Phenomenology? Some Thoughts on Husserl's Last Part of the *Crisis*." *Southwestern Journal of Philosophy* 11, no. 3 (1980): 67–87.
Taminiaux, Jacques. *Le théâtre des philosophes: La tragédie, l'être, l'action*. Grenoble: Jérôme Millon, 1995.
Valdinoci, Serge. *La traversée de l'immanence: L'europanalyse ou la méthode de la phénoménologie*. Paris: Editions Kimé, 1996.
Valéry, Paul. *History and Politics*. Trans. D. Folliot and J. Matthews. New York: Bollingen, 1962.
Volpi, Franco. "Heidegger et la romanité philosophique." *Revue de Métaphysique et de Morale* 3 (2001): 5–18.
Waldenfels, Bernhard. "Die verachtete Doxa: Husserl und die fortdauernde Krisis der abendländischen Vernunft." *In den Netzen der Lebenswelt*, 34–55. Frankfurt/Main: Suhrkamp, 1994.
———. "Europa angesichts des Fremden." *Topographie des Fremden: Studien zur Phänomenologie des Fremden*, 1:131–44. Frankfurt/Main: Suhrkamp, 1977.
Weidner, Daniel, ed. *Figuren des europäischen: Kulturgeschichtliche Perspektiven*. Munich: Wilhelm Fink Verlag, 2006.
———. "Vorwort." In Weidner, *Figuren des europäischen*, 7–19.
Weill, Nicolas, ed. *Existe-t-il une Europe philosophique?* Rennes: Presses Universitaires de Rennes, 2005.
Wismann, Heinz. "Une introduction." In Weill, *Existe-t-il une Europe philosophique?* 23–28.
Zarader, Marlène. *The Unthought Debt: Heidegger and the Hebraic Heritage*. Trans. B. Bergo. Stanford, CA: Stanford University Press, 2006.

Index

Abraham, 277, 279
Achilles, 374n2
Aeschylus, 13
Agenor, 10, 12
Alcibiades, 222, 223
Allemann, Beda, 378n31
Alliez, Eric, 391n23
Anaximander, 100, 101
Anselm of Canterbury, 13
Antigone, 123, 132, 138–40, 157, 181–91, 200, 373n22, 374nn27, 28, 375n7
Aquinas, Saint Thomas, 13
Arendt, Hannah, 177, 300, 314, 368n36, 371n8, 372n11, 377n24, 383–84n3, 388n8, 393n34
Aristotle, 10, 13, 140, 141, 167, 174, 175, 217, 324, 357n30, 370n40, 374nn29, 2, 377n23, 381n7, 391n14
Augustine, Saint, 13, 245, 387n6
Aurelius, Marcus, 339

Baas, Bernard, 366n24
Bach, Johann Sebastian, 13
Badiou, Alain, 9
Beethoven, Ludwig von, 13
Biemel, Walter, 37
Blochmann, Elisabeth, 364n5
Blumenberg, Hans, 362n8
Böhlendorff, Casimir Ulrich von, 151, 191, 193–98, 202

Borradori, Giovanna, 299, 392n26
Boyle, Robert, 359n9
Brague, Rémi, 13, 389–90n11, 394–95n52
Burckhardt, Jacob, 177, 179

Caesar, Julius 14
Cassirer, Ernst, 359n9
Cassin, Barbara, 391n23
Celan, Paul, 315, 317
Cervantes, Miguel de, 13
Cho, Kah Kyung, 364n3
Chuang Tzu, 206
Chvatík, Ivan, 261
Cicero, Marcus Tullius
Cohen, Hermann, 26, 354n10, 359n9
Creon, 138–40, 184, 185, 373n22
Crépon, Marc, 212, 213, 382n23

Dante Alighieri, 13
Dastur, Françoise, 103, 355n13
De Gandt, François, 359–60n9
Democrates, 381n7
Demph, Alois, 383n2
Derrida, Jacques, 2, 5, 9, 51, 57, 100, 105, 106, 127, 237, 265–338, 340, 341, 345, 346, 351n22, 352n2, 355nn12,14, 357nn28,34, 359n8, 363n20, 363–64n21, 370n43, 379n35, 385–86n18,

409

386nn1–3, 388nn8,9,1, 389nn4,6,9, 389–90n11, 390–91n12, 391n23, 391n27, 392–93n26, 393nn29,30, 38, 394nn40,46, 395nn52,54, 395–96n57, 396n58
Descartes, René, 41, 126, 359n9, 362n10, 384n3
Dike, 139, 140, 184
Diner, Dan, 350n5
Duns Scotus, 387n6

Elijah, 328
Empedocles, 154
Enkidu, 383n29
Erasmus, Desiderius, 13
Euripides, 13
Europa, 10–12, 350n17

Fink, Eugen, 25, 251
Fleck, Ludwik, 360n10
Franck, Didier, 372n14

Gadamer, Hans-Georg, 316, 386n2
Galileo Galilei, 49, 50, 52, 53, 55–62, 102, 260, 358n6, 359–60n9, 360n14
Garrido, Juan Manuel, 354n10, 382n26
Gasché, Rodolphe, 349n1
George, Stefan, 152
Gilgamesh, 383n29
Goethe, Johann Wolfgang von, 13, 138
Granel, Gérard, 349n1
Guénoun, Denis, 9, 11, 350n9, 351n22

Han, Byung-Chul, 394n46
Hedio, Caspar, 95
Hegel, Georg Wilhelm Friedrich, 13, 97, 138, 139, 140, 202, 265, 336, 373n22
Heidegger, Martin, 2, 5, 9, 95–207, 211–14, 216, 217, 228, 229, 237, 239–41, 249, 255, 265, 267–69, 271, 278, 279, 291–93, 296, 297, 304, 312–15, 322, 324, 340, 341, 345, 355n14, 356–57n27, 357n34, 361nn3,5, 364nn4,5, 364–65n7, 365nn9,18, 366nn24,26–29, 367nn31–34, 368nn35–37, 369–70n38, 370nn39,43, 371nn7–9, 372nn10,14,15, 373nn21,22, 374nn28,1,2,4, 375nn7,10,12, 376n16,19, 377nn20,22,25, 377–78n27, 378nn29–31, 379n35, 381n11, 389n9, 393n38
Held, Klaus, 42, 393n34
Hellingrath, Norbert von, 152
Heracles, 383n29
Heraclitus, 129–33, 142, 150, 155, 188, 365n7, 373n16, 374n28
Herodotus, 11
Hestia, 378n29
Hitler, Adolf, 369n38
Hobbes, Thomas, 384n3
Hölderlin, Friedrich, 95–97, 104, 141, 147, 150–56, 158, 165, 178, 191–99, 201–3, 298, 365n7, 375nn7,10, 378nn30–32, 386n1
Homer, 12, 13, 135, 146, 152, 158, 174, 300, 374n2
Horace, 13
Hume, David, 330
Husserl, Edmund, 1, 2, 4, 5, 9, 17, 21–91, 96, 99, 104, 105–9, 111–13, 126–28, 144–48, 154, 159, 175, 200, 211–17, 220, 221, 227–29, 231, 237, 239–43, 265, 268, 269, 271, 276, 280, 288–93, 295, 296, 303–7, 310–12, 322, 323, 332, 340–43, 346, 349n1, 352nn1, 352–53n2, 353nn3–5, 354nn10, 354–55n11, 355nn12–15, 355–56n16, 356nn17,19,22,24, 357nn30, 34, 36, 38, 358nn40,4, 359n7,8, 359–60n9, 360n13, 361nn17,1, 361–62n5, 362nn6,8,10, 363nn11,12,16,19,20, 363–64n21, 366n24, 371–72n9, 374n1, 379n1, 380n2, 381n11, 382–83n28, 386n3, 389nn4,9, 393n38
Huygens, Christiaan, 359n9

Isaac, 277, 279
Ismene, 140, 184

Jaspers, Karl, 13, 298, 358n39

Jesus Christ, 385n13, 387n6
Johnson, David E., 396n63
Julian the Apostate, 253

Kant, Immanuel, 13, 17, 34, 83, 87–89,
　91, 286, 304, 307, 310, 312, 334, 336,
　351n28, 354n10, 387n6, 392n26
Kapuściński, Ryszard, 349n3
Kepler, Johannes, 359n9
Kierkegaard, Søren, 267, 279
Kleist, Heinrich von, 138
Kuhn, Helmut, 309
Kuki, Shūzō, 206

Lacoue-Labarthe, Philippe, 114, 136,
　366n20, 370n38, 371n8, 371–72n9
Lawlor, Leonard, 316
Lao Tzu, 206
Le Goff, Jacques, 389n11
Leibniz, Gottfried Willhelm, 14, 65,
　108, 113, 127
Leonardo da Vinci, 13
Lessing, Theodor, 379n35
Levinas, Emmanuel, 267, 279, 294, 310
Liddell, Henry George, 305
Losurdo, Domenico, 365n18, 367n33
Löwith, Karl, 372n11
Luther, Martin, 95, 127

Marramao, Giacomo, 128, 372n11
Marx, Karl, 271
Michelangelo, 13
Moira, 374n28
Molière, 13
Mozart, Wolfgang Amadeus, 13

Naas, Michael B., 395n54
Nancy, Jean-Luc, 11, 12, 33, 102, 347
Natorp, Paul, 359n9
Newton, Isaac, 102, 359n9
Nicolas Cusanus, 13
Nietzsche, Friedrich, 2, 101, 120, 127,
　158, 194, 260, 296, 298, 366n20
Novalis, 2

Oedipus, 137, 383n29
Ogawa, Tadashi, 33
Orth, Ernst Wolfgang, 353n4
Otto, Rudolf, 163, 255

Parmenides, 37, 129–33, 135–37, 140,
　141, 146, 150, 154, 155, 204, 367n34,
　373n16, 375n12
Pascal, Blaise, 13
Patočka, Jan, 2, 5, 9, 59, 127, 145,
　146, 211–62, 266–84, 291, 293,
　304, 312, 313, 326, 340, 341, 371n6,
　380n1, 380–81n2, 381n7,11–13,15,16,
　382nn17,27, 383nn29–32, 383n2, 383–
　84n3, 384nn4,5,8,9,10 385nn12,16,18,
　386nn3,4, 386–87n6, 388n8,
Paul, Saint, 240, 350n9, 372n14, 385n13
Phidias, 13
Pindar, 192, 378n32
Plato, 13, 135, 167, 174, 175, 213, 214, 221,
　222, 224, 226–28, 231, 233, 238, 239,
　241, 243, 245–47, 249–56, 258–62,
　267–77, 279–85, 300, 374n2, 378n29,
　382–83n28, 383nn31,32, 384nn5,8,
　385nn12,18
Plotinus, 13
Pöggeler, Otto, 151, 165, 375n7, 376n16
Prince von Hamburg, 139
Pythagoras, 354n9

Racine, Jean, 13
Ramnoux, Clémence, 354n9
Redfield, Marc, 394n46
Reinhardt, Karl, 138, 139, 151, 373n22
Rembrandt, 13
Reynold, Gonzague de, 12, 379n35
Rheinberger, Hans-Jörg, 360n10
Ricoeur, Paul, 38, 42, 67, 126, 214, 217,
　271, 360n14, 382–83n16
Riedel, Manfred, 104
Ritter, Joachim, 396n1
Rosenberg, Alfred, 114
Rougemont, Denis de, 379n35

Scheler, Max, 311, 322, 356n16, 385n13, 387–88n6
Schleiermacher, Friedrich, 354n10
Schelling, Friedrich Wilhelm Joseph, 202
Schiller, Friedrich, 138
Schlegel, Friedrich, 2
Schmeling, Max, 369n38
Schmidt, Dennis J., 372n15
Schumann, Karl, 37
Scott, Robert, 305
Shakespeare, William, 13
Ströker, Elisabeth, 304, 359n9
Socrates, 222–24, 247, 267, 382n23
Sophocles, 13, 123, 133, 134, 137–41, 150, 151, 154–57, 165, 170, 174, 175, 177, 178, 181, 183, 189–92, 198, 372n15, 375n7, 376n16, 378n32
Spengler, Oswald, 97, 365n9
Spinoza, Baruch, 13

Taminiaux, Jacques, 139
Tasso, Torquato, 139

Telephassa, 10
Thales, 354n9
Trakl, Georg, 100

Valéry, Paul, 9, 11, 205, 265, 324, 327, 328, 379n35
Velásquez, Diego, 13
Vieta, Franciscus, 360n9
Virgil, 13
Volpi, Franco, 370n5
Voltaire, 13

Waldenfels, Bernard, 357n30
Wallenstein, Albrecht von, 139
Wolff, Francis, 391n23

Xenophanes, 354n9

Zarader, Marlène, 128, 136, 383n1
Zeus, 11, 12, 139, 184, 378n30

MERIDIAN

Crossing Aesthetics

Bernard Stiegler, *Technics and Time, 2: Disorientation*

Bernard Stiegler, *Acting Out*

Susan Bernstein, *Housing Problems: Writing and Architecture in Goethe, Walpole, Freud, and Heidegger*

Martin Hägglund, *Radical Atheism: Derrida and the Time of Life*

Cornelia Vismann, *Files: Law and Media Technology*

Anne-Lise François, *Open Secrets: The Literature of Uncounted Experience*

Jean-Luc Nancy, *The Discourse of the Syncope: Logodaedalus*

Carol Jacobs, *Skirting the Ethical: Sophocles, Plato, Hamann, Sebald, Campion*

Cornelius Castoriadis, *Figures of the Thinkable*

Jacques Derrida, *Psyche: Inventions of the Other*, 2 volumes, edited by Peggy Kamuf and Elizabeth Rottenberg

Mark Sanders, *Ambiguities of Witnessing: Literature and Law in the Time of a Truth Commission*

Sarah Kofman, *The Sarah Kofman Reader*, edited by Thomas Albrecht, with Georgia Albert and Elizabeth Rottenberg

Hannah Arendt, *Reflections on Literature and Culture*, edited by Susannah Young-ah Gottlieb

Alan Bass, *Interpretation and Difference: The Strangeness of Care*

Jacques Derrida, *H. C. for Life, That Is to Say . . .*

Ernst Bloch, *Traces*

Elizabeth Rottenberg, *Inheriting the Future: Legacies of Kant, Freud, and Flaubert*

David Michael Kleinberg-Levin, *Gestures of Ethical Life*

Jacques Derrida, *On Touching—Jean-Luc Nancy*

Jacques Derrida, *Rogues: Two Essays on Reason*

Peggy Kamuf, *Book of Addresses*

Giorgio Agamben, *The Time that Remains: A Commentary on the Letter to the Romans*

Jean-Luc Nancy, *Multiple Arts: The Muses II*

Alain Badiou, *Handbook of Inaesthetics*

Jacques Derrida, *Eyes of the University: Right to Philosophy 2*

Maurice Blanchot, *Lautréamont and Sade*

Giorgio Agamben, *The Open: Man and Animal*

Jean Genet, *The Declared Enemy*

Shosana Felman, *Writing and Madness: (Literature/Philosophy/Psychoanalysis)*

Jean Genet, *Fragments of the Artwork*

Shoshana Felman, *The Scandal of the Speaking Body: Don Juan with J. L. Austin, or Seduction in Two Languages*

Peter Szondi, *Celan Studies*

Neil Hertz, *George Eliot's Pulse*

Maurice Blanchot, *The Book to Come*

Susannah Young-ah Gottlieb, *Regions of Sorrow: Anxiety and Messianism in Hannah Arendt and W. H. Auden*

Jacques Derrida, *Without Alibi*, edited by Peggy Kamuf

Cornelius Castoriadis, *On Plato's 'Statesman'*

Jacques Derrida, *Who's Afraid of Philosophy? Right to Philosophy 1*

Peter Szondi, *An Essay on the Tragic*

Peter Fenves, *Arresting Language: From Leibniz to Benjamin*

Jill Robbins, ed. *Is It Righteous to Be? Interviews with Emmanuel Levinas*

Louis Marin, *Of Representation*

Daniel Payot, *The Architect and the Philosopher*

J. Hillis Miller, *Speech Acts in Literature*

Maurice Blanchot, *Faux pas*

Jean-Luc Nancy, *Being Singular Plural*

Maurice Blanchot / Jacques Derrida, *The Instant of My Death / Demeure: Fiction and Testimony*

Niklas Luhmann, *Art as a Social System*

Emmanual Levinas, *God, Death, and Time*

Ernst Bloch, *The Spirit of Utopia*

Giorgio Agamben, *Potentialities: Collected Essays in Philosophy*

Ellen S. Burt, *Poetry's Appeal: French Nineteenth-Century Lyric and the Political Space*

Jacques Derrida, *Adieu to Emmanuel Levinas*

Werner Hamacher, *Premises: Essays on Philosophy and Literature from Kant to Celan*

Aris Fioretos, *The Gray Book*

Deborah Esch, *In the Event: Reading Journalism, Reading Theory*

Winfried Menninghaus, *In Praise of Nonsense: Kant and Bluebeard*

Giorgio Agamben, *The Man Without Content*

Giorgio Agamben, *The End of the Poem: Studies in Poetics*

Theodor W. Adorno, *Sound Figures*

Louis Marin, *Sublime Poussin*

Philippe Lacoue-Labarthe, *Poetry as Experience*

Ernst Bloch, *Literary Essays*

Jacques Derrida, *Resistances of Psychoanalysis*

Marc Froment-Meurice, *That Is to Say: Heidegger's Poetics*

Francis Ponge, *Soap*

Philippe Lacoue-Labarthe, *Typography: Mimesis, Philosophy, Politics*

Giorgio Agamben, *Homo Sacer: Sovereign Power and Bare Life*

Emmanuel Levinas, *Of God Who Comes to Mind*

Bernard Stiegler, *Technics and Time, 1: The Fault of Epimetheus*

Werner Hamacher, *pleroma—Reading in Hegel*

Serge Leclaire, *Psychoanalyzing: On the Order of the Unconscious and the Practice of the Letter*

Serge Leclaire, *A Child Is Being Killed: On Primary Narcissism and the Death Drive*

Sigmund Freud, *Writings on Art and Literature*

Cornelius Castoriadis, *World in Fragments: Writings on Politics, Society, Psychoanalysis, and the Imagination*

Thomas Keenan, *Fables of Responsibility: Aberrations and Predicaments in Ethics and Politics*

Emmanuel Levinas, *Proper Names*

Alexander García Düttmann, *At Odds with AIDS: Thinking and Talking About a Virus*

Maurice Blanchot, *Friendship*

Jean-Luc Nancy, *The Muses*

Massimo Cacciari, *Posthumous People: Vienna at the Turning Point*

David E. Wellbery, *The Specular Moment: Goethe's Early Lyric and the Beginnings of Romanticism*

Edmond Jabès, *The Little Book of Unsuspected Subversion*

Hans-Jost Frey, *Studies in Poetic Discourse: Mallarmé, Baudelaire, Rimbaud, Hölderlin*

Pierre Bourdieu, *The Rules of Art: Genesis and Structure of the Literary Field*

Nicolas Abraham, *Rhythms: On the Work, Translation, and Psychoanalysis*

Jacques Derrida, *On the Name*

David Wills, *Prosthesis*

Maurice Blanchot, *The Work of Fire*

Jacques Derrida, *Points . . . : Interviews, 1974–1994*

J. Hillis Miller, *Topographies*

Philippe Lacoue-Labarthe, *Musica Ficta (Figures of Wagner)*

Jacques Derrida, *Aporias*

Emmanuel Levinas, *Outside the Subject*

Jean-François Lyotard, *Lessons on the Analytic of the Sublime*

Peter Fenves, *"Chatter": Language and History in Kierkegaard*

Jean-Luc Nancy, *The Experience of Freedom*

Jean-Joseph Goux, *Oedipus, Philosopher*

Haun Saussy, *The Problem of a Chinese Aesthetic*

Jean-Luc Nancy, *The Birth to Presence*

The authorized representative in the EU for product safety and compliance is:
Mare Nostrum Group
B.V Doelen 72
4831 GR Breda
The Netherlands

www.ingramcontent.com/pod-product-compliance
Lightning Source LLC
Chambersburg PA
CBHW021140240426
43661CB00075B/1595